The INS on the Line

Published in cooperation with the William P. Clements Center
for Southwest Studies, Southern Methodist University

The INS on the Line

Making Immigration Law on the US–Mexico Border, 1917–1954

S. DEBORAH KANG

OXFORD
UNIVERSITY PRESS

OXFORD
UNIVERSITY PRESS

Oxford University Press is a department of the University of Oxford. It furthers
the University's objective of excellence in research, scholarship, and education
by publishing worldwide. Oxford is a registered trade mark of Oxford University
Press in the UK and certain other countries.

Published in the United States of America by Oxford University Press
198 Madison Avenue, New York, NY 10016, United States of America.

© Oxford University Press 2017

Library of Congress Cataloging-in-Publication Data
Names: Kang, S. Deborah, 1970- author.
Title: The INS on the line : making immigration law on the US-Mexico border,
1917–1954 / S. Deborah Kang.
Description: New York, NY : Oxford University Press, 2017. | Includes
bibliographical references and index.
Identifiers: LCCN 2016040692 (print) | LCCN 2016048283 (ebook) |
ISBN 9780199757435 (hardback) | ISBN 9780190655235 (Updf) |
ISBN 9780190655242 (Epub)
Subjects: LCSH: Border security—Mexican-American Border Region. | Immigration
enforcement—Mexican-American Border Region. | Mexican-American Border
Region—Emigration and immigration. | Mexicans—Legal status, laws, etc.—United States. |
Border security—Government policy—United States. | United States. Immigration and
Naturalization Service. | Emigration and immigration law—United States. | United
States—Emigration and immigration--Government policy. |
BISAC: HISTORY / Latin America / Mexico. | HISTORY / United States /
20th Century. | LAW / Legal History.
Classification: LCC JV6565 .K36 2017 (print) | LCC JV6565 (ebook) |
DDC 363.28/50973—dc23 LC record available at https://lccn.loc.gov/2016040692

1 3 5 7 9 8 6 4 2
Printed by Sheridan Books, Inc., United States of America

Portions of chapters in this book have been adapted from "Crossing the Line: The INS and the Federal
Regulation of the Mexican Border," *Bridging National Borders in North America*, edited by Benjamin Heber
Johnson and Andrew R. Graybill, 167–198. © 2010, Duke University Press, and "Implementation: How the
Borderlands Redefined Federal Immigration Law and Policy, 1917–1924," *California Legal History:
Journal of the California Supreme Court Historical Society* 7 (2012).

CONTENTS

ACKNOWLEDGMENTS

I would not have had the wonderful opportunity to write this book without the support of many institutions, colleagues, and friends. From start to finish, the Clements Center for Southwest Studies has been a tremendous source of support, providing a postdoctoral fellowship that allowed me to begin the process of transforming my PhD dissertation into a book and a generous subvention that facilitated the production of the manuscript. Grants from the Huntington Library and California State University, San Marcos made it possible for me to conduct additional archival research in Arizona, California, and Washington, DC. For fifteen months, the Center for Comparative Immigration Studies at the University of California, San Diego was my home away from home. I will always be grateful to David FitzGerald, John Skretny, Ana Minvielle, and Marisa Evanouski for supplying me with an office and a peaceful place to write as I finalized the revisions to the manuscript.

This book is so much the better thanks to the assistance and expertise of numerous archivists and librarians throughout the country. At the National Archives in Washington, DC, Suzanne Harris's efforts on my behalf were nothing short of Herculean. Marian Smith, Zack Wilske, and Charlaine Cook shared their unparalleled knowledge of immigration policy history as well as the resources housed in the US Citizenship and Immigration Services History Office and Library. Archivists at the following institutions also provided invaluable assistance: the Arizona Historical Foundation at Arizona State University; the Arizona Historical Society; the Bancroft Library at the University of California, Berkeley; the Charles E. Young Research Library and the Chicano Studies Research Center at the University of California, Los Angeles; the Department of Archives and Manuscripts at Arizona State University; the El Paso Public Library; the Georgetown University Law Library; the Huntington Library; the Japanese American Historical Society of San Diego; the Library of Congress; the San Diego History Center; the United States Border Patrol Museum in El

Paso, Texas; the Special Collections at the University of Arizona; the Special Collections and Archives at the University of California, San Diego; and the Special Collections at the University of Texas, El Paso.

I also greatly benefited from the insightful commentary of colleagues who read various portions of this work. Brian Balogh, David Gutiérrez, Benjamin Johnson, Andrew Needham, Monica Perales, Sherry Smith, the late David Weber, and members of the academic community from Arlington and Dallas, Texas graciously provided extensive recommendations during a manuscript workshop hosted by the Clements Center for Southwest Studies. Through an incredibly enriching symposium series, Bridging National Borders in North America, initiated by Benjamin Johnson and Andrew Graybill and sponsored by the Clements Center, I had the chance to present various versions of chapter 1. Lizabeth Cohen's Graduate Student Workshop in Twentieth-Century United States History at Harvard University kindly reviewed an early version of chapter 2. At the University of California, Berkeley, Mark Brilliant and Brian DeLay created opportunities for me to present my work in the Department of History, and at the 2012 Annual Meeting of the American Society for Legal History as well as the 2012 Annual Meeting of the Organization of American Historians. In these venues, I received invaluable feedback from Reuel Schiller, Katherine Benton-Cohen, and Pekka Hämäläinen.

In the Department of History at California State University, San Marcos, Anne Lombard, Michael Henderson, Katherine Hijar, and Olga Gonzalez-Silén helped me to improve the introduction, while Jeff Charles and Jill Watts supplied essential advice regarding the production of the manuscript. Philip Wolgin, a former classmate from graduate school and the managing director for the immigration policy team at the Center for American Progress, encouraged me to think more rigorously about the implications of my work for policymakers and policy historians. Illuminating conversations with Andrea Geiger, Raphi Rechitsky, Martin Shapiro, and Rachel St. John helped me to reframe various aspects of the book. In my immigration history classes at Harvard University and the University of California, Berkeley, and my Chicano/a history class at California State University, San Marcos, my students taught me just as much as I taught them about what it means to be an immigrant in America. Their insights on US immigration policy and personal experiences with the INS and the Border Patrol transformed my own perspectives on these subjects. The anonymous readers at Oxford University Press offered deeply substantive remarks that guided the revision of the manuscript. Susan Ferber, my editor at the Press, prepared comments and line edits that were breathtaking in their genius.

I am very grateful to Jeremy Toynbee and his team at Newgen UK for their expert handling of matters related to the production of the book. I would also like to thank Patty Cañas, California State University, San Marcos, for her deft management of the complex administrative issues surrounding my research travel. Ruth Ann Elmore at the Clements Center for Southwest Studies assisted me with the subvention and, more importantly, supported me without fail these many years. Several research assistants played vital roles in the completion of this book. At Harvard University, Paul Mathis did an outstanding job of unearthing local archival materials for the project. At California State University, San Marcos, Zane Cooper provided research assistance on chapter 4. Meanwhile, Jonathan Barsky, a student at William and Mary Law School, prepared the bibliography in a precise and efficient manner.

Finally, this book owes its very existence to several colleagues and friends. At those inevitable moments in the revision process when I felt anxious and uncertain, I thought of the late Jon Gjerde, my dissertation chair, and recollected his faith in this project and in me. Kerwin Klein read multiple drafts of the manuscript and, despite our disagreements about whiskey and frisée, has been a wonderful advisor, mentor, and friend. Kevin Adams, Patricia Kane, Ellen Huang, and Keeho Kang discussed and reviewed this book with me on too many occasions; I owe them countless thanks for their guidance on this project and everything else.

The INS on the Line

Introduction

It was complained that the presence of the Border Patrol in Nogales, Arizona had a discouraging effect upon business and the patrol inspectors have been taken out of the town with instructions to conduct their operations on the outside.

—Grover C. Wilmoth, District Director,
Bureau of Immigration, May 4, 1928

In 1928 Grover C. Wilmoth, the El Paso district director of the Bureau of Immigration, instructed Border Patrol officers to suspend their pursuit of undocumented immigrants in the border town of Nogales, Arizona. In issuing this order Wilmoth responded to the demands of the Nogales Chamber of Commerce, which, for nearly a decade, routinely opposed the passage of federal immigration restriction laws, alleging that they resulted in the loss of trade and commerce in the region.[1] Echoing the claims made in Nogales, border residents from Texas to California persistently called for the modification and even elimination of the nation's most prominent immigration restrictions, including the Chinese Exclusion Act of 1882, the Literacy Test of 1917, and the national origins quota system of 1924, among others.[2] At stake was not only the economic survival of towns that relied on cross-border traffic but also the transnational social world that, according to local residents, characterized the US–Mexico border region since time immemorial. As their frustrations mounted, residents all along the line went so far as to call for the relocation of the international boundary, a move that would create a zone free from any federal economic and social regulations.[3] While Wilmoth scoffed at these proposals to redraw the map of the US–Mexico border, he used his administrative discretion to address the needs of Nogales residents and temporarily exempted the town from the surveillance of the Border Patrol.

Wilmoth's directive constituted one of many moments in which he refashioned federal immigration restrictions in response to the transnational economy, society, and even geography of the US–Mexico borderlands. While his legal innovations departed from the exclusionary outlook that inspired the passage

1

of early twentieth-century immigration laws, they reflected his view that the borderlands were different. Wilmoth understood that the region presented a unique set of enforcement challenges that would render his officers unable to replicate the achievements and approaches of their peers at Angel Island and Ellis Island, the most restrictive immigration stations in the country prior to World War I.[4] He subsequently explained the need for a distinctive approach to immigration law enforcement in a 1934 training manual: "While the Immigration Service of the Mexican border, of course, conforms to general practice, the wide differences in physical conditions, in the local situations, and in the nature of our contacts with various foreign peoples make imperative noticeable departure from the general practice in several material respects."[5] For much of the twentieth century, immigration officials in the Southwest followed Wilmoth's example by creating numerous local departures from the federal immigration laws.

The INS on the Line traces the ways in which the Immigration and Naturalization Service (INS) on the US–Mexico border made and remade the nation's immigration laws over the course of the twentieth century.[6] In so doing, it argues that the INS functioned not only as a law enforcement agency, but also as a lawmaking body; the agency not only administered the nation's immigration laws, it also made them. These lawmaking endeavors furnished local agency officials with a critical tool, deployed in response to a set of enduring challenges surrounding immigration law enforcement on the US–Mexico border. These included a lack of political, financial, and even moral support from policymakers in Washington, DC; intraagency conflicts and debates; tremendous opposition from border residents, including Asian, European, Mexican, and American nationals living on both sides of the line; and the seemingly impossible task of policing the rugged terrain of the 2,000-mile international boundary. In the face of these obstacles southwestern agency officials amended, nullified, and even rewrote the nation's immigration laws, producing new laws and policies for the border region. As early as 1920, the agency's resort to legal innovations was so extensive that one local immigration leader observed that a "sectional" immigration policy existed in the borderlands.[7]

Yet despite the contingent and local quality of these legal innovations, they shaped the capacities of the American state on the US–Mexico border. Over time, the agency's repeated resort to the law resulted in the creation of a complex approach to immigration regulation in the borderlands. This approach closed the border to unwanted immigrants but simultaneously opened it for the benefit of local residents, tourists, and trade. Meanwhile the Border Patrol, the mobile enforcement unit of the INS, redefined the border as a policing jurisdiction, stretching the geographical limits of its authority to pursue undocumented immigrants from the international boundary to public and privates spaces far north of the line. More broadly, the agency's legal innovations constructed the border as an impermeable sovereign boundary, a permeable socioeconomic zone, and a vast policing jurisdiction. While this composite approach often frustrated nativist policymakers, it defined the mission of the INS on the US–Mexico border for much of the twentieth century.

Over the past fifty years, INS operations on the US–Mexico border have generated much interest among scholars, policymakers, and pundits. Despite their different approaches to the study of the agency, their works have produced two competing and even contradictory interpretations. One argues that the INS was weak and ineffectual and failed to seal the border against the entry of unwanted immigrants.[8] The other casts the INS as a strong and effective agency that developed highly aggressive tactics to deter illegal border crossings.[9] For decades, these two interpretations have regularly traded places as the prevailing account of the agency's history. Yet this bipolar characterization of the INS obscures a more nuanced understanding of agency operations in the Southwest. As policymakers in Washington, DC debated (and continue to debate) the successes and failures of border enforcement, American immigration law and policy quietly and steadily took shape in the hands of borderlands administrators. While outsiders often construed the work of the INS in narrow enforcement terms, the agency on the US–Mexico border defined itself not only as a law enforcement agency, but also as a lawmaking body. As such, the agency played a profound role in shaping our conceptions of immigration law and policy, immigrant rights, and the border.

As a lawmaking entity, the INS is no different than the many bureaucracies that populate the American administrative state. Its lawmaking authority has its origins in Progressive-era notions regarding the role of expertise in American governance.[10] Defenders of administrative agencies specifically argued that the courts and Congress lacked the capacities to understand and regulate a complex modern society. Regulation, then, belonged in the hands of experts trained in the social sciences, who possessed specialized knowledge about the various facets of the nation's economic, political, and social institutions.[11] At the turn of the last century, Congress charged these experts to address some of the nation's most pressing crises as bureaucrats within the fledging administrative state. By delegating its lawmaking authority to the new administrative agencies, Congress ensured that agency administrators had the authority to translate their ideas into laws and public policies.[12]

While the INS shared with other administrative agencies the ability to make law, over the course of the late nineteenth and twentieth centuries, its very approach to lawmaking gradually departed from the mainstream of American administrative practice. In the late nineteenth century, as the federal courts began scrutinizing the lawmaking authority of the nation's administrative agencies, the Supreme Court, in a series of now foundational cases referred to as the Chinese exclusion cases, largely exempted the Bureau of Immigration from judicial review of its admissions and deportation procedures.[13] By the early twentieth century, the Court also excused the agency from the application of constitutional norms to its own internal hearing procedures.[14] The explosive growth of the administrative state during the 1930s prompted a fresh round of criticisms regarding its impact on representative government and individual rights.[15] In response, Congress passed the Administrative Procedures Act of 1946 (APA), which articulated a basic set of standards regarding agencies' lawmaking activities, specifically their rule-making procedures and internal hearing practices.[16] In an ideal world these standards would ensure that agencies, as they devised laws and policies, remained responsive to the American public.[17] Yet the INS remained exempt from the provisions of the APA.[18] Unconstrained by the procedures stipulated by the APA and judicial review of its administrative practices and internal adjudications, the INS became, in historian Lucy Salyer's words, an " 'outlaw' in American legal culture."[19]

These legacies of the Chinese exclusion era and the New Deal created the framework within which Bureau of Immigration officials in the Southwest made the nation's immigration laws. Cognizant of the breadth of their authority, immigration inspectors and Border Patrol officers devised a wide array of policies pertaining to admissions, deportation, enforcement, and even immigrant rights. To a great extent, these lawmaking activities resembled those described by histories of agency operations on Angel Island and Ellis Island.[20] In these locales as well as along the US–Mexico border, the INS relied heavily on its administrative discretion, interpreting the nation's immigration laws in the broadest terms possible so as to maximize their restrictive impact.[21] Yet these works fail to recount the many other forms of lawmaking undertaken by the INS in the borderlands. This book fills this gap by describing the varied uses of administrative discretion in the Southwest that simultaneously enhanced and diminished the exclusionary aspects of federal immigration laws. In addition, southwestern immigration officials played a central role in the preparation of internal agency regulations, which effectively constituted an operations manual for the agency, and the drafting of federal immigration statutes.[22] Finally, local agency officials engaged in legal debates that informed conceptions of immigrant rights and, ultimately, curtailed the already limited constitutional status of immigrants in the United States.[23] Through these disparate means, the INS in the borderlands demonstrated the breadth and depth of its ability to make the law.[24]

While the agency's lawmaking endeavors were unmoored from the oversight of Congress and the courts, they were not conducted in a vacuum. Instead, the agency's legal innovations responded to and reflected the complexities of the US–Mexico borderlands. INS officials stationed in Arizona, California, and Texas—a region long distinguished by its cultural diversity, transnational infrastructure, global trading partners, world-renowned tourist industries, and multinational labor force—recognized the dissonance between the neat dividing lines delineated by the federal immigration laws and the global realities on the ground. Despite their own attempts to defend the nation-building enterprise of immigration restrictionists, southwestern immigration officials quickly realized that they were unevenly matched against the sheer volume of migrants who sought to cross the line each day and the global economic and social forces that brought them to the nation's borders in the first place.[25] Federal policies that fostered cross-border connections for the sake of the regional economy and US foreign relations with Mexico compounded the challenges of immigration law enforcement. Finally, in the first half of the twentieth century, local INS officials believed that the very geography of the border—its sheer expanse, its difficult terrain, and its harsh climate—rendered unimaginable the idea of closing the international line to unwanted immigration.[26]

In this transnational world, INS border enforcement efforts were characterized not by strength but by struggle. Many of these efforts were so haphazard that the INS in the Southwest came to resemble a Rube Goldberg agency.[27] Exasperated by the seeming impossibility of exerting any control over the border, some immigration inspectors simply gave up and neglected their enforcement responsibilities altogether. Dissatisfied with their lack of autonomy and political legitimacy, members of the Border Patrol vented their frustrations in acts of racial violence, whereby Mexican immigrants and Mexican Americans became the focus of the unit's aggressive enforcement campaigns.[28] Meanwhile, other INS officials resorted to the law to address the challenges of border enforcement. This book focuses on these agency administrators, describing how they created a complex set of policies that closed the line to unwanted immigrants, opened it for the sake of the regional economy and society, and redefined it for the benefit of the Border Patrol.

In the simplest terms, *The INS on the Line* is an institutional history of the INS on the US–Mexico border. As such it offers a holistic account of the agency, producing one of the first comprehensive accounts of its admissions, deportation, and enforcement procedures on the nation's southern line.[29] It also recounts changes in the agency's mission and operations over time, particularly with respect to its border crossing policies, the guest worker programs of World War I and World War II, its strategies for border policing, and, most prominently, its lawmaking activities. Through a detailed examination of agency operations in California, Arizona, and Texas, this book affords comparisons and contrasts between the regional branches of the agency as well as the conflicts that suffused the relationship between the local and national offices. Finally, as a study of the agency's lawmaking functions, it primarily follows the work of entry and mid-level agency officials. While agency leaders, particularly General Joseph Swing, participated in the law and policymaking process, they typically served temporary and highly symbolic posts at the pleasure of the president and Congress.[30] In contrast, mid-level INS managers, as civil servants whose jobs were often shielded from the vagaries of the election cycle, possessed decades of experience with the agency's daily operations and were best positioned to define its policies for the long haul.[31]

In broader terms, this book underscores the role of the INS in state-building on the border. In so doing, it shifts the locus of immigration law and policy formation from the nation's center to its peripheries. These regions, as historian Richard White has famously observed, served as the "kindergarten of the American state."[32] In the American West, numerous administrative agencies played a key part in the conquest and settlement of the region and, in the process, grew the capacities of the American state with respect to the distribution and sale of land, the management of natural resources, the expansion of the agricultural and industrial economies, and its relationships with Native Americans and immigrants.[33] For these bureaucracies, capacity-building required agency officials to not only enforce the laws dictated by Congress and the courts, but also to exercise their administrative discretion in order to make them.[34] INS operations on the US–Mexico border serve as a perfect illustration of this phenomenon, providing many examples of the ways in which the agency built the border management capacities of the American state.

This focus on state-building from the margins also exposes the fractures in the federal immigration power. While in theory the federal government possesses the exclusive authority to regulate immigration, in practice local and global forces continually impinged upon that power.[35] In the Southwest, the INS, despite its status as a federal agency, routinely translated the needs and concerns of local, regional, and international forces into federal policies and laws. While it would be an overstatement to say that local and international imperatives superseded federal immigration laws, a history of American immigration law and policy would be incomplete without considering how subnational and supranational concerns contributed to policy formation. *The INS on the Line* argues that the nation's immigration laws emerged—and continue to emerge—as a result of conversations and debates between local, national, and global state and nonstate actors.

Although it played an extensive role in shaping the immigration capacities of the state on the border, the INS in the Southwest was a weak agency for much of its history. While in the popular and scholarly imagination the INS is characterized as a strong bureaucracy, this book draws attention to the liabilities that plagued the agency for much of the century. These included a lack of external support among federal policymakers and local residents for its border enforcement mandate, as well as the environmental challenges presented by the climate and terrain along the line. Pervasive internal weakness also hamstrung agency operations; perhaps most prominently, long-standing institutional differences between the immigration inspection force at the border ports of entry and the Border Patrol led the two units to work at cross-purposes—the former often waived the immigration laws to sustain the transnational character of the borderlands while the latter sought to close the line to unwanted immigrants. Taken together, these political, social, and institutional weaknesses rendered the agency's lawmaking endeavors a conflict-ridden and haphazard process.

Despite the reactive and chaotic quality of the agency's legal innovations, they ultimately served as the building blocks of the nation's regulatory capacities along the US–Mexico border. Some of these local innovations became long-standing procedures due to ignorance and inertia; a lack of oversight by Congress, the courts, and agency leaders in Washington, DC meant that INS officials had little incentive to change local institutional customs. Other local practices were incorporated into the federal immigration statutes thanks to the vigorous lobbying efforts of southwestern agency leaders such as Wilmoth. While expertise, rational decision-making, and neat organizational designs are said to have informed the shaping of the American administrative state, in the immigration policy context sheer incompetence, conflicts among and between social, political, and institutional actors, and a highly disorganized administrative agency served as the foundations of the state in the Southwest.[36]

Given the vigilance of border residents and border businesses with respect to any changes in the nation's immigration laws or local INS practices, this book also traces the relationship between the state and society in the borderlands. In the process, it argues that border residents were far from passive recipients of the nation's immigration laws. Instead, through an active and regular dialogue with local INS officials, they deeply influenced local INS operations and effectively reshaped many immigration laws and policies. Obtaining exemptions to virtually every immigration restriction law passed in the twentieth century, their efforts also underscore the importance of economic and diplomatic (specifically, the border economy and US foreign relations with Mexico) as well as cultural factors in immigration policy formation. Over the course of the century, locals' repeated protests helped to carve out an important regional exception to the federal restriction laws and sustain the transnational character of the US-Mexico border.

INS operations in the Southwest not only reflected the needs and interests of border residents; they also redefined the US–Mexico border. The agency's legal inventions effectively transformed the border from a line into a space or rendered it akin to a series of zones that served a variety of purposes, whether economic, military, political, or social.[37] The agency created these zones in a piecemeal fashion so that by mid-century it defined the border in multiple and even competing ways as a geopolitical boundary, a transnational economic and social zone, and a vast jurisdiction for the policing of unwanted immigrants. In effect, the agency achieved a modicum of control over the border and the surrounding region through the legal conquest or redefinition of space. These legal definitions of the border never replaced alternative conceptualizations of the line as an invisible boundary, a site of conquest and violence, and a zone of cultural interaction and even mixing.[38] But to the extent that the agency's exercise of power at the nation's borders and beyond them have gone unchallenged, these legal constructions of the borderlands stand as potent reminders of the agency's ability to make the law.

The INS on the Line draws upon a variety of archival sources from Arizona, California, Texas, and Washington, DC, relying most heavily upon the agency's own policy, or correspondence, files.[39] Even though these files primarily convey the viewpoints of the agency, they offer a wealth of detail regarding its daily operations. For instance, they allow one to discern the differences between agency offices in Texas, Arizona, and California; observe the competition for resources and prestige that frequently occurred between the immigration inspection force and the Border Patrol; and track developments in the agency's admissions, deportation, and enforcement policies over time. Critically, they record disagreements and conflicts between the agency's central office in Washington, DC, its regional branches in the borderlands, and border residents living on both sides of the line. These disputes form the core of this narrative, for they reveal how local immigration officials departed from the federal immigration laws and, conversely, how national immigration policies evolved from what were once local and improvised administrative practices.

This book begins in the borderlands, with an account of the social, political, and even geographical challenges faced by immigration officials in the first decades of the twentieth century. In the first three chapters, I explain how immigration inspectors and Border Patrol officers in the Southwest responded to these obstacles by devising new policies pertaining to admissions, deportation, and enforcement. Chapter 1 describes how the bureau, through the World War I agricultural labor program, border crossing cards, and what I refer to as a literacy test waiver, sustained the transnational character of the borderlands for the benefit of local residents. By 1924 Congress, as I explain in chapter 2, created the Border Patrol, a mobile enforcement unit charged with the duty of closing the line to unwanted immigrants. Yet the unit found itself working at cross-purposes with immigration inspectors who promoted the regional economic boom of the 1920s by creating new border crossing procedures. In response, the Border Patrol began a thirty-year effort to expand its legal jurisdiction beyond the international boundary and well within the nation's interior. Lacking the political support of local and national policymakers, southwestern Patrol officers resorted to the law to define an institutional identity and enhance their enforcement capacities. But by the 1930s, the agency's enforcement practices, particularly its deportation procedures, drew the criticism of reformers both inside and outside the bureau. As I discuss in chapter 3, the agency, unbound by the oversight of the courts and Congress, developed a highly aggressive approach to border enforcement. As a result, for a moment in its history the INS in the Southwest considered the implications of its policies and procedures for immigrant rights and instituted a series of reforms. More broadly, these reforms revealed the range of the agency's lawmaking activities. Local INS officials not only devised internal agency procedures and drafted congressional statutes; they also played a role in shaping and, ultimately, constricting constitutional norms pertaining to unauthorized immigrants.

By the 1940s, the reform movement of the 1930s gave way to the sheer logistical demands presented by the Bracero Program and the unprecedented increase in the number of immigrants who entered without inspection. Chapter 4 describes how the INS, once again, found itself operating from a position of weakness and buffeted by competing pressures. On the one hand, growers demanded that the border remain open to bracero workers while, on the other hand, the Mexican government emerged as the most vocal proponent of an aggressive enforcement policy and a closed border. Yet as I explain in chapter 5, the contingencies and crises generated during the first decade of the Bracero Program led the INS to change, engaging in a series of lawmaking activities that bolstered the immigration enforcement capacities of the American state in the borderlands. More specifically, southwestern agency leaders sought political support at the national level, particularly from the executive branch, for its border enforcement duties. In the process, they successfully lobbied for legislation that rendered local practices national policy and federal law. Among these included procedures once excoriated by legal reformers and the INS itself in the 1930s. By the 1950s, all the tactics that local immigration officers had devised over the years were put into play with the sanction of Congress and the president in a mass deportation campaign known as Operation Wetback, which I discuss in chapter 6. The campaign not only legitimized mass deportation as a response to undocumented immigration, it also institutionalized a regulatory approach to border enforcement, an approach that simultaneously closed the line to the entry of unwanted immigrants and opened the border for the sake of labor and trade.

The conclusion provides an overview of developments in contemporary American immigration policy from 1954 to the present. Faced with the same dilemmas—how to open the borders to the free flow of trade, travelers, and

commerce while closing it to the entry of undocumented immigrants and security threats, immigration policymakers relied on old solutions. Border Patrol
raids, legalization programs, guest worker agreements, and border crossing cards
have been and continue to be central features of American immigration policy
today. Yet by adopting the once ad hoc practices created by local immigration
inspectors and Border Patrol officers, national policymakers also inherited their
costs and consequences, the most serious of which included the arbitrariness,
corruption, and even violence surrounding Border Patrol operations. Given the
longevity and scope of the agency's ability to define the law on its own terms, I
conclude by arguing that any comprehensive immigration reform package must
include not only a revision of our nation's immigration laws, but also a fundamental reform of the INS and the Border Patrol.

A Sectional Immigration Policy

> ... no regulatory measures could possibly be devised on this border
> in any way affecting the freedom of movement of the people living on
> the border or touching their financial interests which would not be the
> object of attack and criticism. Every innovation of such a character, of
> which the Public Health Quarantine measures, head tax and illiteracy
> provisions are notable examples, have evoked similar protest.
> —George J. Harris, Acting Supervising Inspector of the El Paso
> District, Bureau of Immigration, November 28, 1917

The exasperated declaration of George J. Harris expressed what many Bureau of Immigration officials in the Southwest accepted as a fact of life along the US–Mexico border.[1] Prior to 1917 geography, institutional weaknesses, and local custom all contributed to the lax enforcement of immigration laws on the international line. Few appeared troubled by the unfettered crossing and recrossing of thousands of Mexicans at points all along the border each day. Indeed, the opposite attitude seemed to prevail, as recounted by an El Paso community leader and lifetime resident in the early 1900s: "There were no restrictions as to crossing the bridge, or passports or anything like that. Everyone was happy, coming and going without any customs restrictions, any immigration restrictions, any health department restrictions."[2]

The First World War transformed this orientation toward the border, raising concerns about a foreign invasion along the southern line and compelling southwestern Bureau of Immigration officials to take their jobs more seriously. In response to this wartime threat Congress passed a set of laws, specifically the Immigration Act of 1917 and the Entry and Departures Control Act of 1918 (also known as the Passport Act), which created a new tapestry of regulations along the US–Mexico border.[3] As southwestern immigration officials began administering these new laws, their efforts were hampered by a lack of money, manpower, and materiel as well as enormous opposition from border residents (whether Asian, European, Mexican, or American) who were accustomed to crossing the international boundary without restriction.[4]

Without the resources and, many times, the will to adequately enforce the new laws, southwestern immigration officials facilitated the waiver of old policies or creation of new policies that made their lives and the lives of border residents much easier. The most prominent of these was the wartime labor importation program, initiated to overcome the objections of southwestern industries to the restrictive provisions of the Immigration Act of 1917 and the Passport Act of 1918.[5] In addition, the service modified the new laws for ordinary border residents as well as the rich and powerful. When thousands of locals complained about the literacy test provisions of the Immigration Act of 1917, the bureau created "border waivers" for illiterate Mexican nationals who lived on both sides of the border. As the administrators of the Passport Act of 1918, southwestern immigration officials devised additional exemptions, specifically a border crossing card program for local residents. Although the border crossing card primarily assisted Mexican nationals and Mexican Americans, it also benefited Americans and Europeans, as well as Asian, Asian American, and Asian Mexican merchants. Together, these policy innovations—to the chagrin of anti-immigration advocates—sustained the transnational character of the borderlands.

All of this is not to deny the bureau's vigorous efforts to bar Mexican, Asian, and European nationals from admission for permanent residence or to expel unwanted immigrants in this period. Instead, during World War I and well into the 1920s, the bureau was concerned not only with the restriction of immigrants but also with the regulation of the local border population. While immigration historians have provided extensive accounts of those migrants seeking entry for permanent residence (formally referred to as "immigrants" by the Bureau of Immigration), this chapter shifts the focus of attention from immigrants to border crossers (officially categorized as "nonimmigrants"). This population typically included laborers, tourists, local residents, dignitaries, and businessmen who crossed and recrossed the border on a regular basis for short periods of time. Their presence led the agency to construct an immigration policy for the borderlands, a policy that departed from the restrictionist tenets of the federal immigration and passport laws but met the needs of border society and its economy.

Until World War I, the economic and social needs of the borderlands, rather than immigration regulations, served as the forces driving migration between Mexico and the United States. As historian Mario T. García explains, Mexican immigration was "inextricably linked with the growth of American industrial capitalism."[6] The primary southwestern industries—railroads, mining, ranching, and agriculture—met their labor needs with migrant workers.[7] As these industries triggered the growth of border towns, immigrants, once again, met the burgeoning demand for workers in both the primary (the rail, mining, and ranching industries) and secondary economic sectors (including manufacturing, wholesale and retail trade, and construction).[8] Given the proximity of Mexico, the passage of the Chinese exclusion acts (which barred the entry of Chinese laborers in the late nineteenth century), and political upheavals in early twentieth-century Mexico (including the land policies of the Díaz regime and the Mexican Revolution), Mexican nationals comprised the bulk of the immigrant work force.[9]

Recognizing the importance of immigration to the border economy, federal officials took a highly uneven approach to border enforcement at the turn of the last century.[10] While immigration inspectors were vigilant in the application of the Chinese exclusion laws, they simultaneously adopted a laissez-faire stance toward Mexican migration across the line.[11] Indeed, at the urging of corporations such as the Southern Pacific Railroad, Congress exempted Mexican immigrants from the head taxes stipulated under the Immigration Acts of 1903 and 1907.[12] Even though southwestern officials possessed other statutory means to restrict Mexican immigration, they chose not to exercise this authority on a regular basis.[13] Instead, they allowed most Mexican immigrants to cross the international line without inspection.[14] Some immigration officials, according to historian George Sánchez, even recruited migrant workers for southwestern industries in exchange for bribes.[15] As a result of its lax approach to immigration law enforcement, the Bureau of Immigration itself sustained the transnational character of the borderlands.

The porousness of the border not only facilitated the migration of Mexicans north to the United States, but also allowed them to return home or engage in an ongoing pattern of circular migration. Indeed, while many of the 1.5 million Mexican nationals who entered the United States between 1910 and 1920 settled permanently, demographers and historians agree that hundreds of thousands more entered on a temporary basis, crossing and recrossing the border as laborers, merchants, or casual visitors.[16] This category of migrants, referred to by the Bureau of Immigration as nonimmigrants or nonstatistical entrants, outnumbered immigrants (or those entering for permanent residence) by a factor of three to one.[17] These massive demographic shifts attested to the openness of the border in this period and, more broadly, played a pivotal role in the formation of transnational communities all along the international line.

While Mexican nationals constituted the largest group of migrants crossing and recrossing the border each day, Anglo-Americans, Asian Americans, Europeans, Japanese and Chinese nationals, and Japanese and Chinese Mexicans, among others, also took advantage of the border's permeability.[18] In the late nineteenth century, many of these migrants traveled back and forth across the border to fill the unskilled job needs of the mining, rail, and agriculture industries that had developed, sometimes in tandem, on both sides of the line.[19] Given the racial segmentation of the workforce, these industries sought

Anglo-American workers to fill skilled and managerial posts north and south of the border.[20]

As Asian, European, and Mexican nationals settled in border communities, they often lived transnational lives. Mexican nationals regularly crossed the line to shop for subsistence items in the United States; indeed, these crossings were an absolute necessity, as one State Department official observed, "if they [Mexicans] are refused entry into the United States the Mexican population along the border would starve and the greater number of the shop keepers on the American side would be bankrupted."[21] At the same time, Mexican immigrants and Mexican Americans in El Paso retained their ties to Mexico thanks to Spanish-language newspapers that provided news coverage about Mexican politics and advertisements from Mexican business establishments.[22]

As Chinese and Japanese migrants established their own businesses (including laundries, restaurants, grocery stores, pool halls, barber shops, boarding houses, farms, and ranches, among others) on both sides of the border, regular border crossings became essential to the success of their enterprises.[23] Merchants in Mexico, for example, sought to replenish inventories through large purchases north of the line.[24] Meanwhile, Chinese business owners, in an effort to evade the American prohibition against the admission of Chinese laborers, frequently transported their Chinese employees north from Mexico. Finally, the very financing of many border business was dependent upon the pooling of resources among relatives and friends in the United States, Canada, Mexico, and Asia.[25] Perhaps most important for the purposes of this chapter, the social status of Chinese and Japanese merchants widened the possibilities for their physical mobility across the nation's borders. While the Chinese exclusion acts and the Gentlemen's Agreement of 1907 barred the entry of Chinese and Japanese laborers, both laws contained exceptions for the entry of merchants.[26]

Leisure, as well as labor, led primarily Americans and Mexicans to cross and recross the border each day. The entertainment industry drew Americans south of the line, particularly with the start of Prohibition in 1920; as historian David Romo writes of the port of entry at El Paso:

> It was no longer arms smugglers, spies, soldiers of fortune, journalists and revolutionaries crossing the lines. Suddenly the ludic zone across the border became packed with American tourists. Between 1918 and 1919, about 14,000 tourists crossed the border into Mexico; a year later the official U.S. Customs tally was 418,700.[27]

As Ciudád Juárez drew thousands of casual visitors, Tijuana surpassed all other border towns, north or south of the line, as a tourist attraction.[28] Indeed, given the volume of traffic flowing from north to south, Tijuana identified

Figure 1.1 The international boundary between Nogales, Arizona and Nogales, Sonora in the early twentieth century. Courtesy of the National Archives, Washington, DC.

itself less with Mexico than with California.[29] Seeking to take advantage of the tourist trade in Tijuana, Americans, Mexicans, Armenians, Syrians, Japanese, Spaniards, Italians, and Chinese all launched successful businesses.[30] As an acknowledgment of the increasingly multinational character of the borderlands, one Tijuana school opened its doors to the children of these tourists and traders.[31]

Taken together, these cross-border demographic, economic, and social ties led local residents to construe the border as an "imaginary line."[32] Yet on the eve of World War I, these very ties generated concerns about border security among federal officials in the Southwest and Washington, DC. In particular, the cross-border raids of Mexican revolutionaries exposed the weaknesses of federal authority and the strength of binational loyalties to the rebellion. In American border towns, revolutionary forces found a safe haven to retreat from advancing Mexican federal troops, moral support for their political cause, and even a supply of arms and basic necessities.[33] While these cross-border raids had been a feature of the Revolution from its inception, by 1913 a violent regime change intensified political rivalries and military hostilities within Mexico and along its northern frontier.[34] By 1916, the increase in border raiding drew the fixed attention of Washington officials as they sought to bring order to the region.[35] In pursuit of revolutionary leader Pancho Villa and his forces, President Woodrow Wilson sent General John Pershing and ten thousand troops into Mexico in retaliation for the *Villistas* attacks on American citizens.[36] Yet Pershing's punitive expedition failed to establish peace along the border and instead, brought the nation to the brink of war with Mexico.

At the same time, national anxieties about border security were only exacerbated by World War I. Under pressure from German submarine warfare in the Atlantic, federal officials expressed concerns about enemy incursions through the nation's seaports and land borders.[37] The Zimmerman Telegram lent credence to fears about a possible German invasion from Mexico.[38] In addition, federal officials suspected that Mexican revolutionaries, acting to avenge Villa's defeat, would assist Germany in this effort. Finally, the persistence of the overlapping geographical, social, and economic networks between border towns rendered them "logical haven[s]" for enemy aliens as well as revolutionary forces.[39] According to Romo, the Emporium Bar in El Paso served as a meeting place for Pancho Villa and a German spy who allegedly sought leasing rights to submarine bases in Baja California.[40]

At the local level, the apprehension surrounding Villa's raids and the war increased public antagonism toward Mexican immigrants and, in turn, led to a tightening of border inspection procedures. In an atmosphere of paranoia, El Paso city officials alleged that the thousands of refugees fleeing the Revolution would trigger a public health crisis, specifically a typhus epidemic.[41] As a solution, they initially proposed a quarantine of all new arrivals.[42] In lieu of the quarantine, city officials ultimately conducted health inspections of all the homes in Chihuahuita (the largest Mexican neighborhood in El Paso), which was considerably less drastic than El Paso Mayor Tom Lea's proposal to destroy them altogether.[43] By 1917 local representatives of the United States Public Health Service adopted more austere measures, subjecting 127,173 Mexican entrants to a delousing and bathing procedure followed by a rigorous physical and mental examination.[44]

Like their local counterparts, federal officials demonstrated a more enforcement-minded orientation toward the border during World War I, launching cavalry patrols and air surveillance teams in search of revolutionaries and German spies.[45] Congress also enacted statutory measures, specifically the Immigration Act of 1917 and the Passport Act of 1918, to secure the line against alien enemies and unwanted immigrants. In this wartime context, southwestern Bureau of Immigration officials changed their lax orientation toward immigration law enforcement and, for the first time, took seriously their responsibility to enforce the new laws vis-à-vis Mexican nationals. In so doing, they attempted to impose a new web of regulations upon a population long accustomed to crossing the border without any restrictions.

In 1917, Congress passed the Immigration Act of 1917, an omnibus bill that consolidated immigration legislation from the prior three decades.[46] Its passage marked an apex in Progressive-era efforts to restrict immigration from Southern and Eastern Europe and Asia. It accomplished the latter by excluding immigrants from a geographic area labeled the "Asiatic Barred Zone" that included all of Asia except for Japan and the Philippines. In order to limit entrants from Europe, the act created a literacy test for all individuals seeking admission into the United States.[47] Despite President Wilson's veto of the new immigration act (Wilson was unwilling to reverse a campaign promise not to restrict European immigration), Congress overrode his veto and passed the bill on February 5, 1917.[48]

Even though the Immigration Act of 1917 was not conceived as a wartime measure, policymakers later relied on its provisions to implement a domestic defense policy within the nation and at the borders. Indeed, once the country entered the war (one month after the act's passage), Wilson's concerns about the entry of radicals "dominate[d] the politics of immigration policy."[49] As a result, federal officials relied upon the looser deportation standards created by the new act to expel suspected alien enemies and subversives throughout the country.[50] In the Southwest, the Bureau of Immigration began to reverse its long-standing practice of letting Mexican nationals freely cross the border, attempting to control and restrict their movement under the authority of the new immigration law. For the first time in its history, the service enforced the head tax in conjunction with the new literacy test provisions of the Immigration Act of 1917 vis-à-vis Mexican immigrants.[51]

In order to control the entry and departure of suspected alien enemies, federal officials initially relied on the immigration statutes. They found, however, that the immigration laws failed to provide the regulatory authority necessary to restrict and supervise this category of foreign national. An assistant to the attorney general observed:

> When we got into the war we were met, of course, immediately with the necessity of supervising exit from the country and entrance into the country of undesirable persons, and the only law on the subject that came anywhere near reaching them was the immigration law, which was not designed to fit a situation in which spies were moving to and from the country, because the tests prescribed by the immigration statutes for admittance to the country were, of course, simple and designed to meet certain requirements of intelligence, character, previous history, etc.[52]

In response to this lack of authority, Congress passed the Passport Act to prevent the entry of alien enemies. The act specifically required foreigners and US citizens to present passports for inspection at the nation's ports of entry for the duration of the war.[53] This act constituted another new layer of restrictions that would have a serious impact on the movement of populations across the US–Mexico border.[54]

The administration of the passport law was divided among several federal agencies, including Justice, Labor, Commerce, and State. While the State Department was responsible for the issuance of passports and visas, the Bureau of Immigration was responsible for the actual enforcement of the passport law. Thus prior to conducting their usual immigration inspection, immigration officers would act as passport agents, inspecting passports and visas, collecting visa fees, and taking declarations of foreigners and US citizens entering and departing the country. The new duties increased the workload of an agency lacking the resources to fulfill its own mandate to enforce the nation's immigration laws.[55] And this, in turn, would compound the problems faced by the Bureau of Immigration in expanding the presence of the federal government in a community long accustomed to its absence.

Initially, the new immigration restrictions had a significant impact on immigration, specifically those individuals seeking entry for permanent admission, across the US–Mexico border. The literacy test plus the head tax created serious obstacles for Mexican immigrants, particularly agricultural workers who, for the most part, were poor and illiterate.[56] For the first few months that the new law was in operation, Mexican immigration declined sharply from the same period the previous year. Historian Lawrence Cardoso reports that only 31,000 Mexicans emigrated to the United States in 1917 whereas 56,000 had entered the year before.[57] By 1918, 1,771 Mexicans decided against emigrating due to the literacy test as the Immigration Service rejected the applications of 5,745 for failure to pay the head tax.[58]

While the new immigration and passport laws closed the border for some, other border residents refused to accept the new restrictions. Some expressed their discontent by crossing and recrossing the line without an official inspection. As a result, the bureau reported that the undocumented entry of Mexican nationals—an issue the agency had mostly ignored prior to 1917—had become one of its greatest concerns; as the supervising inspector for the Mexican Border District wrote in his annual report, "The suppression of attempted illegal entry of countless aliens of the Mexican race, excluded or excludable, under what they deem to be the harsh provisions of the immigration act of 1917, has constituted one of the most difficult problems with which this district has had to contend in the past year."[59]At the same time, thousands of local residents, as both the State Department and Bureau of Immigration reported, protested repeatedly and vehemently about the ways in which the Immigration Act of 1917 and the Passport Act of 1918 disrupted the transnational character of their daily lives.

Locals complained about the new laws in a variety of ways: writing letters to state and federal politicians; sending telegrams, letters, and petitions to local and federal Bureau of Immigration and State Department officials; publishing editorials in opposition to the new regulations; and arguing with immigration inspectors at the gates. In the Southwest, those industries reliant on Mexican labor were the most vocal and politically powerful opponents of the restrictions imposed by the immigration and passport acts.[60] Southwestern farmers, for example, repeatedly called for exemptions to the new laws, knowing that they would bar the entry of Mexican workers.[61] In addition to southwestern industries, ordinary individuals—including those traveling from Mexico to shop, work, patronize entertainment venues, or socialize with friends and family—all protested, either in writing or in person.[62] Among the protesters were American citizens who lived in Mexico but worked in the United States as well as Asian nationals, Asian Mexicans, and Asian Americans, domiciled in Mexico, who sought a relaxation of the immigration and passport laws for business reasons.[63] Despite the authority possessed by bureau officials, many border residents, as one inspector reported, did not hesitate to criticize the new laws and even verbally abuse immigrant inspectors at the gates.[64]

The bureau's detractors included not only locals who sought crossing privileges from Mexico to the United States, but also those domiciled in the United States with business and personal interests in Mexico. In San Diego, American backers of a Tijuana race track were vehement opponents of the passport laws, arguing that these regulations would deter patrons from traveling south of the border and instead draw them north to competing entertainment venues in Los Angeles.[65] American tourists and border residents rallied to Tijuana's cause with their feet, defying the warnings of dry advocates about the dangers of Mexican leisure and liquor and overwhelming immigration inspectors at the gates with their demands to depart and re-enter the country.[66] Representatives from the Imperial Irrigation District protested that the passport law would halt construction of a canal project in Mexico (by delaying the entry of American skilled laborers) and thereby hurt American farmers who relied on the water from the canal to irrigate their crops.[67] Also engaged in binational ventures, an Arizona mining company requested exemptions for its Mexican workers who hauled ore mined north of the border to a processing facility south of the border.[68] Meanwhile, in Texas, the bureau received complaints about the passport laws from American ranchers who grazed their stock in Mexico.[69] Affecting small and large businesses alike, the passport law elicited objections from an American dentist who saw many patients south of the border and a request for an exemption from an American doctor who also needed to care for his patients in Mexico.[70]

In the borderlands, the new immigration and passport laws seemed to inconvenience everyone; as a State Department official explained, the passport law "cause[d] a considerable amount of irritation on both sides of the Border. The Mexicans, in ignorance, feel that it is a measure directed especially against them, to cause them annoyance and prevent them from purchasing the food and supplies they greatly need. The American merchants are dissatisfied because of the loss of trade."[71] In the face of this widespread opposition, bureau officials began the work of enforcing the Immigration Act of 1917 and the Passport Act of 1918.

In 1918, Commissioner General Anthony Caminetti asked how the agency could create an immigration policy that closed the border to subversives and unwanted immigrants but, at the same time, kept it open for the benefit of local residents who had legitimate reasons for crossing and recrossing the border each day.[72] In response, southwestern immigration officials developed new ways of managing the huge populations that crossed the border. Addressing the demands of local residents, border officials used their administrative discretion to waive or amend the rules set forth in the Immigration Act of 1917 and the Passport Act of 1918. In turn, they helped to fashion a series of policies, including the wartime agricultural labor program, the border crossing card, and a waiver to the literacy test that facilitated the movement of locals across the international boundary.

These administrative devices were significant because they effectively nullified the restrictions imposed on the US–Mexico border by the Passport Act and the Immigration Act. The wartime agricultural labor program rendered inoperative the head tax, contract labor laws, and literacy test on the US–Mexico border.[73] The border waiver to the literacy test further diluted the exclusionary intent underlying the Immigration Act. Meanwhile, the Section 13 certificate (and the subsequent exemptions to the Section 13 certificate itself) removed any incentive for individuals to procure passports. Yet it is important to note that these exceptions to the new regulations did not generate a condition of lawlessness on the US–Mexico border. Instead, immigration officials in the Southwest effectively created a set of immigration policies that were tailored to the needs of border residents and sustained the transnational character of the borderlands.

In shaping an immigration policy for the Mexican border, the Bureau of Immigration relied on the language of the Immigration Act of 1917, specifically the Ninth Proviso of its third section. This proviso stated that the "Commissioner General of Immigration with the approval of the Secretary of Labor shall issue rules and prescribe conditions, including exaction of such bonds as may be necessary to control and regulate the admission and return of otherwise inadmissible aliens applying for temporary admission."[74] In other words, the Ninth Proviso authorized the Secretary of Labor to waive the immigration laws for those migrants who would not pass an immigration inspection (and thereby qualify for permanent residence in the United States), but who demonstrated a need to be in the country for short periods of time. Thus while nativism inspired its drafting and passage, the Immigration Act of 1917 afforded Bureau of Immigration officials the administrative discretion to unravel the restrictionist spirit of the law.

The most famous invocation of the Ninth Proviso occurred during World War I when the Secretary of the Labor created the nation's first Mexican agricultural labor program. Due to enormous pressure from southwestern growers who claimed wartime labor shortages, the Secretary of Labor temporarily admitted Mexican farmworkers, exempting them from a formal immigration inspection and, more specifically, waiving the literacy test, head tax, and contract labor clauses. Under this program, employers in need of agricultural labor applied to the Department of Labor stating the number of workers required, the duration of the work period, and the wages and hours. They were also to maintain certain standards regarding wages and housing and working conditions.[75] In order to ensure that Mexican agricultural laborers returned to Mexico, wages were withheld from their monthly pay and distributed upon their departure from the country.[76] As an additional precaution against the permanent settlement of these Mexican nationals, immigration inspectors also possessed the authority to deport those who quit their jobs or sought work with a nonapproved employer.

Despite its efforts to maintain a restrictive immigration policy, the Department of Labor was under constant pressure to admit even more Mexican workers into the country. This was particularly the case during a 1917 draft scare, when thousands of workers hired under the wartime labor program left for Mexico.[77] Growers capitalized on this scare to ask the Department of Labor to alter the program in several ways: first, to loosen the provisions regarding the surveillance of workers; second, to allow Mexicans to work in nonagricultural occupations; and third, to extend the laborers' period of stay.[78] Growers also argued for the suspension of the head tax vis-à-vis Mexico altogether so as to facilitate the northward migration of farmworkers. Finally, they proposed that the federal government take a more active role in providing them with laborers by stationing officials in border towns to direct Mexican immigrants to agricultural employers.

In response, President Wilson extended the stay of Mexican agricultural laborers for the duration of the war. He also permitted Mexican nationals to work in nonagricultural industries such as the railroads and the coalmines. Later they were authorized to work on other mining operations and construction jobs throughout the Southwest. Finally, Wilson approved the posting of additional immigration inspectors along the Mexican border to assist in the admission of Mexican immigrant workers.[79] At the war's end, Wilson ended the temporary admissions program. But the protests of Southwestern growers led to the extension of the program through June 30, 1919. Two more extensions were granted through January 1921, when employers were instructed to return their workers to Mexico.[80]

The temporary admissions program proved a boon to Southwestern agriculture. It enabled growers to keep wages low despite an overall rise in agricultural wages over the course of the war. A representative from the Arizona Cotton Growers' Association estimated that the wartime labor importation program saved growers \$28 million in labor costs from 1919 through 1921.[81] Given these benefits, Southwestern growers lobbied for the permanent suspension of the immigration laws; on their behalf, Congressman Claude B. Hudspeth of Texas introduced a joint resolution exempting Mexican nationals from the literacy test and contract labor provisions of the Immigration Act of 1917. What growers wanted even more, however, was a return to the pre-1917 Immigration Act "policy of an open Mexican border."[82] Assuaging the fears of nativists, supporters of this bill argued that those Mexicans admitted would not become permanent residents; instead, Congressman John Nance Garner of Texas "contended that 80 percent of the Mexicans admitted to the United States would eventually return to Mexico and that never more than 2 percent would leave Texas for other states."[83] In the end, however, the House Committee on Immigration and Naturalization tabled Hudspeth's resolution, adopting the views of the American Federation of Labor that a sufficient labor force was already present in Southwest. Furthermore, under pressure from Hawaiian growers to admit Chinese immigrants as agricultural laborers, the Committee feared setting a precedent along the US–Mexico border that would open the door to Chinese immigration in Hawaii.

As bureau officials satisfied the wartime demands of one border constituency, they recognized that they also had to address the vehement demands of ordinary border residents for exemptions to the new literacy test. Indeed, immigration inspectors in the Southwest observed that for the first year after the passage of the literacy test, the "pressure, protests and complaints" were "well-nigh irresistible."[84] Thanks to the bureau's long-standing practice of excusing border residents from the head taxes and qualitative restrictions of the immigration laws, border residents had grown accustomed to crossing and recrossing the international boundary without hindrance. F. W. Berkshire, supervising inspector for the Mexican Border District, was keenly aware that the agency itself had perpetuated this state of affairs—allowing border residents, in his words, to "go and come in the course of their social and business intercourse with the least possible interference and friction." Thus upon the passage of the 1917 immigration law, Berkshire expressed uncertainty as to whether the agency ought to maintain what he referred to as its "time honored custom" by excusing border residents from the literacy test.[85]

Between 1917 and 1924, Berkshire and southwestern immigration inspectors addressed this question by again relying upon the discretionary authority afforded by the Ninth Proviso of the third section of the Immigration Act of 1917. As the commissioner general wrote in 1923, "there is no question under the Act and the Regulations as to the propriety of permitting entry of illiterates for purely temporary purposes."[86] Despite the authority provided by the Immigration Act of 1917, the bureau did not create a holistic waiver, or a general exemption from the literacy test, right away. Instead, southwestern agency officials began in a more limited and even tentative fashion, granting waivers to those illiterate migrants who lived in the United States but who, for personal or business reasons, crossed the border on a regular basis.[87] Concerns that locals domiciled in Mexico would use any literacy test exemption to evade a formal immigration inspection and settle permanently in the United States led bureau officials to prohibit the issuance of literacy test waivers to nonresident aliens. In addition, wartime fears about the entry of enemy aliens and long-standing concerns about illegal Chinese immigration also informed the bureau's decision to create a limited waiver in 1917.[88]

Border residents, however, remained highly dissatisfied by this initial modification of the literacy test. Bureau officials reported that thousands of locals continued to lobby immigrant inspectors at the gates for a complete suspension of the test. In response, immigration inspectors temporarily admitted thousands of illiterate Mexican nationals (domiciled south of the border) so that they could purchase a "loaf of bread, a cake of soap, a pound of starch, a quart of kerosene, a pound of sugar, a pound of flour, a pound of lard, etc."[89] As some inspectors admitted border residents on an unofficial basis, others conducted full-fledged hearings by a Board of Special Inquiry (BSI) to formalize these literacy test waivers.[90] Because these hearings required the participation of southwestern immigration inspectors and their supervisors, the collection of character references from local citizens, and a formal review by bureau officials in Washington, DC, they consumed much time and many resources.[91] Given the overwhelming demand for more relaxed border crossing privileges and the burdens of BSI hearings, southwestern immigration officials themselves proposed changes to the exception to the literacy test. In a 1920 report titled "Recommendations and Suggestions for the Betterment of the Service and for Remedial Legislation," southwestern agency officials called for the admission of illiterate border residents who routinely crossed the line for business or personal reasons. In addition, they advocated lenient inspections for illiterate alien residents of the United States who, upon their return home from Mexico, lacked proof of their domicile. Together, these amendments would remove some of the "irritating consequences" of the reading test.[92]

By 1923, the ongoing protests of border residents led the bureau to seek ways to broaden the exceptions to the literacy test on the US–Mexico border. As the bureau observed, "various chambers of commerce and individual concerns along the Mexican Border are taking concerted action in petitioning both the bureau direct and through Congressmen and Senators for modification of existing regulations that will permit temporary admission of illiterates for trading purposes."[93] In defense of this proposal, the bureau itself argued that any new exemption would not only benefit the economy of the border region but also promote American foreign relations with Mexico, as the commissioner general wrote:

> It is the opinion of the Bureau that in view of the close relations necessarily existing between the neighboring countries of Canada and Mexico and our own country, that some modification of existing practice along the Mexican Border is most desirable that will permit, under proper safeguards, the temporary entry of illiterate aliens for purposes of trade and other sound reasons.[94]

Finally, an official literacy test waiver would allow the bureau to standardize procedures on the Mexican and Canadian borders. Since the inception of the literacy test in 1917, Bureau of Immigration officials excused Canadian residents seeking temporary entry to visit "sick friends, or relatives, by reason of death, or funerals, or weddings, or business or family affairs, etc."[95] After soliciting specific proposals from its southwestern offices, the bureau, in 1923, authorized officers stationed on the Mexican and Canadian borders to admit "illiterate citizens or subjects of Canada and Mexico" who sought temporary entry for personal or business reasons.[96] In sum, these amendments to the literacy test created what one bureau official termed a "sectional" approach to immigration policy in the borderlands.[97]

Bureau of Immigration officials not only eased the restrictive provisions of the Immigration Act of 1917 for the benefit of border residents; in conjunction with State Department officials, they also addressed locals' concerns regarding the Passport Act of 1918. While these two agencies would engage in bitter disagreements about the implementation of the Passport Act of 1918, they agreed to develop an exemption to the act itself, specifically a border crossing card.[98] The border crossing card owed its origins to Rule 13 of the *Immigration Laws and Rules*, which provided that US citizens and foreigners who lived in close proximity to either side of the border and who frequently crossed the border for "legitimate pursuits" could receive a pass (a border crossing card), enabling them to cross the line without embarrassment or delay.[99] By 1918, State Department officials incorporated Immigration Rule 13 into their own regulations regarding the administration of the Passport Act.[100] Referred to as Section 13 certificates, they excused immigrants from paying the head tax,[101] and they were issued due to wartime exigencies, primarily for the benefit of Europeans who were unable to obtain passports from their home countries.[102]

In the issuance of these cards, the State Department and Bureau of Immigration tried to balance the nation's security needs and the borderlands' economic and social interests.[103] Thus State Department and Bureau of Immigration officials agreed that Section 13 certificates, particularly in the case of foreign nationals, were not intended to replace passports; as one State Department official wrote, aliens' identification cards were only "valid for a sufficient period for them to procure passports of the country to which they owe allegiance."[104] As a further security precaution, alien and citizen recipients of the Section 13 certificates were required to be residents of the border region where "residence on the border means residence at no greater distance than ten miles from border."[105] Moreover, these border crossing cards limited the radius of travel: US citizens and aliens were restricted to a ten-mile radius north and south of the line.[106] Finally, border crossing cards were not issued to American citizens who made more frequent trips to nonborder, or interior, regions of Mexico; these individuals were required to obtain passports.

Despite these wartime safeguards, the Immigration Service eventually relaxed the regulations and began issuing cards to those for whom they were not intended. As a Prohibition measure, the agency originally denied identification cards to "pleasure seekers[,] tourists[,] idlers[,] gamblers[,] race horse followers and the like."[107] Yet in 1919, after much protest from border residents and proprietors of the entertainment industry, the Immigration Service instituted a tourist pass system for those wishing to travel south of the border.[108] Tourist passes, initially good for a single day but later extended for ten-day use, allowed visits "in the border zone on either side of the Mexican border, whether such persons reside within or without the zone [the ten-mile limit], provided their identity, nationality and bona fides are established to the satisfaction of permit agents [immigration officials]." These permits were limited to American citizens, but immigration officials could, at their discretion, issue these permits to foreign nationals.[109]

The bureau and Department of State also made exceptions to the passport law on an ad hoc basis, again to cater to the needs of local communities. In Nogales, Sonora, the local American consul issued 4,000 provisional passports to Mexican citizens so that they could cross the line into Nogales, Arizona in order to shop. Under pressure from local businessmen who complained that passport regulations caused a downturn in the border economy, local immigration and State Department officials agreed to repeated extensions of these provisional passports.[110] In 1920 (when passport regulations had loosened somewhat, but still required nonborder residents from Mexico to present visaed passports), the State Department authorized the issuance of identification cards to visitors from nonborder (interior) regions of Mexico attending fairs in El Paso and Dallas.[111]

The bureau also conferred border crossing privileges upon Japanese and Chinese merchants living on both sides of the line.[112] While the immigration laws had long permitted these merchants to cross and recross between Mexico

Figure 1.2 San Ysidro border port of entry viewed from the Mexican side of the line, c. 1920. Courtesy of US Citizenship and Immigration Services History Office and Library, Washington, DC.

and the United States to purchase subsistence items or to engage in trade, these laws imposed strict requirements on their entry and departure. To ensure the latter, the service had to escort each Japanese entrant out of the country. For the Chinese, the regulations were even more stringent and required a tremendous amount of administrative work for the bureau.[113] For example, before approving the entry and departure of a Chinese transit, the bureau needed to conduct medical and background investigations, verify residency in the United States if the entrant claimed to be a US resident, complete in triplicate a description, with photo, of the Chinese transit upon entry, and arrange for an official escort upon departure.[114] The Passport Act threatened to impose a new set of restrictions upon these merchants and, from the perspective of local residents, impede border trade.

Indeed, both Japanese and Chinese merchants had strong advocates in border communities; thus, for example, the Bisbee Chamber of Commerce issued a complaint to Congressman Henry Ashurst about the inability of J. F. Hung, a Chinese Mexican merchant, to cross the line to trade. While the Bisbee Chamber of Commerce made no mention of the racial discrimination encountered by Chinese immigrants on both sides of the line, it protested that "the merchants of Bisbee are being discriminated against."[115] Chambers of commerce in El Paso, Nogales, and Los Angeles, among others, made similar requests on behalf of Chinese merchants.[116] In response to these demands, the Bureau of Immigration, by 1924, had authorized the issuance of border crossing cards to Chinese merchants living on either side of the border and who agreed to enter and depart the country from specific ports in Arizona, California, and Texas.[117] Like the shifts in the agency's border crossing policies, the designation of these ports, which came to include Laredo, Eagle Pass, El Paso, Nogales, Calexico, and Tijuana, was the result of intense lobbying efforts by border chambers of commerce.[118]

All of this is not to say that southwestern immigration officials suspended their concerns about the enforcement of the Chinese exclusion laws or their own anti-Asian sentiments. Instead, it is to say that southwestern border officials created class-based exceptions for a small group of Asian, Asian American, and Asian Mexican merchants and, in so doing, acknowledged the importance of creating an immigration policy that did not obstruct border trade. As the commissioner general himself explained in the case of a Chinese national who obtained border crossing privileges, "Wong J. Hong did not claim citizenship, but admitted, on the other hand, that he is an alien. So extensive were his business interests in Mexicali and the country lying below that city, and so necessary did it appear for him to enter and depart from the United States at will in connection with his business enterprises that the Department made his case an exception." To underscore the highly limited nature of this exemption, the commissioner general noted that the case of Wong J. Hong was not publicized so that "it might not be regarded as a precedent by other Chinese."[119]

As a further reflection of the bureau's ongoing concerns about Chinese immigration, the border crossing privileges issued to merchants of Chinese descent (residing in the United States) differed from those granted to non-Chinese immigrants.[120] American, European, Mexican, and Japanese nationals obtained border crossing cards under Rule 13 of the *Immigration Laws and Rules*. While at least one Chinese American merchant sought to obtain a Section 13 border crossing card,[121] the bureau ultimately chose to issue these merchants "citizens' return certificates" under the more stringent Chinese exclusion laws. At the same time, Chinese national merchants domiciled in the United States received Section 6 certificates (or "exempt return certificates"), which also were stipulated by the Chinese exclusion acts.[122] Because both certificates were only valid for six months, Chinese merchants seeking additional crossing privileges would have to reapply and undergo another extensive examination verifying their merchant status, US residency, and, if applicable, US citizenship. Once in possession of these certificates, Chinese merchants were required to cross and recross the border at designated ports so that the Bureau of Immigration could continually verify the merchant status of these men.[123]

Even though the Immigration Service relaxed border crossing regulations for their benefit, border residents continued to complain about the impositions of the law. Furthermore, despite wartime concerns about border security, local residents demanded fewer restrictions and even an open border. Writing on behalf of San Diego's business community, William Kettner, Congressman for the Eleventh District of California, called for "discontinuing war time restrictions against American citizens going into Mexico," since San Diego businessmen were "at peace with the people of Lower California."[124] According to Kettner, "full ingress and egress" was essential to the San Diego tourist industry, especially since the town was losing business to Los Angeles under the wartime passport and immigration restrictions. Even San Diego labor unions encouraged a relaxation of passport restrictions as a stimulus to the local economy.[125] Similarly, B. Rojo, ad interim chargé d'affaires for the Mexican Embassy, requested a loosening of border crossing regulations between Presidio, Texas and Ojinaga, Mexico for the benefit of Mexican businesses.[126] As the bureau itself realized, any reprieve from the law failed to quell the complaints of border residents and only led to more calls for leniency.

Although southwestern immigration officials created new policies for the benefit of border communities, they were not beholden to local interests. They had their own administrative reasons for pursuing alternative policies. Section 13 certificates, the temporary admissions program, and the literacy test waivers were intended to make life easier for the Immigration Service. No longer would the agency have to deal with the daily press of peoples seeking entry without a passport or seeking the promise of work. No longer would bureau officials have to hold BSI hearings for illiterate border residents requesting special permission to shop or visit family members across the line. But instead of making things easier, these exemptions only made things worse. For example, Supervising Inspector Berkshire observed that the relaxation of passport regulations perpetuated the very problem it purported to solve:

> Paradoxical as it may seem, every modification in the [passport] regulations made with a view to facilitating travel across the Border merely adds to the difficulties encountered. The reason is very simple. Relaxation inevitably increases the volume of travelers to be handled and there is a physical limit to the number of travelers who can be handled by a permit agent under the most favorable circumstances.[127]

Along with the exemptions to the passport laws, the agricultural labor program and the literacy test waivers generated more work for the Bureau of Immigration in the Southwest.

While the bureau undertook extensive efforts to implement the Immigration Act of 1917, the Passport Act of 1918, and the exemptions to both statutes, it conceded that those efforts could not succeed without more money, manpower, and materiel.[128] This is not to say, however, that southwestern immigration officials gave up. Instead, they called for an end to their responsibilities under the passport law, which, among all of their administrative duties, they blamed for diverting their attention and resources away from immigration law enforcement.[129] More important, it was the agency's experience with the border crossing card program, the agricultural labor program, and the literacy test waivers that led it to call for the formation of a roving police unit that became the Immigration Border Patrol.[130]

The wartime mandates increased the responsibilities of the Immigration Service on the Mexican border. The border crossing card and temporary admissions program placed a huge new population under the administrative supervision of the Bureau of Immigration. Migrants, including agricultural laborers, border crossers, and American citizens, among others, that the bureau once ignored now had to be processed, surveyed, and policed. Under the temporary admissions program 72,862 Mexican farmworkers were admitted.[131] Upon the inception of the Passport Act, one State Department official estimated that 100,000 to 200,000 border crossers would need to obtain appropriate border crossing identification (be it in the form of passports, identification papers, or alien declarations).[132] Bureau figures further attest to the heavy workload created by the Passport Act. Between September 15, 1918 and June 30, 1919, the service in District 23 (the Mexican Border District) issued 12,917 border permits to alien residents of the United States; 22,693 border permits to residents of Mexico; 15,413 citizens' identity cards to those residing in the United States; 362 citizens' identity cards to those residing in Mexico; and 14,130 one-trip tourist passes. During the same period, the service reviewed the passports of 6,663 US citizens entering the United States and 7,526 US citizens departing the country.[133]

Successful fulfillment of these tremendous responsibilities required an administrative infrastructure that did not exist. In its enforcement of the passport laws, labor importation program, and the immigration laws, the bureau, time and again, found itself underfunded and understaffed. Furthermore, the exemptions to the Passport Act and the Immigration Act of 1917 had a negative impact on the bureau's budget. Dependent primarily on head tax revenue and administrative fines, the Section 13 certificates and temporary admissions programs left the bureau strapped for cash by waiving the head tax. These fiscal shortfalls, along with federal budget cuts and the wartime draft, prevented the bureau from hiring more inspectors. Thus at many ports of entry, the service had no more than two inspectors on duty at a time processing applications, renewals, or cancellations of passport documents, in addition to handling regular immigration work.[134] Some southwestern offices tried to ease their workloads by temporarily hiring army and customs personnel, but their lack of familiarity with the immigration and passport laws often created confusion for immigrants.[135] The general weaknesses of the agency lowered morale within the force and, as a result, some officers took a lax approach to passport enforcement so as to complete their immigration duties.[136] It also led to ad hoc, delayed, or inconsistent implementation of the ever-changing passport policies, immigration laws, and the exceptions to both at the border.[137]

The lapses in the agency's approach to border enforcement along with the repeated modifications of the Immigration Act of 1917 and the Passport Act of 1918 rendered the agency the subject of harsh criticism. Some attacked it for failing to close the nation's borders to the entry of alien enemies, as one border resident observed:

> The immigration officials here make an effort to be as lenient as possible in the interpretation of the laws and the terms of the treaty existing between Mexico and the United States. Liberal instructions are given the field men in this respect. Inspectors and patrol officers are urged to cooperate with the local Mexican emigration authorities. There seems to be a tendency to lean ever backwards in this—as for example, the waiving of literacy requirements, the recognition of identification cards, permits, and the like in the case of temporary entry of visitors and laborers.[138]

This approach to immigration and passport law enforcement deeply concerned military officials. A Navy officer crossing the border at Laredo was shocked to find himself summarily waved across the line without an inspection. Writing to his superiors in the War Department, he noted, "it is a dangerous way to run such a service during war times and particularly on a frontier such as that of Mexico, which country harbors within its borders many of our enemies."[139]

The Immigration Service itself was also fully cognizant of the ways in which its administration of the laws left the border open to unwanted immigrants and potential alien enemies.[140] The temporary agricultural labor program sparked an increase in legal and undocumented Mexican immigration that, according to the 1920 annual report, placed a "severe tax" on the service.[141] Similarly, southwestern immigration inspectors reported that both official and unofficial literacy test waivers had been used by immigrants to achieve permanent domicile in the United States; as George J. Harris wrote in 1923, upon the inception of the literacy test in 1917 "thousands of aliens pleaded for and secured admission on the pretext that they were coming merely temporarily to make small purchases or to visit friends or relatives and took advantage of the opportunity to remain permanently."[142]

Immigrants also used their border crossing cards to circumvent the laws. In California, the bureau discovered that Hirochi Nagasaki, a Japanese national residing on the US side of the border, used his border crossing card to recruit Japanese immigrant laborers in Mexico to work on a 360-acre Calexico ranch that spanned the US–Mexico border. Nagasaki was only one of a hundred Japanese agriculturalists to whom the bureau had issued border crossing cards for the purpose of traveling to Mexico to lease or purchase agricultural lands.[143] Alarmed immigration agents wrote that Nagasaki had initiated a "Japanese invasion" of undocumented workers. To redress the problem, these particular agents did not call for the revocation of border crossing cards. Instead, they called for the creation of a border patrol.[144]

Multiple calls for a border patrol were made by various immigration inspectors posted along the US–Mexico border. Bureau officials who administered the passport laws and the border crossing cards, inspectors who issued literacy test waivers, and inspectors who tried to enforce the provisions of the agricultural labor program independently concluded that a roving patrol force was necessary for effective border enforcement.[145] This consensus reflected their shared understanding of the obstacles and problems surrounding immigration law enforcement on the US–Mexico border. Indeed, in calling for a border patrol, these bureau officials acknowledged that taken literally, the task of closing the nation's borders to unwanted immigrants was impossible. As a result, in the minds of these immigration officials, an effective border enforcement policy needed to take place at the border itself and beyond. A mobile patrol force, operating in the nation's interior, would be able to monitor and apprehend those immigrants

Figure 1.3 Japanese farmers in Chula Vista, California, c. 1920. Reproduced by permission of the Japanese American Historical Society of San Diego.

who had not only violated the letter of the immigration laws but also benefited from the exemptions to the Immigration Act of 1917 and the Passport Act of 1918—exemptions created by the Bureau of Immigration itself.

Even though the Immigration Act of 1917 sharply curbed the numbers of Mexican immigrants seeking admission for permanent residence, it did not diminish the number of border crossers. By the mid-1920s, the regulation of these nonimmigrant border crossers, rather than the restriction of immigrants, became the central concern of the Bureau of Immigration. In 1928, the commissioner general of Immigration underscored this point when he observed that the nation's borders had surpassed Ellis Island as the major ports of entry. On the Mexican and Canadian borders, he continued, "a great change has been taking place . . . steadily are they approaching a place of first importance in the scheme of things from an immigration standpoint. The fiscal year just closed witnessed a movement back and forth across these frontiers made up of citizens and aliens aggregating 53,000,000 entrants. Many of these, of course, were commuters, visitors, excursionists, etc."[146] Their numbers, as Table 1.1 illustrates, would remain just as substantial well into the 1950s.

Table 1.1 Inward Movement of Aliens and Citizens over International Land Boundaries: Years Ended June 30, 1928 to 1953[1]

Period	All arrivals			Via Canadian Border			Via Mexican Border		
	Total	Aliens	Citizens	Total	Aliens	Citizens	Total	Aliens	Citizens
1928–1953	1,587,082,113	806,765,760	780,316,353	742,028,412	334,431,156	407,597,256	845,053,701	472,334,604	372,719,097
1928	53,539,702	30,162,945	23,376,757	26,410,720	12,823,162	13,587,558	27,128,982	17,339,783	9,789,199
1929	57,905,685	31,562,934	26,342,751	30,854,674	15,221,215	15,633,459	27,051,011	16,341,719	10,709,292
1930	59,276,639	30,034,301	29,242,338	32,251,548	14,498,083	17,753,465	27,025,091	15,536,218	11,488,873
1931–1940	477,022,589	255,240,806	221,781,783	252,372,946	117,878,795	134,494,151	224,649,643	137,362,011	87,287,632
1931	52,991,765	26,481,279	26,510,486	28,939,718	12,929,750	16,009,968	24,052,047	13,551,529	10,500,518
1932	46,858,719	22,862,697	23,996,022	23,592,271	10,275,347	13,316,924	23,266,448	12,587,350	10,679,098
1933	40,662,207	20,560,826	20,101,381	18,877,956	8,434,715	10,443,241	21,784,251	12,126,111	9,658,140
1934	40,749,632	21,627,711	19,121,921	19,608,768	9,105,383	10,503,385	21,140,864	12,522,328	8,618,536
1935	43,424,920	23,497,061	19,927,859	21,707,282	10,165,762	11,541,520	21,717,638	13,331,299	8,386,339
1936	46,152,918	25,739,288	20,413,630	24,965,327	11,861,161	13,104,166	21,187,591	13,878,127	7,309,464
1937	51,722,089	28,841,066	22,881,023	29,022,710	13,669,009	15,353,701	22,699,379	15,172,057	7,527,322
1938	52,993,989	28,651,501	24,342,488	29,970,636	14,230,131	15,740,505	23,023,353	14,421,370	8,601,983
1939	51,363,952	28,858,336	22,505,616	28,631,775	14,141,028	14,490,747	22,732,177	14,717,308	8,014,869
1940	50,102,398	28,121,041	21,981,357	27,056,503	13,066,509	13,989,994	23,045,895	15,054,532	7,991,363

(continued)

Table 1.1 **Continued**

Period	All arrivals			Via Canadian Border			Via Mexican Border		
	Total	Aliens	Citizens	Total	Aliens	Citizens	Total	Aliens	Citizens
1941–1950	628,278,660	308,083,624	322,195,036	267,883,986	110,511,592	157,372,394	360,394,674	195,572,032	164,822,642
1941	38,974,008	18,617,633	20,356,375	15,454,432	4,096,470	11,357,962	23,519,576	14,521,163	8,998,413
1942	43,679,900	20,975,281	22,704,619	17,480,723	5,253,535	12,277,188	26,199,177	15,721,746	10,477,431
1943	40,717,372	20,378,438	20,338,934	14,806,312	5,623,592	9,182,720	25,911,060	14,754,846	11,156,214
1944	46,243,243	22,441,827	23,801,416	18,228,744	7,621,217	10,607,527	28,014,499	14,820,610	13,193,889
1945	55,801,140	27,395,495	28,405,645	23,515,596	10,482,226	13,033,370	32,285,544	16,913,269	15,372,275
1946	74,240,190	37,085,718	37,154,472	30,163,138	13,443,528	16,719,610	44,077,052	23,642,190	20,434,862
1947	77,350,266	38,921,170	38,429,096	34,839,194	15,773,964	19,065,230	42,511,072	23,147,206	19,363,866
1948	78,362,207	38,892,545	39,469,662	34,888,274	15,535,509	19,352,765	43,473,933	23,357,036	20,116,897
1949	85,400,278	40,077,743	45,322,535	39,736,497	16,054,649	23,681,848	45,663,781	24,023,094	21,640,687
1950	87,510,056	41,297,774	46,212,282	38,771,076	16,626,902	22,144,174	48,738,980	24,670,872	24,068,108
1951......	92,400,356	44,620,010	47,780,346	41,341,410	18,680,987	22,660,423	51,058,946	25,939,023	25,119,923
1952......	103,712,099	51,129,142	52,582,957	44,212,088	20,898,541	23,313,547	59,500,011	30,230,601	29,269,410
1953......	114,946,383	57,931,998	57,014,385	46,701,040	23,918,781	22,782,259	68,245,343	34,013,217	34,232,126

[1] Inward movement of aliens and citizens over international land boundaries first recorded in 1928. Each and every arrival of the same person counted separately.

Source: US Department of Justice, Immigration and Naturalization Service.

In response to these conditions, Bureau of Immigration officials, for the remainder of the twentieth century, exercised their administrative discretion and constructed distinctive immigration policies for the borderlands. By carving out exceptions to the nation-bound premises of federal immigration laws, these policies reflected the agency's own recognition that statutes alone could not halt the circulation of peoples at the border. Between 1917 and 1924 at least three policy innovations—the wartime agricultural labor program, the literacy test waivers, and the border crossing card—were devised to satisfy the immediate needs of border residents and border officials rather than the aspirations of immigration restrictionists.

Yet these amendments to the immigration and passport laws only generated new quandaries, such as heavier workloads, and aggravated old ones, particularly undocumented immigration. The bureau's own policy innovations created the very phenomenon—the so-called problem of illegal immigration—that it was mandated to resolve. As one solution, the bureau in 1924 created the Border Patrol, a mobile unit that would shore up the weaknesses in the agency's enforcement capacities along the nation's borders and beyond.

2

The Battle for the Border

It was this same element who sometime past sent to the Bureau a resolution asking that the international boundary line be moved back to the
outskirts of Calexico. This petition seemed so ridiculous that we paid
very little attention to it as we could not conceive that any American
city really desired to become a Mexican city which, in the last analysis,
the granting of the petition would be.
—Harry E. Hull, Commissioner General, January 28, 1926

In the 1920s, local residents from California to Texas demanded that the Bureau
of Immigration move its operations away from the border, redrawing the geopolitical boundary between the United States and Mexico.[1] In Arizona, the Nogales
Chamber of Commerce boldly proposed the relocation of the port of entry
from the international line to the northern boundary of town.[2] The Governor
of Arizona endorsed a similar plan, proposing the creation of a "state free or
trade zone" extending one mile north of the international border in which the
Immigration Service would cede to the State of Arizona control over immigration regulation.[3] In California, Calexico residents went so far as to ask that the
international boundary line itself be resituated to a point north of the city.[4]

These conceptions of the border, as a contingent and even portable boundary,
would pose serious challenges for the Border Patrol, a mobile enforcement unit
created in 1924 to harden the line to the entry of unwanted immigrants. Well
into the 1920s, border residents continued to resist the imposition of federal
authority along the nation's southern line, expressing their opposition to the passage of a fresh set of immigration restriction laws in Congress. These measures
included the Immigration Act of 1924 (which created the national origins quota
system), the Appropriations Act of May 28, 1924 (which created the Border
Patrol), and the Act of March 4, 1929 (which created the first criminal penalties
for undocumented immigration).[5] While many border residents shared the nativist sentiments that inspired the passage of these laws, others thought mainly
about their pocketbooks. The new immigration laws would interfere with their
ability to take advantage of the regional economic boom that resulted from the

passage of the Volstead Act in 1919, a measure that would enforce the prohibitions against the manufacture, sale, or transportation of alcoholic beverages in the United States, as stipulated under the Eighteenth Amendment.[6] Faced with the enduring defiance of locals, the Border Patrol recognized that it would have to posit its own vision of the border.

This chapter traces the early history of the Border Patrol and its battle for the border. In its effort to close the line to unwanted immigrants, the unit redefined and relocated it, transforming it from a line into a space or from an international boundary into a legal jurisdiction, which began at the border and extended far within the nation's interior. Within this jurisdiction or border zone the Border Patrol developed a broad array of policing powers vis-à-vis undocumented immigrants, including the authority to pursue, search, and arrest these individuals without regard for the Fourth Amendment prohibition against unreasonable searches and seizures.[7] Yet in the 1920s, this conception of the border failed to supplant the competing visions of the international line. Instead, the Patrol's legal construction of the borderlands contributed another layer of meaning to the developing genealogy of the border. In this period the US–Mexico border region was also construed as a geopolitical boundary, a transnational social space, a vice-free zone, an economic free trade zone, and a symbol of national sovereignty.

The multiple challenges faced by the early Border Patrol and its efforts to overcome them are the themes of this chapter. It first focuses on the ways in which border residents and southwestern immigration inspectors pursued open border policies so as to sustain Prohibition-era economic growth. Their vision of the border as an economic zone would fuel local opposition to the emergence of the Border Patrol. Federal as well as local officials presented additional quandaries for the new unit. The second part of the chapter describes how federal ambivalence regarding the very creation of the Border Patrol left it without the resources necessary to carry out its mandate. In an effort to compensate for all of these weaknesses, the unit, as described in the third part of the chapter, resorted to the law, exercising its administrative discretion to devise a broad vision of border enforcement. Yet as the final part of the chapter explains, the Patrol's efforts only generated more debates about the nature of immigration law enforcement and the very meaning of the border.

In the 1920s border residents gave voice to the saying that the more things change, the more things stay the same. Their persistent and vociferous calls for the creation of an open border or a border zone repeated analogous demands made during World War I in response to the passage of the Immigration Act of 1917 and the Passport Act of 1918. Yet local residents made these proposals in a period of enormous change. Thanks to the passage of the Volstead Act, the border region witnessed the rise of a binational tourist industry that fueled economic growth over the course of the decade. Seeking pleasure or profit, millions of tourists, businessmen, workers, and settlers flocked to the region in the 1920s. Their substantial contributions to the local economy led border residents to vehemently protest the creation and enforcement of any crossing restrictions. Thus as nativists and moral reformers successfully lobbied for the passage of border crossing curfews, the Immigration Act of 1924, the creation of the Border Patrol, and the Act of March 4, 1929, border residents repeatedly obtained exemptions to these measures. The exemptions afforded by the Bureau of Immigration were so extensive that despite its concerns about unauthorized entry, it played a pivotal role in creating the very border zone sought by local residents.

While the Mexican Revolution and World War I drew the nation's attention to the border as a sovereign space, Prohibition added another dimension to Americans' image of the border, as it became a major tourist destination for the remainder of the 1920s.[8] Travelers from all over the country visited Mexican border towns where they could escape the strictures of Prohibition in a variety of entertainment venues, including saloons, dance halls, gambling parlors, and racetracks.[9] In 1920 alone, approximately 420,000 tourists crossed the border, an explosive increase from 14,000 the prior year.[10] Joining their ranks were saloon proprietors, liquor manufacturers, entertainment purveyors, and liquor smugglers who relocated their businesses south of the border.[11] While the vast majority of these proprietors were American, Mexicans, Europeans, and Asians also opened small businesses in Mexican border towns.[12]

As Americans traveled south of the border to imbibe, Mexicans traveled north to meet their subsistence needs and to find work. Although Prohibition facilitated the industrial and agricultural development of Mexican border towns, their ongoing focus on the sale and manufacture of alcohol meant that residents had to travel to American border towns to purchase a wide variety of everyday items, including food products, household goods, and clothing.[13] By 1926, Juárez residents spent $1.56 million on consumer goods purchased south of the border and $15 million in El Paso.[14] Similar disparities appeared in other twin-city complexes along the border: in 1926, residents of Nogales and Mexicali spent $26,000 on consumer goods in Mexico and $10.5 million in the United States; in Tijuana, virtually all consumer goods were purchased north of the line.[15] The lack of economic diversification in Mexican border towns also led many to commute across the border for work.[16] Here, they were drawn by the rapid growth of southwestern agriculture, mining, manufacturing, and transportation industries in the 1920s.[17] Indeed, in the Southwest, the demand for workers was so great that the numbers of agricultural and industrial workers in the region increased during a period in which their numbers declined in the nation as a whole.[18]

Figure 2.1 Agua Caliente Racetrack, Tijuana, Baja California, c. 1920. Reproduced by permission of the San Diego History Center, S-653.

Vice brought profits as well as people to the borderlands. At both the federal and local levels, taxes on liquor production, licensing fees imposed upon entertainment establishments, and tourist expenditures provided a critical source of revenue in Mexico. In 1923, taxes on liquor production alone constituted 5 percent of federal revenues; over the course of the decade in Mexicali, entertainment industry concessions constituted anywhere from 9 to 48 percent of city revenues.[19] The funds in turn allowed federal and state governments to make infrastructural improvements, financing the construction of public works such as schools, libraries, and roads.[20] North of the line, American border towns, automobile clubs, and railroad lines sought to capture the attention and dollars of tourists headed to Mexico. Through national advertising campaigns, they highlighted the amenities, historical attractions, and pleasant climate of the region, encouraging tourists to make a stay in an American border town one stop in their journeys south of the line.[21] These efforts paid off, sparking the growth of the service and retail sectors, including the hotel, restaurant, real estate, and banking industries in the Southwest.[22] Finally, sustained by a Mexican national workforce, the agriculture, ranching, and mining industries, which were of far greater economic significance to the region than tourism, also flourished during Prohibition.[23]

In the midst of this economic boom, anti-vice forces from both the United States and Mexico tried to close the line.[24] American prohibitionists worried that the Mexican vice industry threatened the moral and physical health of its American patrons and undermined their broader reform campaign at home in the States.[25] They asked the Mexican government to deny licenses to American businesses and called for the creation of a fifty-mile dry zone, or what effectively would constitute a vice-free zone in the region adjacent to the border.[26] In Mexico, reformers objected to the vice industries for nationalistic as well as moral reasons. Prohibition, as historian Oscar Martínez observes, drew Mexican border towns into "the economic orbit of the United States": in Juárez and Tijuana, for example, Americans owned most of the entertainment venues, hired American citizens, and served a predominantly American clientele.[27] In response, Mexican reformers demanded protections for Mexican employees and the increased hiring of Mexican nationals, as well as the closure of American entertainment establishments.[28]

The reformers' campaign reshaped border crossing regulations on both sides of the line. To deter the entry of unwanted pleasure seekers, Mexico, throughout the 1920s, passed laws that criminalized the narcotics trade, regulated the

Figure 2.2 A casino in Tijuana, Baja California, c. 1920. Reproduced by permission of the San Diego History Center, S-659.

prostitution industry, taxed entertainment venues, and established early closing hours at a few border ports of entry.[29] In order to diversify the predominantly American workforce in Mexican border towns, a Mexican court in 1925
required companies to ensure that at least half of their employees were Mexican
nationals.[30] On the US side of the border, the Treasury Department, between
1925 and 1930, increased the number of customs inspectors on patrol from 111
to 723.[31] Searching travelers and their vehicles for illicit contraband, they made
the border crossing experience more "intrusive and time-consuming" than ever
before.[32] At the behest of local reformers, customs officials instituted early closing times at the border ports of entry until the demise of Prohibition in 1933.
Although there was much variation in these curfews, they shared the same purpose: to drive Mexican vice industries out of business by cutting off their primary source of revenue—the American tourist.[33]

In some border towns, the early closing hours had a dramatic impact. In
Tijuana, for example, the liquor, gambling, and prostitution industries experienced a 50 percent decline in business.[34] Yet the demands of American and
Mexican moral reformers never trumped the economic interests of border communities and their national governments, particularly when the vice industry
generated so much profit. As a result, the vice controls established by both governments, as historian Rachel St. John observes, were "conditional."[35] On both
sides of the line, federal curfews were occasionally suspended at the request of
local elites or for special events such as conventions, holiday celebrations, major
horse races, or boxing matches in Mexico.[36] American and Mexican officials also
took particular care to enforce the vice laws in ways that would not disrupt the
entry of presumably benign migrants such as merchants, workers, local residents,
and nonvice tourists who promoted the economic development of the region.[37]

In this period, the Bureau of Immigration played a central role in ensuring the
free flow of traffic through the border ports of entry. In so doing, immigration inspectors, as in World War I, remained highly responsive to the demands of border
residents, despite the passage of the Volstead Act in 1919 and a series of new
immigration measures in the 1920s. These measures included the Immigration
Act of 1924, the Act of March 4, 1929, and the Border Patrol, which was created
in 1924. Although Mexican nationals were exempted from the national origins
quota system mandated by the Immigration Act of 1924, they remained subject
to the qualitative restrictions stipulated in the Immigration Act of 1917. Border
residents repeatedly protested its bans on the entry of those deemed mentally,
physically, and morally undesirable; persons likely to become a public charge;
persons suspected of entering in violation of the contract labor provisions; and
persons unable to pass the literacy test. As in World War I, border communities
charged that immigration restrictions, in general, hindered trade and good relations between the United States and Mexico.[38] In further support of their cause,

they argued that very exclusion of Mexico from the 1924 quota laws underscored their point that national immigration laws had no place in the Southwest.[39]

While the bureau repeatedly rejected requests to waive the immigration laws altogether, correspondence from the 1920s highlights the agency's willingness to implement old and new strategies to promote the development of the border economy.[40] Immigration officials, as in World War I, exercised their administrative discretion to facilitate the crossing and recrossing of border residents. El Paso District Director Grover C. Wilmoth, for example, authorized the relaxation of the literacy test requirements and the quota provisions of the Immigration Act of 1924, permitting the entry of illiterate Mexican merchants and inadmissible Europeans for the sake of the local economy. In a similar spirit, he authorized the temporary entry of Mexican businessmen, Mexican government officials, and all foreigners personally known to immigration inspectors without any form of identification.[41]

Wilmoth also responded to the demands of border communities in novel ways. In 1928, the Nogales Chamber of Commerce complained that personnel changes at the border ports of entry left the impression that the immigration laws had changed, deterred border crossing, and, ultimately, hurt local business. As a solution, the chamber proposed the installation of an immigration inspector "familiar with local conditions and the people who most frequently cross and re-cross the line."[42] Even though Wilmoth would become one of the most vocal advocates of a strong border enforcement policy, as a young, new leader in the agency, he acceded to the demands of border businessmen, agreeing to place on line duty only those officers familiar with local circumstances and needs.[43]

For the benefit of local residents, the Bureau of Immigration in the Southwest built new ports of entry along the line so as to facilitate local border crossings. Residents from Texas to California pressured the Immigration Service for the creation of these ports, arguing that they were essential to the economic development of their towns.[44] In Yuma, Arizona, for example, locals demanded a new port at San Luis "upon necessity for movement of Mexican laborers back and forth across the International boundary for agricultural purposes, and upon the revenue received by Yuma commercial interests from residents of the San Luis district."[45] Often, as was the case in Yuma, the bureau was unable to satisfy local demands for a new port due to insufficient border traffic, a lack of manpower, or both. Yet in lieu of official ports of entry, the agency responded to local concerns by creating various informal entry points along the border. For example, in San Ygnacio, Texas, the service operated what it referred to as an "unofficial crossing place" that permitted locals to complete their shopping north of the line.[46] In Ysleta and Fort Hancock, Texas, the service opened what it termed "limited" or "modified" ports of entry. Manned by three federal officials representing Customs, Immigration, and Public Health, it served Mexican residents south of the

Figure 2.3 A Bureau of Immigration inspector looking into the window of a Pickwick Stage coach, Southern California, 1927. Courtesy of US Citizenship and Immigration Services History Office and Library, Washington, DC.

border who had regularly crossed north to purchase subsistence items.[47] Finally, at established ports of entry such as Calexico, the bureau bolstered its inspection infrastructure by building a new gate. More important, the agency built the gate at a site favored by the local chamber of commerce.[48] Whether informal or formal, the new border entry points served as vivid illustrations of the ways in which southwestern immigration inspectors literally constructed the border as a binational economic zone.

In the 1920s southwestern agency officials continued to facilitate the entry not only of visitors, dignitaries, and merchants, but also farmworkers, especially given the postwar growth of the agribusiness industry. Wilmoth, in particular, did everything in his power to ensure the seamless entry of Mexican laborers for the benefit of farmers and ranchers. In 1928, he openly admitted that his officers in Texas turned a blind eye to the illicit crossings of Mexican workers: "We have made no special effort to disturb these local crossers who for years have been accustomed to come to the American side to work."[49] He also actively discouraged immigration inspectors in Arizona from searching farms and ranches for undocumented immigrants.[50] All of his efforts underscored the agency's role in fostering regional economic development.[51]

Yet for both border residents and officials, administrative grace had its limits. While southwestern immigration agents and local residents welcomed the temporary visits of tourists, merchants, and laborers, they did not demonstrate the same attitude toward immigrants, including Chinese, European, and Mexican nationals, who sought permanent domicile in the United States.[52] Ethnic Chinese expelled from Mexico during the late 1920s and early 1930s, in particular, faced hostility north of the line, as both local residents and immigration officials advocated their deportation from the United States.[53] Even border chambers of commerce, which had fought vigorously for the establishment of crossing policies, made a distinction between nonimmigrants and immigrants. For the benefit of the former, J. B. Bristol of the Nogales Chamber of Commerce requested the complete suspension of the immigration laws, but he did not support the loosening of inspection standards for Mexican immigrants.[54] Moreover, he encouraged the expeditious deportation of Mexican nationals held in Arizona state penitentiaries, hospitals, and asylums because they allegedly constituted a burden on the public fisc.[55] The bureau concurred with Bristol's views and created a two-tiered inspection policy that welcomed the admission of businessmen, shoppers, and tourists but required comprehensive investigations for those seeking admission for permanent residence.[56]

In the 1920s, the Border Patrol would assume a major role in the enforcement of the immigration laws along the US–Mexico border.[57] As the agency's inspection force manned the ports of entry, the Border Patrol would monitor the spaces between and beyond them. Yet the agency's legal innovations, especially its border crossing policies, generated quandaries for the Border Patrol. The unit discovered that the constant protests of border residents and the confusion surrounding the repeated modifications to the immigration laws created a sense of frustration among some immigration inspectors. At other border ports of entry, Border Patrol officers found that immigration officials ceased their inspection duties altogether. These lax inspections undermined the work of the Patrol, as one official observed, "as the matter then stood aliens entered the United States without inspection through the regular crossing places and afterwards on the same date were apprehended by patrol inspectors and brought to the immigration office for return to Mexico."[58] In these cases, federal courts exposed the weaknesses of the agency's enforcement capacities by refusing to uphold prosecutions for unauthorized entry when those entries resulted from the dereliction of the immigration inspection force.[59]

Confronted by these social and institutional obstacles to immigration law enforcement, the Border Patrol had a number of incentives to devise a set of enforcement practices that took place not only at the international boundary but also far beyond it. While the orientation of immigration inspectors at the border ports of entry might have been local, the Border Patrol, during the twentieth century, developed a vision of border enforcement that would become national in scope. In the process, the unit would reconstruct the border once again.

When it was created in 1924, the Border Patrol was not new. Wartime concerns about border security highlighted the importance of border policing; as a result, US military, customs, and immigration officials launched their own respective border patrol units during World War I. Decades earlier in 1904, the agency created the Mounted Guard, a mobile force charged with patrolling the borders and the highways and rail lines that ran beyond them, that was the direct precursor of the Immigration Border Patrol.[60] While the Mounted Guard focused on restricting the flow of Chinese immigrants crossing the nation's borders,[61] the Border Patrol also pursued European immigrants (who, through surreptitious border crossings, sought to avoid the qualitative restrictions of the 1917 immigration act or the quota systems of the 1921 and 1924 immigration acts) and Mexican immigrants (whose entry was limited by the provisions of the 1917 law and the visa requirements of the 1924 immigration act).

Despite the resemblances between the Border Patrol and earlier border policing units, the creation of the Border Patrol marked an important turning point in American immigration law enforcement. The early weaknesses of this new unit led it to seek an unprecedented expansion in its authority to pursue and apprehend unwanted immigrants. In the process, Border Patrol officials in the Southwest played the primary role in reshaping the policies and, in turn, the statutes pertaining to immigration law enforcement. In the most basic terms, these statutes extended the jurisdiction of the Border Patrol, authorizing it to monitor not only the international boundaries but also the interior spaces, both public and private, of the nation. Construed more broadly, these legislative reforms transformed the border from a geopolitical dividing line into a space in which the Border Patrol could justify under law a highly aggressive approach to immigration law enforcement.

In the 1920s, the Border Patrol was beset by liabilities, whether legal, institutional, or social. The unit's very creation was not momentous but instead seemed like an afterthought as Congress slipped the authorization for the Patrol into an appropriations act that said virtually nothing about its mission, organization, or operational procedures.[62] The Appropriations Act of May 28, 1924 simply allocated one million dollars for the creation of a border patrol to enforce "Section 8 of the Immigration Act of February 5, 1917 (39 Stat. 874), which prohibited smuggling, harboring, concealing, or assisting an alien not duly admitted by an immigrant inspector or not lawfully entitled to enter or reside in the United States."[63] Given the vagueness of the statute, the Border Patrol struggled to form a new, cohesive, and effective policing unit.

When the first part of the appropriation was made available in June 1924, the bureau was given only three weeks to get the force in the field—issuing rules and regulations, purchasing supplies, and hiring and assigning men. Since there was not enough time to draft and administer a civil service exam specifically for Border Patrol officers, the first recruits were selected from a list of those men who had passed the civil service exams for railroad mail clerks and immigration inspectors.[64] Others were former members of the Mounted Guard (which was dissolved upon the creation of the Border Patrol), who had the most experience conducting border surveillance.[65] The first Border Patrol force was composed of 450 men, of whom approximately 250 were stationed on the Mexican border.[66]

These initial hires from the railway postal registers proved unqualified and unaccustomed to working long hours in harsh outdoor conditions. Thus the bureau advertised for new officers and attempted to recruit a different type of man:

> The patrol, which is a branch of the immigration service will accept no man unless he is big and strong and fearless. He must have experience in cowboy work, tracking and general border occupations and he must have had service in some highly organized police unit or in some regular army.[67]

Furthermore, the ad required three years' experience in ranch work along the border since the primary duty of the officers would be to ride along the line on horseback. As a result, the Immigration Service "hired former cowboys, skilled workers, and small ranchers as its first patrol officers in the Mexican border district."[68] Many of them also had former military experience, having served in the armed forces during World War I, or police experience as former Texas Rangers.[69] Within a few years, the force grew to 1,000 patrol officers.

In fulfilling their enforcement duties, the first Patrol officers obtained little guidance from the original Border Patrol statute or their peers and supervisors in the Bureau of Immigration.[70] Describing his first day of work in Del Rio, Texas on July 28, 1924, officer Wesley Stiles found that "no one knew what we were supposed to do or how we were supposed to do it."[71] When the new recruits asked for instructions, they were told to "catch aliens." Stiles observed that they caught a few "just by main strength and awkwardness," but for the most part, "all of August we didn't do anything, we just wandered around town here." By October, several of his fellow officers decided to take an unauthorized vacation.[72] Meanwhile, Border Patrol officers on the Canadian border found themselves similarly perplexed; as a result, one official drafted his own Border Patrol procedures regarding pursuit strategies, arrests, and detentions and sent them to the commissioner general for his review.[73]

The early Border Patrol recruits were also hampered by a lack of resources. They were provided with what Stiles laughingly referred to as "old relics" for weapons. Nor were they given uniforms or badges, which made it difficult for them to assert their authority; Stiles noted, "we didn't have a darn thing to show who we were or what we were supposed to do . . . [no one in the general public] knew what it was all about."[74] No Border Patrol school or training program existed. "None of us," Stiles admitted, "spoke any Spanish to speak of and somebody suggested, we'd better get you a speaking dictionary . . . But anyway, we didn't have any schooling. No one knew what to do. That was the big trouble." Stiles also recounted that he and his fellow recruits had no place to live, so "the sheriff gave us a place to sleep in the jail." Having nothing to eat, "we finally made arrangements to eat with E Troop of the Fifth Cavalry. They charged us I believe it was $.35 a meal to eat there." Also, in its first year, Patrol officers had no means of transportation and had to conduct patrols on foot.

Conditions improved somewhat by the following year; Stiles received a badge, uniform, and monthly fuel allowance of thirteen dollars.[75] By then the government also purchased approximately one vehicle for every five officers.[76] Stiles and his partner were among those who did not receive a government vehicle, so they bought an automobile together to use when on duty. Yet at their office in Nogales, use of the car was limited to 1,000 miles per month or an average of 33 miles per day so as to limit government fuel reimbursements. An inspection of the Nogales Border Patrol operations noted, "to limit the use of a car in this manner simply limits the activities of the patrol inspectors." When these officers exceeded the mileage allowance, they resorted to using their own cars or simply patrolling on foot.[77]

As a result of these initial problems, 25 percent of the new hires left in the first few months.[78] For some of those who remained the job offered social mobility, especially since the Border Patrol paid a decent salary at the time.[79] In the early days, it was also a job that attracted men who had a love of adventure. In his diary, Officer Dogie Wright observed, "Laying in on a wet river bank or in a wet cotton field is one thing that will separate the men from the boys."[80] In 1927, the commissioner general characterized Patrol officers as follows: "The border patrol is a young man's organization; it appeals strongly to the lover of the big outdoors . . . the business upon which it is engaged calls for manhood, stamina, versatility, and resourcefulness in the highest degree."[81]

It was this very love of adventure, however, that contributed to the lack of professionalism within the unit. Corruption was noticeably acute in the Texas offices of the Border Patrol. During an inspection tour of these offices, Clifford Alan Perkins discovered inspectors aiding and abetting immigrant and liquor smugglers.[82] In addition, he found Border Patrol officers stealing from undocumented European immigrants prior to their arrest.[83] Early recruits fashioned themselves after the Texas Rangers and were reported "drinking on the job, reading and socializing with friends while on duty, reckless driving, rumor-mongering, and accepting gratuities from aliens."[84] The presence of ex-Rangers, well known for their violent vigilante campaigns against ethnic Mexicans, on the Border Patrol force also fostered an aggressive orientation toward the pursuit and apprehension of Mexican immigrants.[85] According to historian Mae Ngai, these attitudes resulted in the arrest of "nearly five times as many suspected illegal aliens in the Mexican border area as it did in the Canadian border area."[86]

Yet in its first year of operation, Border Patrol officers recognized that their immigration enforcement capacities were hamstrung by the unit's own enabling statute: the Appropriations Act of May 28, 1924 gave them no authority to pursue undocumented immigrants. Upon his discovery of this problem, the commissioner general wrote, "If the Bureau is right in its understanding of the matter, the border patrols are now without the slightest authority to stop a vehicle crossing the border for the purpose of search, or otherwise, nor can they legally prevent the entry of an alien in violation of law."[87] Under the statute, immigration officials only possessed the authority to apprehend immigrant smugglers or those offering assistance to individuals attempting to cross the line without inspection.[88] In this situation, Border Patrol officers exercised those powers available to them. First, they pursued immigrant smugglers under the original Border Patrol act. Second, even though the Border Patrol could not pursue an individual undocumented immigrant under the immigration laws, they could do so under the Passport Act of 1918, which rendered entry without inspection a criminal act.[89] Finally, officers exercised the common law right of peace officers and citizens to arrest on sight (that is, without warrant) those they witnessed in the commission of a crime (specifically those infractions defined as felonies under law).[90]

Due to these institutional weaknesses, the Border Patrol, in its first year, devoted little time to immigration law enforcement and instead focused its efforts on Prohibition enforcement.[91] Southwestern Border Patrol officers enjoyed the adventure, publicity, and glamour surrounding chases and gun fights with rum-runners. Moreover, the Patrol discovered that they had more legal authority to arrest a liquor smuggler than an undocumented immigrant. Under the common law, Patrol officers arrested hundreds of liquor smugglers, seized just as many cars, and destroyed (under the terms of the Volstead Act) thousands of dollars worth of contraband.[92] In enforcing the Prohibition laws, the Patrol "gained a reputation as a fast-shooting and deadly unit."[93] Having discovered that liquor smugglers were often armed and dangerous, Border Patrol officers responded with an equal measure of force.[94] As a result, violence pervaded the early years of the Patrol; until the end of Prohibition in 1933, the Border Patrol in the El Paso district averaged one gunfight every seventeen days.[95] In the long term, the

Patrol's experiences with Prohibition law enforcement set a precedent for its subsequent immigration enforcement operations.[96]

The aggression with which the Patrol administered the Volstead Act caught the attention of agency administrators and legislators. Indeed, the Bureau of Immigration expressed concern that Border Patrol officers, lacking the statutory authority to pursue liquor smugglers and immigrants, exposed themselves and the agency to the risk of civil suits initiated by citizens.[97] As the commissioner general wrote:

> They [the Border Patrol] possess no more powers than does the ordinary citizen, who can exercise police powers only at the request of a duly constituted officer of the law, or to prevent the commission of a felony. Should they, in attempting to prevent a violation of the immigration laws, attempt to hold up a person who offers resistance, or even should a person attempting to cross the border, even though he did not offer resistance, bring action for assault against a patrol inspector who placed any restraint upon him, it is believed that the officer would be guilty of assault, and called upon to defend his action, as under their present title.[98]

Thus, agency officials and legislators sought an amendment to the original Border Patrol act in order to encourage Border Patrol officers to exercise caution in their pursuit of citizen violators of the Volstead Act.[99] Even more important, bureau officials sought to shift the focus of the unit's operations from Prohibition enforcement to immigration law enforcement. In short, at the same time the new legislation would limit the repercussions of Border Patrol practices against United States citizens, it also would enhance the power of the Border Patrol vis-à-vis immigrants.

The new Border Patrol law, the Act of February 27, 1925, would fill the gap left by the original legislation by giving the unit the power to pursue undocumented immigrants at the border and, eventually, beyond it.[100] As one member of Congress recalled:

> If you will remember the history of this thing [the Border Patrol], we set up the Border Patrol by appropriation, and not by a law. Then when we found out that we could not do much with it, we went to the Senate with something written in this committee and put in a rider on the appropriation [the Act of February 27, 1925].[101]

The new act clarified the Patrol's status as an immigration enforcement agency. It conferred upon Bureau of Immigration officials the "power without warrant,"

> (1) to arrest any alien who in his presence or view is entering or attempting to enter the United States in violation of any law or

regulation made in pursuance of law regulating the admission of aliens, and to take such alien immediately for examination before an immigrant inspector or other official having authority to examine aliens as to their right to admission to the United States, and (2) to board and search for aliens any vessel within the territorial waters of the United States, railway car, conveyance, or vehicle, in which he believes aliens are being brought in to the United States; and such employee shall have power to execute any warrant or other process issued by any officer under any law regulating the admission, exclusion, or expulsion of aliens.[102]

More specifically, the act expanded the bureau's authority with respect to immigration law violators, allowing it to pursue foreign seamen, individuals who had entered without inspection, and smugglers.[103] In addition, it gave the Border Patrol the authority to enforce the immigration laws along the nation's coastlines.[104] Finally, the measure conferred upon the unit the power to arrest without warrant those immigrants attempting to enter the United States in violation of any provision of the immigration laws.

Like its predecessor, the new Border Patrol law was slipped into an appropriations bill at the last minute, and, until its revision in 1946, the act served as the primary legislative language spelling out the scope of authority of the organization. Despite the brevity of the new act, its provisions, particularly those regarding warrantless searches and seizures, conferred upon the Border Patrol sweeping operational powers between the ports of entry. These powers were so broad that in the 1930s, legal reformers and scholars raised questions regarding the constitutionality of the warrantless search, seizure, and arrest provisions of the act; more specifically, they asked whether the statute violated the Fourth Amendment prohibition against unreasonable searches and seizures.[105] Yet in 1924, there was virtually no debate in Congress regarding the measure, and the House and Senate committees on immigration unanimously approved the bill prior to its introduction in the House.[106] A few legislators recognized that administrative officials might rely on its warrantless search and arrest provisions to abuse their authority. Yet in response to these concerns, Senator Reed of Pennsylvania reassured the membership that the act applied only to noncitizens in the process of crossing the border, not to citizens or immigrants already present in the United States. He stated:

It applies only to the arrest of aliens in the act of entering the country. There has been some doubt about the authority of those men to make arrests. We want to make it very clear that they have no right to make arrest except on sight of a violation of the immigration law as to illegal entry. They have no right to go into an interior city and pick up aliens in the street and arrest them, *but it is just at the border* where they are patrolling that we want them to have this authority.... It must be in sight of the officer himself; otherwise he has to get a warrant. We are all on the alert against granting too much power to these officials to act without warrant.[107]

Under the Act of February 27, 1925, the Border Patrol wielded a tremendous amount of power to conduct warrantless searches, seizures, and arrests at the border. Conducted here, warrantless searches and seizures could be justified as a legitimate exercise of national sovereignty.

At the international boundaries and coastlines, the authority of the Border Patrol derived in part from long-standing legal doctrines that exempted the unit, the Bureau of Immigration, and other federal agencies from the Fourth Amendment guarantees against unreasonable searches and seizures. Since the nation's founding, Congress and the courts have taken this exception as a given, conferring upon customs officials in 1789 the power to search without warrant "any ship or vessel" entering the United States.[108] Not only did this exception apply to ships and vessels, but also to persons. In 1925 the Supreme Court, in *Carroll v. United States*, 267 US 132,[109] held that "travelers may be ... stopped in crossing an international boundary because of national self-protection reasonably requiring one entering the country to identify himself as entitled to come in, and his belongings as effects which may be lawfully brought in."[110] Until 1973, the courts upheld the statute (the Act of February 27, 1925 and, later, its amendment, the Act of August 7, 1946) as sufficient authority for Border Patrol operations at the international line, creating what contemporary legal scholars call a "Fourth Amendment exemption" or the "border exception" to the Fourth Amendment.[111]

In the debates over the Act of February 27, 1925, Congress did not sanction the untrammeled exercise of searches, seizures, and arrests without warrant vis-à-vis immigrants. Yet even though the drafters of the law promised the exercise of prudence, the Border Patrol used it to justify and fight for the widest possible operational capacities beyond the border. Indeed, the very language of the act granted the Patrol a great deal of latitude in its pursuit of unauthorized immigrants. In 1930, Commissioner General Hull acknowledged that the brevity of the legislation raised more questions than it settled and noted that more congressional direction was desired.[112] Assistant Commissioner General Harris acknowledged that although the authority of Border Patrol officers to make arrests without warrant at the nation's borders was clear, the status of that authority became "more complicated" the further the officer traveled from the international line.[113]

The Border Patrol frequently resolved these so-called complications in its favor by relying on its own interpretation of the statute. Thus, while a literal reading of the law would suggest that a Border Patrol official had to witness an illicit crossing prior to engaging in a pursuit or arrest, the unit chose a broader interpretation. On the Canadian border, District Director Alfred Hampton noted that such a literal reading of the statute was simply incorrect; he advised his employees:

> You ask if your assumption is correct, that under Clause (1), the phrase "who in his presence or view" is intended to be taken literally, thus only empowering patrol inspectors to make arrests without Departmental warrants in those cases in which they have actually witnessed an illegal entry, or in which such entry was made in their presence. While the language quoted is fairly specific, I do not believe you are correct in placing such a literal interpretation upon same.[114]

In his testimony before the House Committee on Immigration and Naturalization, Commissioner General Harry Hull acknowledged that Border Patrol officers conducted pursuits north of the border without a warrant of arrest. Even though he doubted the legality of this practice, he justified Border Patrol interior operations without a warrant because "they find under the general law that an officer has a right to arrest a lawbreaker." In theory, Hull continued, the Border Patrol was to be more sensitive about exceeding their legal authority in pursuing immigrants. In practice, Hull concluded, "generally speaking, though, the people do not object to border patrol men going back if they are in pursuit of somebody, even going back 50 or 100 miles."[115]

As Hull defended the Patrol's interior operations by recourse to a general notion of lawbreaking, others relied on the ambiguity in the new statute, stretching the meaning of the phrase "entering or attempting to enter the United States" to justify warrantless searches, seizures, and arrests miles beyond the border. As a source of authority for its interpretation of the statute, the Patrol cited to the definition of "entry" in *Lew Moy v. United States*, 237 Fed. 50 (1916), a decision of a federal court in Texas. In *Lew Moy*, the court held, "the expression 'entering the United States' has been construed by the courts to mean that an alien is engaged in the act of entering until he reaches his intended destination."[116] While bureau officials later doubted the sufficiency of this case as authority for Border Patrol practices, Border Patrol officers in the 1920s devised the theory that "entry" was not complete as long as the individual was still in transit and had not reached his final destination, even if that destination was hundreds of miles from the border.

The Patrol argued that sheer practical necessity, as well as the Act of February 27, 1925, justified its operations beyond the border. In the Patrol's most ideal enforcement scenario, individuals attempting to cross the line without a formal immigration inspection would be spotted by officers and apprehended straightaway. But the bureau and the Patrol long recognized the impossibility of providing enough manpower and resources along the 2,000-mile long border to accomplish this feat; thus, for example, by 1928, the Border Patrol in the El Paso district monitored an 1145-mile stretch of border with approximately 100 men and 39 vehicles. The sparseness of the force led Commissioner Hull to observe, "there are places out in the mountains where nobody can get through and, of course, we have no men there."[117] Border Patrol efforts to seal the border to unwanted entries were also rendered more difficult by the sheer volume of border crossings that occurred each day.[118] The Patrol faced additional obstacles north of line, observing that roads, both paved and unimproved, and railways expedited the migration of undocumented individuals to the nation's interior.[119] Moreover, they noted that industrial centers and farms situated along these major rail lines and roadways served as destinations for out-of-status migrants of all nationalities.[120] Together, roads, transportation systems, and workplaces constituted (to borrow a term from historian Samuel Truett) a fugitive landscape or locales that offered undocumented immigrants refuge from the surveillance of the state.[121] From the perspective of the Border Patrol, effective enforcement, would require a mobile immigration unit to monitor multiple sites north of the line as well as the numerous entry points along the border.[122]

In order to gain control of this vast landscape, the Border Patrol devised a strategy of placing officers at the line and beyond it, creating what they called a "double line of defense" or a "border zone."[123] The precise location of officers detailed at points north of the border depended on the specific topographical features of each region. In border towns such as Nogales, Naco, and Douglas, officers were stationed close to the international line. But because many local roads led from the border to Tucson, officers were also placed at strategic spots between the line and the city. In West Texas, officers were posted in El Paso and at known crossing points on the Rio Grande. And in the Big Bend district, officers were assigned to patrol the tracks of the Southern Pacific, which migrants had to cross in order to proceed north.

Within this area north of the border, the Border Patrol was given a free hand to operate. Jurisdictional boundaries between Border Patrol districts were fluid; tentative Patrol agents were encouraged to cross them in pursuit of undocumented immigrants and smugglers.[124] As one supervisory official observed, "the maximum efficiency cannot be obtained from the border patrol unless it is constituted as a swift moving body."[125] To facilitate the mobility of its officers, Border Patrol leaders routinely wrote to the central office for more cars, specifically Chevrolets, which, by the 1920s, proved to be faster and more durable than the latest Fords.[126] And those who spent their days at a Border Patrol inspection station were chastised for "dig[ging] in" and becoming too familiar with the locals.[127]

By requiring Border Patrol officers to relocate on a regular basis, the bureau further stressed the importance of the unit's mobility. In addition, Border Patrol inspection stations, typically located north of the international boundary, were not fixed. Instead, these stations were opened, closed, and repositioned in response to the movements of smugglers and, more commonly, to the changes in the border transportation network. Tracking the construction of new transborder highways, railways, and bridges, the semiannual reports of the Border Patrol often read like transportation trade journals.[128] More important, these reports reveal that Border Patrol inspection stations themselves were impermanent, closing when a rail line or highway became defunct;[129] opening with the construction of a new road, rail, or bridge that spanned the border;[130] and moving in closer proximity to the major rails and highways of a specific region.[131] By increasing its mobility, the Border Patrol sought to overcome its legal, logistical, and social challenges and to solidify its vision of the border as a zone for the policing of undocumented immigrants.

Even though the Act of February 27, 1925 enhanced the powers of the Border Patrol, the new statute did not settle debates about the scope of the unit's authority and even its very existence. For the remainder of the decade, the Border Patrol faced multiple challenges to its broad vision of border enforcement. As the unit sought to create a policing zone along the US–Mexico border, local residents, border farmers, and their allies in Congress continued to defend their economic interests by pressing for an open border regime. Just as they had challenged the enforcement work of immigration inspectors at the border ports of entry, border residents resisted the development of a strong Border Patrol. At the same time, the Border Patrol faced serious opposition from moral reformers who proposed to eliminate the unit altogether. Seeking to strengthen the enforcement of the Volstead Act, prohibitionists lobbied Congress for the consolidation of the Immigration and Customs Border Patrols into a single organization. Charged with enforcing a variety of federal laws along the nation's international boundaries, the jurisdiction of the new consolidated force would no longer encompass spaces within the nation's interior but instead would be limited to the international boundaries themselves.

In response to these competing demands for open and closed border policies, southwestern agency officials turned to the law once again. To cope with the complaints of border businesses, local Border Patrol officials relied on their administrative discretion and developed a legalization process or what is now referred to as an adjustment of status procedure. Soon after its creation, Congress, with the support of President Herbert Hoover, sanctioned the procedure, passing the Registry of Aliens Act only two days before the Act of March 4, 1929, a measure that created the first criminal penalties for undocumented immigration.[132] Despite its irregular and local origins, the adjustment of status procedure became a regular feature of agency enforcement operations well into the twenty-first century. Meanwhile, in Congress, southwestern bureau officials fought to preserve the very existence of the mobile unit during the consolidation hearings. They not only succeeded in keeping the Immigration Border Patrol intact and distinct from the Customs Border Patrol, they also used the congressional debates to articulate and defend an aggressive conception of border enforcement and an expansive vision of the border as policing zone.

With the emergence of the Border Patrol, border residents applied the same arguments and tactics that they had deployed against the immigration inspection force at the border ports of entry, ceaselessly pressuring both divisions of the agency to relax their enforcement efforts vis-à-vis Mexican migrants. Exemplifying locals' resentment of the Border Patrol, Texas congressman John Nance Garner advised the Patrol that "he had very little use for the work the Patrol was doing and would make the most of every complaint [from farmers and ranchers] to embarrass Republican incumbents in Washington."[133] In many cases border residents simply ignored the new immigration laws as well as the Border Patrol, opting to abide by long-standing custom with respect to the crossing and recrossing of Mexican workers along the border, as San Antonio District Director William A. Whalen explained in 1929:

> Since the first settlers broke the ground and started farming and ranching in the vicinity of the Mexican border they have hired and fired Mexican laborers indiscriminately, without reference to the legality of the residence of the aliens in the United States. This practice has become so well grounded that it has been and in some cases still is difficult to impress upon many of the employers that there is an immigration law and that Mexican aliens are subject to its provisions.[134]

Protests against the Border Patrol were not limited to southwestern growers; representatives of border chambers of commerce from Texas to California who wanted to maximize the benefits of the transnational economic boom routinely argued that Border Patrol operations hurt the economies of their communities. As a solution, local businesses demanded that the Border Patrol suspend its operations in border towns. In some cases border officials even proposed the relocation of the international boundary itself, liberating American border cities from the alleged restraints on trade created by the Immigration Border Patrol.[134]

Like their counterparts in the immigration inspection force, early Border Patrol officials proved highly responsive to the complaints of border residents. As political appointees, chief patrol inspectors in San Antonio, Del Rio, and Laredo addressed the complaints of local farmers and ranchers by relaxing their enforcement efforts.[136] The Patrol stationed at Brownsville, for example, set a daily quota on the arrest of out-of-status Mexicans; in a similar vein, in the San Antonio district, Whalen encouraged Patrol officers to cut back on their enforcement activities.[137] Other agents made informal agreements with farmers to apprehend Mexican laborers only when the harvest season had ended.[138] Finally, in response to the bold—yet persistent—calls for the relocation of the international boundary, Wilmoth instructed Border Patrol officers to operate outside the city limits of Nogales, suspending all enforcement work within the town itself. Even though central office officials recognized the importance of the directive to the border economy, they also observed that Wilmoth had virtually yielded the administration of the immigration laws to local interests.[139]

The Border Patrol's own institutional weaknesses, as well as the needs of the local economy, informed one of the unit's most significant legal inventions. In 1926, Calexico Border Patrol Supervisor I. F. Wixon devised a strategy that served as a precursor to the adjustment of status programs that would become a core and ongoing feature of immigration law enforcement. Fashioned in conjunction with growers and the Calexico Chamber of Commerce, Wixon's regularization plan required employers to withhold twenty dollars from the wages of each undocumented worker; this sum would be put toward the cost of a visa application and payment of the head tax.[140] In return, workers received an identification card that exempted them from apprehension and removal by Border Patrol officers.[141] Historian Mark Reisler reports that in less than six months, 6,500 Mexican workers in the Imperial Valley registered under the legalization program.[142] Despite its success, Wixon characterized the program as a compromise. In his mind, it reflected the agency's inability to deter illicit entries and, more broadly, manage the task of border enforcement on its own; as a result, his legalization plan, like all subsequent adjustment of status plans, divided the burdens of immigration law enforcement among employers, workers, and the agency.[143]

Following the local precedent established by Wixon, federal officials created a formal legalization procedure three years later. Under the Registry of Aliens Act, passed on March 2, 1929, Congress authorized the adjustment of status of those undocumented individuals who had lived in the United States continuously prior to June 3, 1921 and could fulfill the requirements of a moral character test.[144] The measure was supported not only by southwestern agribusiness interests in Congress but also by President Hoover, who did everything he could to guarantee growers a steady supply of workers.[145] Upon passage of the law,

Hoover instructed immigration Commissioner Hull to issue what were lenient evidentiary requirements—two sworn statements from credible citizens—for the character test. Local farmers and Mexican consuls subsequently pursued an aggressive publicity campaign to inform Mexican workers of the legalization procedure. The law ultimately allowed thousands of undocumented immigrants to adjust their status and remain in the United States.[146]

These local and federal interventions on behalf of border businesses inspired the ire of nativists; indeed, anti-immigration forces were livid about the passage of the Act of March 2, 1929.[147] Congressman John Box, a long-standing opponent of Mexican immigration and vocal sponsor of several Mexican quota bills, observed the sheer contradiction in the passage of a bill legalizing the entry of Mexican nationals (the Act of March 2, 1929) and a bill that created criminal penalties for unauthorized entry (the Act of March 4, 1929) within days of each other. In congressional debates concerning the Act of March 4, 1929, Box declared, "This last bill that you have just passed provides that it is a felony to do the very thing for which you grant citizenship in the other bill. For having committed a felony you give him the reward of citizenship."[148] The legalization bill, Box argued, undermined the restrictive intent behind the nation's immigration laws; repeatedly refusing to yield the floor, Box continued, "Its chief purpose is to pardon and reward the illegal entry of all who smuggled themselves into the United States prior to June 3, 1921, and all who have illegally remained after the expiration of the period of their temporary visits."[149]

Nativist legislators also charged that Congress had rendered impotent the Act of March 4, 1929 by failing to provide an adequate appropriation for its enforcement.[150] During congressional debates over the Act of March 4, 1929, Congressman Arthur Free of California argued, "Unless you back it [Act of March 4, 1929] up with the money for enforcement and the protection of your borders it will not mean a thing. . . . Why pass another law when we don't enforce those we already have on our statute books?"[151] Some legislators proposed the consolidation of the Immigration Border Patrol with the Customs border force as a cost effective way of policing the border.[152] Others questioned why Congress did not pass a Mexican immigration quota such as that proposed by Congressman Box.[153] New York Congressman Fiorello LaGuardia responded, "Because the influence of the sugar-beet growers and the railroads is too strong."[154]

As Congress anticipated, immigration officials in the Southwest reported that they were unable to enforce the Act of March 4, 1929 due to a lack of resources and institutional support. Without its own detention facilities, the service had to pay local, state, and federal prisons for the detention and maintenance of unauthorized immigrants while they awaited trial. In addition, the agency discovered that judges and federal prosecutors offered little support for its enforcement mandate. In the Southwest, judges often issued lenient sentences (cognizant that deportations would follow any time served), which diluted the deterrent effect of the law.[155] In order to save their own limited appropriations, federal prosecutors in Arizona and Texas decided to stop indicting immigrants under the Act of March 4, 1929; they specifically observed that the costs of pursuing such cases outweighed the penalties, usually a one-day prison sentence. Local immigration officials in Arizona and Texas discontinued their own enforcement of the act.[156] By 1933, facing Depression-era budget cuts, federal prosecutors and southwestern immigration officials agreed to limit prosecutions to the most aggravated cases, specifically to those undocumented immigrants with prior criminal records.[157] Although the bureau chose not to pursue criminal prosecutions in the remaining cases, it, again to cut costs, handled these cases through the voluntary departure procedure, which required immigrants to leave the country at their own expense.[158]

Because of the lack of consensus at the federal and regional levels for strong border enforcement, the agency in the Southwest devoted just as much if not more time to regularizing the status of Mexican immigrants under the Act of March 2, 1929 as it did to the prosecution of undocumented migrants under the Act of March 4, 1929. An El Paso press report made the following observations on the activity of local agency officials:

> It [a report of Grover C. Wilmoth] demonstrates conclusively that the department is not carrying on a drive to rid the southwest of alien labor. On the contrary, the department is cooperating with chambers of commerce and cooperative organizations to legally help supply such labor as is needed.[159]

In his own response to growers' complaints about the Border Patrol and its apprehensions of their workers, Wilmoth reported to the commissioner general, "it must be conceded that there is much to be said from their point of view."[160]

Seeking to shift the unit's focus from immigration law enforcement to Prohibition enforcement, moral reformers joined the chorus of opposition to the Border Patrol. Thus, as Border Patrol officials hailed the Act of February 27, 1925 as a victory, Prohibition advocates argued that it stripped Immigration Border Patrol officers of any statutory authority to pursue liquor smugglers and weakened Prohibition enforcement on the border.[161] Throughout the 1920s, "dry" forces would present a number of bills proposing the consolidation of the Immigration and Customs Border Patrols in an effort to bolster the weak enforcement machinery of the Volstead Act.[162] They also argued that this combined force would eliminate the duplication of effort between the units, cut costs, and promote the enforcement of all federal laws along the borders. The new border patrol would operate as a general police force for the border analogous to the Royal Canadian Mounted Guard.[163] Opponents of the consolidation bills charged that prohibitionists were attempting to create a "dry army" along the nation's borders.[164] Meanwhile, defenders of the immigration agency, particularly labor unions, averred that the reorganization measures would deprive the bureau of the resources critical to immigration law enforcement.[165] Offering a succinct formulation of the choice facing Congress, Representative Carl Hayden of Arizona, who supported the Immigration Border Patrol, exhorted, "there must be a determination as to what is the most important duty. The man ought to come before the dollar. It is more important to keep aliens out of the United States than it is to collect some revenue."[166]

During these congressional debates, Border Patrol and Bureau of Immigration officials acknowledged the fiscal and law enforcement advantages of combining the various federal agencies on the line. But they generally objected to the reorganization bills because they would fundamentally transform Border Patrol operational strategy and mission. These measures, particularly the 1930 consolidation bill, proposed not only the creation of a general police force, but also a border force that operated at the international boundary.[167] The drafters of the 1930 bill argued that these operational limits would deter the new Border Patrol from inconveniencing legitimate travelers and US citizens with searches and seizures far beyond the border.[168] Describing the advantages of a consolidated patrol, Representative Mills of New York noted, "you will not have a border patrol operating 20 miles inside the United States. You will have a border patrol where it belongs, and that is on the border."[169] In a similar vein, the chairman of the House Rules Committee observed, "There will be no one chasing people for 15, 25 or 40 miles from the border. . . . That is the idea; that the determination of whether persons or goods come in lawfully shall, as far as possible, start and end at the border."[170] In addition, this bill would further preclude the need for Border Patrol operations in the interior by constructing additional ports of entry along the international boundary.[171]

As in the debates over the Act of February 27, 1925, the Border Patrol remained wary about violating the rights of US citizens.[172] Wilmoth worried that one day an immigration officer would mistakenly arrest an "American citizen of foreign appearance" and that the incident would generate publicity causing the service "irreparable injury."[173] Yet at the same time, the bureau sought the broadest operational powers in its pursuit of undocumented immigrants.[174] Border Patrol officials and their supporters testified before Congress that limiting Patrol operations to the international boundaries would impede any effective immigration law enforcement, stating that "the closer to the border the officers operate . . . the larger the force required for equal results, since the points of convergence of the numerous roads and trails leading from the border . . . can be covered with fewer men than would be required" on the line.[175] Commissioner General Hull emphasized the importance of flexibility in Border Patrol operations:

> Now, if we are going to have a unified patrol, and it is going to be sta-
> tioned right on the line and traverse that line, we are going to have
> an enormous leakage . . . We are going to have more smuggling than
> we have ever had before. The proper strategy of effective operation
> without excessive cost is not to attempt to build a hog-proof fence on
> the border; to do that would necessitate placing them within sight of
> each other. Flexibility, mobility, resourcefulness, in short, brains is the
> real solution. There is no other way.[176]

Ultimately, due to some controversial features of the bill and disagreements about which department (Treasury, Justice, or Labor) ought to supervise the new unified patrol, the 1930 consolidation bill did not pass.[177]

The reorganization debates presented Border Patrol officials and their sup-porters with the opportunity to defend the organization and argue for even greater authority under the Act of February 27, 1925.[178] Through these propos-als, the Patrol sought to transform the fugitive landscapes of the borderlands, specifically its roads and private dwellings, into a legal jurisdiction in which it exercised sweeping powers to pursue undocumented immigrants. In 1928, Congressman Box proposed a bill to revise the language of the Act of February 27, 1925, allowing vehicular searches when officers believed that such vehicles were transporting undocumented immigrants, regardless of the driver's intent to violate the law or knowledge of the alienage status of the passengers.[179] In addition, the bill authorized the Patrol to make arrests and to stop and search vehicles not only in the act of crossing the border, but also beyond it, "in the immediate vicinity of the coast or land borders upon probable cuase [sic] for believing that they contain aliens making good or attempting to make good their entry into the United States in violation of law."[180]

Testifying before Congress, District Director Wilmoth pressed the members to augment the Patrol's ability to pursue undocumented immigrants on pri-vate property.[181] Agency officials had the authority to enter private property if they were in hot pursuit of individuals whom they had witnessed crossing the line in violation of the immigration laws. They were also authorized to enter private property with the consent of the property owner in order to arrest an undocumented immigrant under warrant. In both cases, however, officers were not permitted to make a general search of the premises for other out-of-status individuals.[182] To further justify the Patrol's need for a general search power, Wilmoth argued that if customs officials had the authority to obtain warrants to search for illegal contraband on private property, the Patrol ought to have an analogous statutory authority to procure warrants to search for undocumented immigrants on private property.[183]

Although these measures did not pass, by the 1940s the southwestern leaders of the Border Patrol would help to draft legislation that enabled the unit to expand the border zone to both public and private spaces far north of the international boundary. In the meantime, it became standard operating procedure for the Border Patrol to interpret its legal authority to pursue and apprehend undocumented immigrants in the broadest terms possible. In a 1944 Border Patrol training manual, Wilmoth instructed new recruits that

> the expression "entering the United States" as used in this statute is not to be given a narrow construction. The purport of the ruling of the Circuit Court of Appeals for the Fifth Circuit in the case of Lew Moy et al. vs. the United States (273 Fed. 50) [*sic*], is that an alien is entering the United States until he reaches his interior destination. It is understood that other courts have held to the same effect. In the Lew Moy case the aliens involved were taken into custody as far in the interior as Las Vegas, New Mexico, some them being destined to Rock Springs, Wyoming.[184]

Heeding Wilmoth's directive, Border Patrol officials exercised their powers under the Act of February 27, 1925 in highly aggressive ways. An internal investigation found Border Patrol officers adopting a strategy known as "putting a man in transit." In this scenario, officers would lure out-of-status immigrants away from their place of employment or home and then arrest them without warrant, arguing that they were still in travel status.[185] While Wilmoth's interpretation of *Lew Moy* may have been suspect, the message it conveyed to officers was clear: the Border Patrol had the power to exercise its power to search, seize, and arrest without warrant not only at the line but far beyond the border.

3

Repatriation and Reform

Communications have been directed from time to time by the Bureau
to field officers of the Immigration Service admonishing them that all
aliens shall be dealt with in a humane and considerate manner; that intimidation, abuse or indignities of any character will not be tolerated;
that the rights of aliens will be respected.
— George J. Harris, Director, Border Patrol, El Paso,
General Order 21, March 29, 1933

In the 1930s, the Bureau of Immigration was forced to clean house. Depression-
era deportation campaigns, which resulted in the removal of approximately one
million ethnic Mexicans, sparked vociferous protests at home and abroad. Civil
libertarians raised questions about the scope of the agency's authority and its
impact on individual rights. Commissioner General Daniel McCormack excoriated the agency's record on deportation as inhumane and contrary to American
constitutional norms.[1] In response to these critiques, legal reformers and Bureau
of Immigration officials embarked on a sweeping effort to reform agency operations. By the mid-1930s, the agency required its officers to adopt a more humane
approach to deportation, as El Paso Border Patrol Director George J. Harris
instructed in a general order.[2]

Abiding by the recommendations of legal reformers and the central office,
southwestern agency officials initially implemented a series of changes to the
Border Patrol's pursuit and apprehension procedures. Yet a combination of factors, including nativism and the enforcement priorities of the Border Patrol,
eventually led southwestern immigration officials to challenge the mandates proposed by the central office. They ultimately paid lip service to the reform direc-
tives issued by their superiors in Washington, DC. By the onset of the Bracero
Program, the intransigence of agency officials in the borderlands reversed the
achievements of the reform movement and paved the way for the circumscription of immigrant rights. Indeed, by the 1950s, the positions articulated by
southwestern INS officials, particularly with respect to Border Patrol arrest practices, would be formalized or incorporated into the federal immigration statute.

The reform efforts of the 1930s revisited some of the claims raised by the Chinese litigation earlier in the century.[3] Yet they also raised new legal and constitutional questions, particularly with respect to the Border Patrol, a unit that did not exist during the Chinese exclusion era. Moreover, the very impetus for reform emerged from within the INS itself, rather than from external actors such as private citizens, immigrants, the courts, and Congress. As such, the reform campaign of the 1930s underscores the ways in which agencies not only create the rules, regulations, and laws necessary for their daily operations, but also engage in their own oversight.[4]

This chapter focuses on one moment in the immigration agency's effort at self-regulation and even reform. While not diminishing the well-documented accounts of the abuses committed by the Border Patrol, it aims to demonstrate how INS officials thought in constitutional terms about the limits of their authority and the impact of agency practices on the legal and constitutional rights of immigrants.[5] Ultimately, the reform efforts of supervisory officials in Washington, DC failed in the 1930s due to the opposition of INS officials in the Southwest. And this failure manifested the authority possessed by borderlands officials to define administrative practices as well as conceptions of administrative justice and immigrant rights.

The Great Depression led to a revival of anti-immigrant sentiment. In an editorial published in the *Saturday Evening Post*, Congressman Martin Dies of Texas argued that the nation's unemployment crisis would have never materialized if the twenty million immigrants who had arrived in the United States since 1880 had never been admitted.[6] In the Southwest, Japanese farmers in San Diego, who were themselves the targets of anti-immigrant sentiments during the Great Depression and World War II, threatened to have Mexican workers deported as a means of asserting control over their labor force.[7] Nativism not only found expression among members of the general public but also served as the basis for policy proposals made by local, state, and federal officials. These included a complete ban on immigration for two years; a Western Hemisphere quota; the registration of all immigrants in the country; the denial of citizenship to immigrants seeking employment in the United States;[8] and the mass deportation of immigrants on relief.[9] At the same time, the bureau found itself under tremendous pressure to use the immigration and deportation laws to address the nation's economic woes.[10]

In 1929, the bureau responded to public pressure by implementing a nationwide deportation drive instigated by President Herbert Hoover's Secretary of Labor, William N. Doak. Both Hoover and Doak believed that they could create jobs for native-born Americans by ousting undocumented immigrants from the country.[11] Doak, relying on Bureau of Immigration employees, conducted a nine-month, cross-country search for deportable immigrants in 1931.[12] In the Southwest, Doak's raids had a disproportionate impact on Mexican immigrants.[13] By the end of the year, the federal deportation drive created a public relations crisis by damaging the nation's image abroad.[14] In defense of its nationals in the United States, Mexico threatened to deport American citizen workers from its boundaries and replace them with Canadian workers.[15] At the same time, federal officials recognized that the deportation drives would tarnish the forthcoming 1932 Los Angeles Summer Olympics.[16] Finally, the election of Franklin Delano Roosevelt and his appointment of progressive leaders to the Department of Labor and the Bureau of Immigration precluded the instigation of any additional federal deportation efforts. For the remainder of the decade, the federal government would play a limited role in the removal or deportation of immigrants from America.

Deportation, however, did not become obsolete in the 1930s. Indeed, during the Great Depression, the deportation of immigrants reached an all-time high. An estimated one million Mexican immigrants and Mexican Americans were forcibly removed from the United States in the 1930s.[17] As historians Francisco Balderrama and Raymond Rodríguez have demonstrated, local and state officials, rather than the federal government, took the lead in removing unwanted immigrants from the country.[18] In response to these massive deportation drives, the INS, constrained by Depression-era fiscal shortfalls and political pressures from the Roosevelt administration, took the path of least resistance, effectively devolving to the states and localities the responsibility for removing hundreds of thousands of immigrants. While this allowed the agency to cut costs, it also led it to sanction and adopt procedures that diminished the already limited constitutional status of immigrants in America.

Throughout its history, the INS had been reluctant to take on the administrative, fiscal, and legal tasks associated with deportation.[19] Formal deportation was a detailed, lengthy, and expensive process that usually began with the discovery of a suspected undocumented immigrant in the field; a preliminary, on-site investigation to determine the individual's status; an application to the central office for an arrest warrant (a process that itself involved several steps); the formal apprehension under warrant of the immigrant; a preliminary hearing conducted by local officers in a Board of Special Inquiry; the preparation of a hearing record by the presiding officer; the review of the record by the examining division of the central office; adjudication by the Board of Review of the central office; approvals by the assistant commissioner of the legal division at the central office and the secretary of labor; and, finally, the actual transportation of the immigrant out of the country.[20] Additional steps and delays arose if the immigrant requested a translator at any stage of the process; counsel at the preliminary hearing; oral argument before the Board of Review; or filed a writ of habeas corpus to contest his or her arrest in a court of law.[21]

The Immigration Service sought to minimize the costs of deportation in several ways. Upon the termination of the World War I agricultural labor program, the service devolved the responsibility and expense of removal to private parties, specifically the farmers' and growers' associations who had hired these laborers. When such efforts failed, the bureau instituted deportation proceedings as a last resort. In some cases, service officials formally admitted laborers so as to avoid the time and expense of deporting them.[22] By the 1920s, the Immigration Act of 1924 and the Act of March 4, 1929 facilitated deportation and created criminal penalties for undocumented entry, but the service did not have the resources to prosecute and deport on a large-scale basis. Thus in 1929, the service ordered local officials to report only the most aggravated cases for prosecution.[23] All others would be "expelled immediately" under the voluntary departure procedure.[24]

By the 1930s, conditions had not changed. Grover C. Wilmoth observed, "This district has never had sufficient immigration allotment to handle all deportable aliens in formal warrant proceedings."[25] During the economic crisis, the service attempted to save money, encouraging the expeditious deportation of those held at the bureau's expense to cut detention costs.[26] Later that same year, the bureau decided to release those in deportation proceedings "under bond, on their own recognizance, or paroled to a responsible person or organization"[27]— again, so as to save on the costs of detention. Border Patrol inspectors also carried out their operations with cost-savings in mind, focusing on the most likely apprehensions first. In addition, Patrol inspectors, without additional compensation, assumed responsibilities as immigration inspectors and, in at least one district, naturalization examiners.[28]

Seeking ways to trim administrative budgets, Congress once again proposed consolidating the Immigration and Customs Border Patrols. The Immigration Service and the Patrol vehemently opposed these measures, arguing that Border Patrol operations were vital to the protection of the US economy.

> Not since our restrictive laws were placed upon the statute books has there been greater need for a trained and efficient Immigration Border Patrol. We cannot safely entrust the protection of our borders to a force which by its record of accomplishments offers so slight a protection as has the Customs Border Patrol, but instead every logical reason prevails why the Immigration Border Patrol should be continued as an auxiliary of the Immigration Service proper so that the two working in conjunction with one another will give us some measure of security against an invasion of aliens who add nothing to our economic well-being, but

on the contrary, bid fair to deprive our people of the opportunity for a means of livelihood to which they are rightfully entitled.[29]

But while the work of the Border Patrol was seen as pivotal to reviving the Depression-era economy, it did not have the resources to conduct the kinds of enforcement operations, such as large-scale deportation campaigns, that would allegedly protect the American labor force.

The bureau also tried to avoid deportation proceedings altogether by resorting to cheaper removal options such as voluntary departure and repatriation. In 1918, bureau officials in the Southwest exercised their administrative discretion to create an expedited procedure known as voluntary departure. As Grover Wilmoth explained it:

> In a voluntary departure procedure there is more or less informal inquiry by the arresting officer, repeated at patrol headquarters, and the examination of the immigrant inspector before the voluntary departure privilege is accorded is apt to be somewhat perfunctory despite all admonitions to the contrary.[30]

By requiring immigrants to leave the country at their own expense, voluntary departure also reduced the Bureau's transportation costs and the maintenance and detention costs of holding individuals awaiting a deportation hearing.[31] Because there was no statutory authority for voluntary departure, the Bureau tried to reserve the procedure for those foreigners who had merely violated a technical provision of the immigration laws.[32]

When funds ran particularly low, immigration officials in the borderlands implemented an even more abbreviated form of the voluntary departure procedure. Wilmoth authorized his Border Patrol officers to return straightaway and without any process those undocumented Mexican immigrants apprehended in the act of crossing the line.[33] Moreover, Wilmoth, in testimony before Congress, admitted that his office offered less process to Mexican immigrants than European immigrants. When his office ran out of funds for deportation (typically during the fourth quarter of the agency's fiscal year), it resorted to voluntary departure in Mexican deportation cases. In contrast, Wilmoth continued to remove undocumented European immigrants through formal deportation proceedings because the distance between the United States and Europe served as a logistical obstacle to the creation of swift removal procedures and because Mexico refused to accept European deportees.[34]

By 1931, the bureau decided to rely on a little used section of the Immigration Act of 1917 that permitted the repatriation of foreigners who had "fallen into distress or need [of] public aid within three years of their entry."[35] Under this provision, eligible immigrants would apply to the bureau; the bureau would investigate applications for fraud (by identifying those individuals who sought repatriation for reasons other than destitution); and then the agency would return approved applicants and their families to their country of birth at the government's expense.[36] As a voluntary procedure initiated by immigrants themselves, the federal repatriation program, the bureau hoped, would allow it to avoid negative publicity. In addition, the agency believed that by removing entire families, it could avoid the impoverishment of wives and children that resulted after Doak's raids separated male breadwinners from their families. Due to these perceived advantages, the bureau distinguished repatriation from deportation and presented the former as a humanitarian measure, providing destitute foreigners and their families an opportunity to seek better circumstances elsewhere.[37]

Predictably, the bureau favored the measure because it was cheaper and easier than deportation. The repatriation procedure itself was, in the agency's words, "simple in procedure and free from legal technicalities."[38] The service estimated that the average cost of repatriation would equal $90 per person whereas deportation would amount to $100 per person, plus the cost of detention.[39] The service pursued additional cost savings by removing repatriates in large groups and negotiating discounts with railways transporting immigrants to their ports of departure.[40] Under this program, over 8,500 immigrants returned to their countries of birth during the 1930s.[41] In order to increase the potential number of repatriates, the commissioner general proposed a two-year suspension of the three-year statute of limitations on repatriation and a five million dollar appropriation.[42]

The bureau also relied on other federal and state agencies to respond to public demands for the removal of unwanted immigrants. At the federal level, the State Department further reduced the number of visas issued to Mexican workers on the grounds that they would become public charges. This policy was so effective that the Bureau of Immigration stopped calling for a Mexican quota.[43] In identifying foreigners eligible for federal repatriation, the service often depended upon information received from state and local welfare agencies rather than its own investigations.[44] At the state and local levels, the bureau sanctioned repatriation campaigns that resulted in the departure of an estimated 400,000 Mexicans.[45] Most historians acknowledge that these state and local efforts, rather than federal endeavors, generated the bulk of repatriations and removals to Mexico.[46] While the bureau publicly disclaimed any responsibility for these campaigns, it supported them as a legitimate means of addressing the nation's unemployment crisis. The district director of immigration for Detroit wrote to the commissioner general:

It is felt by the writer that, if possible, the Bureau . . . should enter wholeheartedly into this movement and extend the Governor of . . .

Michigan all of the co-operation that is possible under the scope of the authority of the Bureau, for the elimination of such a large number of alien laborers and mechanics will work a tremendous benefit not only to the economic situation in . . . Michigan insofar as it concerns the welfare expenditures, but will remove from the economic field a group that . . . is able to get first consideration in employment . . . and by their removal the openings in industry will be left for residents and citizens of the United States.[47]

Finally, the bureau found that state and local repatriation efforts freed the agency from the negative publicity that would most likely follow any major federal deportation drive.

Bureau officials sanctioned these local removal campaigns for economic as well as political reasons. They instructed immigration inspectors to pass on as many of the costs of repatriation to states and localities:

Wherever possible, arrangements should be made with charitable or other public organizations to have aliens delivered at the port of embarkation without cost to the Government, and where that is not practicable, attempt should be made to have such organizations provide attendants, likewise without cost to the Government.[48]

But the service was authorized to provide assistance to state and local organizations as long as its own costs were kept to a minimum.[49] In Detroit, bureau agents worked as guards on the trains conveying repatriates to Mexico.[50] When the Mexican government, coming to the aid of Mexican nationals in the United States, initiated its own repatriation movement, the bureau provided transportation for approximately 1,200 Mexicans from Texas to the border at Brownsville.[51] Yet on other occasions the bureau refused to remove unemployed Mexicans at the request of state and local governments. In these instances, which occurred in Nebraska, Colorado, California, Arizona, Michigan, and Texas, the bureau discovered that many of the unemployed ethnic Mexicans were US citizens or legally resident aliens.[52]

In Los Angeles, the bureau made its most infamous contribution to the repatriation effort. Inspired by federal initiatives, such as Doak's raids, to address the unemployment problem, Los Angeles civic and business officials created their own citizens' relief committee.[53] As their leader, Charles P. Visel sought assistance from the federal government to implement a removal program in Los Angeles County. More specifically, Visel proposed that the bureau, with cooperation from local police and sheriff's offices, conduct a publicity campaign surrounding the prosecution and deportation of a select number of undocumented immigrants. These deportations would serve as a lesson to the immigrant communities of Los Angeles about the consequences of unauthorized immigration, both scaring immigrants into leaving Los Angeles and deterring new immigration into the city.[54]

Responding to Visel's requests for aid, the bureau sent Supervising Inspector W. F. Watkins to Los Angeles. Watkins found Visel's claims to be specious and unfounded. As historian Abraham Hoffman notes, "Watkins soon learned that Visel had no basis for his assertion that 20,000 deportable aliens were in the Los Angeles area. The plan to scare Mexicans out of the city without the bother of formal deportation hearings was grounded in vagueness and lacked specific evidence."[55] Watkins even doubted that such tactics would make an impact on undocumented immigration. Instead, he believed that Visel's plan would drive immigrants to other parts of the country. Despite these reservations, Watkins conducted deportation raids in the city, suburbs, and farms of Los Angeles County. During the raids, he rounded up approximately 3,000 to 4,000 individuals, 389 of whom were prosecuted.[56] While both local and federal officials claimed to target only undocumented immigrants, Mexicans and US citizens of Mexican descent were singled out during the raids.[57] By the end of the federal repatriation drive, Watkins reported that seven out of ten deported were of Mexican descent.[58]

By early March 1931 (two months after the inception of Visel's raids), apprehensions declined as worried Mexicans and Mexican Americans left the area, repatriated on their own accord, or prepared themselves for the raids by providing head tax receipts as proof of legal entry.[59] In addition, the national press, civil libertarians, and the Los Angeles Bar Association mounted intense criticism of the drive, charging officials with apprehending individuals without a warrant, inspecting them without counsel, and procuring a warrant of arrest based on evidence obtained under duress. Even the central office questioned the purpose of and procedures used during the raids. Ultimately, however, the bureau held the Los Angeles Chamber of Commerce responsible for the raids and for exaggerating the scope of the crisis in Los Angeles County.[60]

Although federal participation in the deportation drive came to an end, it achieved Visel's goal of scaring immigrants out of the Los Angeles area. By March 1931, Spanish-speaking charitable organizations in the county were conducting their own repatriation campaigns. By the end of the year, between 50,000 and 75,000 Mexicans and even Mexican Americans left Southern California. By 1933, Los Angeles County had conducted fifteen repatriation drives. Indeed, they had become so regular that the local press stopped its coverage of the drives.[61] While no other community was as aggressive as Los Angeles in its effort to repatriate Mexican nationals, the drives created a model followed by the rest of country.[62] By 1937, the Mexican government, frustrated with the hostility directed toward its nationals, came to the aid of Mexicans living in the United States and began conducting its own repatriations.[63]

Contrary to popular perception, the INS played a secondary role in the mass repatriation campaigns of the 1930s due to budget constraints and fears of the public relations consequences.[64] Yet it was this very passive approach to deportation that resulted in the circumscription of immigrant rights. The agency's focus on cutting costs facilitated the development of expedited removal procedures at the federal level and unprecedented, mass deportation drives at the local and state levels.

Federal, state, and local deportation drives triggered vocal opposition from Mexican officials, humanitarian organizations, administrative law reformers, and the repatriates themselves.[65] As Balderrama and Rodríguez explain, the Los Angeles repatriation drives were deeply humiliating and insulting to Mexican immigrants "because they viewed themselves as honest, industrious workers."[66] In Mexico, the press made similar arguments, emphasizing the ways in which Mexican immigrant labor had sustained numerous sectors of the American economy.[67] As it became clear that Mexican immigrants were disproportionately impacted by local and state removal campaigns, the repatriates and their advocates in Mexico could only conclude that racism had instigated the repatriation movement.[68]

Other organizations expressed their opposition to the deportation campaigns by seeking to defend immigrants' humanitarian interests. Mexican consular officials assisted repatriates by "pressuring local authorities to provide better care and treatment for Mexican Nationals and their families."[69] In El Paso, Cleofas Calleros, leader of the National Catholic Welfare Conference (NCWC), declared the repatriation drives to be one of the " 'blackest pages in American history for Mexicans and Mexican Americans.' "[70] He worked to prevent the deportation of ethnic Mexicans and helped others obtain their citizenship papers so as to avoid the removal drives altogether.[71] Calleros also joined Commissioner General MacCormack and a number of other immigrant advocacy organizations in calling for more humanitarian deportation proceedings and a general reform of the nation's deportation laws.[72]

While local and state repatriation campaigns continued for the remainder of the decade, the Roosevelt administration by 1933 adopted a new orientation toward federal deportation policy.[73] The administration was responding not only to the public outcry regarding the recent deportation drives, but also to a demographic shift wrought by the economic crisis. Because the Great Depression deterred new immigration, by 1931 the number of persons leaving the country exceeded the number of individuals seeking admission. In 1934, Commissioner General MacCormack could even declare: "Quantitatively and for the present, at least, we have no immigration problem."[74] In so doing, he created a propitious context in which to undertake a review and reform of the agency's deportation practices and procedures.

The first commissioner general with no ties to organized labor, MacCormack unequivocally refused to satisfy public demands for the mass deportation of Mexican immigrants.[75] Moreover, he publicly criticized the agency's deportation operations as inhumane and in violation of fundamental constitutional norms regarding procedural due process and individual rights.[76] In cooperation with Frances Perkins, Progressive-era reformer and secretary of labor, MacCormack sought to investigate and change the bureau's policies and procedures.[77] As a result of their efforts, service officials from the central office to the local offices evinced a more humanitarian and fair-minded approach toward deportation. During the 1930s, the agency's own effort at self-regulation served as an unexpected restraint, checking the emergence of a more aggressive federal deportation policy. Indeed, as historian D. H. Dinwoodie concludes, the post-1933 decline in deportations and voluntary departures was due, in part, to the reform-minded policies of Commissioner General MacCormack.[78]

The bureau's own internal review of its procedures was one of a number of reform efforts initiated by legal reformers and social welfare advocates in the 1930s. Their work resulted in the publication of several reports including *The Deportation of Aliens in the United States to Europe* by Jane Perry Clark, a Barnard political scientist; *The Administrative Control of Aliens: A Study in Administrative Law and Procedures* by William Van Vleck, dean of the George Washington University Law School; and a report by the National Commission on Law Observance and Enforcement (also known as the Wickersham Commission).[79] Each of the three investigations reached the same general conclusions about deportation. The reformers noted that the bureau demonstrated few concerns regarding the consistency and fairness of its deportation proceedings, particularly when it came to its use of the public charge provisions of the immigration laws.[80] The service drew upon the prohibition against the admission of public charges to deport immigrants, such as unwed mothers, petty thieves, and adulterous husbands, who had not committed deportable offenses.[81] In effect, the service used conditions that had arisen subsequent to entry as justification for an ex post facto determination of inadmissibility under the "liable to become a public charge" clause.

When it came to the deportation hearing itself, reformers charged that the service "operated in the breach of established traditions of Anglo-American jurisprudence."[82] Reformers found that immigrants were detained without warrant and often lacked the benefit of counsel during the deportation hearing.[83] These hearings were held by local Boards of Special Inquiry, administrative tribunals that had no statutory basis and, in the eyes of the courts, were not equivalent to judicial proceedings. As such, they loosely conformed to the standards of administrative and judicial procedure, if at all.[84] At the hearing, the presiding officer played multiple and conflicting roles in the case, usually having served as arresting officer, prosecutor, and judge. Relying on information gleaned from anonymous tips or agency informants, Boards functioned without regard for formal rules of evidence.[85] They also allowed the introduction of new charges against the immigrant during the course of the hearing itself.[86] Finally, deportable immigrants had few options to appeal their cases because the courts, since the late nineteenth century, had limited the conditions under which it would review agency operations.[87]

All of the reformers recognized that the courts generally sanctioned as sufficient the process offered by the deportation statute.[88] This was particularly the case given that deportation was a civil, not criminal procedure, and thereby held to lower procedural standards. Yet the reformers' arguments were premised on the assumption that while deportation was not a form of punishment under law, it operated as such in practice. As a result, they argued that the deportation hearing needed to adhere to higher standards of due process, if not the same standards that applied in a criminal proceeding. In one way or another, all the reformers recommended that deportation hearings more closely resemble formal judicial proceedings; Clark suggested that a jury trial replace Board of Special Inquiry hearings, while Van Vleck and Wickersham proposed the creation of a new, independent judicial body to hear deportation cases.[89] As the process stood in the 1930s, however, reformers found that deportation proceedings maximized the "powers in the administrative officers" while minimizing the "checks and safeguards against error and prejudice."[90]

In the face of these criticisms and under the leadership of MacCormack and Perkins, the bureau appointed an outside committee dubbed the Ellis Island Committee, which was composed of administrators and experts who investigated deportation procedures. In March 1934 the committee published its findings, which led the service to implement its recommendations. Evaluating the results of the committee's work, MacCormack concluded that its reforms "have materially reduced the sum total of inconvenience, friction, and human suffering incident to the enforcement of the law."[91] The first set of reforms suspended the practice of arresting suspected undocumented immigrants without an arrest warrant. The service also found that immigrants awaiting a deportation proceeding had been held in jail for upward of a year or more. Releasing these detainees on bail or to the custody of friends, the service saved $150,000 a year.[92] With respect to the hearing, the bureau divided the investigation, prosecution, and adjudication functions among three different officers.[93] In general, the bureau advised officers to use greater restraint and caution in the conduct of deportation hearings; they were instructed to "use every endeavor to so conduct hearings as to preclude any justifiable grounds for complaint."[94]

MacCormack and Perkins also attempted to reform the legislation surrounding deportation, which the commissioner general described as "rigid in the extreme."[95] He thus encouraged the passage of legislation that would permit the suspension of deportation in cases where the individual was found to be "of good moral character" and had not been convicted of a crime. In the absence of such legislation, however, MacCormack and Perkins devised administrative means of granting discretionary relief such as authorizing the stay of deportation warrants in cases involving family separation; legalizing the status of those who had violated a technical provision of the deportation laws and for whom deportation would constitute a hardship; and by 1940, suspending orders of deportation.[96] This last provision also permitted immigrants to reapply for admission after deportation.[97] Together, Perkins and MacCormack "took seriously the criticisms that had been mounting against the Immigration Service's practices."[98]

The impetus for reform generated by the central office spread to the local offices as well. Indeed, despite the prevalence of Depression-era xenophobia, service officials at both the national and local levels demonstrated a newfound concern for the treatment of Mexican immigrants.[99] Much of this concern was sparked by the persistent protest of Mexican consuls along the border who voiced two main criticisms, both relating to the rights of Mexican nationals in a deportation hearing. First, they demanded notification when any adverse proceeding was instituted against a Mexican national. Second, they demanded to be admitted to the Boards of Special Inquiry if their presence was requested by the immigrant.[100] In addition, the Mexican Embassy charged the service with unnecessary delays and detentions, accusing it of holding Mexican nationals for up to ten months before handing down a decision.[101] Local and national officials appeared responsive to these criticisms. Southwestern agency administrators recommended that consuls be given notice of deportation proceedings, and Commissioner General MacCormack released deportees held in prison for lengthy periods of time.

The Immigration Service also dispatched George Coleman to conduct an investigation of border conditions. He produced a lengthy, fascinating report that serves as a counterpart to the investigations of the central office and the East Coast reformers. Coleman's conclusions were eye-opening. While he found immigration inspectors at the ports of entry to be professional and courteous, he could not say the same for the Border Patrol. Coleman characterized Border Patrol officers "as a whole a different type than the immigration inspectors."[102] He discovered that Border Patrol officers abused Mexican immigrants both verbally and physically. At the immigration office, inspectors resorted to aggressive interrogation tactics—"Anything to get them to confess."[103] Coleman obtained a statement from Calexico attorney Alfred Blaisdell that Border Patrol officers relied on intimidation, openly displaying their revolvers and handcuffs while

Figure 3.1 Border Patrol, El Paso, Texas, 1931. Courtesy of US Citizenship and
Immigration Services History Office and Library, Washington, DC.

conducting searches on ranches and farms. Blaisdell also observed that officers'
"Spanish is usually poor and only sufficient to ask ordinary questions, so a real
investigation is a farce."[104]

Like the national reformers, Coleman recommended that the Border Patrol
stop its practice of making arrests without warrants and refrain from relying on
anonymous letters or informants with personal vendettas. The remainder of his
recommendations further revealed the free-wheeling, if not lawless, approach to
law enforcement taken by the Border Patrol. He called on Border Patrol officers
to treat immigrants with more courtesy and emphasized the need for officers to
learn or improve their Spanish-speaking abilities. He also admonished the Patrol
for misrepresenting the voluntary departure procedure as one that would enable
a problem-free return to the United States and ordered officers to cease shooting
immigrants fleeing from the scene.[105]

The Border Patrol responded to these criticisms and those of the national
reformers. For example, the Wickersham Commission raised objections to
Patrol officers' undisciplined use of firearms. It also observed the inconveniences
and dangers caused by the promiscuous stopping of citizens on the highways.[106]
As a result, the service curtailed its traffic checks, concerned about their legal
validity.[107] Furthermore, with the repeal of Prohibition in 1933, the service decided to put an end to the Border Patrol's "fast-gun reputation."[108] Commissioner
General MacCormack created a series of lectures to standardize immigration inspector and Border Patrol officer training.[109] As part of a review of the Patrol's
policies and procedures, the service interviewed all Patrol inspectors and tested

their fitness for office. Former officer Dan R. Roberts recalled one of the interview questions as follows:

> One question concerned what the Inspector would do if he encountered an alien crossing the border who had previously murdered the Inspector's partner. Most of the hard-bitten veterans answered that he would shoot the so and so and kill his ghost if he came back as well. All who gave answers like that were discharged.[110]

The repeal of Prohibition, these internal and external reviews of Border Patrol policy and practice, and the new emphasis on professionalism marked the end of an era for the Border Patrol.

With respect to deportation policy, southwestern officials of the Immigration Service followed the lead of Commissioner General MacCormack. El Paso District Director Wilmoth encouraged a more humanitarian orientation toward deportation, particularly when the procedure separated families or affected those experiencing hardship. Rather than blindly apply deportation for every infraction, Wilmoth instructed his officers to consider the merits of each case. Whereas Wilmoth and the bureau once considered adultery, unemployment, and petty crime as material to a showing of deportation, they now sought mitigating circumstances in these cases. In a remarkable change of course, Wilmoth advised officers to treat each immigrant on a case-by-case basis, rounding out the details of their presence in the United States by determining their work histories, how they supported themselves, and whether or not they had dependents in the country. Wilmoth observed,

> It is noted that many of the warrant records covering aliens arrested in this district are too meager as to personal and family circumstances, concerning which the Department is entitled to enlightenment, for the purpose of enabling it to determine whether to extend special consideration by way of granting the voluntary departure privilege, or canceling the warrant, or placing the alien on probation, or permitting him to register.[111]

While the effort to reform deportation policy and procedure may have been initiated by northern progressives, urban elites, and central office administrators, and while the reform movement may have primarily benefited European immigrants, it did reach the Southwest in both spirit and practice.[112] Taking a cue from central office administrators, Southwestern officials conducted their own internal investigations and appeared willing to liberalize their approach to deportation.

There were, however, limits to reform. Nativism precluded any substantial and wide-ranging reforms of Border Patrol and Immigration Service policy and practice toward Mexican nationals in the Southwest. While the national decline in deportations was mirrored in the Southwest, most deportations occurred in this region due to the large Mexican immigrant population.[113] Balderrama and Rodríguez note that "during the period from 1930 to 1939, Mexicans constituted 46.3 percent of all the people deported from the United States. Yet Mexicans comprised less than 1 percent of the total U.S. population."[114] Furthermore, such reforms could not and did not reach state and local removal actions against Mexican immigrants. It is clear that Mexican immigrants and even Mexican Americans continued to bear the brunt of both legal and extralegal expulsion campaigns at the local, state, and national levels.

Opposition from local immigration offices constituted another major obstacle to reform in the Southwest. While local immigration officials made an effort to mitigate some of the harsher features of deportation procedure (particularly those affecting the welfare of families), their new reform orientation never trumped their enforcement priorities. This was most evident in southwestern officials' resistance to the new warrant policy that prohibited the detention of an immigrant without an arrest warrant issued by the central office. Contrary to current historical accounts, the new warrant procedure was not a fait accompli in the Southwest; local office correspondence reveals the interagency debates about the new requirements and the intransigence of local officials in implementing new procedures.[115]

In a 1933 conference, bureau officials expressed deep concerns about the legality of Patrol operations beyond the border. To bureau officials, it was clear that the Patrol had a broad yet legitimate power to make arrests and conduct searches and seizures without warrant at the border.[116] It was not clear, however, whether the Patrol had the same power to arrest without warrant at points beyond the line. The statutes regarding the Border Patrol failed to illuminate the issue, and the deportation statutes were just as vague on this point.[117]

To date, the courts had not penalized officers for making arrests without warrant, nor had they used it as a basis to release detained immigrants on a writ of habeas corpus. But the bureau felt that "the time is coming . . . when the attorneys in this country are going to sue and hold these men liable for these arrests."[118] Keenly aware of the legal problems surrounding the practice, Commissioner General MacCormack was determined to make a change, noting that, "It appears to me that we can not escape the conclusion that the Department has been consenting to apprehensions without due regard for our constitutional procedure and that there is, in many of the cases, distinct lawlessness."[119] Later that summer, the commissioner requested a legal opinion on the issue of arresting immigrants without warrant. The report concluded that beyond the border, "there is no authority under existing law to arrest or detain an alien prior to the receipt of a proper warrant."[120]

Reformers like MacCormack believed that warrantless arrests raised not only liability questions for immigration officers but also fundamental questions of fairness and due process. They argued that the investigation and arrest comprised two of the most important facets of deportation procedure prior to the deportation hearing itself. As one reformer noted, "The preliminary phases of enforcement of the deportation laws are all focused upon the effort to obtain sufficient evidence to justify the issuance of a warrant."[121] More important, the warrant was the only procedural safeguard for the immigrant prior to the deportation hearing. Arrest warrants could not be issued arbitrarily but instead had to be supported by sufficient evidence, as one observer wrote:

> Plainly enough the [deportation] statute, in referring to a warrant, does not mean a writ arbitrarily issued without consideration. What is contemplated is the exercise of a responsible judgment affording reasonable assurance that no person will be called upon to defend himself in formal proceedings save where a *prima facie* case against him exists.[122]

Reformers found, however, that warrants were not issued on the basis of consistent or principled evidentiary standards. Immigration officials often questioned immigrants without regard to any formal procedure, failed to procure sufficient evidence, relied on anonymous tips, and, when applying to the central office for an arrest warrant, condensed the rationales for such warrants down to a series of code words, as opposed to a detailed statement of the facts and evidence.[123] In his examination of 605 bureau arrest warrants, Van Vleck found that the "definiteness and particularity of an indictment or of a complaint in a civil case are lacking. The warrant does not apprise the alien of the exact charges against him."[124] As a result of findings like these, reformers concluded that the most egregious aspects of the deportation proceeding surrounded the investigation and the arrest.[125] A warrant properly issued ensured that an immigrant's arrest and detention were justified under law. A warrant improperly issued and executed was simply an abuse of power.

Given these concerns, the commissioner general, on June 16, 1933, issued confidential orders to all district directors prohibiting the apprehension of immigrants without an arrest warrant. (Warrantless arrests continued to be permitted when officers witnessed foreign nationals in the act of surreptitious entry or were in continuous pursuit of such immigrants.[126]) This new instruction flew in the face of long-standing practice in the Southwest, and predictably, local officials railed against it. Border Patrol Supervisor I. F. Wixon noted, it was a "procedure which has been followed practically ever since we have had immigration laws on our statute books of detaining aliens by whatever means may be available until warrants could be secured."[127] Southwestern officials relied on the procedure for logistical reasons—immigrants would abscond in the 24 to 48 hours it took for officers to procure an arrest warrant from Washington, DC.[128] Others acknowledged that the detention and subsequent examination were necessary so that officers could collect the requisite evidence for issuing a warrant. Border Patrol Supervisor W. F. Kelly observed that once caught, "not one alien in a hundred so encountered [beyond the border] will immediately admit to the patrol inspector either that he is an alien or that he entered without inspection, and usually they have to be subjected to rigid questioning or even taken into custody before they will confess."[129]

The differences of opinion essentially centered on the question of speed. The changes implemented by the reformers slowed down the process of deportation at each and every stage. Reformers called for deliberation, careful adherence to standards, and checks and balances within the process, as Van Vleck emphasized, "there is no need that accuracy and justice be sacrificed to speed."[130] This ran counter to the ways in which southwestern immigration officials and, in particular, Border Patrol officers were accustomed to working. Contemporary commentators observed that the ambiguity of the deportation statute, the dearth of its provisions regarding due process, enabled a fast procedure.[131] Furthermore, field officers had long sought to execute deportation with the same expeditiousness

Figure 3.2 Border Patrol inspectors talking with Mexicans over wire fence at Border Monument #11, Cordova Island, 1940. Courtesy of US Citizenship and Immigration Services History Office and Library, Washington, DC.

that immigration officers exercised the exclusion power at the ports of entry.[132] In 1921, George J. Harris, acting supervising inspector of the Mexican Border District wrote to the commissioner general:

> Would not the vesting in district heads, at least, of the same discretion with respect to the deportation of aliens, as is lodged in port of entry officers respecting the exclusion of alien applicants for admission better serve the situation, and result in an increased capacity of the Service as a whole?[133]

The reformers in the 1930s, however, made a distinction between exclusion and deportation, asserting that deportation created much greater hardships than exclusion. As one official explained, "Deportation, at least of resident aliens, is in terms of human consequences one of the most serious forms of the exertion of governmental power—far more serious than mere denial of entry."[134] As a result, reformers strenuously argued for a slower process.

With a few exceptions, southwestern officials appear to have complied with the terms of the experiment and instructed their officers not to arrest without warrant.[135] Field offices concluded that the warrant requirement prevented overly aggressive Border Patrol tactics. W. F. Kelly even complained that the new procedure made his officers too tentative, "not wishing to chance jeopardizing their positions by taking any action, consequences to them of which they are uncertain."[136] Southwestern officials also found that without the power to make an immediate arrest, immigrant workers fled to neighboring farms or further into the interior during the time required to petition the central office for an arrest warrant.[137] The district director at El Paso reported:

> For the first half of July 1933, 164 aliens were apprehended by patrol officers and delivered to administrative officers, as compared with 321 for the first half of June 1933. It is believed that it is safe to say that this decrease of 50% was due almost entirely to the limitations placed upon the officers as to the manner in which they may arrest aliens.[138]

F. W. Berkshire of the Los Angeles office noted that 100 to 200 immigrants evaded arrest under the new procedure.[139] In 1934, Wilmoth reported that "2,000 more aliens would have been apprehended had authority existed to detain aliens for twenty-four hours."[140] Both he and W. F. Kelly argued that this new procedure was the primary cause of the decline in apprehensions for fiscal year 1934, and that, if eliminated, would greatly improve immigration enforcement.[141] In its 1934 annual report, the central office concluded that 2,600 persons avoided arrest under the new warrant requirement.[142]

In 1934, the service ended its investigation of the new warrant procedure and implemented it as official policy.[143] In an attempt to increase the number of arrests, however, the agency streamlined the warrant procedure. The service had always relied on the telegraph to issue warrants of arrest in cases where speed was of the utmost importance.[144] In these cases, the district offices would telegram the central office with a warrant request and the central office would telegram back a warrant.[145] (Before instituting the warrant requirement, the service detained immigrants in their own facilities or had the local police hold them on a technical charge for the 24 to 48 hours it took to receive the warrant.[146] Either way, the service admitted that it was arresting without a warrant.)

By creating an even more expedited form of the warrant procedure, the service hoped to evade the legal consequences of detaining without a warrant and to reduce the incidence of flight risks.[147] Since government radiograms proved too slow and even inaccurate, the service contracted with private telegraph companies.[148] It also eliminated the number of people involved in processing the telegraphic warrant, from the initial application to its issuance. Furthermore, a clerk was hired to process requests on weekends.[149] In order to accommodate the time difference between the east and west coasts, legal advisor R. J. Powers recommended that a clerk be hired to work until 8:00 p.m. EST to process requests that came in from the West Coast. This would enable these offices to receive same-day, rather than next-day, service.[150] Finally, since the commissioner general was not always available to personally sign the telegraphic warrants of arrest, he agreed to make available presigned blanks to be used in his absence.[151]

The central office requested a time study of apprehensions made under the revised telegraphic warrant procedures.[152] In an evaluation of the new procedure, the central office concluded that the new system saved 1.5 to 2 hours; cut down the number of staffers involved in the processing from five to two; enabled the service to issue warrants on the weekend; and saved the service money since private telegraph companies cut their rates in order to obtain the government's business.[153] Yet when it came to the most important question—whether the new procedure enabled the service to forego its policy of arresting without a warrant (that is, enabled the service to quickly issue warrants for flight risks without having to detain them)—legal advisors to the service concluded in the negative:

> Rather reluctantly, I must express my personal opinion, after reviewing the reports from the field . . . that a system cannot be made to work so that some aliens will not decamp during the period that elapses between preliminary statement and the time when the telegraphic warrant is received. . . . Mr. Wixon's memorandum discloses that . . .

approximately one hundred thirty-six warrants remained unserved during the period reported on because of the new procedure.[154]

As a possible solution, Powers recommended that district directors be given the power to issue warrants of arrest. He expressed reservations about the delegation of such power: district directors might be swayed by local sentiment; they might not have the legal acumen to properly issue a warrant in certain cases; they would not have the luxury of turning to the solicitor's office (as did the warrant division at the central office) for legal advice; and uniformity in the issuance of warrants might be lost. Finally, he noted, the immigrant improperly arrested would suffer unnecessarily.

Despite these reservations, Powers ultimately favored the proposal. He observed that "the issuance of telegraphic warrants here in Washington is now a more or less pro forma matter; that is, a warrant is issued on the assumption that the immigration officer who requested it has made out a prima facie case."[155] In issuing an arrest warrant, the district director would perform the same rubber-stamping function as the commissioner general (who approved warrants without reviewing the applications from the field).[156] Powers admitted that this procedure would not stop immigrants from fleeing after the preliminary examination and prior to the issuance of the arrest warrant. He hoped, however, that it would ameliorate the problem to some extent.

On October 21, 1933, Commissioner General MacCormack implemented two of Powers's proposals. First, he advised that telegraphic warrants of arrest would be issued from 4:30 p.m. to 8:00 p.m. EST, except on weekends. Second, he instructed officers not to use government telegraph services to apply for arrest warrants.[157] The Los Angeles office reported that these new procedures "greatly reduce[d] the number of aliens, who were found subject to arrest, who actually escaped."[158] By 1941, the bureau authorized district directors to issue warrants of arrest in emergency cases only—in the event that it appeared to the district director that the immigrant was "prima facie subject [to] deportation and may excape [sic] arrest unless warrant immediately issued."[159]

In response to proposals to confer the power to issue arrest warrants upon more minor district office employees, the central office expressed the same reservations that Powers had articulated with respect to the district directors. As a result, in 1941, the central office declined to grant such authority to lesser officials. Yet by 1948, the central office delegated to subdistrict officers, specifically assistant district directors and officers-in-charge of southwestern Border Patrol sectors, the authority to issue warrants of arrest.[160] Indeed, by the 1940s, southwestern immigration officials adopted operational practices that reversed the reforms of the 1930s, making arrests without warrant, procuring arrest warrants from district directors (rather than the central office) in all cases rather than emergency cases, and seeking explicit legislative sanction for warrantless arrests through an amendment of the Border Patrol legislation (the Act of February 27, 1925).

In 1940, Secretary of Labor Frances Perkins conducted another investigation into immigration practice and procedure. She appointed Marshall E. Dimock, former professor at the University of Chicago and assistant secretary of labor, to oversee a new study, which became popularly known as the Dimock Report. While the Dimock Report noted that the service responded to the criticisms raised by Clark, Van Vleck, the Wickersham Commission, and the Ellis Island Committee, it concluded that not much had changed:

> A characterization found in Jane Perry Clark's volume is almost as valid today, we are sorry to say, as it was when she wrote it: "It must be conceded that the present procedure affords opportunity for deprivation of rights considered fundamental to Anglo-Saxon law where personal liberty is involved. Deportation may technically not involve punishment, but practically a procedure where anonymous reports are received, where complete information against a person may be obtained from him and others before his right to counsel is made known to him, where the hearing is held in secret and where appeal to the courts is so rigidly restricted as in deportation cases, savors in actual practice of lack of due process of law."[161]

When it came to warrant procedure, Dimock found field officers requesting telegraphic warrants of arrest before procuring any evidence, relying on confidential informants, and issuing telegraphic warrants in regular cases as well as exceptional ones.[162]

With respect to the deportation hearing, Dimock discovered that the service continued to vest in a single officer the roles of prosecutor and judge.[163] Furthermore, many officers assigned to the Boards of Special Inquiry had no experience with administrative tribunals; they were placed there because the service considered them "misfits," unqualified or too old for other posts within the service or the Patrol.[164] On this point, the report noted:

> The most serious problems of exclusion hearings are problems of personnel. It is common practice to place the most competent men on primary inspection, relegating to the hearing chamber those who have difficulties of personality or who have grown old in the Service. Every district, apparently, has its "misfits"; we were several times told that the board of special inquiry is the best place to dispose of such persons. "We tell them just to sit and keep their mouths shut"—a warning, needless to say, given not to the chairman of the board, who does practically all of the

Figure 3.3 Marshall Dimock, Assistant Secretary of Labor, 1939. Courtesy of Prints and Photographs Division, Library of Congress, LC-H22-D-5608.

questioning, but to the second or third members. Correction of this difficulty is not an easy matter, since misfits cannot readily be discharged.

Hearings were conducted in an unprofessional manner. Making an exception for the Board of Special Inquiry at Ellis Island, the committee characterized the remaining boards as

> desultory, discursive, sadistic hearings which take place in some other jurisdictions. We have both read and witnessed such proceedings. The inspectors, on occasion, are seemingly actuated by a desire to learn all the intimate details of the alien's life. If resentment is shown they attempt to "crack down" on him. We have read some cases in which the officials commented upon the "non-cooperative" attitude of the alien when it seemed that any self-respecting person would have responded to the question in precisely the same way. Hence the irony of inadequate exclusion hearings; persons of self-respect and spirit who are the best of material for citizenship may be the very ones who are excluded.[165]

The Committee also observed a lack of consistency between central office and field office practice and procedure. It criticized field offices for the "mistaken initiation of deportation proceedings which ultimately must be quashed [by the central office]."[166] In theory, the warrant division of the central office was to oversee field office warrant procedure. But, the committee found that the central office failed to scrutinize both telegraphic and mail warrant requests. In effect, the central office issued warrants on blind faith that the field offices performed their jobs correctly.

The committee attributed this disparity between central office and field office procedure to the lack of an administrative manual. While the agency's *Immigration Laws and Rules* provided an outline of the immigration statutes, the bureau failed to provide a detailed and comprehensive operations manual. Dimock found that what operational instructions did exist—general orders, central office circulars, and district office circulars—were in a state of complete disarray. As late as 1940, none of these had been compiled, indexed, cross-referenced, or updated. They covered a variety of subjects, dealing with "everything under the sun, from the trivial and non-recurrent, to important instructions relative to practice and procedure . . . [and] interpretations of substantive law."[167] Multiple officials had the authority to issue the circulars and orders, and none were required to have their instructions approved by a higher authority. Inevitably, instructions issued by one official conflicted with those of another. Furthermore, none of these documents, including the *Immigration Laws and Rules*, were issued to the service as a whole. Those who were lucky enough to obtain a copy of the *Immigration Laws and Rules* were expected to update the manual independently and by hand.[168] When it came to other sources of authority for the Immigration Service, specifically court decisions, Board of Review cases, and opinions of the solicitor of the Department of Labor, there were no compilations or digests. During the 1941 Annual Service Conference, one INS official explained the necessity for just such a compilation, "We [field officers] are told to do a thing and we don't know why, what the need or purpose is."[169] Noting that calls such as these, specifically proposals for an administrative manual, had been made as early as 1915, Dimock wrote, "It is literally astounding that so much time should have elapsed without the intention expressed in 1915 ever having materialized."[170]

The tenets of legal realism informed the reform efforts of Clark, Van Vleck, Wickersham, and MacCormack; each believed that a more humanitarian deportation policy rested upon the expertise of administrative officials who considered the specific facts of each case rather than a blind application of the law.[170] Immigration officials themselves had long argued that certain congressional enactments pertaining to deportation were too rigid and, if strictly applied, would create unnecessary hardships for otherwise deserving immigrants, especially those with families or long-term residents of the United States who could establish good moral character.[172] As a solution, they proposed that immigration officers have more authority to exercise their administrative discretion, reviewing cases on an individual basis and excusing meritorious claims from deportation.[173] When it became apparent that congressional amendments to the deportation laws were not forthcoming, bureau officials relied on just such discretion to suspend deportation in hardship cases.

Yet in the Southwest, administrative discretion functioned as a double-edged sword. On the one hand, Wilmoth, who concurred with the humanitarian aspirations of MacCormack and Perkins, used his discretionary powers to alleviate the hardships of deportation for families and deserving individuals. On the other hand, southwestern immigration officials sought the widest possible discretion in the exercise of their enforcement powers against undocumented immigrants, chafing against the warrant reforms implemented by MacCormack. By the 1940s, Wilmoth himself was responsible for letting these reforms fall by the wayside and allowing Border Patrol officers to revert to their old practices. In his investigation, Dimock found that this attitude was typical among field officers. Many were reluctant to enforce the law in strict accordance with any set of rules or principles but instead preferred to act as the circumstances dictated. Dimock quoted one of these officers in his report:

> Every once in a while someone gets the idea that everything should be standardized, that we should promulgate rules, interpretations and procedures which are uniform throughout the country. This sounds nice, but it is not workable, it is not desirable. There is too much variety in this work for that. Every case is different. Some people get worked up because they read two cases that are as much alike as two peas in a pod and yet the determination is different: one is rejected and the other is let in. That's all right. . . . We don't want to be bound by past determinations; we refuse to be . . . If he tried to decide the case on the basis of Central Office regulations, he would never get anywhere—he would simply flounder. So, it is better that he should exercise a sound discretion . . . The discretion is broad. Yes, it is. But someone must exercise it.[174]

Dimock concluded that this attitude created "inertia" within the service and long prevented the expression and standardization of agency practices. Under these conditions, Dimock asserted that the law was effectively enforced by "laymen" and, more important, "the correct and even-handed application of the law is not possible."[175] In the southwestern field offices, the problem with deportation policy was not only the inflexibility of the law with respect to hardship cases but also the virtual lawlessness of its execution with respect to undocumented immigrants. What was required in the latter case was less discretion and more law.

If Dimock had looked further back into the institutional history of the bureau, he would have found many parallels between agency practices in the 1930s and agency practices at the turn of the century with respect to the Chinese. Historian Lucy Salyer explains that Immigration Service policies vis-à-vis the Chinese set a precedent for service operations toward all other immigrants:

> The doctrines established in the early Chinese and other immigration cases had served to loosen immigration procedures from constitutional moorings. By 1905, the summary administrative hearing, devoid of most procedural protections, coupled with the agency's broad discretion to interpret and administer the law, characterized proceedings involving admission as well as deportation, Chinese as well as non-Chinese.[176]

Indeed in the 1930s, southwestern officials within the service often referred to the Chinese precedents to argue against the reform of warrant procedures. Wilmoth protested Commissioner General MacCormack's order to suspend all warrantless arrests by arguing that the bureau's power to arrest illegal Chinese immigrants without warrant served as a legal basis for the arrest without warrant of undocumented immigrants in general.[177] While MacCormack rejected his arguments, Wilmoth's resistance to reform reflected a long-standing orientation among service officials in the Southwest.

INS efforts at self-regulation and reform in the 1930s proved incomplete and fleeting. The new standards surrounding the agency's warrant procedure were never incorporated into the immigration statutes nor articulated as judicial precedents. Over time, the high-minded ideals and well-intentioned aspirations of the central office gave way to the more mundane and practical concerns of southwestern officers in the field—how to prevent flight risks, how to minimize one's workload while making as many apprehensions as possible, and how to trim expenses when funds ran low at the end of the year. These concerns became even more pressing when immigration officials found themselves confronted by the unprecedented logistical demands of the Bracero Program. As a result, encouraged by those very officers who implemented the reforms of the 1930s, southwestern agency officials, by the 1940s, reverted to their old ways. Exercising their enforcement authority in a highly discretionary fashion, a haphazard, extralegal, and local form of immigration administration would become the law of the land once again in the US–Mexico borderlands.

4

An Agency in Crisis

People today are more Federal minded than ever before. Today even
our local papers have more Federal news than local news and with that
change I find that people are hungry for Federal information.
—Edward Shaughnessy, Commissioner General,
INS Annual Service Conference, 1944

Edward Shaugnessy's observation during the 1944 INS Annual Service
Conference reflected the new realities of the American state.[1] The Great
Depression and World War II expanded and transformed the role of the federal
government. Through national work programs such as the Civilian Conservation
Corps and the Works Progress Administration, home and farm mortgage relief,
and social security, the New Deal administration used the powers of the federal government to protect ordinary individuals from unpredictable shifts in the
economy.[2] The growth of the American state, however, did not necessarily in-
stantiate a more efficient and rational bureaucracy.[3] Instead, conflict and contingency suffused the nation's administrative agencies, both old and new. As Ellis
Hawley observes in his classic study *The New Deal and the Problem of Monopoly*,
agencies rarely were able to effectively implement their administrative mandates
on the ground.[4]

The INS at mid-century shared much in common with other federal agencies. Its participation in the Bracero Program, a labor importation program that
employed approximately 5 million Mexican nationals from 1942 until 1964,
threw the agency into a state of disarray. Whereas the Bureau of Immigration
during World War I had struggled to close the line to unwanted immigrants,
the INS during World War II lacked the institutional capacities to open the
border under the aegis of the Bracero Program. Cognizant of the agency's organizational weaknesses, INS leaders repeatedly challenged their participation
in the Program. As an immigration agency charged with monitoring the arrival
and departure of foreigners at the nation's ports of entry, the INS, agency leaders argued, did not have the experience or resources to oversee an agricultural
employment program. Meanwhile, the Border Patrol struggled to control the

unprecedented number of unauthorized entries triggered by the bracero agreement. Confronted by a set of countervailing priorities, it was not uncommon
for the Patrol, in the 1940s, to relax the enforcement of the laws at the behest of
local farmers at the very same time that it engaged in wide-ranging deportation
campaigns at the request of the Mexican government.[5]

The very conflicts and weaknesses surrounding immigration law enforcement in the 1940s led to change within the INS. Indeed, the lapses of the agency,
exposed during its administration of the Bracero Program, ultimately refocused
its mission as a whole. The agency assumed a much more aggressive orientation
toward immigration law enforcement, which continues to characterize the INS
to the present day. At the beginning of the decade, the INS remained the disorganized, apathetic, and locally minded agency of the 1920s and 1930s. By the
end of the 1940s, what was once considered peripheral to the administration of
American immigration law, specifically law enforcement along the US–Mexico
border, became the central concern of the agency.

Most of the accounts of the Bracero Program characterize the INS in one of
three ways—first, as a pawn of southwestern agribusiness that opened the border
to Mexican migrants; second, as an agency that pursued its own institutional
interests in immigration law enforcement and thereby closed the border to undocumented Mexican nationals; and third, as one of several state and nonstate
actors complicit in the exploitation of ethnic Mexican workers.[6] This chapter
argues that the agency was all of the above and more. Yet the conflicts, contra-
dictions, and failures that pervaded INS operations during the bracero era ought
not to be dismissed as irregularities or signs of the agency's impotence. Instead,
they ought to be construed as critical building blocks in the construction of the
state's regulatory capacities along the US–Mexico border.

In elucidating the mid-century transformation of the INS, this chapter begins
by describing the global, national, and local imperatives that strengthened economic, political, and social relationships across the line. In this context, southwestern agribusiness and local border residents lobbied for the creation of new
policies, including border crossing regulations and the Bracero Program. While
the Bracero Program reflected the aspirations of the United States and Mexico to
strengthen cross-border connections, it presented the INS with the messy realities surrounding this transnational endeavor. The INS lacked the resources to
manage the Bracero Program and the dramatic increase in undocumented entries
that followed in its wake. As a result, for much of the decade, the agency administered the Program with great reluctance and little administrative finesse. At the
same time, the Border Patrol found itself working at cross-purposes, opening the
border for the benefit of southwestern growers and closing it in response to the
demands of the Mexican government. Among contemporaries, the haphazard
quality of INS operations reinforced the image of the agency as unfocused and

ineffectual, incapable of closing the border to undocumented immigrants and opening it to legal guest workers.

In 1944, INS Commissioner General Earl G. Harrison and his wife toured the border in order to see first-hand the problems facing US immigration agents, Mexican immigration inspectors, and Mexican immigrants. At a banquet hosted by Sanchez Taboada, the governor of Lower California, Harrison delivered a speech expressing the wish of the immigration agency to create "a good understanding and feeling between the Mexican and American citizenry on the border."[7] Upon the conclusion of his tour, Harrison, along with Deputy Commissioner Joseph Savoretti and Los Angeles District Director Albert del Guercio agreed that the end of the war and the close relationship between the United States and Latin America necessitated the easing of American and Mexican immigration regulations. The INS leadership specifically proposed to lift all the documentary requirements for local border crossers and to eliminate the visa fees for all other Mexican nationals visiting the United States. As a reciprocal gesture, they recommended that Mexican immigration officials institute reforms for the benefit of American travelers, specifically the creation of consistent inspection policies and the elimination of corruption and bribery.

Harrison's tour reflected not only the wartime softening of American immigration laws but also a transformation in the nation's relationship with Latin America. The war conferred a sense of urgency on the Good Neighbor policy, a diplomatic posture that moderated the aggression underlying America's empire-building exploits in general and the language of 1904 Roosevelt Corollary (which stipulated that the United States could resort to military intervention to maintain order in the Western Hemisphere), in particular.[8] While seeds of the policy emerged by the second decade of the twentieth century, it found its clearest expression in the administrations of Herbert Hoover and Franklin Delano Roosevelt.[9] Rejecting the martial spirit of the Roosevelt Corollary, President Hoover actively sought to rectify the nation's image as the "'Colossus of the North.'"[10] FDR expanded upon Hoover's efforts by explicitly adopting a policy of military nonintervention, a stance that, according to historian Lars Shoultz, "became the defining characteristic of FDR's Good Neighbor policy."[11]

As World War II erupted in Europe, FDR refashioned the Good Neighbor policy in order to forge hemispheric solidarity. A series of trade agreements between Germany and Latin America led FDR to focus in particular on the development of military alliances and a hemispheric response to the Axis threat.[12] Upon America's entry into the war, the administration had posted military advisors in every Latin American nation, gained access to air and naval bases in Mexico and Brazil, and built a new base in Cuba.[13] German victories against Poland, France, and the Low Countries propelled the Roosevelt administration to fortify hemispheric relationships even further through the Office for the Coordination of Commercial and Cultural Relations between the American Republics (OCCCRBAR), later known as the Office of the Coordinator of Inter-American Affairs (OCIAA).[14] As the agency's director, Nelson Rockefeller created an economic aid program that addressed public health, infrastructure, and educational needs in Latin America, and relied on cultural vehicles, including magazines, newspapers, films, radio broadcasts, music, and art, to emphasize the region's shared interests in freedom and democracy.[15]

Roosevelt's Good Neighbor policy also improved the fraught relationship between the United States and Mexico.[16] American interests in obtaining access to Mexican air bases in 1941 served as the final impetus for the resolution of the conflict between the two nations over the Mexican oil expropriation crisis.[17] The creation of binational economic programs further signaled the strength of US–Mexican relations during the war. These endeavors included the US–Mexican Commission for Wartime Cooperation, which assisted Mexico in the development of railway lines essential for the transportation of war materiel, and the Mexican-American Commission for Economic Cooperation, which financed infrastructure and industrial projects as compensation for Mexico's provision of war supplies to the United States.[18] These collaborations between the United States and Mexico not only grew but also consolidated both nations' economies. Thus, for example, a representative from the Rockefeller Foundation came to occupy a position within the Mexican Agriculture Ministry and promoted the development of large-scale irrigation projects in the Mexican northwest.[19] These projects, in turn, drew southwestern growers into cooperative arrangements over financing, production, processing, packing, and shipment with Mexican growers who had benefitted from the Rockefeller Foundation's largesse.[20]

Mirroring the sentiments of their national governments, local and state governments on both sides of the border demonstrated a heightened spirit of friendship and cooperation during the war years.[21] Border towns such as El Paso and Juárez memorialized their nations' defensive alliance by regularly observing each nation's holidays.[22] Meanwhile, locals in Arizona–Sonora took the defense of the border in more literal terms, proposing to conduct state level policing exercises that would assist federal agencies in monitoring the border for wartime enemies.[23] Yet as in the past, apprehensions about border security competed with concerns about the health of the border economy. As a result, while the onset of World War II led to the creation of various restrictions on border crossing, the familiar demands of local residents led to their undoing. To boost the local economy, in February 1942 Mexican officials negotiated with their American counterparts to lift the ban on the border crossing of soldiers from Fort Bliss to Juárez.[24] In order to sate the tremendous consumer demand for subsistence items, such a food, tires, and fuel, rationed during the war, US customs officials could be lenient in their inspections, permitting shoppers to return from Mexico with a quantity of provisions that exceeded the ration set by the Office of Price Administration.[25]

Despite the immigration agency's own concerns about border security, it facilitated border crossings once again by modifying a new set of federal laws during the war. As a border security measure, the State Department, under Section 30 of the Alien Registration Act of 1940 and Executive Order 8430 of June 5, 1940, canceled all nonresident alien border crossing cards; in order to obtain a new card, nonresident aliens were required to present valid passports and visas.[26] Yet at the same time, resident aliens found themselves exempted from these wartime border crossing restrictions; the Alien Registration Act of 1940 rendered the border crossing card a valid entry document for resident aliens, and Executive Order 8430 excused resident aliens from the wartime documentary requirements.[27] Even German and Italian resident aliens, who were explicitly barred from receiving border crossing cards during the war, could be granted discretionary relief if they could establish a legitimate business purpose north of the line.[28]

Long accustomed to the border crossing card system that had been established during World War I, nonresident aliens protested their disparate treatment under these new travel restrictions.[29] Popular opinion held that the US government instituted the visa requirement to extract money from Mexican border crossers.[30] On the US side of the border, local businesses worried about the impact of the new regulations on the economy; Chris P. Fox, manager of the El Paso Chamber of Commerce, argued that the new nonresident rules were unnecessary given that those subject to its terms had already crossed the border, had formal records of previous lawful admission, and sometimes were personally known to immigration officials.[31] In his 1943 annual report, El Paso District Director Grover Wilmoth concluded that the new crossing restrictions undermined the wartime spirit of cooperation between the United States and Mexico: "Business people on the Mexican Border chafe under the continued application of regulations considered to be too severe for governing travel between two friendly countries jointly engaged in war against common enemies." He then continued by strongly encouraging the dismantling of wartime regulations at the earliest possible date, urging, "it is not too soon to consider post-war measures to regulate Border travel."[32]

In the meantime, local INS officials, having anticipated these protests, built in some leniency to the new rule, permitting appeals (and, in most cases, the service ultimately issued a nonresident border crossing card) and allowing those already in possession of a card to retain them (although without the possibility of renewal).[33] But given the continued complaints, local officials created ad hoc exemptions that were later effected into law. For example, agency officials used their administrative discretion to excuse illiterate nonresident aliens from the literacy test requirement.[34] By 1944, this once makeshift and local exemption was adopted as a formal policy, as central office officials amended the agency's internal regulations to permit the issuance of nonresident alien border crossing cards under the Ninth Proviso.[35] Also, by 1944, the ongoing protests of local residents as well as the agency's own workload concerns led it to eliminate the renewal requirement and thereby render indefinite the validity of nonresident border crossing cards.[36]

During the war the border remained open not only to local border cross- ers, but also to Mexican agricultural and rail workers who were admitted to the United States under the international bracero accords. Despite the repatriation drives of the 1930s and its ongoing opposition to the bracero agreement, the Camacho administration ultimately perceived the farm labor program as vital to Mexico's own foreign policy interests during the war.[37] Indeed, Germany's re- cent attack on Mexican ships in the Caribbean and its subsequent blockade of trade in the region created popular support for these wartime mandates.[38] More broadly, the Mexican government saw its participation in the rail and agricul- tural bracero programs as a way of strengthening hemispheric relations, particu- larly with the United States, in the spirit of the Good Neighbor policy.[39]

Mexico and the United States agreed to the terms of an agricultural labor pro- gram and signed the bracero agreement on August 4, 1942. President Franklin D. Roosevelt introduced the Bracero Program as a pivotal wartime measure that bore "eloquent witness" to Mexico's participation in the "war of [food] produc- tion, upon which the inevitable success of our military program depends."[40] Approximately eight months later, Congress formally sanctioned the agreement when it passed Public Law 45 on April 29, 1943. Under its terms, both govern- ments would play a role in the enforcement and implementation of the Program. On the American side, the Department of Agriculture held primary responsi- bility for the administration of the Program. The United States Employment Service (USES), a division of the Department of Agriculture until 1949, would certify that labor shortages existed in a particular area and specify the number of braceros required for a certain time period. In Mexico, the Bureau of Migrant Labor (under the Ministry of Foreign Affairs) allotted bracero quotas to its states. Both Mexican and American immigration officials selected workers from recruitment centers located in Mexico City. Once chosen, the workers signed employment contracts with the US government (specifically, the Farm Security Administration, a division of the Department of Agriculture), traveled to the United States (at the expense of the American government and growers), and then were placed on farms.[41]

On paper, the bracero agreement allayed the humanitarian concerns of the American and Mexican governments.[42] The agreement established standards regarding wages and working and living conditions. Braceros were to be paid at the same rate as domestic workers performing similar jobs and, at a minimum, no less than thirty cents per hour.[43] They were guaranteed food and housing facilities equal to those granted domestic farmworkers, the same protections against disease and accidents afforded domestic farm laborers, and transportation to and from Mexico. Also, Mexican workers were not to be subject to racial discrimination. Until 1954, Mexico reserved the right to blacklist American states, counties, or employers from the receipt of workers if they discriminated against Mexican nationals.[44] For this reason, until March 1947, Mexico excluded Texas from participation in the Bracero Program.[45] In general, Mexico hoped that the government-administered contracts would afford greater protections to its nationals than private contracts between growers and workers.[46]

The inception of the Bracero Program reflected the broader changes in US–Mexican relations during World War II. Yet while the Program symbolized a spirit of unity and cooperation, both American and Mexican critics exposed the ways in which the bracero accords perpetuated long-standing social, political, and institutional problems—the very same problems surrounding the World War I agricultural labor program. Despite the standards created, Mexican farmworkers again encountered poor living and working conditions.[47] Moreover, the INS found itself without the resources to manage the Bracero Program and to deter the subsequent increase in undocumented immigration. These difficulties led southwestern agency officials to raise questions about the open border regime created by the international agreement. As domestic forces, particularly southwestern agribusiness, obstructed the passage of federal regulations regarding the Bracero Program and border enforcement, Mexico emerged as a vocal advocate of bracero workers and border control. Ironically, it would be in the spirit of the Good Neighbor policy that the United States and Mexico would collaborate to harden the international border and, in turn, transform the institutional orientation of the INS.

In the 1930s and early 1940s, the INS expressed numerous reservations about southwestern growers' calls for a new farm labor program. In a 1941 review of petitions from Texas, the service determined that no labor shortage existed in that state. In Arizona, the service concluded that shortages could be filled by labor sources from surrounding states, Works Progress Administration rosters, and Native Americans recruited by the Bureau of Indian Affairs. The report also emphasized Mexico's staunch opposition to the use of its nationals as agricultural laborers in the United States.[48] Throughout their correspondence, service officials expressed their unwillingness to import Mexican labor and thereby create a competitive threat for domestic workers. Indeed, immigration officials emphasized that "alien contract labor laws were enacted purposely to avoid the importation of labor which would lower the standard of living in the United States."[49] For the same reason, the Departments of Agriculture and Justice also denied southwestern agribusiness requests for a labor importation program in 1941.[50]

Yet by 1942, the US entry into the war rendered a farm labor shortage a real possibility. Federal agencies, including the INS, began to concur with the growers' earlier predictions regarding a wartime decline in the domestic labor supply.[51] Thus in April 1942, the INS and the Departments of State, Labor, Agriculture, and the War Manpower Commission devised a wartime labor importation program. Even before the international bracero accords were signed, however, high-ranking INS officials continued to express their concerns about the revival of a guest worker program. Grover Wilmoth personally opposed its creation for both humanitarian and institutional reasons. He argued that the Bracero Program would limit employment opportunities for domestic workers and, at the same time, place foreign workers in "peonage."[52] Recounting the agency's experiences with the World War I labor importation program, he reminded State Department officials that the INS did not possess the enforcement capacities to monitor admitted workers and, as a result, only 35,000 of the original 70,000 braceros returned to Mexico on schedule.[53] The Border Patrol, Wilmoth observed, spent years locating and deporting those who remained. Wilmoth and other agency officials warned that the Bracero Program would also reproduce the most serious of the legal and institutional problems of the World War I program; that is, the agency, which continued to lack adequate resources, would find itself tasked to track, apprehend, and deport the undocumented migrants who would inevitably cross the nation's borders upon the start of the Program.[54]

Despite the agency's various objections, by September 1942, it found itself administering the terms of the international bracero accords. And, as agency officials anticipated, the Bracero Program recreated the logistical problems of the World War I agricultural labor program. Once again manpower and materiel shortages prevented the service from adequately fulfilling its responsibilities. When the central office instructed Wilmoth to send inspectors to Mexico City to select and recruit workers,[55] he telegrammed that he did not have the personnel; "[it] has been impossible to fill immigrant inspectors vacancies and but few immigrant inspectors this district can be spared from regular work to handle farm laborers in Mexico is it possible to detail inspectors from other districts."[56] A dearth of information about the Program led many growers to mistake the INS as the agency in charge and place their requests for labor with it rather than the USES. Indeed, there was confusion within the service itself on this point; Wilmoth himself inquired whether employers ought to apply to the INS or the USES for permission to import agricultural labor.[57] And when growers faced delays in recruitment,

Figure 4.1 Bracero Program recruiting center in Monterrey, Mexico, c. 1950. Courtesy of US Citizenship and Immigration Services History Office and Library, Washington, DC.

they singled out the INS, rather than the other multinational agencies involved in the Bracero Program, as the cause.[58]

Also as in World War I, southwestern growers asked agency officials to use their administrative discretion to overcome the so-called red tape surrounding the bracero accords. Some specifically requested that the service grant them workers under the Ninth Proviso of the immigration laws or under a border crossing card system.[59] While these demands were not met, the administrators of the Program did everything they could to ensure a steady supply of labor for the growers. Leon Brody, Immigration Service representative stationed in Mexico City, observed that the sugar beet growers' representative at the Mexico City recruitment center did not hesitate to accept Mexicans without the requisite agricultural labor experience.[60] Z. B. Jackson of the San Francisco office reported that

> the majority of the imported workers were never agricultural workers. They are better described in most instances as "dead end kids" from Mexico City. Their numbers include ex-deportees, persons posing as others when entering, and even in some instances persons neither of Mexican race or nationality although they managed to obtain documents of Mexican nationality. The local Mexican Consul, in commenting on a group of 22 in our custody, called them a bunch of "no good tramps."[61]

The service further exercised its administrative discretion on growers' behalf by authorizing the transfer of braceros from one place of employment to another and obtaining extensions of stay for workers in the United States.[62]

As the service anticipated, its heaviest responsibilities pertained to enforcement rather than recruitment. During the course of the Bracero Program, its enforcement efforts would focus primarily on two classes of undocumented immigrants: first, those who breached the terms of their contracts by leaving the job site; and second, the thousands of Mexican nationals who crossed the border, drawn by the promise of work but unable to secure bracero contracts.[63] Yet as in 1917, the service found itself without the institutional capacities to enforce the laws. With respect to those braceros who violated their work contracts, the INS quickly discovered that it had had no plan in place for their apprehension; as one immigration official observed, the Bracero Program "[had] been handled [without] any serious thought as to the problem of apprehending those who disappear."[64] Initially, INS officers kept agricultural workers under surveillance in order to prevent desertions. But the central office, seeking to limit the responsibilities of the service under the Program, instructed its inspectors to oversee only the admission and departure of workers.[65]

This policy, however, left surveillance responsibilities in the hands of Farm Security Administration officials whose own institutional mission—to defend the rights of migratory workers—prevented it from sharing the enforcement priorities of the INS.[66] Immigration inspectors noted that the FSA's haphazard recordkeeping undermined their enforcement efforts; from San Francisco Jackson reported, "FSA does not submit centralized or regular reports of missing workers. They maintain no complete and current list of missing men, but depend on their several field offices to report."[67] As a result, the service discovered that one-third of the men on one FSA list had already returned to Mexico. INS officials also believed that the FSA intentionally adopted a lenient approach to the apprehension and repatriation of contract violators. In response to these problems, one official proposed stationing a few Border Patrol officers at FSA field offices as an intimidation tactic, reminding Mexican braceros of the consequences of desertion.[68]

In the first year of the labor program, the service discovered that it needed a detention as well as an apprehension strategy for bracero contract violators. Thus, while holding thirty-one braceros at Sharp Park, California, I. F. Wixon, San Francisco district director, anticipated a public relations nightmare. In what he referred to as an "extremely bad situation," Wixon reported that detained braceros were engaging in organized protests against the Bracero Program. Wearing handmade signs that read "Esclado [sic] No. —," these former bracero workers argued that they had not been treated fairly by the FSA and the growers who employed them. Moreover, according to Wixon, some appeared to be working in the detention camps alongside enemy aliens. Even though detention officers reassured Wixon that these braceros were working voluntarily, he worried that outsiders would misconstrue the situation, believing that bracero detainees were forced to work as a form of punishment.[69]

Wixon also doubted the legality of the arrest and detention of braceros in the first place. Having apprehended the migrant workers without a warrant, Wixon wrote, "I feel that we should not be called upon to detain these Mexican workers unless we resort to deportation proceedings. It is not seen how we otherwise enter into the picture . . . in the final analysis we have no authority to hold them in custody without warrants."[70] He also asked whether the INS was responsible, in the first, place for the detention and subsequent deportation of these workers. If so, Wixon noted that these duties would consume much of the agency's time, money, and manpower. Indeed, given the volume of bracero workers crossing the border each day, Wixon emphasized that the agency's pursuit of bracero contract violators would leave time for little else.[71] In effect, the service would become a functionary of the FSA and the Bracero Program. As he observed, "It is much to be regretted that we must spend so much time and effort on this class of aliens, as we are more or less acting in the capacity of retrievers for the Farm Security."[72]

In response to Jackson's reports and Wixon's complaints, service officials met in March 1943 to define a set of admissions and enforcement policies under the Bracero Program. First, in order to insure that the braceros had the requisite work experience, the service proposed that the Mexican Labor Department submit a descriptive list of workers. Officials in El Paso would then conduct an immigration "background check" for each worker. Second, it was recommended that the FSA contact the service when braceros refused to move from one work assignment to another and when they refused to be repatriated.[73] Third, in the case of deserters, the service would not abide by FSA practice and return workers to their jobs.[74] Instead, the INS insisted that the FSA follow through on its responsibility to send these individuals back to Mexico. If these workers refused repatriation, the immigration agency would issue arrest warrants and proceed from there. Fourth, in the case of braceros who left their jobs for wartime defense industry positions, the service hoped to obtain the cooperation of the Social Security Administration in finding contract violators.[75]

Yet the agency's efforts to enhance its enforcement capacities under the Bracero Program were quickly checked by southwestern growers. By March 1943, agribusiness interests, displeased with the FSA's efforts to improve the working and living environments of both foreign and domestic farmworkers, succeeded in removing it from oversight of the Bracero Program.[76] Highly responsive to its agribusiness constituencies in the Southwest, Congress transferred jurisdiction over the Program to the new War Food Administration (WFA) in the Department of Agriculture.[77] Appointed as head of the new agency was

Chester C. Davis, former chief of the Agricultural Adjustment Administration and an ally of southwestern growers and their congressional representatives.[78] While growers desperately sought federal assistance and federal funding for the procurement of Mexican agricultural labor, they vehemently opposed anything that smacked of federal control over agricultural production. Growers strove to revamp the Bracero Program in ways that limited its centralizing features and enlarged local control.

Under the WFA, the Bracero Program gave growers more control over the hiring and management of labor. The war food administrator had the discretion to select the public or private agencies that were to implement the Program on a day-to-day basis.[79] When it came to the determination of wage rates and labor shortages, Davis chose to place that authority in the hands of state and local branches of the USES, which were beholden to agricultural interests.[80] As a result, growers effectively controlled the establishment of wage rates for Mexican braceros. Growers, moreover, ensured that no domestic laborers would be available to perform agricultural work by setting wages low. They further depressed farm labor earnings by generating a surplus of Mexican agricultural workers, routinely requesting and receiving more Mexican recruits than they actually needed.[81] By removing the FSA, growers were able to limit government supervision of braceros' workplaces and housing; as a result, they often failed to meet the humanitarian provisions of the Bracero Agreement regarding wages, and working and living conditions. As historian Richard Craig notes, growers "either ignored them or fulfilled them in a manner more to their liking."[82] Finally, with respect to enforcement, the WFA transferred responsibility for worker surveillance from the FSA to private growers. They were to report to the service those braceros who failed to remain on the job.[83] Predictably, growers were negligent in this regard.

As a testament to growers' increasing power, the agency relied on Public Law 45 (signed one month after Congress ousted the FSA from the Bracero Program) to satisfy agribusiness demands for border recruitment. While Mexico, under the bracero accords, objected to border recruitment (concerned that it would siphon away workers needed in Mexico and burden Mexican border towns with large numbers of bracero aspirants), growers perceived border recruitment as a way of circumventing the time and expense of the Program's binational inspection procedure.[84] To lower the barriers to bracero hiring even further, growers asked that the INS take charge of any border recruitment scheme and the Bracero Program as a whole. Based on their earlier wartime experiences with the agency, growers believed that an INS-administered Bracero Program would involve less red tape and oversight.[85] Despite the agency's initial objections to the administration of another farm labor program, by April 1943, it wielded its administrative discretion (as authorized under Public Law

45) and launched a border recruitment drive.[86] Under this campaign, growers could directly recruit workers at the border, avoiding all the administrative processing required by the Bracero Program.[87] Mexico vehemently objected to the 1943 border recruitment drive as a violation of its positions on grower–bracero contracting, border recruitment, and the Texas blacklist. Indeed, these braceros were contracted for the express benefit of Texas growers.[88] When Mexico threatened to withdraw from the Bracero Program altogether, the service halted the 1943 border recruitment campaign. Yet that incident served as a sign of things to come—a postwar Bracero Program that reflected growers' demands for easier access to labor, the institutional weaknesses of the INS, and the role of the Mexican government in reshaping immigration enforcement policy in the borderlands.[89]

In 1942, the INS was loath to be perceived as the agency in charge. But within a few years the service took charge, using the Bracero Program to meet its own institutional interests in stemming the tide of undocumented immigration sparked by Public Law 45.[90] Southwestern immigration officials believed that both strong enforcement and the Bracero Program were necessary to controlling the problem of unauthorized immigration. Wilmoth, for example, argued that a guaranteed supply of legal workers in conjunction with regular expulsion and legalization campaigns would deter growers from hiring unauthorized migrants.[91] Even though the INS, upon the creation of the peacetime Bracero Program in 1947, began envisioning it as one component of a broader enforcement strategy, the agency remained unwilling to manage the Program on a daily basis. Yet, due to unregulated nature of the postwar Program, INS officials increasingly found themselves not only supervising the entry and departure of guest workers but also defining policy—specifically agricultural employment policy—in ad hoc ways.

From 1947 until 1951, the peacetime Bracero Program further reinforced grower influence and control.[92] Under the Program's authorizing statutes and the international accords, growers were permitted to contract directly for braceros, eliminating the government-sponsored contracts preferred by Mexico.[93] In addition, no minimum wage was specified, employer oversight was undefined, and no formal compliance procedure had been created.[94] The looser contracting arrangements and weak government supervision resembled the terms of the World War I program preferred by growers.[95] The federal government also signaled a hands-off attitude toward the peacetime Program by appropriating a relatively small sum for its administration, especially in comparison to the wartime appropriations.[96]

Despite the agency's continuing reservations about the Bracero Program, the INS agreed to its extension because its own institutional interests coincided with

Figure 4.2 An immigration inspector and a bracero applicant, 1957. Courtesy of US Citizenship and Immigration Services History Office and Library, Washington, DC.

growers' demands for a cheap and plentiful supply of labor.[97] Given its limited resources, the service recognized that it would be easier to permit wartime braceros to remain in the country under the authority of the Ninth Proviso rather than bear the costs of removing them and, most likely, reprocessing them as agricultural workers.[98] The agency raised the same point in justifying its support of successive extensions of the peacetime Bracero Program. Furthermore the service believed that continued participation would enable it fulfill its enforcement mandate to prevent unauthorized immigration.

Although the INS may have saved itself the time and expense surrounding the repatriation of wartime farmworkers, it took on new responsibilities under the postwar Program. On paper, the agency's duties remained the same as in the wartime Program, limited to the admission and deportation of Mexican immigrant laborers. Other functions, including the determination of wage rates, the inspection of working and housing conditions, and the drafting of contracts between growers and workers, fell under the purview of the United States Employment Service.[99] In practice, however, the agency took on many of the duties of the USES, effectively operating as an agricultural employment agency.[100] Moreover, given its lack of institutional capacities for the very management of the farm labor program, the INS, once again, relied on its administrative discretion and devised makeshift agricultural employment policies.

Under the peacetime Bracero Program, the INS received, reviewed, and approved applications for the importation of labor. Rather than issue standardized applications, the agency instead asked growers to submit their requests in petition or affidavit form stating their efforts to procure local labor, the wage they intended to pay and evidence that it met the prevailing wage for the area, the type of work to be performed, and the time period such workers were needed. The agency then processed these applications in a decentralized way, devolving the responsibility to the district directors who, in turn, based their decisions on the investigations of subordinate officers in the field, many of whom were sympathetic to grower interests and needs.[101]

Not only did the agency process grower requests for labor, it also assumed the task of determining the existence of labor shortages and prevailing wage rates. When no other agency was available to perform these functions, the INS decided to conduct its own investigations regarding local labor needs and farmworker wages. These determinations were far from scientific and often worked to the advantage of the growers. William A. Whalen, the INS district director in San Antonio, instructed his officers to interview farmers so as to ascertain the prevailing wage.[102] After soliciting the personal opinion of a Texas State Employment officer and the testimony of farmers, and concluding that local labor organizations would remain quiescent in the face of additional importations, an immigration officer in San Antonio decided that there was a local labor shortage and approved several applications for bracero workers.[103]

While the central office raised no objections to the methods and conclusions of this officer, outside observers later criticized INS officials for setting wages. In his testimony before the President's Commission on Migratory Labor, Grover Wilmoth reported that while the 1947 agreement stipulated the payment of the prevailing wage, no agency took responsibility for determining that wage. Thus, he admitted that he set the prevailing wages himself. But he based his determination on past wage rates paid to undocumented workers—a rate that turned out to be lower than the prevailing wage. He then noted, "I was later informed that I had exceeded my authority in fixing *any* wage."[104]

Under the postwar Program, the INS also found itself having to determine what constituted agricultural employment. Even though there was an official definition of agricultural labor, its broad, almost tautological quality provided little guidance to INS officers. The 1948 bracero agreement defined the term as follows:

> The term agricultural labor, as defined in Public Law 229, . . . is under-
> stood to mean services performed in the employ of any person, trust,

estate, partnership, or corporation in connection with farming in all its branches, if such services are performed as an incident to farming operations, including preparation of fruits and vegetables for market or for delivery to storage of carriers, or the transportation and the operation, management, conservation, improvement, or maintenance of tools and equipment used in connection with these operations. In brief, agricultural labor within the meaning of this program will include any practices performed by a farm operator on a farm as an incident to or in conjunction with farming in all its branches.[105]

Rather than rely on this provision, Immigration Service officials used their own discretion in defining agricultural employment. As a result, the INS classified a variety of occupations as agricultural jobs. Reports from the field indicated that agency officials permitted the hiring of Mexican braceros in the construction, manufacturing, and dairy industries. Stapled to these reports was a handwritten note that read, "The attached indicates the need of a clear definition of 'agricultural laborer' in our new instructions info. bulletin."[106] In Texas, one immigration official assiduously studied statutes, court decisions, and the opinion of a Texas State Employment official to formulate a definition of agricultural labor. Written in technical legal prose, none of these sources clarified the matter. More often, they obscured the issue by providing a definition and numerous exceptions to that very definition.

Other service officials also found the provisions pertaining to worker housing to be vague.[107] This ambiguity, in addition to the weaknesses of the inspection system, enabled growers to interpret the statute as they pleased and to the detriment of Mexican braceros. Indeed, J. F. Delany, Officer in Charge in New Orleans, was dismayed to find "twelve to fourteen laborers housed in a one room cabin approximately 15 x 20 feet, where they all slept and did their cooking and eating."[108] Delany attempted to rectify the situation by issuing a set of housing guidelines to growers and by reporting infractions in detailed memoranda to his supervisors. Growers objected to Delany's supervision, charging that he had overstepped the boundaries of immigration law enforcement and usurped the jurisdiction of the USES (which most likely would have taken the growers' position in any debates about adequate housing conditions).

By October 1948, service officials in Mississippi reported with relief that local USES officials were "prepared to take over supervision of the conditions under which these laborers are being employed."[109] The INS, they continued, "assumed responsibility for it for the reason that we were the only agency with personnel available, and, in the emergency, someone had to do the job."[110] USES supervision would free Border Patrol officers to focus on their enforcement duties, as one district director wrote, "the Patrolmen may be withdrawn from this work and, if kept in the areas, should devote their time principally to the apprehension of aliens who desert their employment."[111] Growers in Mississippi and Arkansas were also pleased that the INS planned to curtail its role in the Bracero Program, hoping that this would put an end to Delany's "investigations and checks . . . and requirements."[112]

In the absence of any other federal authorities, the Immigration Service took responsibility for virtually all aspects of the Bracero Program, identifying the existence of labor shortages, processing recruits in Mexico and at the border, setting wages, inspecting job sites and dwellings, apprehending deserters and undocumented immigrants, and conducting deportations. Yet the service did not take on these tasks in consistent ways, let alone on an agency-wide basis. It appears that district directors and lower-level officials took on these additional duties at their own discretion.[113] In general, however, agency officials saw their agricultural employment responsibilities under the Bracero Program as a burden that prevented them from enforcing the immigration laws. Commissioner General Miller noted that the determination of wages, working, and living conditions all fell under the purview of the USES, not the INS.[114]

Summarizing the unregulated character of the postwar Bracero Program, the President's Commission on Migratory Labor wrote, " 'Following the war . . . we virtually abandoned effective scrutiny and enforcement of the Individual Work Contracts to which private employers and individual Mexican aliens were the parties."[115] Given their own experiences managing the peacetime Program, immigration officials in the 1940s suggested a number of solutions to this lack of organization and oversight. Delany recommended the appropriation of more resources to those agencies, particularly the USES, directly responsible for enforcing the bracero accords.[116] Others proposed the creation or assignment of a single agency that would have jurisdiction over the day-to-day operations of the Program; some recommended that the INS serve as that agency.[117]

Advocates of the latter proposal argued that, if placed in charge of the Bracero Program, the INS would have the power to enforce not only the immigration provisions of the labor accords but also its humanitarian terms, thereby protecting the wages, and working and living conditions of bracero migrants. El Paso officer A. S. Hudson proposed to Wilmoth that if farmers refused to pay a fair wage (determined by the INS) or provide adequate housing, the Border Patrol "concentrate on his farm so that he will not be able to make use of additional illegal laborers."[118] Wilmoth himself proposed that the INS take charge of the Bracero Program to enforce these same provisions:

Apparently some agency should have authority to take immediate action to remedy situations of this sort, when found to exist, (a) to

prevent loss of work and wages to the laborers, (b) to prevent employers from mistreating other recruited laborers, and (c) as a warning to
other employers; it is believed that this Service is the logical agency to
be vested with that authority.[119]

By the 1950s, the bureau took increasing control over the agricultural employment aspects of the Bracero Program, but not for the humanitarian reasons
envisioned by Delany, Hudson, and even Wilmoth. For Commissioner General
Swing, INS supervision over the Bracero Program served as one means of
achieving his main goal—controlling the problem of unauthorized immigration.

As immigration inspectors in the Southwest found themselves consumed by
the administration of the Bracero Program, Border Patrol officers shouldered
many of the agency's wartime responsibilities.[120] Patrol officers stepped in as
immigration inspectors when there were staff shortages, supervised some of
the wartime detention camps, assisted the Army and Navy in patrolling the
Atlantic and Gulf Coasts in response to the German U-boat campaign against
Atlantic shipping, and helped to administer the Bracero Program.[121] But as early
as 1941, the Border Patrol reported that its focus had shifted from the entry of
Axis spies to the undocumented migration of agricultural workers.[122] By 1945, as
the unit suspended its wartime operations, another kind of war seemed to have
just begun.[123] Left to manage the rapidly growing migration of undocumented
workers across the nation's southern line, the Border Patrol, in the words of one
officer, recognized that "the illegal entrant at the Mexican border presents the
most serious problem confronting the Border Patrol."[124]

In their effort to enforce the immigration laws, Border Patrol officers faced
the same pressures as immigration inspectors who administered the terms of the
Bracero Program. On the one hand, growers and their congressional representatives actively undermined Border Patrol efforts to close the nation's borders to the
entry of undocumented workers; on the other hand, the Mexican government
pressured the agency to deter unauthorized immigration and uphold the terms
of the bracero accords. As a result, the Patrol found itself, as its leaders put it,
"caught in the middle"—enforcing the laws at the behest of the Mexican government one day while standing down in response to grower complaints the next.[125]
Yet due to this haphazard and reactive approach to immigration law enforcement,
the Border Patrol, in the 1940s, attained the image, in historian Manuel García y
Griego's words, of "an inept, slovenly, and ineffective branch of government."[126]

The Bracero Program created the conditions for an unprecedented increase
in undocumented immigration from Mexico to the United States. The bureaucratic regulations surrounding the Program inspired resistance among aspiring
braceros as well as southwestern growers. Given the hiring quotas established by

the bracero accords, Mexican nationals quickly discovered that positions were extremely difficult to obtain. In some regions, twenty applications were received for each available contract.[127] In addition to the quotas set by the Mexican federal government, provincial and local governments, in an effort to protect their own industries, adopted limits on bracero hiring. These included outright bans on bracero recruitment, the rejection of bracero quotas issued by the national government, the creation of additional fees for bracero applicants, and, by the 1950s, a requirement that applicants first work on Mexican farms, in a kind of internal bracero program, for a set period of time.[128] Those who won a county lottery (through which bracero quotas were distributed) then found themselves having to undergo an expensive and time-consuming inspection process that took place on both sides of the border.[129] Corruption and abuse, on both sides of the line, only aggravated the difficulties surrounding the recruitment process. In Mexico, bribery became an accepted means of obtaining a bracero quota.[130] In the United States, workers were subjected to intrusive health inspections, which included a "delouse[ing] with DDT,"[131] and a demeaning selection process whereby growers sought to hire those men who appeared most compliant.[132] After enduring these procedures, bracero contracts were still not guaranteed; US officials reserved the right to return applicants to Mexico if they expressed radical political beliefs or showed symptoms of any medical ailment.[133] These extensive and humiliating examinations served as powerful incentives for Mexican migrants to circumvent the formal recruitment process and cross the border without inspection.

For many, the rewards of a surreptitious crossing appeared to outweigh the risks. The Bracero Program inspired hope and desire among many in Mexico, particularly given that the Mexican economy, even after experiencing a revival during the war years, failed to provide enough jobs to meet demand.[134] Thus, as the first wave of braceros sent their earnings home, their families gained "economic breathing room" or material improvements in their quality of life.[135] Witnessing the increased purchasing power of braceros in their families and communities, many more Mexican nationals sought employment in the United States and joined the numerous chain migrations, both legal and undocumented, headed north.[136] Southwestern growers only fueled migrants' aspirations by asking workers, particularly former employees originally hired as braceros, to return to the United States outside the requirements of the bracero accords.[137] Their invitations sent a clear message to Mexican nationals that jobs were readily available for those willing to take a chance on an illegal border crossing.

Because the Bracero Program generated so many incentives for undocumented entry, the number of out-of-status workers, according to historian Kitty Calavita, "far exceeded the number of legal braceros."[138] INS apprehension statistics further attest to the unprecedented nature of undocumented migration during the bracero era. By 1949, the El Paso district reported that its Border Patrol unit "apprehended more persons than did the Border Patrol for the entire Service in any of the fiscal years 1939 to 1944 inclusive."[139] In each successive year of the decade, the Patrol reported a new record in apprehensions, and each record shattered the 1929 record of 35,000 apprehensions that stood between 1924 and 1943.[140]

In its effort to control undocumented entry across the nation's southern line, the Border Patrol operated from a position of weakness during the bracero era. The unit repeatedly found itself challenged by farmers and ranchers who staunchly defended their use of undocumented Mexican labor and vigorously protested any INS efforts to enforce the law. In frequent contact with their congressional representatives, southwestern agribusiness interests compared Border Patrol roundups to the workings of a fascist state. Others boldly argued that the best way to redress alleged labor shortages was to make the Border Patrol cease its apprehension of undocumented Mexican workers.[141] In response to these complaints, southwestern legislators made sure that the Border Patrol never had the appropriation to effectively enforce the immigration laws. In 1944, Congress cut more than 100 posts from the Border Patrol (despite, or perhaps as a result of, the dramatic rise in apprehensions between 1943 and 1944), thereby reducing the size of the unit by 10 percent.[142] As Congress reduced the appropriation for the Border Patrol, it simultaneously increased service appropriations for the administration of the Bracero Program.[143]

Pro-bracero legislators also defended the interests of borderlands growers in more pointed ways, issuing explicit warnings to Immigration Service officials. When the Border Patrol conducted a roundup in Texas, Representative Lloyd Bentsen, having received numerous complaints from farm constituents, threatened to initiate an investigation of Border Patrol practices.[144] In 1951 Congressman Poage of Texas, the vice chair of the House Committee on Agriculture, secured a guarantee from Border Patrol supervisor Willard F. Kelly that the Patrol would not disturb the undocumented immigrant population on the US–Mexico border.[145] Other legislators had personal motivations for supporting a relaxation of Border Patrol enforcement. Through a staff member, Senator Eastland of Mississippi contacted the INS to follow up on a promise that "he would get 50 Mexican laborers from Monterey." In lieu of these legally contracted workers, however, Eastland's office indicated that the Senator could procure "50 'wetbacks'" from his uncle who had a ranch in Texas.[146]

Federal courts also demonstrated an unwillingness to take a strong stand on enforcement by declining to prosecute undocumented immigrants or by issuing suspended sentences under the criminal penalty provisions of the Act of March 4, 1929.[147] The Los Angeles district reported that the United States Attorney refused to prosecute not only undocumented entrants but also smugglers (under the anti-smuggling clauses of Section 8 of the Immigration Act of 1917) except in the most aggravated cases.[148] In San Antonio, District Director Whalen explained that courts demonstrated leniency due to the sheer volume of cases and because they were sympathetic to the farmers and ranchers.[149] District Director Wilmoth observed a similar situation in El Paso where sympathetic grand juries "declined to indict . . . even after they [undocumented immigrants] had made written and signed confessions of their guilty implications in alien smuggling transactions."[150] As a further reflection of the reluctant enforcement of the Act of March 4, 1929, one federal judge in San Diego proposed that the INS legalize workers by making them available for hire as braceros after their convictions.[151] By 1949, the service itself decided not to pursue prosecution except in the most aggravated cases, which included "those who are criminals, those who falsely claim United States citizenship, and those who reenter more than four times during any six months' period after voluntary departures."[152]

Throughout the duration of the Bracero Program, various factions, in both the United States and Mexico, challenged southwestern growers, objecting to their reliance on undocumented labor. For over a decade, American and Mexican unions demanded a place at the bracero negotiating table and stronger protections for foreign and domestic workers in the United States.[153] Their activism not only reflected the binational interest in the humanitarian plight of farmworkers, but also produced transnational reform proposals. For example, in a 1953 meeting of the Inter-American Regional Organization of Workers (of the International Confederation of Free Trade Unions, an international labor organization which included members of the AFL, CIO, and United Mine Workers Association) the unions recommended that Mexican braceros be admitted to American labor unions,[154] and that the principles of Mexican labor law "be incorporated into the US–Mexico contract agreement when a higher legislation does not exist in the United States."[155] In addition, the conference proposed a binational approach to border enforcement, calling upon the Mexican government to penalize Mexican nationals who illegally emigrated to the United States and calling on the US government to pass sanctions against employers who hired undocumented workers.[156]

Even though these proposals paralleled those made by the Mexican government and prominent liberal politicians in the United States, labor unions did not find a sympathetic ear in Congress until the 1950s.[157] Indeed, even when the Truman administration sought to draw attention to the problems surrounding migratory agricultural labor, whether foreign or domestic, and documented or undocumented, Congress continued to ignore the humanitarian crises facing the nation's farmworkers. Beholden to agribusiness interests, Congress, as Ellis Hawley writes, ignored almost completely the proposals of labor groups and liberal congressmen for stringent safeguards and new curbs on the wetback traffic. It paid little attention to the recommendations of the President's Commission on Migratory Labor. And it refused to go along with the proposals of the Department of Labor for the recruitment, transportation, and protection of domestic as well as foreign workers. Such an approach, the farm spokesmen insisted was impractical, bureaucratic, and unneeded.[158]

Given the political weaknesses of American and Mexican labor organizations, the Mexican government, for much of the 1940s and 1950s, would be the most vocal advocate for undocumented and bracero labor in the United States.

In a context in which many American policymakers ignored the issue of undocumented immigration, Mexican government efforts to address the problem stood in sharp relief.[159] There were several reasons underlying Mexican concerns about unauthorized immigration. First, Mexican officials were embarrassed by the mass departure of their nationals. Second, they feared the loss of a cheap labor source for Mexico's own agricultural and industrial economies.[160] Third, they argued that the employment of undocumented immigrants would lower wage rates and diminish working and living conditions for all Mexican workers, both legal and undocumented, in the United States.[161]

To support their case, Mexican officials recounted the experiences of Mexican workers in Texas. Excluded from the bracero accords, Texas farmers and ranchers relied primarily on undocumented immigrants whom they subjected to low wages, harsh working conditions, and discriminatory, if not violent, treatment.[162] Indeed, the discrimination faced by Mexican farmworkers was an extension of the Jim Crow racism faced by all persons of Mexican descent.[163] As historian Justin Hart observes, "Mexican braceros complained about all sorts of unequal treatment, such as receiving a 'lower rate of pay for the same work'; on-the-job segregation between Mexicans and Anglos; separate recreational and toilet facilities; and a glass ceiling that prevented them from advancing beyond 'certain low-paying jobs.' "[164] Despite the efforts of the State Department and the Fair Employment Practices Commission (FEPC) to rectify the discrimination faced by these workers, Mexico insisted on stronger measures.[165]

In order to assist undocumented workers, Mexico adopted a two-prong approach, advocating for the humanitarian needs of persons of Mexican descent in the United States and demanding stronger border enforcement. With respect to the former, the Mexican government repeatedly insisted upon the inclusion of working and living guarantees in the international bracero accords. Using its participation in the Bracero Program as leverage, the Mexican government also negotiated with the American federal government and the state of Texas to address the discrimination faced by Mexican Americans and Mexican immigrants.[166] Thus during the 1940s, Mexican officials actively lobbied Texas legislators to pass anti-discrimination laws, particularly measures that would include penalties for violators. In the spring of 1943, the Texas legislature ultimately responded by passing House Concurrent Resolution 105, the "Caucasian Race—Equal Privileges" resolution, which expressed the rights of Caucasian persons to equal access to public facilities and declared denials of those rights to be violations of the Good Neighbor policy.[167] Disappointed by the weakness of this resolution, particularly the absence of penalty provisions, the Mexican government, by June 1943, decided to ban Texas farmers from the receipt of bracero contracts.[168] In response, Texas sought to appease Mexico by making several concessions, proclaiming the state's official advocacy of the Good Neighbor policy and creating the Good Neighbor Commission (which implemented an education campaign to encourage Texans to end the discriminatory treatment of Hispanics).[169] Even though Mexico continued to insist that Texas pass penalty legislation, it hesitantly accepted the programs developed by the Texas Good Neighbor Commission and, by 1947, authorized bracero contracting in Texas.[170]

Mexico also sought to protect its nationals by preventing their unauthorized migration into the United States in the first place. In addition to local and provincial regulations surrounding bracero contracting, the Mexican federal government by 1950 established fines and prison terms for individuals facilitating undocumented emigration.[171] On the international stage, the Mexican government entered into a series of bilateral conferences on the issues of unauthorized immigration and the Texas ban, the first of which took place in June 1944 and at intermittent points until 1947.[172] During these conferences, Mexican concerns about undocumented immigration served as the basis for that country's repeated insistence that bracero recruiting take place at interior points of Mexico; that the US Border Patrol strengthen its enforcement efforts; and that the United States agree to legalize and hire out-of-status immigrants as braceros. In return, the Mexican government promised to beef up its own enforcement efforts. In the June 1944 bilateral conference held in Mexico City, Mexico agreed to use its military authorities to prevent the unauthorized departure of its nationals, to modify its passport system, and to create penalties for undocumented emigrés.[173] Yet Mexico failed to strengthen its own border patrols and pass the penalty legislation. Once again, after the United States and Mexico agreed to a 1945 bilateral roundup operation, Mexico failed to satisfy its commitment to transporting apprehended immigrants from the border to the interior.[174] Similar promises were made, but yet again unfulfilled, in 1946 and 1947.[175]

Despite the lack of assistance from Mexican officials, the Border Patrol initiated most of its enforcement campaigns at the insistence of the Mexican government. Whenever Mexico threatened to back out of the bracero

accords—claiming that the United States failed to uphold its contractual ob-
ligation to prevent unauthorized border crossings—the Immigration Service
increased its enforcement efforts. In the summer of 1944, Mexico promised
continued participation in the Bracero Program if the United States removed
the estimated 22,000 undocumented Mexicans in the country. In response, the
Border Patrol conducted a number of roundups throughout the Southwest that
resulted in the apprehension of over 45,000 laborers.[176] Once again in 1949, as
the United States and Mexico were engaged in negotiations over a new bracero
agreement, the service conducted roundups in response to Mexican criticism
about the issue of unauthorized immigration. Upon completion of the operation at the end of May 1949, the service reported the apprehension of 2,883
immigrants.[177] In August 1949, the United States and Mexico signed another
guest worker agreement that lasted until 1951.

These roundup efforts were always compromised. At the request of growers, central office officials, and national politicians, the Border Patrol stayed
off farms and ranches while conducting its removal drives.[178] As a result, the

Figure 4.3 One of the removal campaigns conducted by the INS during the Bracero
Program, Hidalgo, Texas, 1948. Courtesy of US Citizenship and Immigration Services
History Office and Library, Washington, DC.

service grappled with the competing demands of the Mexican government and Southwestern farmers:

> The Mexican government on the one hand is recommending that we apprehend and deport their nationals, while the farmers on the other hand are asking that they be permitted to employ in the planting and harvesting of their essential food crops Mexican nationals, regardless of whether they entered the United States illegally. The Service is in the middle.[179]

Yet outside of peak harvest periods, the service augmented its efforts to control unauthorized border crossings, transferring men from other stations to assist in roundup efforts and apprehending immigrants both on and off the fields and ranchlands.

Also at the instigation of the Mexican government, the Border Patrol undertook several legalization campaigns as another approach to redressing the issue of undocumented immigration. The Mexican government strongly advocated legalization because it felt that the procedure, by placing workers under the protective mantle of the bracero accords, would improve the working and living conditions for out-of-status migrants in the United States.[180] To this end, Mexico repeatedly refused to sign any new bracero agreement unless American officials agreed to regularize the status of those undocumented workers already in the United States.[181] Thus on April 10, 1947 the United States and Mexico set up processing centers (one along the California–Mexico border, and two along the Texas–Mexico border) to adjust the status of the reported 119,000 undocumented immigrants who remained after the termination of the wartime Bracero Program.[182] The 1947 legalization campaign, in turn, opened the door to new negotiations between the United States and Mexico and facilitated the signing of the 1948 agreement. The two countries would agree to additional regularization drives in 1948 and in 1949.[183] Ultimately, regularization became one of the distinguishing characteristics of the peacetime bracero agreements between 1947 and 1949.[184]

Mexico was mistaken in believing that legalization would improve conditions for out-of-status workers, particularly those in Texas. Here, farmers and ranchers refused to abide by the terms of the bracero accords regarding wages and working conditions and, instead, claimed to follow the dictates of Texas state law, which imposed less onerous requirements on agricultural labor matters.[185] Moreover, Mexico, according to historian Peter Kirstein, was naive to think that legalization would solve the problem of undocumented immigration. A government investigation of migratory labor in the United States later cited to the procedure as one of the primary causes of unauthorized immigration.[186] If anything, the possibility of legalization only served as an additional incentive for surreptitious crossings.

While regularization failed to meet Mexico's law enforcement expectations, it satisfied growers' demands for a steady supply of Mexican labor.[187] Growers quickly realized that it was easier to procure labor through the legalization procedure rather than the formal bracero recruitment process (there were fewer steps and less paperwork) and increased their requests for these workers.[188] As a result, the service found that "employers are more successful in collecting qualified laborers [undocumented laborers who had entered prior to August 1, 1949] than we are in apprehending them."[189] Further attesting to the popularity of the program among farmers, between 1947 and 1949, 142,000 undocumented immigrants were legalized while 74,000 Mexicans were recruited under the terms of the Bracero Program.[190]

Despite these unanticipated consequences, the service continued to rely on the legalization procedure, even going so far as to regularize workers without the sanction of the Mexican government. During the infamous "El Paso Incident" of October 1948, the INS opened the border to 7,000 Mexicans who had gathered upon word that the United States and Mexico were in negotiations to open a border recruitment center. Although Mexico agreed to the recruitment of 2,000 workers from Ciudad Juárez, formal hiring never began as waiting workers "stormed the border."[191] A few days later, the INS took unilateral action by opening the line to the unauthorized entry of the gathered applicants.[192] Service officials arrested them on the spot and then paroled them to waiting employers. Grover Wilmoth justified the maneuver as a "humanitarian gesture because both the laborers and farmers were 'desperate.'"[193]

The El Paso Incident prompted the withdrawal of the Mexican government from the Bracero Program—at least publicly.[194] Historians report that the United States conducted the Bracero Program on a unilateral basis for eight months after the El Paso Incident.[195] Yet it appears that only two months later, the Mexican government entered into secret negotiations to regularize the status of 4,000 undocumented laborers to work on farms in California and Arizona. Furthermore, Mexico took the unprecedented step of agreeing to legalize these workers at points far from the border—in Sacramento, Fresno, and Phoenix.[196] Given that this operation contradicted their official opposition to the El Paso Incident, Mexico insisted on confidentiality. Under this program, farmers not only brought their undocumented workers to be processed but the Immigration Service also made "available for contracting Mexican nationals apprehended while illegally employed in agriculture."[197] By July 25, 1949, the service reported that 1,500 workers had adjusted their status under this secret agreement.[198]

At the very same time that the service undertook this clandestine legalization program, it was in the midst of conducting the spring 1949 roundup campaign, also at the request of the Mexican government, which resulted in the apprehension of almost 3,000 out-of-status workers and the signing of the August 1949 bracero agreement. In short, in 1949, the INS carried out two campaigns that worked at cross-purposes with each other—one deported undocumented immigrants, while the other regularized their status. Although the spring 1949 legalization program remained confidential, the August 1949 bracero agreement institutionalized its terms, authorizing the processing of undocumented immigrants who entered before August 1, 1949.[199] Subsequent negotiations resulted in repeated extensions of the cut-off date for the contracting of undocumented workers.[200]

The President's Commission on Migratory Labor excoriated the legalization programs. These, it emphasized, constituted flagrant violations of the immigration laws; the commission wrote:

> In the contracting of wetbacks, we see the abandonment of the concept that the ninth proviso authority is limited to *admission*. A wetback is not admitted; he is already here, unlawfully. We have thus reached a point where we place a premium upon violation of the immigration law.[201]

INS officials would broach no disagreement with this characterization. A few years earlier, Border Patrol supervisor Kelly admitted that in the face of the sheer logistical demands presented by the Bracero Program, "It is clear that our law enforcement machinery has broken down almost completely." [202] Yet, the crises the agency faced in the 1940s would motivate a new round of reforms focused on building an immigration enforcement strategy for the US-Mexico border.

5

Making the Local National

Because this report so remarkably reflects the logic and persuasion of
Mr. Wilmoth, it is, in fact, a monument to the finest of a long line of
brilliant achievements.
           —Argyle R. Mackey, Commissioner General, May 7, 1951

When El Paso District Director Grover C. Wilmoth passed away in 1951,
Commissioner General Argyle Mackey sent a copy of the final report of the
President's Commission on Migratory Labor along with his condolences to
his widow. Mackey characterized the report as the "last great effort in the field
of immigration to which Mr. Wilmoth contributed so much during his lifetime."[1] A forty-three year veteran of the agency, Wilmoth was a driving force
not only in the enforcement of the immigration laws in the borderlands but
also the drafting of the laws that continue to inform the letter and spirit of
American immigration policy. As such, the El Paso district director actively
participated in the policymaking process at the local, regional, and national
levels. In the 1930s, he prepared a training manual for southwestern Border
Patrol officers and a 115-page report on potential communist threats in the
United States for the central office.[2] When he died of a sudden heart attack in
Mexico City, Wilmoth was serving as part of an American delegation renegoti-
ating the bracero accords.[3] For several years he had played a pivotal role in the
President's Commission on Migratory Labor, launched by President Truman
to investigate the condition of domestic and foreign agricultural workers in the
United States. Although Wilmoth initially doubted that the INS could make
any impact on the commission, he ultimately shaped its vision of immigration
law enforcement.

The President's Commission on Migratory Labor gave Wilmoth an unprecedented opportunity to express his views on immigration law reform. In the halls
of Congress and the office of the president, Wilmoth articulated a highly aggressive approach to border enforcement that unraveled the reforms of the 1930s.
This approach was motivated by the problems surrounding the implementation
of the Bracero Program, specifically, the question of how to locate, pursue, arrest,

detain, and deport hundreds of thousands of unauthorized immigrants with a limited budget and a small staff. In response, the agency restored old practices and created new procedures that circumscribed immigrant rights. The old strategies included roundup, or mobile task force, operations and warrantless arrests beyond the border. The new strategies expedited deportation procedures and relied heavily on military technology.

While the humanitarian reforms of the 1930s never achieved the status of law, Wilmoth ensured that his own reform program would not meet the same fate. Through his legislative efforts, Congress, in 1946, passed Public Law 613, which legalized warrantless searches, seizures, and arrests beyond the international line.[4] His extensive testimony before the President's Commission on Migratory Labor eventually led to the passage of S. 1851 in 1952, which expanded the Border Patrol's authority to operate far beyond the international line and well within the nation's interior. More broadly, Wilmoth developed a border enforcement strategy that was contingent upon the conquest of space—upon the agency's ability to pursue undocumented immigrants far within the nation's interior and without regard for any legal or constitutional constraints.

This chapter traces the ways in which Wilmoth, a local INS official, played a pivotal role in defining and advancing the enforcement priorities of the INS among politicians and policymakers in Washington, DC. In contrast to agency leaders who had limited periods of time in which to absorb and promote their agencies' agendas, Wilmoth's four decades of service with the INS in the Southwest rendered him particularly qualified to speak to the issue of immigration law enforcement along the US–Mexico border.[5] Timing, as well as experience and expertise, enabled Wilmoth to win support for the agency's enforcement goals. An executive branch responsive to immigration reform supplied Wilmoth and the INS with a powerful and long-sought political advocate in the nation's capital.[6] Joining the office of the president were liberal legislators who, for economic and humanitarian reasons, supported strong border enforcement. In the 1950s, the INS would work alongside the executive branch and these liberal legislators to revamp the nation's immigration enforcement policies. In so doing, the INS shaped the work and findings of President Truman's Commission on Migratory Labor.[7]

Wilmoth's endeavors not only illustrate the policymaking function of local and regional agency administrators; they also underscore the importance of contingency in the state-building process.[8] Wilmoth's blueprint for border enforcement was an attempt to create some kind of order out of the disorder that permeated agency operations during the first decade of the Bracero Program. Through Wilmoth's efforts, the INS by the early 1950s possessed a broader set of legal tools, including expedited removals, the statutory authority to arrest without warrant all unauthorized immigrants (whether in transit or domiciled), and the reasonable distance rule, with which it could pursue, detain, and arrest undocumented immigrants at the border and far beyond it.

For most of the decade, the annual reports of the southwestern border districts plus the semiannual inspection reports of the Border Patrol division attested to the shortage of personnel and supplies for enforcement. Budget cuts and the loss of men to the military and better paying wartime industries meant that the unit had to make do with sparse resources. In the face of this budget crisis, in 1949 C. E. Waller, the chief budget officer for the Patrol, argued that the Border Patrol had been asked to do the impossible—halt the ever-increasing flow of undocu-mented immigration with a perpetual decline in manpower. He warned, "We are now ATTEMPTING to apprehend about 300,000 aliens per annum with 100 fewer officers than we had in the fiscal year 1943 when we apprehended but 16,330 aliens and 63 alien smugglers."[9] Patrol operations were affected not only by staffing reductions but also by a dearth of housing for Border Patrol offi-cers, adequate training for new recruits, and equipment, such as radios and auto-mobiles.[10] The Border Patrol also discovered that it could not afford the high purchase and maintenance costs surrounding new surveillance technologies, specifically airplanes and radar, adopted during World War II.[11] As a result, de-spite the promising use of the patrol planes, fiscal limits prevented the contin-uous use of aerial surveillance during the 1940s and early 1950s.[12]

It was in this context that service officials restored policies attacked by reform-ers and rendered defunct by Commissioner General MacCormack in the 1930s. These were tactics that enabled the INS to apprehend and remove large numbers of immigrants quickly and cheaply. In his 1944 lecture on Border Patrol duties (ironically, this was one of a series of lectures originally commissioned in the 1930s as part of an effort to educate and reform Immigration Service officers), Wilmoth encouraged the use of confidential informants and noted that the ser-vice had set aside funds for their use. He also encouraged officers to interrogate detained immigrants regarding the presence of other undocumented immigrants on or in the vicinity of their place of employment; Wilmoth referred to this as an "endless chain system" whereby the arrest of a single individual would lead to the identification of other suspects for apprehension.[13] In contravention of MacCormack's prohibition against warrantless arrests, Wilmoth recommended that officers be given permission to "take deportable aliens into custody without warrants of arrest."[14]

Perhaps most infamously, in the 1940s the Border Patrol fine-tuned a removal procedure that allowed small teams of Border Patrol officers, later referred to as "task forces," to apprehend a large number of deportees in a short period of time.[15] While it achieved notoriety during the 1954 mass deportation campaign known as Operation Wetback, the strategy was not new. Since its creation in

1924, Border Patrol officers operated in a semimobile fashion, organized into units that were shifted from place to place for both tactical and financial reasons. The regular transfer of officers enabled the service to make do with a limited number of men. Thus, for example, a task forces operation conducted in 1944 tripled the agency's apprehensions; in 1943 the Border Patrol apprehended 11,715 individuals, while in 1944 that number rose to 31,174.[16] The strategy also reflected the long-standing view of many service officials regarding the agency's inability to deter undocumented immigration at the international boundary itself.[17]

Even though the reformers of the 1930s excoriated the lack of process surrounding deportation, the agency by the 1940s sacrificed immigrant rights in the interest of speed. Although the INS would publicly deny any wrongdoing, local residents wrote to agency officials protesting the treatment of Mexican Americans and Mexican immigrants by Border Patrol officers.[18] Attesting to the rapidity with which deportations occurred, Richard J. Hanavan of Fresno, California wrote:

> Citizens of Mexico, who have illegally entered this country, or have illegally remained after expiration of visas, are being deported indiscriminately as soon as they are "caught." This deportation is apparently a very rapid process. The specific "roundups" that I am familiar with . . . indicate that the alien is deported within 24, or at most 48 hours after apprehension.[19]

E. T. Yates, an attorney in Brownsville, Texas, also criticized the agency's deportation procedures and made recommendations that echoed those of Commissioner General MacCormack and Secretary of Labor Frances Perkins. Based on his own observations, he charged that local Border Patrol officers had deprived immigrants of their right to an attorney and failed to advise them of their right to pursue a suspension of deportation. Yates emphasized that the latter was particularly necessary in the case of those immigrants who had lived in the country for several years, married American citizens, raised children in the United States, and lacked a criminal record. Perceiving a difference in the institutional culture between Border Patrol and immigration officers, Yates recommended that apprehended migrants be turned over to immigration inspectors for a full examination of their cases.[20]

Despite these criticisms, the agency continued to rely on the roundup procedure throughout the 1940s. At the same time the strategy allowed the agency to compensate for some of its weaknesses, it exposed others, which led southwestern immigration officials to further undermine the reforms of the 1930s. The volume of apprehensions generated by the roundups stretched thin the agency's detention capacities. Although the INS constructed its first immigration detention center in El Centro, California in 1941, it continued to require additional detention space throughout the 1940s.[21] But the service argued that due to ongoing fiscal shortfalls, it could not bear the cost of maintaining detainees for an extended period of time. As I. F. Wixon, the district director at San Francisco, pointed out, "To equip these camps with beds, linen, kitchen utencils [sic] and the like would mean a considerable outlay. To secure cooks, laborers and possibly security officers on a temporary basis would be well-nigh impossible."[22] Wixon also anticipated that his office would be unable to spare the administrative personnel necessary to finalize the deportation of detainees.[23]

In response to this crisis southwestern agency officials innovated once again, authorizing the use of expedited warrant procedures and mass voluntary departures in lieu of formal deportation. Whalen justified the use of these procedures by saying, "There is not sufficient personnel to make warrant cases in all cases when aliens are apprehended in such large numbers at one time. Another reason for granting additional voluntary returns is that there are no jail facilities for holding aliens awaiting deportation."[24] Even though voluntary departure itself was an expedited removal procedure, the number of voluntary departures was so great during the bracero era that district directors agreed to streamline the process even further. Service officials authorized field agents to make an abbreviated record in voluntary departure cases so that they could devote more time to apprehending immigrants, as Whalen instructed:

> Wherever extremely large numbers of aliens are apprehended, we have to refrain from making as good records as is desirable. To hold them up for this purpose would mean excessive cost of detention, with no place to detain, and in addition it would mean that our officers would not be able to be at work apprehending aliens due to the work necessary in processing."[25]

Underscoring the value of speedy removals to the agency, Whalen effectively gave his field officers carte blanche to use the procedure as they saw fit.[26] Although legal reformers in the 1930s stressed the need for more process in Immigration Service deportation proceedings, southwestern immigration officials, buckling under the logistical demands of removing thousands of undocumented immigrants, authorized the curtailment of that process. As Whalen instructed his officers, "In short, it is almost impossible to foretell many of the types of cases in which the informal quick process would be advantageous, and that, in itself, would seem to be sufficient reason to broaden the field authority to the extent here suggested."[27]

By the 1940s, the practical needs of the agency overrode the principles under-lying the reforms of the 1930s. Without the manpower, materiel, and money to control the unprecedented flow of undocumented migration triggered by the Bracero Program, southwestern Border Patrol officers implemented old and new procedures that expedited immigrant apprehensions and removals. As Border Patrol officers in the Southwest used their administrative discretion to devise new practices and procedures, Grover Wilmoth sought legislative reforms that reversed the policies of the 1930s and greatly expanded the authority of the agency to pursue undocumented immigrants far beyond the nation's borders. In the 1930s Wilmoth had agreed to abide by MacCormack's recommendations; but he, as well as other southwestern agency officials, did so half-heartedly. By the 1940s, southwestern INS leaders, such as San Antonio District Director William A. Whalen, and Border Patrol supervisor Willard F. Kelly continued to express attitudes toward border enforcement that reformers had tried to weed out among the rank-and-file in the previous decade. During the 1944 Annual Service Conference, Wilmoth strongly opposed raising the standards for Border Patrol intelligence tests, and in his annual report for 1949, he complained that Border Patrol officers were burdened by paperwork.[28] Wilmoth also resuscitated an older vision, dating back to the 1920s, of Border Patrol officers as men of action:

> Patrol officers are outdoor men; to a certain extent they are gunmen; their work is arduous and hazardous; they must lie in concealment on an eight-hour stretch, in rain, hail, sleet and snow, waiting for smugglers and smuggled aliens; they constantly deal with criminals and frequently must engage in dangerous physical encounters and shooting affrays; in short, they are and must be a bit "tough" to say the least.[29]

Moreover, Border Patrol officers were "essentially different" from other employees in the agency, particularly immigration inspectors whom Wilmoth described as "soft," "indoor [men]."[30]

During the 1944 Annual Service Conference, Wilmoth openly criticized the Wickersham Commission. Acknowledging that it had made some necessary changes, he argued, "[I do not] think there were as many inequities perpetrated under our system as they would have us believe."[31] In particular, Wilmoth and southwestern Border Patrol officials chafed against MacCormack's ban on war-rantless arrests. Upon its implementation, Wilmoth and other Patrol officers averred that the procedure impaired their effectiveness, cutting apprehensions in half. As Border Patrol supervisor W. F. Kelly wrote, "It is an utter impossi-bility for the patrol at its present size to function effectively if the only aliens it may arrest without warrants are those who, in its 'presence or view' are entering unlawfully."[32] Held to MacCormack's requirement, officers found that undocumented immigrants often escaped during the time it took for them to procure a warrant for their arrest. Thus, INS officials vigorously argued for the restoration of their ability to make arrests on the spot without a warrant.

As early as 1941, Wilmoth sought not only the revival of this practice but also its explicit legal sanction. He wrote, "I have not quit worrying about what I consider to be the need of additional legislative authority to arrest aliens without warrants."[33] The Bracero Program gave new impetus to Wilmoth's calls for legislative reform. Beyond their sheer numbers, what concerned Border Patrol officers even more was the possibility that bracero contract violators and undocumented migrants would find both a literal and legal refuge in the nation's interior.[34] By making their way far north of the line, immigrants evaded detection by the Border Patrol, whose operations were concentrated in the border region.[35] In the nation's interior, undocumented immigrants, Border Patrol officials feared, would achieve domicile, obtain jobs, homes, and families, and, as a result, become eligible for a suspension of deportation.[36] While such suspensions had been granted on a discretionary basis since 1903, the Alien Registration Act of 1940 allowed administrative grace in cases where immigrants had demonstrated "good moral character" for the previous five years, and the McCarran-Walter Act of 1952 offered relief for those who faced extreme hardship as a result of the deportation.[37] From the perspective of the Border Patrol, then, domicile offered undocumented immigrants a potential legal refuge. Moreover, even if domiciled immigrants were found ineligible for a suspension of deportation, this status functioned like an unwanted brake on INS removal operations. As Collaer, the chief of the Border Patrol, observed, domicile increased the costs and legal complexity of deportation cases:

> When they reach large cities or industrial areas they are more difficult to apprehend while many will have recognizable equities under the laws precluding their deportation or necessitating much more clerical work on the part of the Service. Furthermore, the cost to the Service of deporting such aliens formally from northern industrial areas is much greater than to accord them voluntary departure from points comparatively close to the border.[38]

Wilmoth's efforts, if successful, would strip immigrants of this refuge, rendering domicile ineffectual as a defense against warrantless apprehensions and removals.

Between 1941 and 1944 Alexander Holtzoff, special assistant to the attorney general, worked with Wilmoth to discuss and draft legislative amendments to the Act of February 27, 1925. Before, during, and after the passage of the bill (H. R. 386), Wilmoth and other Border Patrol officials sought the broadest possible operational powers. Acting Commissioner Joseph Savoretti proposed extending the power of immigration officers to make warrantless arrests from felony cases to misdemeanor cases. This would enable the Patrol to arrest without warrant first-time offenders, who comprised the majority of undocumented immigrants.[39] Savoretti then sought an even broader, if not ambiguous, power to arrest without warrant those individuals who had committed what he called an "offense."[40] Holtzoff responded to these suggestions:

> While I realize the utility of such an extension of the authority to make arrests, I desire to call attention to the fact that traditionally it has never been the practice to confer on any arresting officer the power to make an arrest without a warrant for a misdemeanor not committed in his presence. The common law did not permit such arrests, nor do the State laws permit such arrests. No Federal agents, such as Agents of the Federal Bureau of Investigation, Secret Service, Alcohol Tax Agents, etc., are granted authority to make arrests without warrants for misdemeanors not committed in their presence.[41]

So as to ensure the passage of H. R. 386, the INS dropped these recommendations and decided to seek further amendments after the bill had passed.[42]

In May 1944, Holtzoff submitted a set of amendments that Congress passed with very little debate as Public Law 613 in 1946.[43] The act gave statutory sanction to the warrantless arrest of undocumented immigrants beyond the border.[44] More important, it stretched the concept of "entry," specifically stating that the INS had the power without warrant

> to arrest any alien who in his presence or view is entering or attempting to enter the United States in violation of any law or regulation made in pursuance of law regulating the admission, exclusion, or expulsion of aliens, or any alien who is in the United States in violation of any such law or regulation and is likely to escape before a warrant can be obtained for his arrest.[45]

As Holtzoff explained, the act created a "continuing violation of the law on the part of . . . an alien remaining in the United States, so that when an officer of this service encountered him and learned of his illegal entry, the officer could take him immediately into custody."[46] This language made it clear that immigration officers would have the power to arrest without warrant long after an undocumented immigrant had achieved "entry" or established domicile.

During the deliberations regarding H. R. 386, Wilmoth not only recommended the reversal of the ban on warrantless arrests, he also successfully fought
to confer the authority of law upon its very practice. As a result of his efforts,
Congress in 1946 passed Public Law 613, the first major revision of the Border
Patrol statute, the Act of February 27, 1925. Unlike the earlier enactment, Public
Law 613 was not drafted with the express intent to restrain Border Patrol operations. Instead, its provisions authorizing the warrantless searches, seizures,
and arrests of all undocumented immigrants, whether "in transit" or domiciled,
vastly expanded the agency's legal authority at the border and far beyond.

In drafting H. R. 386, Wilmoth attempted to thwart the various means by which
undocumented immigrants evaded the Border Patrol beyond the international
line. Once the measure passed, it rendered domicile obsolete as a defense against
warrantless Border Patrol apprehensions. Yet Wilmoth long recognized that undocumented migrants avoided the Patrol not only by achieving domicile but
also by finding physical and legal refuge on the nation's highways and on border
farms and ranches. As he explained in a 1940 Border Patrol training manual,
"Aliens who evade the immigration officers at the international line do not all
take refuge in nearby houses and on adjacent premises. Many of them use the
highways from the Border in proceeding to the interior of the United States."[47]
Early drafts of H. R. 386 contained proposals to secure these locales, but ultimately Public Law 613 did not incorporate all of Wilmoth's proposals, specifically those pertaining to the search of private property. Despite this defeat, the
measure still bolstered the agency's legal authority to apprehend undocumented
immigrants in public spaces at and beyond the border.

Since 1924, a variety of factors had increased the "many ground routes of escape from the border," as explained by N. D. Collaer in a report to W. F. Kelly.[48]
These included the ongoing modernization of the nation's road system, which
placed the Border Patrol at a disadvantage in deterring undocumented immigration. As Collaer observed, "Vehicular traffic over dirt roads was formerly the
rule, whereas in all sections we now have networks of vast paved highways to and
paralleling in close proximity the international boundaries. This is particularly
true on the Mexican border."[49] On the unpaved roads, the Patrol discovered that
it was unable to keep up with immigrant smugglers, some of whom had managed
to obtain four-wheel drive vehicles once owned by the US Army.[50] Lacking the
funds to purchase and maintain new vehicles and to pay the per diem and over-
time salaries of mobile officers working away from home, the agency found itself
unable to effectively patrol the nation's roads.[51] By 1949, Collaer, in a survey of
border conditions, would conclude, "All who have given the matter of patrolling
our international boundaries serious study must agree that we have lost greatly
in mobility since the early days of the Patrol."[52]

Legal, as well as logistical, considerations further checked agency surveillance of the highways. Concerned about lawsuits and criticized by legal
reformers, the Border Patrol, at one point in the 1930s, ceased its car search
operations.[53] By the 1940s, however, Wilmoth and Kelly sought to license what
they themselves characterized as questionable practices through an amendment to the Border Patrol statute.[54] As Kelly stated, "[patrol] officers' authority
to stop vehicles promiscuously on the highways leading away from the border
has been questioned innumerable times, yet we have continued to act without
proper authority."[55] Even though the Border Patrol statute stipulated minimal
standards for car searches (Border Patrol officers had to have some reason to
believe that the vehicle was transporting undocumented immigrants), Kelly
admitted that in practice, Border Patrol officers stopped cars with little or no
discrimination:

> As you are aware, our methods of operation have been such during
> the past ten years, and from the period between 1924 and 1931, that
> in no one case out of one hundred could our officers show reasonable
> cause to believe that the vehicles they stop contain aliens who are being
> brought into the United States.[56]

Rather than train officers to abide by reasonable cause standards during a car
stop, Kelly sought a legislative amendment that would sanction standing procedures. Specifically, these authorized indiscriminate car stops and searches within
a zone one hundred miles north of the border. As Kelly described the procedure, "the actual practice for years has been for Border Patrol Units established
at strategic points on highways leading away from the International boundaries
(at some points as remote as 100 miles or more from the boundary), to stop and
inspect all traffic coming from the direction of the border."[57] Under this policy,
the Border Patrol estimated that officers stopped an average of 3,323,488 motor-
ists per year.[58]

Public Law 613 sanctioned this approach to Border Patrol vehicle stops.
Specifically, it eliminated the language from the old Border Patrol statute, granting INS officers the power "without warrant to board and search for aliens, any
vessel within the territorial waters of the United States, railway car, conveyance,
or vehicle, in which *he believes* aliens are being brought into the United States."[59]
The new language of Public Law 613 substituted the belief provision with the
reasonable distance rule:

> (2) to board and search for aliens any vessel within the territorial waters
> of the United States, railway car, aircraft, conveyance, or vehicle, within
> a reasonable distance from any external boundary of the United States.

Figure 5.1 Border Patrol traffic check, Chula Vista, California, c. 1940. Reproduced by permission of the National Border Patrol Museum, El Paso, Texas.

Under this provision, Border Patrol officers were freed from making a determination of probable cause or reasonable suspicion for a stop. Instead, they were given broad authority to stop, search, seize, and arrest within a specific geographic area beyond the border.[60] This area was determined administratively by the district directors to be one hundred air miles from the international line. There were, however, exceptions to this rule. The central office gave district directors the administrative discretion to extend this boundary, allowing

> that whenever in the opinion of a district director, a distance in his district of more than 100 air miles from any external boundary of the United States would because of unusual circumstances be reasonable, such district director shall forward a complete report with respect to the matter to the Commissioner of Immigration and Naturalization, who may, if he determines that such action is justified, declare such distance to be reasonable.[61]

This discretionary authority was used by the El Paso district director to request that Pecos, Texas, Globe, Arizona, Phoenix, Arizona, and Albuquerque, New Mexico be deemed within a "reasonable distance" from the US–Mexico border.

In the San Antonio district, Mason, San Antonio, Austin, and San Angelo, Texas, were declared to fall within a reasonable distance of the US–Mexico border.

Beyond the one hundred-mile boundary (or other boundary administratively established under the reasonable distance rule), Border Patrol officers continued to possess the authority to arrest without warrant. Here, the service determined that Section 16 of the Immigration Act of 1917 provided adequate legal authority for its employees to arrest without warrant those travelers believed to be in the United States in violation of the immigration laws.[62] In other words, north of the one hundred-mile boundary, Border Patrol officers had to have reasonable cause, as a 1950 traffic inspection manual explained:

> It will be seen that under Section 16 of the Immigration Act of 1917, not only immigration inspectors, but patrol inspectors and other authorized employees, have no limitation imposed upon them as to the distance from the border where the boarding and searching [of any vessel, railroad car, or other conveyance or vehicle] may be conducted *provided they believe*, and with reason, that aliens are being transported in the manner indicated.[63]

In conjunction with the border exception to the Fourth Amendment, reasonable cause and the reasonable distance rule would serve as the bases of the Border Patrol's authority to conduct vehicular searches at the international boundary, in the borderlands, and the nation's interior for the next two decades.

Through H. R. 386, Wilmoth sought to augment the jurisdiction of the Border Patrol in private spaces, such as border farms and ranches, as well as in public spaces, such as the nation's highways. Border Patrol officials often expressed their frustration with their lack of legal authority to pursue immigrants in these locales, knowing that most undocumented migrants could elude detection there. General concerns about trespassing on private property posed the strongest deterrent to Border Patrol searches of farms and ranches.[64] Cognizant of the Patrol's wariness, growers encouraged their workers to remain on their property, as Wilmoth explained:

> All of the farmers and ranchmen seem to be aware of the fact that the officers of this Service may not go upon their property unless in possession of warrants of arrest, and they apparently are taking advantage of that situation by advising the deportable aliens to remain on the property and impressing them with the thought that they will be arrested and deported if they do not do so.[65]

Service officials felt particularly powerless with respect to those immigrants who crossed illegally onto farms adjacent to the border.[66] Border Patrol farm operations were further limited by supervisory officials themselves who, at the behest of southwestern growers and politicians, instructed the unit to stay off the farms and ranches or temporarily cease its enforcement efforts altogether.[67]

A few exceptions, however, accorded the Patrol some authority in these spaces. The provisions of the bracero accords allowed the agency to enter farm property to apprehend and remove undocumented workers.[68] Under the Border Patrol statute (the Act of February 27, 1925), officers were permitted to enter farm property if they were in continuing pursuit of an immigrant whom they had witnessed in the act of illegal entry. If they lost sight of the immigrant, however, they were not authorized to continue the pursuit on private property.[69] Also, the INS general counsel advised that a Patrol officer was permitted to enter private property when "he knows or has good reason to believe that a deportable alien is thereon and will escape if not immediately taken into custody."[70]

Fearful of lawsuits filed by growers, agency officials declined to rely on any of these as a source of authority for their pursuit of undocumented immigrants on private property. Wilmoth later explained to the President's Commission on Migratory Labor that INS officials doubted the legal validity of the Bracero Program provisions and instructed officers not to act on their basis.[71] They were also hesitant about relying on either the Border Patrol statute or the determination of the general counsel to pursue immigrants on farms and ranches. Instead, agency officials chose to take the most cautious approach by procuring arrest warrants or obtaining the consent of the landowner or manager of the property prior to entry.

Yet by the 1940s, southwestern agency officials grew increasingly impatient with this approach, discovering that it made their officers tentative and that it limited the Patrol's apprehension rate.[72] The arrest warrant itself limited apprehensions to those individuals named in the warrant. It did not confer upon agency officials the authority to conduct a general search of the premises for other undocumented immigrants.[73] Although growers once consented to agency searches, this consent was increasingly less forthcoming.[74] As historian Kelly Lytle-Hernández explains, two factors sparked growers' hostility: the roundup campaigns of the 1940s and a hiring initiative in the 1950s that transformed the composition of the Patrol. Once made up of local men who were responsive to growers' demands, the Border Patrol of the 1950s became the domain of outsiders with a more professional orientation toward their duties.[75] Growers reacted to these developments by refusing to grant their consent to agency searches. Moreover, they actively resisted the enforcement efforts of the Patrol, constructing fences, blocking private roads, and posting "no trespassing" signs on their property.[76] They also wrote protest letters to their local Congressmen and, in a few cases, filed lawsuits.[77]

Through both administrative and legislative means, the Patrol sought to rectify these limits to its search powers.[78] In order to detect and apprehend migrants on farms, Border Patrol officials traversed the rights-of-way along irrigation canals lying within a farm or drainage ditches next to a farm, arguing that such areas were public property. One former Border Patrol officer observed, "The ditch banks in some areas, of course, belonged to the Bureau of Reclamation, and that was government property. So you'd catch 'em coming across the ditch bank or going from field to field across the public road and sack them up. And of course that irritated the farmers, but you still weren't on their farms."[79] When local INS officials sought administrative sanction for this practice, however, the central office dismissed their arguments and instructed officers to stay off the rights-of-way.[80]

The Border Patrol also lobbied for increased statutory powers to search farms and ranches. Wilmoth recommended that INS officials attain the power to issue search warrants so as to overcome the limits of the arrest warrant. As he wrote, "A law authorizing the officers of this Service to obtain search warrants would enable our officers to control the alien smuggling situation on the Border, provided of course we would not be required to particularize as to each individual alien in order to secure the warrants."[81] Kelly proposed that Border Patrol inspectors be granted the authority to "enter upon or pass through private property adjoining the international boundary (at least property other than a dwelling or house) in the performance of his official duties."[82] He also suggested that farm and ranch owners be held accountable by increasing the penalty for harboring and concealing undocumented immigrants.[83] Yet both Kelly and Wilmoth chose to set aside these proposals, fearing that they would jeopardize the passage of the bill as a whole.[84]

Public Law 613 dramatically extended the jurisdiction of the Border Patrol while limiting the domains in which immigrants once found a safe harbor from the surveillance of the state. Yet Wilmoth remained dissatisfied with his legislative victory. In the wrangling over H. R. 386, he had failed to win for his officers the statutory authority to search private property adjacent to the border and within the nation's interior. In 1951, he would pursue additional amendments to the Border Patrol statute that would expand the border zone once again. In the interim, Wilmoth would find an unexpected set of allies among liberal immigration reformers and an unanticipated venue—President Truman's Commission on Migratory Labor—through which he advertised the agency's border enforcement agenda.

During the Cold War, immigration reform gained a powerful advocate in the executive branch. Two presidents—Truman and Eisenhower—expressed deep concerns about the impact of America's race-based immigration policy on efforts to win the loyalties of incipient Communist states.[85] In the debates surrounding the McCarran-Walter Act of 1952, a measure that ultimately retained the national origins quota system, Truman repeatedly highlighted the contradiction between the racism of the quota system and the principles of American democracy. As Truman exhorted during his veto of the McCarran-Walter Act, "We are asking them [Italy, Greece, and Turkey] to join with us [in the North Atlantic Treaty Organization] in protecting the peace of the world. We are helping them to build their defenses, and train their men, in the common cause. But through this bill we say to their people: You are less worthy to come to this country than Englishmen or Irishmen."[86] As part of a broader effort to burnish America's image and to win the world for democracy, both the Truman and Eisenhower administrations would seek to rectify the discriminatory features of the nation's immigration laws.

Although Truman's immigration reform proposals had the vocal support of congressional liberals, they did not possess the votes or the key committee chairmanships necessary to pass immigration legislation on their own terms. Until 1965, a coalition of conservative politicians would continue to dominate the politics of immigration policy; since the 1920s, this faction had refused to remove the barriers to entry for southern and eastern Europeans and repeatedly voted against immigration law enforcement measures.[87] To achieve his immigration reform agenda, Truman skirted Congress and expanded the powers of the executive branch. For example, he used his parole powers to overcome the restrictions of the national origins quota system to admit hundreds of thousands of European refugees.[88] In the process, he set a precedent for successive administrations whose immigration platforms continued to be blocked by restrictionist legislators in Congress.[89]

The executive branch, then, opened up another avenue for immigration policy formation. Liberal reformers and politicians would turn to the office of the president to devise and implement immigration policies, particularly with respect to refugee law, that mitigated the harsh restrictions imposed by the national origins quota system. More broadly, the Truman administration, in conjunction with liberal legislators, expressed a powerful alternative vision of American immigration law and policy, paving the way for the dismantling of the national origins quota system in the Hart-Celler Act of 1965. This vision was best encapsulated by the final report of the Commission on Immigration and Naturalization, formed by Truman in response to the passage of the McCarran-Walter Act over his veto.[90] Presented on January 1, 1953, the final report of the commission, titled *Whom Shall We Welcome*, rejected the race-based conclusions underpinning the original national origins quota systems of the 1920s. It stated, "The basic racist assumption of the national origins quota system is invalid" and described the ways in which immigrants had contributed to the nation's economy and society.[91] Even though no legislative reform resulted from the publication of this report, it began to soften American public opinion regarding the quota system, generating support for its reform and eventual repeal.[92]

Truman and his supporters in Congress were receptive not only to the liberalization of the nation's admissions policies but also to the strengthening of border enforcement. Under pressure from labor and religious organizations, President Truman, on June 3, 1950, created the President's Commission on Migratory Labor to investigate the condition of domestic agricultural workers, Mexican braceros, and undocumented immigrants in America. Reflecting the progressive outlook of the commission, Truman issued a statement noting that agricultural workers, compared to other occupational groups, endured poor working and living conditions because they were "denied the benefits of federal, state or local social legislation."[93] Truman appointed a chairman, four commissioners, and an executive secretary (an attorney, a member of the clergy, a political scientist, a labor mediator, an economist, and an expert on agricultural affairs) to the commission.[94] To the dismay of labor unions,[95] the president did not appoint any labor representatives, believing that if he did so he would also have to appoint a growers' representative.[96] This, Truman felt, would create untenable divisions among commission members and result in the issuance of several minority reports.[97] The commission held twelve public hearings in Brownsville, El Paso, Phoenix, Los Angeles, Portland, Fort Collins, Memphis, Saginaw, Trenton, West Palm Beach, and two in Washington, DC, where they solicited testimony from local, state, and foreign governments, laborers, labor unions, employers, social workers, health officials, and religious organizations.

Also invited to the hearings were various local, regional, and national representatives of the immigration agency. Initially doubtful that the President's Commission could address the underlying causes of undocumented immigration, INS officials in 1949 focused on implementing old and familiar solutions, backing the renegotiation of the Bracero Program as the best remedy to the crisis.[98] By providing growers with an uninterrupted supply of legal workers, the Bracero Program, agency officials reasoned, removed an incentive for farmers to hire undocumented immigrants.[99] Despite these reservations, Commissioner General Miller hoped that the commission would make findings favorable to the service, particularly drawing attention to its enforcement needs. Due to the efforts of Wilmoth, the commission's final report did just that, stressing the importance of immigration law enforcement and setting forth a series of proposals that would bolster the power of the INS to pursue unauthorized immigrants.

In making these recommendations, Wilmoth dropped the agency's longstanding defense of the Bracero Program as a remedy for undocumented immigration. Instead, his testimony echoed the critiques of the Bracero Program made by labor organizations during the hearings. Criticizing the working and

Figure 5.2 President Harry S. Truman used the powers of the executive branch to spearhead immigration reform. Courtesy of Prints and Photographs Division, Library of Congress, LC-USZ62-117122.

living conditions faced by Mexican braceros, AFL President William Green, for instance, proposed a higher minimum wage for immigrant workers.[100] Drawing on his experience as an administrator of the Bracero Program, Wilmoth came to similar conclusions, admitting that for a time in the late 1940s, he set the prevailing wage in the absence of any federal agencies with the authority to determine wage rates. Farmers further diminished the value of bracero earnings, Wilmoth explained, by coercing them to purchase necessities at inflated prices from on-site commissaries.[101] As a solution, Wilmoth recommended the creation of an agency to determine and enforce the payment of fair wages to Mexican workers.

Government officials also questioned the need for the Bracero Program altogether. The Department of Labor observed that if American growers improved living and working conditions on the farms, they could attract a sufficient domestic work force.[102] Although the department did not call for the termination of the Program, it recommended that foreign labor recruiting take place only during times of national emergency.[103] In his testimony Wilmoth observed that contrary to growers' assertions, domestic labor was often available to fill agricultural jobs, submitting evidence that braceros were not needed in the states of New Mexico and Arizona.[104] Yet he explained that these workers were not hired because federal and state agencies would not "see to it that local labor is fully employed before foreign labor is brought into the area."[105] One Border Patrol investigation also revealed that some Texas farmers fired local workers in order to replace them with Mexican braceros who worked for lower wages.[106] Wilmoth concluded his critique by recommending that the commission find a way to draw domestic laborers back into the agricultural work force.[107]

While Wilmoth's testimony revealed an in-depth knowledge of the labor issues surrounding the Bracero Program, he and other INS officials ultimately participated in the hearings to address the issue of undocumented immigration. Indeed, the President's Commission hearings provided a propitious context for Wilmoth to further the agency's institutional interest in stronger law enforcement. Commissioners made a concerted effort to gather written statements and verbal testimony from southwestern district directors of the INS both on and off the record.[108] Other witnesses, particularly labor unions such as the AFL, demonstrated their support of the agency by castigating the problem of illegal immigration, calling for increased INS enforcement, and recommending the passage of legislation penalizing employers for hiring undocumented immigrants.[109] Representatives from Mexican American organizations such as the American G.I. Forum of Texas and the Mexican-American National Association also called for employer sanctions.[110] George Sanchez, director of the University of Texas survey of Spanish-speaking people, advocated greater controls on undocumented immigration.[111] Liberal politicians and Truman himself also backed these positions. For example, Congressman Emmanuel Celler of New York, in a 1951 statement before Congress, observed, "Again, between March 12 and 25, 8,191 wetbacks were picked up. . . . Five thousand and sixty-two were employed, while many American workers were on relief and out of work, seeking work."[112] As a solution, Celler recommended strengthening the Border Patrol, maintaining the Bracero Program, and passing penalty legislation against employers.[113] As historian Bernard Lemelin observes, other liberal legislators such as Senator Herbert Lehman (D-NY), Senator Hubert Humphrey (D-MN), and Representative Jacob Javits (R-NY) concurred with Celler's call for tougher immigration enforcement as a means of protecting the domestic labor force against competition from foreign labor.[114]

It was in this receptive forum that Wilmoth made his case against undocumented immigration. In doing so, he deflected attention away from the agency's own role in perpetuating the problem (by regularizing out-of-status immigrants or by ignoring the widespread use of undocumented Mexican labor on southwestern farms) and launched an assault on local farmers, blaming them and their unwarranted demands for Mexican labor for the agency's enforcement failures.

In a statement submitted to the commission, Wilmoth wrote, "If it were not for the farm labor situation we could very well guard the Border against illegal entrants."[115] During the course of the hearings, Wilmoth closely monitored the testimony of local officials, farmers, and agency representatives. He was especially diligent about rebutting growers' claims regarding labor shortages by mailing numerous reports from the field to the President's Commission. All made the same point—that there was no need for the importation of Mexican agricultural labor in a particular region.[116] He also emphasized that if local growers paid fair wages, they could find a sufficient supply of domestic agricultural workers.[117]

The central office echoed Wilmoth's assertions about the speciousness of growers' claims regarding a labor shortage. Under the 1949 agreement, the INS admitted more than 50,000 workers and, as a result of the contentions of the Employment Service about continued labor shortages, prepared to admit 25,000 more. While the INS agreed to cooperate with growers and the USES in supplying these workers, Commissioner General Mackey observed, "it is the consensus of opinion among our field officers that these certifications are generally greatly inflated and reports which have been received and certain evidence have provided convincing evidence that the general opinion in this regard is well founded."[118]

Press coverage of the commission hearings afforded the INS an opportunity to publicize its case against the farmers. Often, the agency received the publicity simply by virtue of the fact that the local and national media recounted or quoted statements made during the hearings. In August, the *New York Times* reported that INS officers "charged . . . that a powerful 'pressure group' of farmers annually was forcing suspension of law enforcement against illegal Mexican immigrants in order to get cheap labor."[119] The same article reported that while "higher-ups" within the INS instructed agents to halt deportation operations during peak harvest seasons, the ultimate blame rested with the farmers for placing intense pressure on central office officials to issue such instructions.[120] Another newspaper reported, "The commission found that the Immigration and Naturalization Service was susceptible to political pressure to go easy on deportations until crops were harvested."[121] The press coverage also afforded the agency a chance to present itself in a positive light, as an agency eager to crack down on undocumented immigration but for the opposition of agribusiness and its supporters in Congress. The press reported another immigration officer testifying, "the flouting of the immigration laws is 'a disgrace' . . . All we need is a go-ahead signal—we'll take care of the enforcement."[122]

The agency also used the hearings as an opportunity to lobby for the legislative and administrative tools to fight undocumented immigration and, specifically, to fight that battle on the growers' turf. Two days after submitting his first statement describing the problems faced by agricultural workers, Wilmoth sent several lengthy reports on the enforcement challenges facing the service. He explained to Chairman Van Hecke that he did not want to discuss these issues during the public hearings because his statements would "advertise to the farmers how little real authority is possessed by our officers."[123] Wilmoth's testimony was particularly central to the agency's effort, which began in the 1940s, to gain stronger provisions for the search and arrest of immigrants on southwestern farm and ranch lands. In fact, Wilmoth presented to the commission those proposals he had made, and then deferred, during agency debates over H. R. 386.

Specifically, he sought legislation that would grant INS officers a general power to make warrantless searches of farms, "for inspection purposes, when the farmer is the recipient of *alien* labor under any law, international agreement, or administrative order of this Government."[124] He also sought greater authority for INS officials to make warrantless arrests of unauthorized immigrants on farm and ranch lands. He observed that with an arrest warrant in hand, Border Patrol officers had the authority to enter a farm and arrest those specific persons named on the warrant. Even though INS counsel determined that Patrol officers possessed the legal authority to arrest other undocumented immigrants not listed on the warrant but discovered on the premises during the warrant operation, they refrained from doing so, desirous of a clearer and more explicit legal authority on which to act.[125] In an effort to provide a statutory basis for this authority, Wilmoth drafted an amendment to the Act of August 7, 1946 that would enable Border Patrol officers, in the process of executing a warrant, to make warrantless arrests of other undocumented immigrants found on the property.[126] These two proposals reflected the agency's efforts to gain expansive powers to pursue unauthorized immigrants on southwestern farms and ranchlands.[127]

As the first round of public hearings came to a close in the summer of 1950, it became apparent that the INS played a very large role in shaping the commission's understanding of the problems on the US–Mexico border.[128] INS officials Willard F. Kelley and Harlon B. Carter, both of the Enforcement Division, and Hugh Carter of the General Research Section, prepared a report on undocumented immigration and immigration law enforcement especially for the commission.[129] The President's Commission also initiated a second round of hearings in November 1950 specifically for government agencies such as the INS. The commission asked the INS and other federal agencies to submit written recommendations for legislative and administrative reform that would then be discussed at the November hearings.[130]

The agency took the commission's request as an opportunity to lobby for enforcement measures in addition to those already presented by Wilmoth.[131] INS officials recommended the construction of additional detention facilities, believing that the commission's sanction of the project would increase the likelihood of an appropriation from Congress:

The Service plans to establish two detention camps of 5,000 capacity to cost about $12,000,000. The present law prohibits asking for a deficiency appropriation for such purpose, but the Bureau of the Budget has said that, in the event the President's Commission on Migratory Labor should recommend such detention camps, their recommendation might constructively have the significance of new legislation, and on that basis the Immigration Service might proceed with a request for a deficiency of $12,000,000 to build the two detention camps.[132]

By the fall of 1950, INS cooperation with the commission had paid off; INS officials were confident that some commission members had a clear picture of the problems plaguing the agency. Carter wrote that Varden Fuller, executive secretary of the commission, would advocate for the INS if other members of the commission raised questions about the new facilities: "Should discussion or justification be necessary for the inclusion of this item in the report of the President's Commission, Varden Fuller will likely go along with us if he understands that inclusion of this item in the President's report will be the equivalent, so far as we are concerned, of having new legislation upon which we can base a request for a deficiency appropriation of $12,000,000."[133] In addition to these detention facilities, the service proposed stronger penalties for alien smugglers (through an amendment to Section 8 of the Immigration Act of 1917), and new penalties for those—particularly farmers and ranchers—who employed or transported undocumented immigrants.[134]

The final report of the President's Commission, *Migratory Labor in American Agriculture*, was published in 1951. It concluded that "the needs and problems of migrants were urgent and that they could best be met by broadening and extending them the basic services which are designed to serve the general population."[135] While the commission did not focus solely on the Bracero Program, it devoted one chapter to Mexican braceros and undocumented Mexican workers. With respect to the latter, the commission found that undocumented Mexican workers suffered the worst conditions in every respect, including wages, working environments, housing, health, welfare, and labor relations.[136] It further emphasized that the mass, unauthorized entry of these farmworkers depressed incomes, and employment and living standards for all farm laborers.[137]

With respect to the braceros, the final report observed that while the international agreements and the individual work contracts stipulated protections for foreign recruits, these agreements were not observed in practice. It specifically claimed that the United States government "virtually abandoned effective scrutiny and enforcement of the Individual Work Contracts to which private employers and individual Mexican aliens were the parties."[138] The commission attributed this weak enforcement to a dearth of manpower and disorganization among and between federal and state agencies involved in the Bracero Program.[139] As a result, legal guest workers endured poor working and living conditions.[140] They also received low wages, the commission explained, due to the laxity of Farm Security Administration wage determinations, which were based on farmers' estimates rather than any unbiased source.[141] The report also asserted that the labor importation program worsened the employment prospects of agricultural laborers in general and charged growers with making unfounded claims about farm labor emergencies.[142] Most important, the commission held that if wages and working conditions were adequate, a sufficient supply of domestic labor was available to work on southwestern farms. In short, the report concluded that the Bracero Program was unnecessary.

Of particular interest to the commission was the issue of undocumented immigration. The single chapter devoted to the topic highlighted the scope of the problem; the report stated, "'the magnitude of the wetback traffic has reached entirely new levels in the past seven years. . . . In its newly achieved proportions, it is virtually an invasion.'"[143] The commission found that "United States administrative agencies practically ceased to exert effective effort to preserve the requirements of national immigration policy."[144] On this point, the commission focused on the legalization procedure, criticizing it as a blatant violation of the laws prohibiting unauthorized immigration.[145] It further charged that the repeated legalization of undocumented workers throughout the 1940s only increased the volume of illegal crossings during the 1950s.[146] As one of its final recommendations, the commission categorically declared that the procedure had to be "discontinued and forbidden."[147]

While the commission denounced the abandonment of the immigration laws under the Bracero Program, it was very cautious about placing responsibility on the INS. Indeed, in the two chapters discussing the problem of unauthorized immigration and the Bracero Program, the commission rarely mentioned the INS. For example, when discussing the El Paso Incident, the commission made a curious, if not careful, choice of words that absolved the INS by omission:

> In October [1948], several thousand breached the border patrol lines in the vicinity of El Paso and entered illegally. Instead of deporting the illegally entered Mexican workers immediately, they were by *unilateral action of the United States*, "paroled" to farm employers who wanted their services.[148]

When describing the legalization procedure, the commission relied on the passive voice to describe the role of the INS, implying that it followed orders rather than acting on its own volition:

> A technique more insidious than ingenious was devised and put in effect *by the agencies of the United States Government* having responsibility for law enforcement and procurement of labor. In this improvisation, the Immigration and Naturalization Service *would be allowed* to "deport" the wetback by having him brought to the border at which point the wetback would be given an identification slip. Momentarily, he would step across the boundary line . . . and [then] was eligible to step back across the boundary to be legally contracted.[149]

In the next sentence, the commission continued to mitigate the responsibility of the INS and other government agencies by providing a justification for the legalization programs of the late 1940s: "In fairness to Government officials participating in the practice of contracting wetbacks, it needs to be noted that some limits and qualifications were imposed. These were apparently expected to make the legalization program a substitute for, rather than an accelerator of, wetback traffic."[150] Throughout this brief discussion, the commission placed just as much blame on the Mexican government for the legalization programs as it did the INS and other US government agencies.[151] Later, the commission blamed growers for placing pressure on the INS to "go easy on deportations until crops have been harvested."[152] Far from a direct and incisive condemnation of the INS, these two pages carefully sidestepped the issue of blame and responsibility while attacking the legalization procedure itself.

Curiously absent from the report was any mention of INS laxity (arrangements made between agents and farmers to not deport workers during harvest season), corruption (bribes taken by INS officials at recruiting centers in Mexico to admit unqualified agricultural laborers; bribes taken by INS officials to stay off American farms; undocumented workers procured by INS officials for their own farms), or abuse (in its pursuit and apprehension of Mexican workers) in its conduct of the wartime Bracero Program. During the public hearings, the commission asked one Border Patrol official about allegations of abuse. He simply discounted the charges as false.[153] Also missing from the final report was any reference to the long-standing attitude within the INS that had fostered a lackadaisical approach to enforcement—the refrain that had become so familiar in the agency correspondence of the 1920s and 1940s (when Mexican agricultural labor was most in demand), that the unfettered crossing of Mexican agricultural labor had been part of the natural order of things in the West since time immemorial and ought to be left unimpeded.

The silence of the commission on these points did not mean that Border Patrol abuses, laxity among immigration officers, and cooperation between farmers and the INS were no longer problems. Indeed, at the same time the President's Commission issued its findings, Professor Lyle Saunders at the University of

New Mexico issued a report that was highly critical of the INS, citing incidents of abuse and racial discrimination on the part of the Border Patrol. It also blamed the agency for weak enforcement, describing the de facto understanding between farmers and INS officials that the agency would not conduct enforcement operations during the harvest season and accusing Border Patrol officers of inefficiency and ineptitude. The INS issued a pointed rejoinder, denying most of the accusations and asserting that the rest were exceptions to the rule when it came to officer conduct.[154]

The President's Commission on Migratory Labor may have provided a critique of the wartime Bracero Program, but it did not provide a direct or substantial criticism of the INS. Instead, the report fostered the agency's campaign to obtain more men, materiel, and statutory authority to execute its enforcement mandate. The final recommendations of the commission closely followed the proposals submitted by INS officials. The report enumerated the obstacles facing the service in effectively enforcing the law (again, avoiding any mention of how problems internal to the agency itself may have contributed to lax enforcement): a scarcity of funds and personnel, juries sympathetic to local farmers and unwilling to convict immigration law violators, restrictions on officers' ability to enter private property to search for unauthorized immigrants, and the lack of statutory penalties against the employment of undocumented immigrants.[155] In order to ameliorate the problem of unauthorized immigration, the final report proposed the appropriation of more men and money, passage of additional statutory authority to conduct searches on private property, revised statutory penalties for harboring, concealing, and transporting unauthorized immigrants, and new statutory penalties for employing out-of-status workers.[156]

In concluding its report, the commission recommended that the Immigration and Naturalization Service take charge of the Bracero Program. While the USES would continue to certify the need for workers, it specifically suggested that the "administration of foreign-labor recruiting, contracting, transportation, and agreements should be made the direct responsibility of the Immigration and Naturalization Service. This should be the principle contracting agency and private employers should secure their foreign workers exclusively from the Immigration and Naturalization Service."[157] The commission also proposed that the service supervise the employment of the braceros, manage labor disputes, and terminate contracts as it saw fit.[158] The commission did not recommend the termination of the labor importation program. Instead, the commission sanctioned its extension so long as it included an INS-administered enforcement plan.

As President Truman's Commission on Immigration and Naturalization shifted the tenor of the debate on immigration restriction, his Commission on Migratory Labor transformed the orientation of the state toward immigration

enforcement. Since the 1920s, immigration restrictionists in Congress successfully blocked efforts to construct a strong immigration enforcement infrastructure. Under the Truman administration, pro-enforcement advocates found a
voice, airing their concerns about the problem of undocumented immigration
and calling for increased enforcement measures. As pro-bracero legislators continued to block most of the enforcement proposals of the early 1950s, Truman's
commission lent an aura of legitimacy to the idea and rhetoric of immigration
enforcement. Viewed from this perspective, Wilmoth's contributions to the
President's Commission sounded the alarm on undocumented immigration in
the United States.

While southwestern growers and their allies in Congress would continue to
pose formidable obstacles to the passage of a strong border enforcement policy,
Wilmoth, liberal legislators, and the executive branch rendered the issue a central
element of immigration policy debates at the national level. As such, President
Eisenhower was in no political position to ignore the subject of undocumented
immigration. Responding to pressures from the American public, state and local
officials, federal administrators, the INS, and his attorney general, Eisenhower
sanctioned the 1954 deportation drive that rendered immigration law enforcement on the US–Mexico border the primary focus of INS operations and a fixed
feature of immigration policy debates.

The Federal Regulation of the US–Mexico Border

The border has been secured.
—Immigration and Naturalization Service, *Annual Report*, 1955

In 1953, Attorney General Herbert Brownell devised a plan to post 4,000 military troops along the US–Mexico border to halt the entry of undocumented immigrants.[1] When he discussed the idea with General Joseph Swing, commander of the Sixth Army in California and close friend of President Eisenhower, Swing responded that it was a "perfectly horrible" plan and that an enforcement operation could be conducted with the resources and manpower available within the INS. In response, Brownell named Swing the new commissioner general of the agency, challenging him to "come on down and show us how to do it without closing the border."[2] Swing met Brownell's challenge, launching a mass deportation drive known as Operation Wetback, which resulted in the removal of approximately one million Mexican nationals while at the same time leaving the border open to the admission of Mexican braceros.

Operation Wetback is remembered as an apex in the history of the INS, a sign of the agency's strength, and a measure of its ability to control undocumented immigration along the US–Mexico border. Yet the campaign marked another moment in the agency's battle for the border–another moment when the INS found itself unable to overcome the political opposition of southwestern agribusiness and their allies in Congress in order to set the agenda on immigration law enforcement. As a result of these political liabilities, the agency turned to the law once again, using its administrative discretion to devise Operation Wetback as one approach to border control.

This chapter recounts the long history of Operation Wetback, in contrast to most accounts that trace its roots to the Eisenhower administration.[3] Facing increasing public pressure to address the perceived crisis surrounding unauthorized immigration along the US–Mexico border, the president dispatched his attorney general, Herbert Brownell, on an August 1953 tour of the Southwest to investigate the situation. Shocked by what he found, Brownell described undocumented immigration as the one of the "nation's gravest law-enforcement problem[s]" and formulated a series of solutions, one of which included Operation Wetback.[4] In 1954 the INS, led by Commissioner General Swing, launched what it later hailed as a successful military-style campaign to gain control over illicit migration across the southern line.

While these were the most proximate causes of the campaign, this chapter argues that the road to Operation Wetback was paved during the Truman administration. Truman might not have sanctioned Operation Wetback, but his Commission on Migratory Labor set in motion a series of events that conferred political legitimacy upon an increasingly enforcement-minded posture within the INS. Well into the 1950s, southwestern agency officials sought to solidify these political gains by translating Wilmoth's vision of border enforcement into a reality; more specifically, they lobbied for a legislative agenda that included increased Border Patrol appropriations, employer penalties, and an enhanced search authority. Yet these endeavors, due to the ongoing opposition of southwestern agribusiness, largely failed, resulting in the execution of Operation Wetback. Despite its contingent origins, Operation Wetback drove the agency's institutional development and transformed conceptions of immigration law enforcement by regulating rather than closing the US-Mexico border.

With great reluctance, President Truman, on July 13, 1951, signed S. 984, which served as the statutory framework for the Bracero Program until its demise in 1964.[5] Even though the measure, which became Public Law 78, addressed Mexico's humanitarian concerns (by replacing grower–bracero recruiting with government sponsored contracts and by curtailing use of the legalization procedure), from Truman's perspective, it suffered from many deficiencies.[6] In particular, the new Program failed to heed many of the recommendations of the President's Commission on Migratory Labor. These included proposals regarding labor certification and prevailing wages that would have improved the working and living conditions of Mexican braceros. Truman also underscored the lack of enforcement provisions such as criminal penalties against employers who hired undocumented workers and additional authority for INS officials to search places of employment without warrant.[7]

Even though the President's Commission had drawn national attention to the question of undocumented immigration and cast a sense of legitimacy upon the task of border enforcement, Truman and the INS faced the ongoing opposition of southwestern legislators in Congress. Their demands for the renewal of the Bracero Program, moreover, grew increasingly urgent with the onset of the Korean War in 1950.[8] Lacking the votes in Congress to eliminate or significantly alter the Bracero Program, White House and INS officials pursued legislative amendments to rectify the enforcement gaps in Public Law 78. These amendments pertained to INS appropriations, employer sanctions, and the agency's search powers. Ultimately, Truman and the INS failed to win the requested appropriations and an efficacious employer penalty measure. Despite these legislative defeats, the agency, as it had for much of the century, found other means, both statutory and administrative, of achieving its enforcement objectives. More specifically, because the INS failed to gain any degree of control over the hiring practices of southwestern growers, it augmented its ability to monitor, pursue, and apprehend their workers, whether legal or unauthorized, in an ever-expanding jurisdiction or policing zone.

After Grover C. Wilmoth's death in 1951, INS officials took advantage of the momentum generated by his participation on the President's Commission on Migratory Labor to develop the agency's enforcement capacities. Indeed, upon the publication of the commission's report, agency leaders distributed copies to key members of the House and Senate Appropriations Committee and drew upon its conclusions to plead its case before Congress.[9] Testifying before the House Committee on Appropriations in May of 1951, INS officials characterized the problem of undocumented immigration as a "national disgrace" and blamed the lack of appropriations for creating a "farce of our immigration laws."[10] A month later, the attorney general submitted a detailed wish list to the Bureau of the Budget, outlining the need for stronger enforcement legislation, specifically the creation of penalties for transporting, harboring, and employing undocumented immigrants and the addition of greater search and seizure powers for the Border Patrol.[11]

The White House joined the INS in this lobbying effort. Truman administration officials recognized that they would be unable to stop the renewal of the Bracero Program, but remained committed to a strong immigration enforcement policy. In a July 6, 1951 meeting between White House officials and the INS, David Stowe, assistant to President Truman, advised Border Patrol supervisor W. F. Kelly, "if the bill [Public Law 78] is signed, even though there is a lot of pressure against it, it will give them [growers] a legal way to get laborers. Then he [Stowe] said we should enforce the law and continue to enforce it as hard as we can, and clean out every wetback in the United States, right now."[12]

Days after signing Public Law 78, President Truman requested a supplemental appropriation of $6.5 million for the INS. Writing to Senator Kenneth McKellar, the Chairman of the Senate Appropriations Committee, Truman emphasized that effective enforcement was an essential counterpart to the farm labor importation program:

> Continuation of an adequate system of importing farm labor is essential to the farm areas where large seasonal crops present farm labor problems. On the other hand, as I pointed out in my Message to the Congress, it is essential that we stop the hundreds of thousands of Mexicans, commonly known as "wetbacks," from illegally entering this country from Mexico to the detriment of both countries.[13]

On August 17, 1951, the House Committee on Appropriations recommended a figure of $4 million. But three days later, the House of Representatives deleted the item altogether from the appropriations bill. In 1951, Congress failed to authorize any additional funds for enforcement work in the Southwest.[14] A year later, the Department of Justice requested a $6 million supplemental appropriation that would create 864 new Border Patrol positions, finance the construction of two new detention facilities on the US–Mexico border, and fund the airlift of undocumented immigrants to the interior of Mexico.[15] On June 5, 1952, Congress approved an appropriation for 335 additional Border Patrol officers but revoked the appropriation three weeks later.[16] It did, however, pass a one million dollar appropriation for the construction of two detention facilities (one at McAllen, Texas and the other at Chula Vista, California) and some equipment.[17] By 1953, despite liberals' repeated calls for stronger enforcement, prominent members of Congress defended agribusiness interests by supporting reductions in the Border Patrol budget.

Truman and the INS were also unable to win congressional support for employer sanctions.[18] During debates over S. 984 (which would become Public Law 78), the Senate passed an amendment to the farm labor program sponsored by Senate Democrats Paul Douglas of Illinois and Hubert Humphrey of Minnesota, and Senate Republican Wayne Morse of Oregon, which would have imposed penalties on employers who hired undocumented immigrants. But Senator Ellender, known as an "aggressive [ally] of agribusiness," deleted the amendment in a conference committee.[19] Wielding his authority as the chair of the Senate agricultural committee, Ellender also played a key role in shaping the Bracero Program for growers' benefit, convincing reluctant Mexican officials to sign a new set of bracero accords in 1951, facilitating the swift passage of S. 984 in Congress, denying increased appropriations for the Border Patrol, as well as blocking the employer sanctions amendment to the farm labor bill.[20]

After the defeat of the Democrats' amendment and the passage of S. 984, Truman turned to the Mexican government for assistance, adopting, in historian Robert Robinson's words, the "unusual approach of explicitly enlisting the cooperation of a foreign government to help manage a domestic political fight."[21] Both governments agreed to use the temporary nature of the bracero accords to their advantage, making renewal contingent upon the passage of employer penalties.

During renewal negotiations the following year, Mexico reiterated its demands for penalty provisions and threatened to back out of the bracero accords altogether.[22] In response to the Mexican ultimatum, the State Department reassured Mexico that President Truman and Congress supported such measures and managed to bring Mexico back to the bargaining table.[23] Congress then hastily passed an enforcement bill six days before the expiration of the agreement. Introduced by Senator Harley Kilgore (D-WV), S. 1851 imposed no employer sanctions. Instead, it clarified the penalties for harboring and transporting undocumented immigrants under Section 8 of the Immigration Act of 1917 that were struck down by the Supreme Court in 1948 as void for vagueness.[24] Congressional debates over S. 1851 make its intent perfectly clear: Congress passed the bill in order to ensure the continuation of the Bracero Program. As Senator McFarland (D-AZ) explained to the members, "the bill before the Senate is proposed as stopgap legislation to enable the farmers to obtain the needed labor for another six months."[25]

Congressional liberals, such as Senators Humphrey, Lehman, and Douglas, were emphatic that, without employer sanctions, the bill would do little to stem the flow of unauthorized immigration.[26] Senator Douglas sought an amendment that penalized those who knowingly employed undocumented workers.[27] Grower advocates in the Senate, however, argued that the Douglas amendment would unfairly punish American farmers and successfully prevented its passage.[28] In its place, the Senate approved an amendment that would be known as the Texas Proviso, in reference to the Texas growers who lobbied for the measure.[29] It explicitly excluded employment from the harboring provisions of S. 1851, stating, "for the purposes of this section, employment (including the usual and normal practices incident to employment) shall not be deemed to constitute harboring."[30] In effect, the Texas Proviso would shield from prosecution those farmers who claimed ignorance with respect to the immigration status of their employees.[31]

Shortly after the passage of S. 1851, the INS established explicit guidelines on its implementation. Issued in April 1952, these instructions directed officers to avoid interrogating growers about their knowledge of their employees' immigration status, stipulating, "No investigation shall be made to determine whether the employer was aware of the employment of the illegal aliens. However, any facts at hand bearing on this question shall be reported. No opinion by the officer as to whether, based on the facts developed, the employer is in violation of PL 78 and the Migrant Labor Agreement of 1951 should be expressed."[32] Stripping the agency of the ability to investigate employers, S. 1851 placed substantial limits on the enforcement capacities of the INS.

The Texas Proviso was a significant and precedent-setting defeat for the INS; indeed, it stood as the first of many occasions in which Congress would reject employer sanctions outright or pass these measures in a diluted form. Yet while S. 1851 prevented the INS from investigating employers themselves, it conferred upon the agency the long-sought authority to search for unauthorized workers on farms and ranches in the border region. Construed as a partial victory for the INS, S. 1851 was part of a slow but steady expansion of the agency's jurisdiction, a jurisdiction that once began at the border ports of entry, but later applied to the public spaces between and beyond the border, and, by the 1950s, encompassed a set of private spaces in the borderlands and beyond.

By 1952, Congress, under S. 1851, permitted the warrantless searches of private property within a twenty-five-mile radius along the international line (both Canadian and Mexican).[33] Unsurprisingly, this statutory language incited much protest from growers and their representatives who blocked the passage of employer penalties under the Douglas amendment. They strenuously asserted that it gave the Border Patrol too much power at the expense of individual civil liberties. Congressman Ovie Fischer (D-TX) argued that it violated the Fourth Amendment prohibition against unreasonable searches and seizures to permit INS officers to enter private property and interrogate individuals as to their citizenship status. In the debates over S. 1851, he stressed, "the Constitution authorizes search warrants for the limited purposes of seizing persons or things. It does not authorize fishing expeditions. It does not authorize searches for the purpose of interrogating people."[34] Fischer further insisted that the twenty-five-mile zone effectively granted the INS a license, or what he called a "blank check," to trespass on a huge swath of private property. Such a provision, Fischer alleged, legitimized and even encouraged an established agency practice of entering private property without sufficient legal authority (in the form of an arrest warrant or grower consent).[35]

Demonstrating their support for stronger immigration enforcement, liberal members of Congress were some of the most vocal advocates of S. 1851. In response to the bill's detractors, Representative Celler emphasized that it did not violate the Fourth Amendment because it did not authorize the warrantless search of private dwellings. Reiterating the argument first presented by the President's Commission on Migratory Labor, Celler asserted that farms and ranches were places of employment and, as such, vested with a public interest. Celler further argued that it was unreasonable to construe the entirety of this terrain as private property. He claimed, "To call a ranch of huge dimensions a dwelling is absurd. It has been held that these huge ranches are like a man's castle. He cannot live in all the places that might be deemed houses, or habitations, on the ranch or the plantation."[36]

Celler further backed the agency's enforcement mandate by defending it against charges that the Border Patrol abused its authority. When Fischer accused the agency of issuing arrest warrants on the basis of a "hunch, even a

Figure 6.1 Representative Emanuel Celler (D-NY) was a staunch supporter of a strong border enforcement policy. Courtesy of Prints and Photographs Division, Library of Congress, LC-USZ62-127299.

remote suspicion" rather than probable cause,[37] Celler retorted that Fischer was mistaken and that the INS adhered to standards of probable cause prior to issuing warrants of arrest for undocumented immigrants.[38] When other members of Congress questioned the authority of district directors to issue arrest warrants and proposed that the INS procure judicial warrants instead, Celler explained the importance and necessity of administrative warrants to the agency's enforcement of the law. Faster and easier to procure than judicial warrants, administrative warrants enabled the agency to apprehend potential flight risks more quickly and, in turn, increased the overall apprehension rate.[39]

As Celler rebuffed the legal challenges to S. 1851, other congressional liberals advocated for the measure in broader terms. In defense of domestic workers and small farmers, Congressman John Shelley (D-CA) argued that strong border enforcement laws were needed to "raise the intolerable living standards of American farm labor in [the Southwest], and if we are to keep the millions of legitimately run small farms in this country secure from the merciless competition of the corporation farms."[40] These laws would also serve a humanitarian purpose by ameliorating the exploitation of undocumented workers or what Shelley described as a system of "miserable peonage" run by "slave trader[s]."[41] Given these economic and social concerns, Shelly urged Congress to grant the INS a blanket authority to enter all farms without warrant or risk a scenario in which "practically the whole of the southwest becomes a sanctuary within which the authorities are powerless to act effectively."[42]

Finally, the measure received the approval of staunch anti-communists such as Representative Frances Walter (D-PA), cosponsor of the McCarran-Walter Act of 1952, who argued that strong border enforcement was necessary to protect national security.[43] His claims echoed concerns expressed in a House report on S. 1851 that diminished access to the border farms and ranches rendered the nation vulnerable to the entry of alleged communists as well as undocumented immigrants; the report observed:

> In recent months the activities of the border patrol have in certain areas been seriously impaired by the refusal of some property owners along the border to allow patrol officers access to extensive border areas in order to prevent such illegal entries. This action by property owners is creating an increasingly serious situation, one which endangers the national security. It affects the sovereign right of the United States to protect its own boundaries against the entry of aliens, including those of the most dangerous classes.[44]

Despite proposals to reduce the zone from twenty-five to five miles and to require the INS to procure judicial warrants of arrest, pro-enforcement legislators won passage of this provision of S. 1851 without amendment.[45]

The President's Commission on Migratory Labor and congressional supporters had characterized this measure in a matter-of-fact way. The new provision was required for the sound enforcement of the immigration laws along the international borders. The INS, however, interpreted the statutory language in the broadest terms possible and used it as a license to battle farmers on their own turf. The INS operations instructions encouraged its officers to act assertively under the new law, stating:

> This provision is not construed as limiting border patrol activities as heretofore conducted. Instead, it confers powers in addition to those heretofore exercised by Service officers. In the past if gates on all roads leading to fenced property adjoining the border were kept locked and the use of keys refused, officers patrolling the border were instructed not to cut fences. Now, all methods of persuasion [sic] failing, or the possibility of obtaining relief through court proceedings having been

exhausted, it is the opinion of the Service that officers, where absolutely necessary, may break locks or cut fences in order to have access to the border.[46]

Armed with this new authority, Border Patrol officers regularly searched border farms without warrant, cutting chains and fences that growers had installed to prevent them from entering.[47] Farmers also complained that the unit demonstrated no restraint in driving or running through the fields, and destroying crops in pursuit of fleeing workers.[48] Finally, there were allegations that Patrol officers entered private homes without warrant in search of undocumented immigrants.[49]

The Patrol's orientation toward border farm searches reflected a more aggressive attitude toward enforcement in general, both on and off the fields. Residents of border towns complained about the new tactics. One laundry owner wrote to Congressman Bentsen (D-TX) that Border Patrol officers entered his business and proceeded to question his patrons in a brusque and arbitrary manner about their citizenship status.[50] Another described an incident in which officers rejected his drivers' license as sufficient evidence of his citizenship. As a result, he found himself forced to leave work, accompanied by the Border Patrol officers, to procure additional documentation, specifically his military discharge and a letter from the Veterans Administration, at home.[51] Others accused Border Patrol officers of even more serious infractions. In Cameron County, Texas, a grand jury concluded that a Border Patrol officer stepped far beyond the bounds of his authority when he shot a fleeing Mexican worker in the back. In the same county, a Mexican American filed a civil suit against a Border Patrol officer for physically attacking him. The foreman of the Cameron County Grand Jury observed that Border Patrol officers were either poorly trained or "they are deliberately undertaking to intimidate, terrify, abuse and mistreat persons of Latin American extraction" and even American citizens.[52]

Local farmers and business owners expressed much confusion about the Border Patrol's new tactics. The laundry owner was baffled as to how one of his customers, a Mexican American woman, could receive such harsh treatment at the hands of a Border Patrol officer who was a fellow parishioner at her church.[53] A farmer who had long-standing cooperative relationships with Border Patrol officers (the farmer admitted to "loan[ing]" both legal and undocumented Mexican immigrants to Border Patrol officers who owned their own farms, providing them with advice on growing cotton, and sharing grazing land for their cattle) was perplexed when they harshly questioned and threatened his Mexican American employees, ordered him to remove the locks from the gate to his farm, and threatened to cut off his supply of legal workers because he had hired undocumented immigrants. He felt he was being singled out for the latter offense given that every farmer, he claimed, in the neighborhood hired unauthorized workers.[54]

Local residents expressed great concerns about the implications of the Border Patrol's misconduct for the community-at-large. One Texan wrote, "Ours is not a police state. . . . I want to be sure that any citizen regardless of his color is safe from unjust questioning, that he can walk the streets and not be *required* to *prove* his citizenship simply because he is lighter or darker than most of us."[55] In response to these claims, the INS usually found no wrongdoing on the part of its officers and justified the Patrol's actions as necessary to the proper enforcement of the immigration laws. The agency argued that the destruction of fences, chains, locks, and crops, and the harsh and random interrogation of individuals on private property were necessary for the apprehension of out-of-status workers in the fields.[56]

In 1919, Commissioner General Caminetti outlined an operational procedure for a proposed border patrol force. Recognizing the difficulties of catching all illicit entries at the line, he proposed the creation of what he called a "second line of defense" at strategic points, such as the rails or major roads, by which migrants were most likely to flee on their way north. The third line of defense, Caminetti proposed, "would be created by establishing cooperative informational networks with local farmers and ranchers."[57] By 1953, W. F. Kelly laid out a bolder enforcement strategy than his predecessors:

> The line operation . . . operating within about 25 miles of the border, is to prevent illegal entries of aliens and to apprehend, on or close to the border, those illegally entering. The second is the supporting operation, sometimes called a "back-up operation" in support of the line effort. This supporting activity consists of maintaining blocks or checks upon highways or roads, of inspecting and searching freight trains and inspecting buses and terminals and other means for travel. This activity is carried on generally within a hundred miles of the border. In a few places where arteries of travel from the border come together, they are somewhat more distant. The third activity consists of mopping up or cleaning up the interior areas.[58]

Whereas the first line of defense once referred only to the international boundary, by 1953, it included a radius twenty-five miles north of the line. While INS officials once required reasonable cause to search, seize, and arrest unauthorized immigrants in public spaces beyond the line, no such rationales were needed in a zone that stretched one hundred miles north of the border thanks to the passage of Public Law 613 in 1946.[59] Finally, as an indicator of the strained relations between the Border Patrol and southwestern farmers, the agency's third line of defense would no longer rely upon cooperative efforts with these border residents.[60] Although the agency would never conquer the growers, it would seek to achieve its own institutional interests—the control of undocumented immigration through the Bracero Program and Operation Wetback.

By the early 1950s, the INS sought to manage the movement of workers to and from the farms as well as unauthorized immigration along the international boundary. More specifically, the agency increasingly monitored those individuals it referred to as "skips," or workers who left their places of employment prior to the termination of their contracts or those who failed to return to Mexico after the harvest season had ended. In spite of the agency's ambivalent participation in the Bracero Program, in order to police this new and growing class of undocumented immigrants, it enlarged its authority over the Bracero Program, shaping policies pertaining to both immigration and agricultural employment. As a result, the agency extended its supervisory reach from the ports of entry and the public places between and beyond them onto the farms and the factories. More broadly, the daily management of the Bracero Program, both its immigration and agricultural employment aspects, would become an integral feature of the third line of defense.

Upon the signing of Public Law 78, the INS, as it had in 1942, sought to limit its role in the administration of the Bracero Program. It emphasized that as an immigration agency, it held responsibility only for the admission and removal of Mexican national recruits. Seeking to divest itself of any responsibilities pertaining to the employment of guest workers, the agency insisted that the Department of Labor, not the INS, was to handle the review of applications and the identification of qualified agricultural laborers.[61] It also shirked any role in resolving disputes between laborers and growers and any duties related to contract violators except for their apprehension and transportation to Mexico.[62] If the agency happened to determine that an employer was in violation of the bracero accords, the INS maintained that the USES, rather than the INS, held jurisdiction over the removal of employers from the Program. Finally, given the lack of congressional appropriations, other INS officials made clear that the agency could not bear the costs of housing and feeding the thousands of braceros who arrived at the reception centers on the American side of the border.[63]

Yet as agency leaders continued to object to the scope of their duties under the Bracero Program, they increasingly saw it as a vital component of a larger border enforcement plan. As in the 1940s, agency officials reasoned that they could curtail undocumented entry through what Mae Ngai has referred to as a carrot and stick strategy.[64] On the one hand, the INS would deter growers from hiring undocumented migrants by providing them with a steady supply of legal workers under Public Law 78; on the other hand, the agency would simultaneously punish growers who fell out of compliance by deporting their unauthorized laborers. Los Angeles District Director H. R. Landon summed up this two-pronged strategy as follows: "the problem [of undocumented immigration] can be met only by the utilization of sufficient manpower for line, road block and mop-up operations, an adequate labor program, . . . and a vigorous prosecution and deportation program."[65]

The agency's enforcement aims, however, were confounded by the growing numbers of workers who had violated the terms of their bracero contracts. One INS official acknowledged not knowing how many of these out-of-status individuals remained in the country "because our records are not current." He continued, "many have deserted who have not been reported as such, and no doubt many have departed without their identity being made known as departing workers."[66] In order to rectify this situation, the INS and USES, by the spring of 1952, agreed that that farmers ought to report skips directly to the INS alone.[67] In a further effort to prevent desertion, service officials instructed its agents at recruiting centers in Mexico to reject those applicants who had violated the terms of their work contract.[68]

While these may have been minor instructions, they reflected a shift in the agency's outlook. In the early 1950s, the INS began to administer the employment aspects of the Bracero Program in order to control the growing number of undocumented workers. By 1954, the INS regularly excluded former contract violators for recruitment and created a worker ranking system in order to identify and admit those most likely to stay on the job. Later, the service considered other means of keeping braceros at work, including the issuance of bonuses, an educational program informing workers of their responsibilities under the Bracero Program, financial penalties for desertion, and wage withholding schemes.[69] All of these policies pertained to those aspects of the Bracero Program that the INS once considered well outside of its jurisdiction.

External factors also led the agency to play a larger role in the administration of the Bracero Program and, more importantly, to reverse its prior objections to taking control. Frustrated by Mexican threats to withdraw its workers from the United States in July 1953, immigration policymakers began to take a "hard-line" approach to the Bracero Program.[70] Growers, congressmen, federal administrators, and even President Eisenhower reasoned that if Mexico could threaten unilateral action, the United States could take unilateral control over the Program.[71] When US–Mexico negotiations over the extension of Public Law 78 stalled in November 1953, the attorney general asked the INS to draw up a unilateral recruitment plan overseen by the agency.[72] The service submitted a proposal on December 3, 1953. On January 15, 1954, the attorney general authorized the agency to put the plan into effect and issued regulations effective January 16, 1954.

The unilateral recruitment program led to the second open border incident in which immigration agents had unauthorized immigrants briefly step across the line and then return in order to adjust their status. The incident led to a now infamous situation in which destitute Mexicans attempting to cross and re-cross the border were held back and even beaten by Mexican officials. Historian Richard Craig observes that "perhaps the epitome of absurdity was depicted by a photograph showing a hapless bracero being pulled south by a Mexican border official and north by a United States officer."[73] The unilateral program ended on February 5, 1954 when American officials realized there was no legal authority to expend federal funds on this kind of initiative. In response, Congress passed Public Law 209 five days later, authorizing unilateral recruitment in the event of a future breakdown in negotiations.[74] On March 10, 1954, the Bracero Program was resumed under a new bilateral accord.

With the appointment of Commissioner General Joseph Swing in April 1954, the INS used the second open border incident to lobby for full control over the Bracero Program. The commissioner general wrote to the Office of the Attorney General:

> I have reviewed this background [the commissioner general provided an overview of the agency's role in the second open border incident] for the purpose of showing that your office and this Service have been in agreement in the past that the recruitment and admission of labor-ers from Mexico could effectively function under the Immigration and Nationality Act without regard to Public Law 78.[75]

In 1954, the INS proposed admitting temporary agricultural laborers (with no restrictions as to country of origin) by adding a provision under the McCarran-Walter Act.[76] The provisions of the statutory amendment would make the terms of the Bracero Program a permanent feature of American immigration law.[77] Just as important, the proposal made clear that the INS intended to run any fu-ture labor importation program on a unilateral basis. INS officials instructed the amendment's drafters as follows:

> No Government-to-Government agreement or guarantee with any foreign country. No more than possible routine exchange of notes at diplomatic level. Disregard previous discussion of advisability of amending section 103 of Public Law 414 expressly to give the United States Government or the Attorney General authority to make such agreements.[78]

Under its plan, the INS would hold primary responsibility for the guest worker program. It would select employer organizations eligible to contract agricul-tural laborers and serve an appellate function in disputes between workers and growers. The agency also prepared a budget estimating the cost of taking full control over the Bracero Program.[79] Lastly, INS officials wrote a comprehensive analysis of bracero processing, from the initial certification of need by the Department of Labor, to the recruitment in Mexico, to worker arrival at the reception centers in the United States.[80] In their final report to the commissioner general, the authors concluded that the INS, more than the Departments of Labor and Agriculture, was best suited to run the Bracero Program. This was the case, they reasoned, because, of all the federal agencies, only the INS had the capacity to execute the enforcement aspects of the Program.[81]

Although the INS proposal to take unilateral control of the Bracero Program never came to fruition, it reflected a dramatic shift in the agency's posture. From its reluctance to implement the wartime bracero accords, it came to view the peacetime Bracero Program as essential to its enforcement mandate. By the early 1950s, the agency's responsibilities vis-à-vis the Program only grew; in an effort to obtain greater control over both unauthorized border crossings and contract violators, the INS, under the new leadership of Commissioner General Swing, began to resemble the agricultural employment agency that it was loathe to become in 1942.

When appointed the new commissioner general of the INS in April 1954, General Joseph Swing overhauled the structure and mission of the agency. With respect to the former, Swing reorganized both the administrative and enforcement branches of the INS and maintained close personal supervision over their operations.[82] With respect to the latter, Swing shifted the agency's priorities and budgets to its enforcement arm.[83] By expanding the agency's enforcement capacities, Swing played a critical role in creating an image of the INS as an aggressive, highly militarized law enforcement organization.

In his restructuring of the INS, Swing greatly benefited from the support of the Eisenhower administration, using it to carve out a degree of autonomy for himself and the agency.[84] In a 1971 interview Swing indicates that with Brownell's approval, he was able to shield the INS from the legal scrutiny of the Justice Department. He also congratulated himself for ensuring that the agency's own legal personnel, particularly the special inquiry officers who oversaw immigrant appeals, were not beholden to the Administrative Procedures Act of 1946 (APA), which articulated a basic set of standards regarding agency hearing practices and rule-making procedures.[85]

Yet even though Swing managed to check external oversight of the agency, he never achieved for the INS the freedom and legitimacy that would allow it to set a policy agenda independent of outside interests.[86] Indeed, Swing was hired to lead the INS because he understood the long-standing challenges facing the agency, specifically the politics of immigration policy formation in

Washington, DC, and the problems surrounding immigration law enforcement in the US–Mexico borderlands. As a result, Swing ultimately generated an enforcement policy that did not close the border, but rather regulated it through the application of expedited removals, adjustment of status procedures, and the Bracero Program.

Upon assuming office, President Eisenhower and his Attorney General Herbert Brownell were relatively uninformed about the subject of undocumented immigration along the US–Mexico border and had no plans to address the issue.[87] But by 1953, in the midst of an economic downturn, the public began to blame undocumented immigrants for the decline. One press report claimed that they had created "a grave social problem involving murder, prostitution, robbery, and a gigantic narcotics infiltration."[88] California Governor Earl Warren complained that Mexican undocumented immigrants burdened state and county public services.[89] The AFL launched a major publicity campaign on the topic while the press published numerous exposés on undocumented immigrants in the border region.[90]

In response to these disparate concerns, Eisenhower dispatched Brownell on a tour of the Southwest in August 1953. Accompanied by Assistant Attorney General J. Lee Rankin and Assistant INS Commissioner Willard F. Kelly, Brownell was shocked by what he found.[91] State and local officials described the economic, humanitarian, public health, and law enforcement problems surrounding undocumented immigration.[92] In addition, Brownell was dismayed by the state of the INS, observing that the Border Patrol had "completely broken down."[93] Agency officials described how a divide between the administrative and enforcement arms of the agency hampered the development of a clear strategy regarding undocumented immigration.[94] Echoing the sentiments of his colleagues, Harlon Carter, chief of the Border Patrol, observed that southwestern INS officials were "dedicated to the admission of people and not their expulsion."[95]

Upon his return to Washington, Brownell was convinced that much needed to be done to address the issue of undocumented immigration and the problems within the INS. Lacking faith in the agency, Brownell put Rankin in charge of formulating an enforcement plan and overseeing INS implementation.[96] By October 1953, Brownell drew upon Rankin's recommendations and proposed a four-point strategy: it included increased appropriations for the Border Patrol, tougher laws against unauthorized immigration, the enactment of state laws against undocumented immigrants, and negotiations with Mexico on the possibilities of binational law enforcement. Eisenhower sanctioned this plan, convinced by Brownell's investigation that undocumented immigration was a matter that required federal attention.[97]

Even though the Eisenhower administration expressed its strong commitment to border enforcement, the politics of immigration policy—specifically, the demands of southwestern growers—impeded the full and immediate implementation of Rankin's plan. Sensitive to grower demands, Brownell vacillated in his support for a strong approach to undocumented immigration. When US–Mexico negotiations over the extension of Public Law 78 stalled in November 1953, Brownell ensured that farmers had a steady supply of labor by authorizing the unilateral recruitment drive on January 15, 1954. Brownell also changed his position on increased funding for the Border Patrol. For example, in August 1953, he proposed increased appropriations for the Border Patrol; but, by December, he called for reductions in the INS budget, concerned that the removal of out-of-status workers might disrupt the agricultural economy.[98] Yet as he refused additional Border Patrol appropriations, Brownell continued to conceive of increasingly aggressive enforcement operations. In 1953, under a strategy code-named "Operation Cloudburst," Brownell proposed posting 4,000 military officials on the US–Mexico border.[99]

Before implementing this plan, Brownell consulted General Joseph Swing who excoriated the idea. Swing convinced him that Operation Cloudburst would create diplomatic tensions between the United States and Mexico. Moreover, he argued that he could run a deportation campaign that cost less money and required less manpower under the aegis of the INS. Impressed with Swing's keen political and organizational sensibilities, Brownell appointed Swing INS Commissioner General.[100] Ultimately, Swing's awareness of the multiple constraints facing the agency—the international repercussions of any mass expulsion drive, the domestic political objections to strong border enforcement, and the institutional weaknesses of the INS—led him to adopt a regulatory approach to unauthorized immigration on the US–Mexico border. Through Operation Wetback, Swing consolidated old legal innovations, including expedited removals, adjustment of status policies, and a guest worker program, and repurposed—or rebranded—them as part of a new and more vigorous immigration law enforcement strategy. Thus while Swing sold Operation Wetback as an enforcement measure that would secure the border, in practice it both closed and opened the line, simultaneously admitting Mexican nationals under the terms of the Bracero Program and removing ethnic Mexicans through a massive federal deportation drive.

Like his predecessors, Swing envisioned the Bracero Program as an integral component of the agency's battle against undocumented immigration. In other words, by providing growers with a guaranteed supply of legal employees, the Program would serve as a disincentive to the hiring of undocumented immigrants. Yet unlike his predecessors, Swing led the agency to take charge of the Bracero Program. Ordering immigration inspectors and Border Patrol officers to involve themselves in the daily operations of the farm labor program, agency officials supervised both its immigration and agricultural employment aspects.

Calavita notes that Border Patrol reports began to "read like farm trade journals, with agricultural conditions traced in detail and the supply and demand for labor carefully calculated."[101] So as to prevent grower reliance on undocumented workers, each month immigration officers calculated whether the bracero supply would suffice to meet grower demands. Swing also solicited statements from INS officers in the field about ways to improve the operation of the Bracero Program.[102]

Swing exerted an unprecedented degree of control over the guest worker program out of the belief that it would only function as a deterrent to undocumented immigration if it worked efficiently. Indeed, Swing, in a further departure from his predecessors, met with growers and shared their concerns regarding the so-called red tape surrounding the hiring of foreign national farmworkers. Demonstrating an understanding of and even empathy for their needs, Swing stated, "You are in business to make a profit. If you lost money on your crops, you would stop trying to produce them. We appreciate that from your standpoint an adequate supply of good labor at a fair competitive cost is a '*must*.'"[103] He then promised to reform the Bracero Program, streamlining recruitment procedures to ensure that growers received an easily accessible, qualified, and plentiful supply of labor.[104]

To this end, Swing authorized agency officials to use their administrative discretion to devise two new innovations, the Specials Program and the I-100 card, that enabled growers to rehire preselected workers outside of the formal recruitment channels of the Bracero Program. Through the Specials Program, the INS permitted farmers to regularize the status of their undocumented workers who, over the course of many years of employment, had developed specific agricultural skills. Swing was fully aware that the Specials Program violated the letter and spirit of Public Law 78, specifically its prohibitions against legalization, and that it represented the kind of unilateral action heavily criticized by the Mexican government during the first and second open border incidents. Yet with much bravado, Swing reassured concerned INS officials, "You must inform the farmers that at present this is unilateral on the part of the Immigration Service, but it is expected that the Mexican government will comply with this proposal."[105]

Growers liked the Specials Program because it allowed them to rehire a wide range of out-of-status workers in an expeditious fashion. Indeed, when the Specials Program began, farmers designated workers as "specials" without any review by the USES or INS.[106] A few weeks later, INS officials became aware of this lapse and hastily cobbled together a procedure for the processing of specials.[107] The procedure, however, imposed few obligations upon growers. Instead, the INS simply rubber-stamped the departure cards (known as I-100 cards) of those workers selected by the farmers (who, per Swing's instructions, submitted a list of names to the reception centers in advance). Farmers were not required to provide evidence that the worker was skilled and, as a result, the INS took for granted that if a worker's name appeared on the list, that worker was qualified as a special. Furthermore, Swing's procedure not only allowed for the recontracting of skilled workers, it also allowed for the rehiring of those unskilled laborers with reliable work histories (Swing dubbed these "Good" workers).[108] Finally, growers liked the Specials Program because it accelerated the inspection process (by exempting rehires from the interior recruitment process in Mexico and the health and immigration inspections in the United States) and allowed growers to contract workers at the border.[109] When State Department and Department of Labor officials noted that border contracting violated the terms of Public Law 78, General Swing responded that these workers "having been previously recruited, are not considered to have again been recruited."[110]

By 1954, the INS adopted a plan initially devised in conjunction with Mexican officials that established an even faster procedure for the entry of specials.[111] Now called the I-100 Program, the procedure continued to mark workers' departure cards (I-100 cards) with an indication as to whether the worker was skilled or satisfactory. Unlike the earlier Specials Program, however, this policy applied only to those workers legally contracted under Public Law 78, not to undocumented immigrants employed by farmers. In addition, the I-100 Program permitted workers to bypass any and all inspections at recruiting centers in Mexico and to head straight for reception centers in the United States where they would be waived through to a predesignated place of employment.[112] These were established when growers sent a request letter and list of former braceros thirty days in advance of their anticipated need to USES officials at the nearest reception center. After USES officials approved the lists, they sent them to the local Mexican consul who also inspected the lists and then mailed postcards to the workers advising them that they had been called up for jobs in the United States.[113] By 1955, farmers were also authorized to place those workers legally employed by other growers on their I-100 lists.[114]

Through the Specials Program and the I-100 Program, Swing not only catered to the interests of southwestern growers but also met the institutional needs of the INS. Swing characterized the Specials Program as a crucial component of his immigration enforcement strategy, specifically the impending deportation drive. By providing employers with a guaranteed supply of legal workers, he hoped to quell any complaints about labor shortages during the course of Operation Wetback. In advance of the campaign, Swing promised growers that he would replace deported workers with braceros as quickly as possible. As the operation began, Swing made good on that promise by initiating the Specials Program and giving farmers a brief period of time in which to legalize their best and most reliable workers. As he explained, "In recognition of the problem of the farmers and the whole general background of wetback labor, the practice that prevailed in the California area of allowing the employer a certain limited time in which to get the so-called 'specials' legalized under the Mexican Agreement was adopted."[115]

Like the Specials Program, the I-100 Program served the agency's institutional interests in curbing unauthorized immigration. By authorizing growers to rehire workers, the service believed that the I-100 system would create a qualified and steady supply of legal workers from year to year.[116] At the same time, the I-100 card would reduce contract violations by offering workers a powerful incentive—the guarantee of regular work—to stay on the job.[117] In addition to deterring undocumented immigration, the agency argued that the card would facilitate its line operations. As a form of identification, the I-100 card enabled immigration officials to make a quick distinction between bona fide agricultural workers and random job seekers as they inspected the thousands of migrants coming through the ports of entry each day.[118] It further prevented congestion at the border, particularly the large gatherings of expectant workers that led to the open border incidents, by allowing workers to remain at home until they were called up for a job by their former employers.

Swing brought as broad and comprehensive a vision to closing the border as to opening it. In refashioning the agency's border enforcement strategy, Swing drew upon his years of military experience and relied on the advice of military leaders and veteran Border Patrol officers.[119] Swing's own military orientation neatly converged with the increasingly combative approach of the INS, which, by the late 1940s, encompassed enforcement scenarios that rendered the US–Mexico border a permanent militarized zone. In 1953, Assistant Commissioner W. F. Kelly, for example, formulated a plan to post military troops under the supervision of the Border Patrol along the southern line.[120] For the California–Mexico border, Los Angeles District Director Landon envisioned a series of fences and towers, manned by units in planes, cars, and on foot. This plan, he believed, would "seal the border area to the highest extent possible."[121] Yet none of these plans were implemented due to the agency's long-standing fiscal, institutional, and political challenges. Conditions had not charged by the time Swing took office and began planning Operation Wetback. Undeterred by the many risks surrounding a mass deportation campaign, he maneuvered past the political complications, if not controversies, surrounding the drive, made do with the sparse resources at hand, and designed the operation in limited terms as one that would prevent undocumented immigration rather than expel all unauthorized immigrants from the county.[122]

Given the domestic and international repercussions of any deportation drive, Swing recognized that he had to inform various constituencies about the campaign rather than launch a surprise attack. In order to avoid a diplomatic crisis with Mexico, the INS and the State Department notified Mexican officials of the impending expulsions months in advance, advising them to be prepared for the return of 1000 individuals per day.[123] Through the creation of the Specials and I-100 programs, his reorganization of the Bracero Program, and his outreach efforts, Swing managed to minimize the resistance of southwestern growers. They came to believe his assurances that upon the start of campaign, their out-of-status workers would be replaced with a plentiful supply of legal braceros.[124] Moreover, many agreed with Swing's reasoning that their participation in the deportation drive would ensure the continuation of the Bracero Program.[125]

In order to head off public opposition, Swing relied heavily on the media to win support for the forthcoming operation. Press releases burnished the agency's image, conveying the message that it was serious about enforcing the immigration laws.[126] In addition, they reiterated a theme conveyed by INS officials since late 1953 that any enforcement effort would seal the border to communist threats as well as undocumented immigrants. Even though southwestern INS officials and Attorney General Brownell, as late as April 1954, reported that no subversives had crossed the international boundary, they used contemporary anti-communist anxieties to garner public support for a federal deportation drive.[127]

Swing also used the local press to facilitate the very implementation of Operation Wetback. Like Charles Visel, the architect of the Los Angeles repatriations of the 1930s, Border Patrol officers, under Swing's orders, used the media to exaggerate the scope of the operation and the size of the force so as to scare undocumented workers into leaving the country on their own.[128] As a result of the publicity, thousands of immigrants fled; in Texas alone, more than 60,000 Mexican nationals repatriated in response to the news of the imminent campaign.[129]

Having sought the cooperation of farmers, the Mexican government, and the general public, Swing prepared the agency itself. Due to budget shortfalls, the agency relied on familiar, cost-saving strategies in conducting Operation Wetback. As District Director Landon explained, "The special operation . . . employed no novel plans of operation. Line operations, road blocks, mop-up crews and removal of aliens from the Border were means that have been employed in this District throughout the years."[130] Central to the drive were the mobile task forces, units created in the 1940s to conduct quick and cheap deportation sweeps. By the early 1950s, the service initiated a program of buslifts and trucklifts to transport undocumented immigrants across the border.[131] As long as funds were available, the agency also conducted trainlifts, boatlifts, and airlifts prior to Operation Wetback.[132] Border Patrol officials incorporated all of these tactics in planning and executing Operation Wetback.

In order to make up for the shortage of Border Patrol personnel, the service transferred officers from other districts and the Investigations Division as it had during the mobile operations of the late 1940s.[133] Local and state law enforcement officials agreed to cooperate, if not participate, in the deportation drives.[134] The agency also solicited the assistance of the public in reporting the whereabouts of undocumented immigrants.[135] In Arizona, manpower shortages led the Border Patrol to hire Native Americans who were paid $2.50 to $3.00 for each out-of-status immigrant apprehended on their reservations.[136] Texans, however, did not offer much cooperation in the early stages of the campaign. Here the media was highly critical of the service, and the public refused to assist officers in carrying out Operation Wetback, even demonstrating overt hostility toward Border Patrol officers.[137] State and local law enforcement officials and the governor, whose own family members employed undocumented workers on their farms, also refused to support the INS.[138]

On June 17, 1954, Swing began Operation Wetback in California with 800 Border Patrol officers organized into twelve-man teams called Special Mobile Forces. These units apprehended immigrants in public spaces, at road blocks, and on the railroads.[139] Many received assistance from air units, which surveyed both

Figure 6.2 INS officials from Niagara Falls, New York, Lyndon, Washington, Glasgow, Montana, and San Diego, California gathered in San Diego to conduct one of the deportation drives under Operation Wetback, June 17, 1954. Reproduced by permission of the San Diego History Center, UT84: 25386.3.

public and private spaces for suspected undocumented immigrants and radioed their location to waiting ground teams.[140] During the first month, these teams worked their way through California, before continuing in Arizona, New Mexico, Texas, and the industrial areas of Los Angeles, San Francisco, and Chicago.[141] The service, in conjunction with Mexican officials, repatriated workers by trains and boats to points in the interior of Mexico.[142] While the majority of those deported were men, the INS began removing entire families in the later stages of the campaign. Between August 5 and 13, 1954, the agency deported from Texas 8,876 mothers, fathers, and children, who were expelled as families.[143]

Figure 6.3 An INS official checks the fingerprints of a hotel employee during Operation Wetback, San Ysidro, California, June 17, 1954. Reproduced by permission of the San Diego History Center, UT84: 25386.2.

Figure 6.4 An INS officer questions a farmworker during Operation Wetback, San Ysidro, California, June 17, 1954. Reproduced by permission of the San Diego History Center, UT84: 25387.1.

By several measures, Operation Wetback was declared a success. The agency claimed that it initially expelled 3,000 undocumented workers per day. Over the course of three months, it claimed to have returned 170,000 to Mexico.[144] By the end of the fiscal year, June 30, 1955, the agency had deported over one million undocumented immigrants.[145] More important than the absolute number of apprehensions and subsequent expulsions was the deterrent effect of the campaign. In this respect, the INS concluded that it had achieved its goal of preventing unauthorized immigration. It defended this claim by noting that as of January 1955, Border Patrol apprehensions dropped to 300 per day compared to 3,000 per day a year before.[146] As further evidence of the deterrent effect, the service pointed to the

Figure 6.5 The INS chartered buses to remove Mexican workers from the United States during Operation Wetback, San Ysidro, June 15, 1954. Reproduced by permission of the San Diego History Center, UT84: 25384.3.

voluntary return of more than 60,000 individuals from South Texas, California, and Chicago. Yet Swing's declarations of success were more rhetoric than reality. In fact, apprehensions declined as a result of a general reduction in Border Patrol enforcement activity after Operation Wetback.[147]

The INS also cited the dramatic increase in bracero recruitment as evidence of the campaign's efficacy. Prior to the operation, the service reported only 1,200 legal braceros working in the Lower Rio Grande Valley of Texas. Afterward, it reported over 60,000 legal workers.[148] Overall, by 1955 the INS recruited 398,650 braceros compared to 201,380 in 1953.[149] In October 1954, immigration officials reported a complete change in attitude among farmers with respect to the hiring of undocumented immigrants: "The general attitude of the ranchers, with the exception of some small operators, now appears to be that as much as they would like to employ 'wets' as before, they do not want to bother with them as they feel certain the 'wets' would be removed by our officers in a short time."[150] The service was so confident that Operation Wetback had achieved the desired deterrent effect that, in January 1955, the agency withdrew its support for two bills (S. 3660 and S. 3661) that would have enjoined noncompliant employers from receiving legal braceros and created additional penalties for transporting undocumented immigrants.[151] One year after Operation Wetback, an official concluded that the INS had "regain[ed] . . . control on the Mexican border. The Border has been effectively closed to the wetback."[152]

Operation Wetback breathed new life into the long beleaguered agency. Prior to the campaign, federal officials considered eliminating the Border Patrol. After the operation, they praised the agency, conferring upon it and its enforcement mandate the political legitimacy that it had sought since the early twentieth century. Signaling its approval of the agency's enforcement mission, Congress approved a $3 million supplemental appropriation for the agency in 1955. Given the success of Operation Wetback and in receipt of the supplemental appropriation, the INS took sweeping measures to shore up its enforcement capacities. In so doing, Commissioner General Swing cultivated within the agency a highly aggressive and increasingly militarized approach to immigration law enforcement.

The effectiveness of the mobile task force units during the federal deportation drive led Swing to adopt them as a permanent part of the agency's enforcement apparatus. On March 3, 1955, the INS activated a special mobile task force composed of 206 officers (later the service attained an additional appropriation which increased the force to 400 men).[153] Split between the San Francisco and San Antonio districts (the two immigration "hot spots"), the force was trained to be ready in under 2 hours to make sweeps in these areas and, when needed, anywhere in the country.[154] By the end of fiscal year 1955, the unit had conducted roundups in Spokane, Chicago, Kansas City, and St. Louis.[155]

Facilitating the operation of this new unit was the reorganized Border Patrol itself.[156] Prior to Operation Wetback, the Patrol along the US–Mexico border was divided among thirteen different sectors and supervised by three district directors. After the restructuring, Border Patrol offices were divided among four regions and the entire southwestern organization was placed under the command of a single Border Patrol official. Whereas Border Patrol officers previously restricted their activities to a single district, the reorganization enabled the force to scout freely along the international line. In addition, the Border Patrol force in the Southwest Region ceased working in pairs and began operating in twelve-man units, modeled after the special mobile task force.[157]

The agency also relied on old and new measures to maintain its surveillance of undocumented immigrants, including those who entered without inspection and those who violated their bracero contracts. Well into the 1950s, the INS continued the I-100 Program, arguing that it promoted the agency's enforcement mandate. By providing growers with an experienced and stable labor force, it served as a deterrent to the hiring of undocumented workers, and it gave braceros a reason to stay on the job.[158] The agency also devised new measures to monitor guest workers. Placing informants in bracero camps, the INS pursued immigrants and potential or actual labor organizers whom the INS, and particularly General Swing, regarded as subversives.[159]

Swing also bolstered the binational dimensions of border policing. Shortly after Operation Wetback, the commissioner sought to fortify relations between the INS and Mexican border control officials. As he observed in a 1971 interview, "So through Congress we succeeded in getting a few extra thousand dollars for the purpose of pushing a . . . program which can't be vouchered, to invite the opposite officials across the border and set them up at a picnic or barbeque, and get a social atmosphere between the two groups."[160] Swing also strengthened the agency's binational enforcement efforts by authorizing the use of undercover agents and informants in Mexico, as well as the United States. In October 1954, for example, Swing planted officers in Mexican bars "to spread rumors . . . that there is no work in the United States for the 'wetback' alien," and that the INS would quickly deport them.[161] At the same time, the service sent an undercover Mexican American officer to Los Angeles to collect "intelligence" on undocumented immigration. This officer also traveled to Mexico in order to attempt surreptitious entries into the United States. As he identified the weak spots in the agency's border surveillance, the INS augmented enforcement at those points.[162] By 1955, Swing institutionalized these strategies by creating an intelligence unit that collected, analyzed, and distributed information pertaining to the smuggling and unauthorized entry of immigrants.[163]

As further indicators of the increasing militarization of the force, the INS constructed new fencing and conducted airlifts on a regular basis.[164] As early as 1925, service officials emphasized the need for the construction of fences and watchtowers along the border.[165] Given the impossibility of patrolling every point along the international line, officials argued that the fence would channel unauthorized border traffic to specific locales at which officers would be posted guard. The fence would also save the bureau some of the expense of apprehending, detaining, and deporting undocumented immigrants beyond the line.[166] Officials further argued that the fences would increase federal revenues by forcing immigrants to cross through a port of entry where they would have to pay head taxes and customs duties.[167] Yet due to the lack of appropriations, the fence was not built. In 1935, service officials once again proposed the construction of fences at six points along the international line. In the midst of the Great Depression, the bureau argued that such barriers would protect the domestic labor force by barring the entry of Mexican workers and save states and municipalities the expense of supporting destitute aliens.[168] Congress passed legislation authorizing the Secretary of State to construct fences on the international boundary with Mexico under the auspices of the Works Progress Administration. Fence construction was authorized not only for the benefit the Immigration Service but also the Departments of Agriculture and the Bureau of Customs.[169]

By the 1950s, the rhetoric about the fence had taken on a new sense of urgency. INS officials insisted that its installation would close the "free zone" and "seal the border."[170] The agency conceived of the fence in highly aggressive terms, transforming the blockaded portions of the US–Mexico boundary into virtual militarized zones. In the 1930s, immigration officials proposed the construction of a single fence, almost eleven feet high.[171] By the 1950s, the INS suggested something much more elaborate: it planned the construction of two eight-foot high fences spaced eight feet apart, topped by barbed wire and rolls of concertina wire. The fence itself would be manned by a series of bulletproof towers (which would be furnished with spotlights), patrol officers on foot, patrol jeeps driving on new roads built adjacent to the fence, and airplanes.[172] The INS also explored the possibility of installing signal devices, which would alert officials of any breaches. Due to the expense, the service decided to forego this option.[173]

For its execution of Operation Wetback, the INS garnered both praise and blame. As Congress demonstrated its support of the INS through increased appropriations, international and domestic actors lauded the agency for its performance during the drive. The American Section of the Joint Migratory Labor Commission, a binational commission formed to investigate the Bracero Program and make recommendations regarding its renewal, commended the INS for the campaign.[174] Drawing upon documents prepared by Commissioner General Swing, the American Section observed that the INS, for the first time in its history, took a "firm stand" against unauthorized immigration.[175] Moreover, it praised the agency for eliciting the cooperation of growers and for treating deportees in a humane fashion. President Eisenhower was also pleased with the outcome of Operation Wetback, especially because it satisfied his wish that any enforcement program toe a fine line between the demands of the American public, southwestern growers, and the Mexican government. Finally, the removals, while short-lived, gave many Americans the impression that the problem of undocumented immigration had been solved or, at least, was under control.[176]

Others, however, reacted quite differently, expressing outrage about the federal removal campaign. Many of those who wrote protest letters agreed that undocumented immigration was a serious problem but, at the same time, they believed that the methods chosen by the INS to address the matter were far too severe. Typifying the sentiments of many individuals, one private citizen wrote to President Eisenhower:

> When men are packed in trucks like cattle and driven forty miles in a
> blazing sun; when Boarder [*sic*] Patrol planes swoope [*sic*] down on

men in a field buzzing them so close to scare them into running until they drop from sheer exhaustion—just for the laughs they get out of it; when wetbacks are mistreated and robbed of their small earnings; I cannot help but wonder why we have bothered with a good neighbor policy only to throw away any semblance of friendship in a few short weeks.[177]

Some members of the press, particularly in California, presented the operation in a favorable light, yet others were harshly critical, as one editorial intoned, "If the wetbacks were public enemies and criminals of the Alcatraz variety there might be some justification for an enormous man-hunt such as we have had thrust upon us by the handmaidens of the labor unions. But what has the wetback done?"[178]

Many expressed concerns that Operation Wetback would fuel anti-American sentiment abroad and incite subversive activity at home, particularly among Mexican immigrants. "The Mexican immigrant is going to tell of the manner of his ejection," an editorial in a Texas newspaper warned, "of the Americanos who profess to be friends of the Mexican but whose government is brutal and ruthless in dealing with lowly Mexican men, women, and children. He is going to listen with more interest when the next communist agitator comes spreading his poisoned words."[179] Farmers accused the Border Patrol of resorting to tactics that belonged in a communist state rather than a democratic one.[180] Labor unions expressed similar sentiments, shocked that a democratic nation would rely on "intimidation," "McCarthyism," and "repressive" policies.[181] Texas farmers, who staunchly opposed the operation, condemned the service not for infringing the rights of Mexican immigrants and Mexican Americans but for what they saw as their right to use undocumented workers. As one news account reported, "They [the farmers] assert boldly that this 3,000 square-mile agricultural empire, with 300,000 inhabitants and an annual income of more than $3,000,000, was built on cheap 'wetback' labor like the Southern slave owners of a century ago—it is a violation of their rights to take it away even if the 'wetbacks' are lawbreakers."[182]

For the Mexican American community, Operation Wetback served as an all too vivid reminder of the mass deportations of the 1930s and the Zoot Suit Riots of 1943, during which Mexicans were terrorized in Los Angeles. According to historian Juan Ramon García, many were frightened into silence, raising few objections to the expulsions.[183] Mexican American organizations, however, did express their opposition to the campaign. While groups such as the League of United Latin American Citizens (LULAC) and the American G.I. Forum initially supported the drive (leading Border Patrol officials to seek their endorsement during the course of Operation Wetback), these organizations soon realized that the roundup had affected their primary constituents, Mexican American citizens, as well as undocumented Mexican immigrants.[184] Furthermore, the removals had broken up, if not deported, entire families whose citizenship status often varied from member to member.[185] As a result, these organizations began to view the fight for immigrant rights as an extension of their struggle for Mexican American civil rights.[186]

In public, the INS claimed that it tried to use the most humane measures possible during the course of the operation, making a particular effort to keep families together.[187] At other times, the service argued that the deportation drive served a humanitarian purpose in and of itself by removing out-of-status workers from exploitative conditions. Garciá also notes that Swing warned INS officials to be careful during the course of the roundup to avoid overly aggressive tactics and to ensure that individuals were undocumented immigrants rather than citizens, particularly given all the media attention on the campaign, much of which he solicited himself.[188] Yet the press and INS records documented several instances of abuse. Ngai reports that Operation Wetback deposited thousands of workers over the border without sustenance or shelter; in one instance, workers were left without food or water in 112-degree heat, resulting in the deaths of eighty-eight braceros.[189] Others discovered Border Patrol officials collecting money from deportees to pay for their transportation home.[190] The agency was later attacked for using ships of questionable seaworthiness to transport Mexicans.[191] The service terminated the boatlift in 1956 when seven immigrants drowned after trying to flee by jumping overboard.[192] The INS generally denied these allegations of abuse.[193] But in his testimony before the Joint Commission on Migratory Labor, Swing was reported to have said, "there is undoubtedly some dirty linen which will have to be washed."[194]

The perceived successes of Operation Wetback led Swing, his contemporaries, and his successors to institutionalize a multilayered approach to immigration law enforcement. To this very day, policymakers on both the left and the right concur that a strong Border Patrol, adjustment of status laws, and farm labor programs are integral to any efficacious border enforcement plan. At the same time, the American public has absorbed the broader legacies of Swing's Operation Wetback, taking for granted the now routine exercise of large-scale expulsions at the international boundaries and throughout the country.

Conclusion

After 9/11, concerns surrounding border security transformed the US–Mexico border once again. Congress reorganized the INS, passed several border enforcement measures, and, for the first time in history, routinely appropriated immigration agencies more money than they requested. By 2012, Congress was spending a record $100 billion per year on immigration and border enforcement. By 2014, US Customs and Border Protection (CBP), the successor to the Border Patrol, was the largest law enforcement agency in the country, employing a total of 60,000 agents and administrators.[1] And by 2012, CBP constructed 651 miles of a 700-mile border fence mandated by the Secure Fence Act of 2006.[2] Accompanying the new fence was an array of surveillance technologies, including predator drones, video cameras, mobile license plate readers, and thermal imaging systems. More than ever before, the border came to resemble a militarized zone.

Despite the unprecedented buildup of the nation's border enforcement capacities after 9/11, the border remained open. CBP, like the immigration officials of the twentieth century, continued to facilitate the flow of local residents, laborers, tourists, and traders. Rather than view this situation with alarm, CBP leaders described it as an integral component of their institutional mission. As the agency's website states: "[CBP] is charged with keeping terrorists and their weapons out of the United States while facilitating lawful international trade and travel."[3] At times, federal agencies have been so sensitive to the socioeconomic needs of the borderlands that they, in the words of Janet Napolitano, former Secretary of the Department of Homeland Security, "emphasized and worked to improve the flow through the border of legal travel and trade" and made border enforcement their second priority.[4]

In a recent expose of the CBP, Garrett Graff, editor of *Politico Magazine*, characterized the agency's dual role as a "quirk."[5] Yet this book reveals that the complexity of CBP practices derives in part from the institutional orientation and legal precedents established by its predecessor, the INS. Over the course of the twentieth century, the INS in the Southwest created laws and policies that opened and closed the border. As nativism and national security informed initiatives to bolster immigration law enforcement, economic, political, and diplomatic imperatives led the agency to devise procedures that sustained the transnational character of the borderlands. These legal innovations reflected the agency's view of the US–Mexico border as much more than a dividing line or symbol of national sovereignty. INS officials also construed and constructed the border as an economic zone, a transnational social space, and a vast legal jurisdiction.

In the popular and scholarly imagination, the INS functioned as a law enforcement agency, fulfilling its mandate to close the borders to unwanted immigrants. This book unsettles this notion, tracing the ways in which the INS served as a lawmaking body as well as a law enforcement agency. While Congress and the courts provided the outlines of a federal immigration policy, local INS officials articulated that policy in more detail, modifying, inventing, and even ignoring it in response to regional and transnational needs. What resulted were laws, policies, and procedures related to the admission of border residents, tourists, and guest workers, including the literacy test waiver, border crossing cards, adjustment of status plans, and the border recruitment schemes of the bracero era; expedited deportation practices including voluntary departure, Border Patrol roundups, and mass removal campaigns; and an aggressive enforcement strategy that hinged upon the agency's exemption from the Fourth Amendment prohibition against warrantless searches and arrests at the international boundaries and far beyond them. Through these legal innovations, the INS in the Southwest played a profound role in shaping the letter and spirit of the nation's immigration laws.

The scope of the agency's ability to make law, however, belied its long-standing weaknesses. Challenging characterizations of the INS as a strong and focused organization, this book has argued that conflict, contingency, and failure pervaded the agency. A lack of support from federal policymakers, resistance to the agency's border enforcement mandate among southwestern businesses and ordinary border residents, internal agency disputes, and the logistics of patrolling the 2,000-mile border prevented local INS officials from closing the line to unwanted immigrants. In reaction to these obstacles, immigration inspectors and Border Patrol officers turned to the law, using their legal innovations to achieve some degree of control over the border. Even though many of these laws and policies were created in a reactive and haphazard fashion, they served as the foundations of state border enforcement capacities in the Southwest.

In the process of building the American state, the INS in the Southwest also re-envisioned the border. It not only reinforced conceptions of the border as a sovereign boundary but also generated legal constructions of the border as an economic and social zone and a jurisdiction for the policing of unauthorized immigration. For much of the twentieth century the INS sustained all three visions of the border, despite their contradictory purposes. Yet if the INS continued to pursue policies that simultaneously opened and closed the line, it did so in response to the complexities of immigration law enforcement in the region. Generation after generation of southwestern agency officials would report that the economic and social realities of the borderlands rendered impossible the literal application of federal immigration restriction laws and the closing of the US–Mexico border. It was in this context that the INS in the Southwest transformed the border into a borderlands.

Contemporary developments continue to reflect the nation's variegated priorities with respect to immigration regulation on the US–Mexico border. On the one hand, the agency, in the years following Operation Wetback, conducted additional enforcement campaigns based upon similar strategies and rationales. Fears about the illicit entry of goods, unwanted immigrants, and security threats, after 9/11, were used as justifications for increased border enforcement. Yet social, economic, and diplomatic concerns continued to inform the construction of open border policies. Global economic imperatives led to the passage of the North American Free Trade Agreement (NAFTA), which lowered trade barriers between Canada, Mexico, and the United States. Meanwhile, domestic demands for immigrant labor resulted in the creation of new guest worker programs and prevented the passage of efficacious employer penalties.

After Operation Wetback, several administrations bolstered the nation's immigration enforcement capacities in response to a series of perceived crises along the border. Relying on tactics devised in the 1954 deportation drive, the Nixon administration, in 1969, launched Operation Intercept to stem the illegal drug trade across the border. The campaign linked the issues of undocumented immigration and drug trafficking in the public mind, a connection perpetuated by the Reagan and first Bush administrations.[6] Indeed, by the 1980s INS officials were deputized as Drug Enforcement Agency officers, expanding the policing dimensions of agency operations in ways not unlike those envisioned by Prohibition advocates of the 1920s.[7] In the 1980s the INS also extended its enforcement efforts to allegedly subversive aliens, specifically Central American refugees.[8] While the interventionist foreign policies of the Reagan administration triggered the refugee crisis, Reagan in 1989 approved the largest removal campaign since Operation Wetback.[9]

In the 1990s, California nativists issued renewed calls for local, state, and federal action on the issue of undocumented immigration. The INS responded to these local pressures by initiating another enforcement drive named Operation Hold-the-Line in 1993. Reversing the strategy of Operation Wetback, the agency did not pursue immigrants beyond the line but instead placed 400 officers on a twenty-mile stretch of the Texas–Mexico border in what it described as a "visible show of force" to block surreptitious entry.[10] A year later the Clinton administration, seeking to seize the initiative for immigration enforcement from conservatives in an election year, took additional steps to address the perceived crisis in the Southwest. Applying the line defense strategy of Operation Hold-the-Line, the administration launched Operation Gatekeeper on the Southern California–Mexico border.[11] Meanwhile, California voters took matters into their own hands by passing Proposition 187, a ballot initiative that denied public services such as education and health care to undocumented immigrants.[12] Even though the federal courts struck down Proposition 187, Congress reiterated the spirit and substance of the initiative by passing the Personal Responsibility and Work Opportunity Act of 1996, a welfare reform law that excluded immigrants from federal benefits.[13]

According to political scientist Timothy Dunn, these late twentieth-century federal enforcement operations militarized the US–Mexico border.[14] But none of these efforts closed the line, particularly to the entry of both legal and un-documented immigrant workers. Private sector demands for immigrant labor and poor economic conditions in Mexico continued to serve as powerful incentives for many noncitizens to cross the border without undergoing a formal immigration inspection. Thus despite the multiple enforcement campaigns that had been conducted after Operation Wetback, apprehensions of undocumented immigrants continued to rise, reaching over one million per year by the late 1970s. The federal government, often working in conjunction with the private sector, created additional channels for the entry of immigrant labor. Even though Congress terminated the Bracero Program in 1964, it continued to afford growers' access to a steady supply of Mexican labor up to the present day.[15] The most prominent of these endeavors were the legalization plan and agricultural labor program mandated by the Immigration Reform and Control Act of 1986 (IRCA).[16] Although it was billed as a piece of border enforcement legislation, IRCA ultimately did more to facilitate growers' demands for Mexican agricultural labor. As the century wore on, other industries, particularly the technology industry, joined growers in lobbying Congress for immigrant labor, reinforcing claims about importance of guest workers to the nation as a whole.[17]

As in the 1950s, congressional legislators in the 1970s and 1980s perpetuated growers' reliance on out-of-status workers by blocking the passage of strong enforcement legislation.[18] Congress, as it had for much of the early twentieth century, continued to provide insufficient funds for the INS and Border Patrol.[19] Moreover, as the Carter administration lobbied for employer sanctions, Congress once again defended the interests of southwestern growers and blocked their passage.[20] In this period Mexican American organizations, having established a viable presence among Washington, DC lobbying firms, joined pro-business forces in their opposition to employer sanctions. They argued that by creating a disincentive for employers to hire anyone of Mexican descent, employer penalties discriminated against Mexicans and Mexican Americans.[21] In 1980, Congress revived debates over employer penalty legislation in response to renewed public concerns about undocumented immigration, spurred by the arrival of 125,000 Cuban refugees in 1980.[22] Yet pro-business legislators and the Mexican American lobby succeeded in eviscerating the terms of the employer penalty measures that were enacted under IRCA after six years of congressional debate.[23] Further weakening the IRCA penalty provisions was the lax enforcement effort of the INS.

While immigration policymakers debated the merits of closing the border to unwanted immigrants, NAFTA opened the borders to the free flow of goods and services. In so doing, it promoted regional integration and grew the border population and economy. From 1994 to 2000, political scientist Joseph Nevins observes, trade between the United States and Mexico increased from $80 billion to $200 billion.[24] Yet a decade later, NAFTA was criticized for failing to live up to its promises to improve the standard of living for Mexican workers, promote economic and infrastructural development in Mexico, and prevent unauthorized entry into the United States.[24] The development gap that emerged between the United States and Mexico constituted what one journalist referred to as a "root cause" of undocumented immigration.[26]

It was in this context that Mexican President Vicente Fox and President George Bush raised the idea of creating a new guest worker program in 2001. Like the Bracero Program, the plan would offer Mexico a safety valve, specifically through worker remittances, for its ailing economy. Mexican officials also cited to humanitarian concerns about the increased dangers of unauthorized entry (increased enforcement efforts led Mexicans to risk crossing the border through the Arizona desert) as a reason to begin another farmworker program.[27] Given his pro-business orientation, Bush proved responsive and proposed a plan whereby undocumented workers already employed in the United States would obtain the sponsorship of their employers for a temporary stay visa.[28] Yet further talks on the guest worker program were interrupted by the terrorist attacks.[29]

A subsequent investigation into the attacks, *The 9/11 Commission Report*, pointed to the persistence of organizational problems within the INS.[30] The report concluded that if the immigration laws had been strictly enforced, fifteen of the nineteen terrorists would have been barred from entry.[31] In response to the report, federal officials handed the INS a fate equivalent to administrative death, splitting it into three new agencies: US Citizenship and Immigration Services (USCIS), which focuses on providing services such as naturalization and work visas; US Immigration and Customs Enforcement (ICE), which combined the forces of the Customs and Immigration bureaus and conducts immigrant removals at and between the nation's ports of entry as well as from the nation's interior; and US Customs and Border Protection (CBP), which consolidated several agencies, including the border immigration inspection force, the Border Patrol, the US Customs Service, and agricultural inspections, to conduct enforcement operations on the international boundary, becoming a "comprehensive border security agency."[32]

This administrative restructuring was accompanied by a series of legislative and executive measures; together, these efforts marked an unprecedented intensification of border enforcement. During the administration of George W. Bush, Congress passed border security measures such as the Real ID Act, which prevented states from issuing drivers' licenses to undocumented immigrants.[33] It also revived long-standing proposals for the construction of a border wall through the Secure Fence Act of 2006.[34] In a sharp break with the past, Congress has funded many of these border enforcement measures, spending more than $100 billion on immigration and border control since 9/11. Conveying the breathtaking scale of this spending, Graff writes, "The United States today spends more money each year on border and immigration enforcement than the combined budgets of the FBI, ATF, DEA, Secret Service and US Marshals— plus the entire NYPD annual budget."[35]

This investment in border security transformed the Border Patrol by creating the kind of consolidated border policing force, the CBP, that prohibitionists repeatedly proposed in the 1920s. As the Border Patrol chafed against its absorption into CBP, its reorganization led to its spectacular growth in the first decade of the twenty-first century; between 2005 and 2012, its budget

Figure C.1 By 2012, the federal government had spent $4.3 million on the "Surf Fence Project," renovating a section of the border fence jutting three hundred feet into the Pacific Ocean, Imperial Beach, San Diego County, December 2014. Photo by author.

increased 85 percent from $6.3 billion to $11.7 billion while its staff grew 50 percent from 41,001 to 61,354. Of these 61,354 employees, 21,370 were Border Patrol officers and 21,186 were immigration inspectors.[36] In sum, according to Graff, the Border Patrol went from a "comparatively tiny, undermanned backwater of the Justice Department to a 21,000-person arm of the largest federal law enforcement agency [the CBP] in the country."[37] Meanwhile, Immigration and Customs Enforcement (ICE), which experienced an 87 percent rise in its own budget since 2005, has steadily increased the number of immigrant detentions from 85,730 in fiscal year 1995 to 429,247 in fiscal year 2011.[38] By the twenty-first century, more individuals, as the Migration Policy Institute (MPI) reported, were "detained in the immigration detention system than are serving sentences in federal Bureau of Prisons facilities for all other federal crimes."[39]

Despite the massive expansion of the nation's immigration enforcement capacities, the border remains porous and open. After 9/11, many border residents wanted it to remain that way, notwithstanding their concerns about terrorism. In 2002, Congressman Bob Filner of San Diego stated that while the Department of Homeland Security's "chief goal is to keep people out," border businesses in San Diego County aimed "to keep the legal people coming across."[40] Underscoring the economic importance of cross-border traffic, one report observed that "as many as 8 out of 10 businesses along that border depend on the daily flow of Mexicans who come seeking blue jeans, designer clothes and Nike sneakers."[41] Reminiscent of their twentieth-century precursors, federal immigration officials themselves struggled to balance the nation's security needs with its economic interests along the US–Mexico border. Of this dilemma, Michael Chertoff, former Secretary of Homeland Security, observed, "I actually could eliminate the risk to the ports. If I shut them, there will not be any risk, but there won't be any ports."[42]

Through the creation of so-called smart borders, federal immigration officials have sought to satisfy both the nation's economic and security concerns along its land and sea boundaries.[43] This approach to border regulation expedites the crossing and recrossing of low-risk travelers, particularly border residents, tourists, and traders, through overseas prescreening procedures and biometric identification systems.[44] NEXUS and SENTRI offer expedited inspections for visitors arriving at the ports of entry on the US–Canadian border and the US–Mexican border, respectively; meanwhile US-VISIT and Global Entry provide analogous services for travelers arriving at the nation's land, air, and sea ports of entry.[45] In order to facilitate the free flow of trade, FAST supplies a streamlined entry procedure for prescreened commercial truck drivers, while cargo release/simplified entry is an accelerated, yet secure, cargo processing system for preselected companies.[46] Finally, DHS modernized the nation's border ports of entry, installing

Figure C.2 Pedestrian and vehicular traffic headed northbound at the San Ysidro–Tijuana border port of entry, December 2014. Photo by author.

fixed and mobile license plate readers, radiation scanners, and RFID detectors (which read and transmit the information conveyed by the wireless RFID chips embedded in most contemporary border crossing documents), among others. These technologies, DHS claims, have reduced the long wait times at the border ports of entry; for example, by 2013, pedestrian processing in El Paso "improved between 16 to 34 percent, depending on the day of the week."[47]

The private sector has also played a pivotal role in keeping the borders open to the free flow of tourism and trade. CBP, for example, developed its post-9/11 border crossing policies in cooperation with private industries; in so doing, it sought to assuage concerns that a border shutdown, such as that which occurred in the immediate aftermath of 9/11 and paralyzed the regional economy, will not occur again.[48] CBP claims that it possesses the institutional capacities to sustain the flow of trade and commerce across North America's borders even in the face of an emergency.[49] The private sector not only has worked with executive branch agencies to construct new border crossing procedures, it also has lobbied Congress for the creation of visa and guest worker programs for the agribusiness, construction, and technology industries, among others.[50] Heightened concerns about border security have not diminished the private sector's pursuit of a cheap and pliable workforce. As a result, two issues—the nation's security and labor needs— have continued to define the parameters of contemporary debates on American immigration policy. Indeed, during the Bush and Obama administrations, each and every major immigration proposal included provisions for stronger border enforcement, adjustment of status measures, and guest worker programs.[51]

The lawmaking activities of the INS have left a mixed legacy for the borderlands. On the one hand, the agency's open border policies reflected its responsiveness to regional economic, political, and social needs. Yet, on the other hand, the violence surrounding Border Patrol practices illustrated the many ways in which the exercise of administrative discretion could go awry. Today, CBP practices, like those of the Border Patrol continue to elicit concerns among legal commentators and civil rights advocates who have drawn attention to the agency's repeated abuse of power. The critiques of the Border Patrol, both past and present, raise broader questions regarding the scope of the unit's authority and the agency's ability to define the law.

For over a decade after its post-9/11 overhaul, the CBP has preserved the cultural and institutional traditions of its predecessor. As one indicator of its reluctance to let go of the past, the Border Patrol refused to adopt the navy blue uniforms of the CBP, instead retaining its familiar olive green issue.[52] The Border Patrol of the twenty-first century bears more than a superficial resemblance to its forerunner. It continues to enjoy a tremendous amount of deference from the legislative, judicial, and executive branches, which have prioritized the defense of national security over the protection of individual rights.[53] As a result, the new unit has repeated past precedent by defining the law on its own terms and in ways that curtail the rights of immigrants and citizens.

Most recently, privacy advocates have observed that the unchecked quality of CBP's authority characterizes its new virtual, or technology-driven, operations.[54] The limits of these operations remain undefined, conferring upon the CBP broad authority to monitor immigrants and citizens long after their entry and exit from the United States. Thus, in order to protect individual privacy rights, some have called for the drafting of statutory language that would articulate the precise limits of CBP authority to collect and disseminate biographical and biometric data, define oversight mechanisms for the agency's surveillance activities, and afford individual redress procedures at the agency level.[55]

Such speculation regarding the CBP's virtual operations is not unwarranted given that, during the Bush and Obama administrations, reports of corruption, excessive use of force, and physical abuse became commonplace.[56] Between 2013 and 2016, five separate investigations confirmed the violence surrounding border enforcement operations and underscored how little the Border Patrol has changed over the course of the last century. The findings of one investigation, conducted by the Police Executive Research Forum (PERF), a nonprofit member organization composed of the chiefs of the nation's law enforcement agencies, was highly reminiscent of the conclusions of the 1931 report of the National Commission on Law Observance and Enforcement regarding the highly aggressive nature of Border Patrol practices. In particular, the report focused on the unit's undisciplined use of firearms, charging:

It appears that CBP practice allows shooting at the driver of any suspect vehicle that comes in the direction of agents. It is suspected that in many vehicle shooting cases, the subject driver was attempting to flee from the agents who intentionally put themselves into the exit path of the vehicle, thereby exposing themselves to additional risk and creating justification for the use of deadly force.... It should be recognized that a .5 ounce (200 grain) bullet is unlikely to stop a 4,000 pound moving vehicle, and if the driver of the approaching vehicle is disabled by a bullet, the vehicle will become a totally unguided threat. Obviously, shooting at a moving vehicle can pose a risk to bystanders including other agents.[57]

PERF concluded that this approach to law enforcement placed both immigrants and agents in mortal danger and cultivated an atmosphere of lawlessness and violence along the US–Mexico border.

CBP, like the twentieth-century Border Patrol, also came under fire for the weak oversight of its officers. PERF, for instance, argued that a lack of accountability fostered a "no harm–no foul" attitude among Border Patrol officers with respect to their resort to deadly force.[58] The remaining four investigations into CBP practices independently concluded that in the vast majority of use of force and physical abuse cases, no action, whether administrative, civil, or criminal, was taken against the unit's officers.[59] The report of the American Immigration Council (AIC) perhaps offered the most pointed synthesis of all five reports when it wrote, "the complaint system is a rather ornamental component of CBP that carries no real weight in how the agency functions."[60]

The numerous reforms recommended by PERF encouraged CBP officers to adopt alternatives to deadly force when faced with nonlethal threats.[61] In response to rocks and other objects thrown at agents by immigrants across the line in Mexico, the report suggested that agents defuse the situation by "taking cover, moving out of range and/or using less lethal weapons."[62] In a similar fashion, the report also urged the agency to adopt the following language as official policy: "Agents shall not discharge their firearms at or from a moving vehicle unless deadly force is being used against the police officer or another person present, by means other than a moving vehicle."[63]

In response to the report, Border Patrol leaders, as Commissioner General Swing had done half a century earlier, sought to shield their officers from scrutiny. The conclusions of the PERF report were so damning that CBP challenged its release to the public until December 2013, twelve months after its completion.[64] When it was finally issued, the Border Patrol refused to release its internal policies on the use of force, a gesture that was *pro forma* for many law enforcement agencies.[65] But several months later, the Border Patrol instructed employees to limit their use of deadly force to those situations in which they feared death or serious injury. Yet in 2014 the ACLU observed that the instruction simply restated existing and, more important, ineffectual Border Patrol policies.[66] As various commentators observed, a long-standing culture of autonomy undergirded the Border Patrol's intransigence in the face of demands for reform.[67] Graff quotes a former DHS employee: "Out in the field, there was a culture to keep things to themselves. You're familiar with 'What happens in Vegas stays in Vegas?' They had a 'What happens in the field stays in the field.'"[68]

Whether these recent investigations of CBP will result in a reform of the agency remains to be seen. Informed by a security-minded approach to border management, anti-immigrant sentiment, or a combination, pro-border enforcement forces for over a decade have adopted an "enforcement-first" position, blocking the passage of any immigration reform measures until their enforcement goals are met.[69] As a result, guest worker programs, adjustment of status proposals, pathways to citizenship, the Development, Relief, and Education for Alien Minors Act (DREAM Act),[70] and institutional reform have failed to make any headway in Congress.[71] Pro-enforcement advocates continued to maintain their stance even as evidence mounted that the federal government, due to the expansion of immigration enforcement capacities after 9/11, had achieved control over the nation's borders. As the Migration Policy Institute observed in a 2013 study of immigration law enforcement, "The report demonstrates that the United States has reached an historical turning point in meeting long-standing immigration enforcement imperatives."[72] Due to the new realities of immigration law enforcement on the US–Mexico border, MPI rejected the assertions of enforcement-first advocates regarding the need for additional border enforcement resources.[73] It further advised policymakers to focus on the nation's other immigration priorities such as the efficient regulation of trade, travelers, and commerce along the US–Mexico border and the creation of a more humanitarian approach to immigration law enforcement.

Recent events illustrate the many ways in which the past has retained its grip on the present along the US–Mexico border. Although 9/11 led to the transformation of the nation's immigration agencies and the US–Mexico border, immigration policymakers continue to raise the same questions and concerns as their peers in the early twentieth century. Janet Napolitano's efforts to regulate—rather than close—the border echoed Commissioner General Anthony Caminetti's 1918 endeavor to create an immigration policy that simultaneously closed the border to unwanted immigrants and security threats yet opened it for the sake of the transnational economy and society.[74] Meanwhile, the scrutiny and censure of the Border Patrol has become a recurring theme in modern United States history, as the Wickersham Commission of 1931, the Dimock Committee of 1940, the Mexican government over the course of the Bracero Program, civil libertarians and private citizens in the aftermath of Operation Wetback, and, most recently, PERF, the *Arizona Republic*, the American Immigration Council, MPI, and the Department of Homeland Security issued damning reports regarding the arbitrariness and aggression of the unit's operations.

Unable to shed the dilemmas of the past, immigration law and policy in the new millennium as well as in the twentieth century defies simplistic renderings. In the Southwest, the nation's immigration agencies continue to implement the immigration laws in ways that cast the border as a sovereign boundary, a transnational economic and social space, and a jurisdiction for the policing of undocumented immigrants. The complexities of immigration law enforcement are unsettling for some, particularly real estate mogul Donald Trump who, during his presidential campaign, proposed the construction of a massive border wall and the revival of federal deportation drives such as Operation Wetback.[75] Yet these are the complexities the nation must face, rather than deny, in pursuing comprehensive immigration reform. The economic and social needs of border communities, the living and working conditions of guest workers, a proposed pathway to citizenship for undocumented immigrants, reform of CBP policing practices, and border security are only a few of the many issues that policymakers must address in making and remaking the nation's immigration laws.

NOTES

Introduction

1. Grover C. Wilmoth, District Director, El Paso to Commissioner General, May 24, 1928, file 55637/640, RG 85, National Archives.
2. Act of May 6, 1882, 22 Stat. 58; Act of February 5, 1917, 39 Stat. 874, §3; Act of May 26, 1924, 43 Stat. 153, §12.
3. J. B. Bristol, Nogales Chamber of Commerce to James J. Davis, Secretary of Labor, Department of Labor, April 19, 1928, file 55637/640, RG 85, National Archives; J. B. Bristol, Nogales Chamber of Commerce to Senator Henry Ashurst, May 7, 1928, file 55637/640, RG 85, National Archives; George W. P. Hunt, Governor, Arizona to James J. Davis, Secretary of Labor, July 23, 1927, file 55301/217, RG 85, National Archives; Harry E. Hull, Commissioner General to I. F. Wixon, Chief Supervisor, Calexico, CA, January 28, 1926, file 55031/81, RG 85, National Archives.
4. Schneider, *Crossing Borders*, 79, 102.
5. Grover C. Wilmoth, District Director, El Paso, "Mexican Border Procedure, Lecture No. 23," November 19, 1934, RG 85, file 55875/23.
6. In 1891, Congress created the Bureau of Immigration as part of a larger effort to centralize immigration control along the nation's land borders and coastlines. Since its founding, the agency has been housed in various departments, including Treasury (1891), Commerce (1903), Justice (1940), and Homeland Security (2003), and reorganized several times. By 1933, the agency permanently assumed a set of naturalization functions, in addition to its immigration duties, and became the Immigration and Naturalization Service (INS). In 2003, the INS was split into three agencies, Customs and Border Protection (CBP), Immigration and Customs Enforcement (ICE), and Citizenship and Immigration Services (CIS), all under the aegis of the Department of Homeland Security. US Congress, Senate, Committee on the Judiciary, Select Commission on Immigration and Naturalization, *History of the Immigration and Naturalization Service*, 3.

   When using the terms, "Bureau of Immigration," "Immigration and Naturalization Service," "border immigration officials," "southwestern immigration officials," or the acronym "INS," I am referring to both the immigration inspection force that manned the nation's ports of entry and the Border Patrol, the mobile division of the agency. When I use the terms "immigration inspection force" or "immigrant inspectors," I am referring to the immigration inspectors stationed at the nation's ports of entry only. When I use the terms "Border Patrol," "Border Patrol officers," or "Patrol officers," I am referring exclusively to employees of the Border Patrol.
7. "Recommendations and Suggestions for the Betterment of the Service and for Remedial Legislation," in Bureau of Immigration, *Annual Report, Fiscal Year Ended June 30, 1920*, 450.
8. See, for example, Scruggs, "The First Mexican Farm Labor Program"; Craig, *The Bracero Program*; Ettinger, *Imaginary Lines*.

9. More specifically, these important studies have drawn attention to the discriminatory and even violent treatment inflicted by the INS upon the ethnic Mexican population in the United States. As a result of the agency's undue focus on Mexican immigrants and Mexican Americans, they became, in Mae Ngai's words, the "iconic illegal immigrant." Ngai, "Illegal Aliens and Alien Citizens," 161. See also Ngai, *Impossible Subjects*; Lytle-Hernández, *Migra!*; Sánchez, *Becoming Mexican American*; Gutiérrez, *Walls and Mirrors*; Balderrama and Rodríguez, *Decade of Betrayal*; Calavita, *Inside the State*.

10. On the limited scope of federal bureaucratic action in particular and the policymaking process in general during the pre–Civil War period, see Carpenter, *The Forging of Bureaucratic Autonomy*, 37–64.

11. Horwitz, *The Transformation of American Law, 1870–1960*, 215; Wiebe, *The Search for Order, 1877–1920*; Skowronek, *Building a New American State*; Skocpol, *Protecting Soldiers and Mothers*; Wilson, *Bureaucracy*; Shapiro, *Who Guards the Guardians?*; Bremer, "The Unwritten Administrative Constitution."

12. Delegation has been a feature of American governance since the nation's founding. See Shapiro, *Who Guards the Guardians*, 43; Mashaw, *Creating the Administrative Constitution*, 290.

   The debates regarding the implications of delegation for a representative democracy are voluminous. For a sampling see Landis, *The Administrative Process*; Horwitz, *The Transformation of American Law, 1870–1960*, 215–216; Schoenbrod, *Power Without Responsibility*; Davis, *Discretionary Justice*; Shapiro, *Who Guards the Guardians*; Mashaw, *Creating the Administrative Constitution*.

13. The Chinese exclusion cases included *Chae Chan Ping v. United States*, 130 US 581 (1888) (more commonly known as the Chinese Exclusion Case), *Fong Yue Ting v. United States*, 149 US 698 (1892), and *Nishimura Ekiu v. United States*, 142 US 651 (1891).

   In the late nineteenth century, concerns about the rise of the administrative state and its impact on democratic processes led to the creation of both internal and external checks upon the decision-making authority of other federal agencies. By the 1890s the courts, for example, exercised a much more vigorous review of the Interstate Commerce Commission, weakening its ability to regulate the nation's railroads. Agencies themselves engaged, and continue to engage, in their own oversight through agency hearing procedures, which are often required by agency enabling statutes, as well as internal agency rules. On the concerns surrounding the rise of the administrative state, see Horwitz, *The Transformation of American Law, 1870–1960*, 215; Shapiro, *Who Guards the Guardians*. On the history of the Interstate Commerce Commission, see Friedman, *A History of American Law*, 451–453. On the origins and debates surrounding agency hearing practices, see Shapiro, *Who Guards the Guardians*, 40. On agency motives for drafting their own internal decision-making procedures, see Riley and Brophy-Baermann, *Bureaucracy and the Policy Process*, 311. On the history of agency self-regulation, see Mashaw, *Creating the Administrative Constitution*; Horwitz, *The Transformation of American Law, 1870–1960*, 215; Shapiro, *Who Guards the Guardians*.

14. Salyer, *Laws Harsh as Tigers*, 29. After filing the Chinese exclusion cases in the late nineteenth century, a new generation of Chinese litigants asked the Supreme Court to compel the agency to abide by fundamental norms of fairness and due process, as articulated by the Fifth and Fourteenth Amendments, in the conduct of agency hearings. In response the Court, by 1924, defined due process as those procedures guaranteed by the immigration statute rather than a set of fundamental rights. In sum, a fair hearing came to be defined as whatever Congress and the INS deemed it to be. See, in particular, *Japanese Immigrant Case* (*Yamataya v. Fisher*), 189 US 86 (1903); *Chin Yow v. United States*, 208 US 8 (1908); Salyer, *Laws Harsh as Tigers*, 179.

15. Schiller, "The Era of Deference," 399–441; Shapiro, *Who Guards the Guardians*, 36–49.

16. Agency adjudications, or agency hearings, pertain to trial-like proceedings conducted by agencies, rather than the courts, to resolve disputes. Rule-making refers to a process by which agencies fashion a more detailed set of rules that, in political scientist Martin Shapiro's words, are "necessary to carry out the general rule" or the statutes. Shapiro, *Who Guards the Guardians*, 41–42.

17. As Shapiro explains, the APA was a "catch-up statute trying to provide law to cover legitimate agency practices" (41). It specifically sanctioned the very conduct of agency adjudications

but stipulated that they abide by the procedures of regular courts and that they be subject to judicial review.

It also legitimized and standardized agency rule-making practices. Prior to the passage of the APA, agency-enabling statutes offered few limits on rule-making procedures; as a result, agencies had few rules for the very making of rules, and few agencies shared the same rule-making procedures. After the passage of the APA, agencies were required to make law through a "notice and comment procedure" whereby they advised the general public of their intent to make a rule and solicited comments from parties affected by the rule. Shapiro, *Who Guards the Guardians*, 41.

APA rule-making procedures, however, did not supplant the rule-making procedures stipulated by agencies themselves or by their enabling statutes. As Shapiro explains, no single statute could provide a comprehensive set of decision-making rules for the ever-increasing number of federal agencies. As a result, agencies were expected to turn to the APA only when their own enabling statutes and internal procedures failed to provide sufficient guidance on rule-making. Shapiro, *Who Guards the Guardians*, 39. See also Rabin, "Federal Regulation in Historical Perspective," 1263.

18. Kanstroom, *Deportation Nation*, 170–176; Schuck, "The Transformation of Immigration Law," 30–33.
19. Salyer, *Laws Harsh as Tigers*, xiv.
20. Lee, *At America's Gates*, 48, 52–58, 72–74; Schneider, *Crossing Borders*, 101; Salyer, *Laws Harsh as Tigers*, 195.
21. Salyer, *Laws Harsh as Tigers*, 195; Schneider, *Crossing Borders*, 76.
22. Since 1938, the *Immigration Laws and Rules* have been incorporated into the *Code of Federal Regulations*.
23. This claim builds upon the work of administrative constitutionalists who posit that agencies make law by defining conceptions of constitutional rights. More specifically, they reveal the ways in which the federal courts drew upon agency practices and customs to expand constitutional norms regarding free speech, equal protection, and privacy. In a similar fashion, this work argues that internal debates within the INS about the constitutional implications of its operations redefined conceptions of immigrant rights under the Fourth Amendment. Yet while these scholars, for the most part, tend to hold a more hopeful view of the role of agencies in expanding constitutional norms (particularly at moments in United States history when the political climate vitiated against the expansion of such norms), this book emphasizes the ways in which the INS functioned to further curtail the legal and constitutional rights of immigrants. See, for example, Metzger, "Administrative Constitutionalism"; Lee, "Race, Sex, and Rulemaking"; Bremer, "The Unwritten Administrative Constitution"; Desai, "Wiretapping Before the Wires."

    All of this is not to say that constitutional norms regarding the nation's immigrants are defined exclusively by the nation's immigration agencies. The rights immigrants possess at any given moment are defined by a variety of institutions and, as legal scholar Linda Bosniak has pointed out, by a competing set of principles, including "the government's broad power to regulate national borders, and . . . the ideal of equal personhood for territorially present persons." Bosniak, "Membership, Equality, and the Difference that Alienage Makes," 1047. In addition, it is important to note that while the scope of constitutional protections afforded to the nation's immigrants *qua* immigrants remains limited, it is not unchanging. On the development of quasi-constitutional norms within twentieth-century immigration law, see Motomura, "Immigration Law After a Century of Plenary Power," 545–613; Motomura, "The Curious Evolution of Immigration Law," 1626–1704.
24. This book does not consider the agency's adjudications procedures, but only what might be broadly defined as its rule-making processes. Because INS lawmaking activities were exempt from the notice and comment requirements of the APA, it did not engage in rule-making per se. But its lawmaking activities—its exercise of administration discretion, the creation of internal agency regulations, and the drafting of federal statutes—required INS officials to engage in the same kinds of interpretive acts as other agency rule-makers. In other words, INS officials devised a more detailed set of rules required to carry out the general rule or the federal immigration statutes.

25. For an account of the nativist attitudes of early Bureau of Immigration officials see Lee, *At America's Gates*, 47–74.
26. G. C. Wilmoth, District Director, El Paso, "Artificial Barriers to Prevent Smuggling," February 6, 1930, file 55688/876, RG 85, National Archives; Congress, House, Committee on Immigration and Naturalization, *Immigration Border Patrol*, 71st Cong., 2d sess., January 15, 1930, 7.
27. In using this term, I am referring loosely to Elisabeth S. Clemens's notion of the Rube Goldberg state in which complexity and disorder, rather than expertise and rationality, characterize the state-building process. Clemens specifically focuses on power sharing arrangements between federal and state officials as well as public and private entities in the arena of public subsidies to illustrate the messiness of American governance. Clemens, "Lineages of the Rube Goldberg State," 187–215.
28. Lytle-Hernández, *Migra!*, 5, 21, 45, 67, 126, 129, 132, 145.
29. Social, cultural, political, and international historians have offered important treatments of the INS. But their accounts are often partial, focusing on one branch of the agency, particularly the Border Patrol, or on one moment in the agency's history such as its participation in the Bracero Program. Other accounts subsume the agency's history within broader narratives about Mexican immigration, racial formation in the United States, or the contingencies of the nation-building enterprise. See, for example, Calavita, *Inside the State*; Ettinger, *Imaginary Lines*; Geiger, "Caught in the Gap"; Lytle-Hernández, *Migra!*; Lee, *At America's Gates*; Ngai, *Impossible Subjects*; Stern, "Nationalism on the Line"; Balderrama and Rodríguez, *Decade of Betrayal*; Hoffman, *Unwanted Mexican Americans*; Garciá, *Operation Wetback*; Gutiérrez, *Walls and Mirrors*; Craig, *The Bracero Program*; Scruggs, "The Bracero Program"; Scruggs, "The First Mexican Farm Labor Program"; FitzGerald, *A Nation of Emigrants*; Tichenor, *Dividing Lines*.
30. For an account of how agency leaders played a prominent role in the enforcement of Chinese exclusion on Angel Island, see Lee, *At America's Gates*, 64–74. I do not ignore agency leaders altogether; in chapter 3, I discuss the reform efforts of Commissioner General Daniel MacCormack and in chapter 6, I focus heavily on the institutional and political changes wrought by Commissioner General Joseph Swing.
31. For a comprehensive history of the role of mezzo-level managers in policy formation, see Carpenter, *The Forging of Bureaucratic Autonomy*, 18–22.
32. White, "*It's Your Misfortune and None of My Own*," 58.
33. These agencies included the Bureau of Indian Affairs, the Bureau of Land Management, the National Forest Service, the National Park Service, and the Bureau of Reclamation, among many others.
34. Carpenter, *The Forging of Bureaucratic Autonomy*.
35. On this point, this study reinforces the findings of various scholars regarding the ongoing role of local and global forces in immigration policy formation. A few representative studies from the fields of borderlands and immigration history include Benton-Cohen, *Borderline Americans*; Truett, *Fugitive Landscapes*; St. John, "Line in the Sand"; Cadava, *Standing on Common Ground*; Geiger, "Caught in the Gap"; Delgado, *Making the Chinese Mexican*; Camacho, *Chinese Mexicans*; Lytle-Hernández, *Migra!*; Lim, "Chinos and Paisanos"; Sánchez, *Becoming Mexican American*; Lee, *At America's Gates*; Calavita, *Inside the State*.

    Legal and political scholars have produced an extensive body of work regarding the role of local forces in shaping the nation's first federal immigration restriction policies in the late nineteenth century; see, for example, Sandmeyer, *The Anti-Chinese Movement in California*; Saxton, *The Indispensable Enemy*; Hirota, "The Moment of Transition"; FitzGerald and Cook-Martín, *Culling the Masses*. Others have traced the contributions of interest groups in immigration policy formation, including southwestern agribusiness and Latino political organizations. See Scruggs, "The First Mexican Farm Labor Program"; Reisler, *By the Sweat of Their Brow*; Craig, *The Bracero Program*; Tichenor, *Dividing Lines*; Gutiérrez, *Walls and Mirrors*. For an account of state alienage laws, both historical and contemporary, and the ways in which they impacted federal immigration policy, see McClain, *In Search of Equality*; Daniels, *The Politics of Prejudice*; Bosniak, "Membership, Equality, and the Difference that Alienage Makes."

By the late twentieth century, legal scholars explored the possibilities of devolving the federal immigration power to the states. Scholarly interest in the subject emerged from widespread discontent among the states regarding the perceived weaknesses of federal immigration law enforcement. (Arizona, California, Florida, New Jersey, and Texas expressed their dissatisfaction by suing the federal government to recoup the costs they incurred in providing services to undocumented immigrants. Meanwhile, California voters took additional steps by passing Proposition 187, a ballot initiative that denied public services to undocumented immigrants.) Spiro, "The States and Immigration in an Era of Demi-Sovereignties"; Schuck, "Removing Criminal Aliens"; Agrawal, "Trusts Betrayed"; Elsberger, "Florida's Battle With the Federal Government Over Immigration Policy Holds Children Hostage"; Note, "Unenforced Boundaries."

Recent events, as well as the legal and historical scholarship, underscore the ongoing role of local forces in immigration policy formation. In the first decade of the new millennium, states, once again, expressed their frustration with the perceived failures of federal immigration law enforcement. In 2005, a Vermont sheriff made use of the state trespass law to arrest an undocumented immigrant, and a group in Arizona assembled a vigilante force over the Internet to deter illicit crossings along the US–Mexico border. The Federation for American Immigration Reform (FAIR), backers of California's Proposition 187, launched another successful initiative movement in Arizona to bar out-of-status immigrants from the receipt of public benefits. Similar proposals, along with a recommendation for the creation of a state-led border patrol, were made in California in 2005. Most recently the state of Arizona, in 2010, passed SB1070, Support our Law Enforcement and Safe Neighborhoods Act, which in part authorized state law enforcement officials to apprehend suspected undocumented immigrants and created criminal penalties for those immigrants who failed to carry their immigration papers. Copycat laws were passed in South Carolina, Pennsylvania, Minnesota, Rhode Island, Michigan, and Illinois. For press coverage of these events, see "'Minutemen' End Unofficial Border Patrol but Plan to Return," 36; Jacoby, "A Line Has Been Drawn in the Arizona Sand," B3; Lawrence, "Curbs on Illegal Immigration Fail," 6; Archibold, "Arizona Enacts Stringent Law on Immigration"; National Conference of State Legislatures, "Arizona's Immigration Enforcement Laws," July 28, 2011.

36. For accounts of state-building that emphasize the role of political institutions, social science experts, and order, see Wiebe, *The Search for Order*; Horwitz, *The Transformation of American Law, 1870–1960*; Skocpol, "Bringing the State Back In"; Skowronek, *Building a New American State*; Orren and Skowronek, *The Search for American Political Development*. For less linear accounts of state development that highlight the contributions of the private and public sector, social and political actors, as well as localities, states, and the federal government, see Clemens, "Lineages of the Rube Goldberg State"; Hawley, *The New Deal and the Problem of Monopoly*; Balogh, *A Government Out of Sight*; Novak, *The People's Welfare*.

37. In making this claim this book draws upon the work of historian Peter Sahlins, who defines border zones as areas that "consist in the distinct jurisdictions that each state establishes near the boundary for the purposes of its internal administration—thus a military zone, a customs zone, and so forth." Sahlins, *Boundaries*, 5.

38. For historical overviews of the border, see Weber, "Turner, the Boltonians, and the Borderlands"; Truett and Young, "Making Transnational History"; Johnson and Graybill, "Introduction: Borders and Their Historians in North America"; St. John, *Line in the Sand*; Klein, "Reclaiming the 'F' Word, or Being and Becoming Postwestern"; Adelman and Aron, "From Borderlands to Borders."

39. Because the National Archives required Freedom of Information Act (FOIA) requests to be submitted for post-1954 files and because the agency was (and is) still in the process of indexing these post-1954 documents, I chose to end this project in 1954.

Chapter 1

1. George J. Harris, Acting Supervising Inspector, El Paso to Commissioner General, November 28, 1917, file 54152/1E, RG 85, National Archives. Earlier versions of this chapter appeared

in "Crossing the Line: The INS and the Federal Regulation of the Mexican Border," in *Bridging National Borders in North America*, edited by Andrew Graybill and Benjamin Heber Johnson, and "Implementation: How the Borderlands Redefined Federal Immigration Law and Policy in California, Arizona, and Texas, 1917–1924," *California Legal History: Journal of the California Supreme Court Historical Society*.

2. Calleros, interview.
3. Immigration Act of February 5, 1917, 39 Stat. 874; Entry and Departures Control Act, 40 Stat. 559 (1918) (hereinafter referred to as the Passport Act of 1918 or the Act of May 22, 1918).
4. George J. Harris, Acting Supervising Inspector, El Paso to Commissioner General, November 28, 1917, file 54152/1E, RG 85, National Archives. See also Calleros, interview.
5. Reisler, *By the Sweat of Their Brow*.
6. García, *Desert Immigrants*, 1.
7. García, *Desert Immigrants*, 3.
8. García, *Desert Immigrants*, 3.
9. The Chinese Exclusion Act of 1882 suspended the immigration of Chinese laborers for ten years. An 1884 amendment required all Chinese nonlaborers to present certificates from the Chinese government and endorsed by the American consul in order to re-enter the country. The Scott Act of 1888 prohibited the return of a laborer once he had left the United States. The Geary Act of 1892 extended the original exclusion act for another ten years, required Chinese immigrants to apply for a certificate of residence, and created the first internal passport system. Finally, the 1904 amendment to the Chinese Exclusion Act permanently barred the admission of Chinese laborers. See Salyer, *Laws Harsh as Tigers*; McClain, *In Search of Equality*; Wunder, "The Chinese and the Courts in the Pacific Northwest"; Saxton, *The Indispensable Enemy*. On the turn to Mexican immigrant labor after the passage of the Chinese exclusion acts, see García, *Desert Immigrants*, 2, 33.
10. Ettinger, *Imaginary Lines*, 123–144.
11. Prior to 1917, the Bureau of Immigration focused its enforcement efforts on the Chinese. For an account of Immigration Service operations on the US–Mexico border in the early twentieth century, see Smith, "Early Immigrant Inspection along the US–Mexican Border," 2; Ettinger, *Imaginary Lines*. But see Delgado, *Making the Chinese Mexican*, 82–84, for a discussion of the contingencies in the enforcement of the Chinese exclusion laws.
12. The Immigration Acts of 1903 and 1907 respectively charged a head tax of $2.00 and $4.00. Cardoso, *Mexican Emigration to the United States*, 34; Lorey, *The U.S.–Mexican Border in the Twentieth Century*, 69–71.
13. Cardoso, *Mexican Emigration to the United States*, 34.
14. Johnson, *Revolution in Texas*, 71–72.
15. Sánchez, *Becoming Mexican American*, 51–53. See also Barrera, *Race and Class in the Southwest*, 71–72.
16. This massive migration was one of the most important events on the US–Mexico border in the early twentieth century. Hall and Coerver, *Revolution on the Border*, 126. Lorey estimates that between 1910 and 1930, "almost 10 percent of Mexico's population migrated north to the United States." Lorey, *The U.S.–Mexico Border*, 69. On the causes of the migration, see García, *Desert Immigrants*, 33; Acuña, *Occupied America*, 145; Barrera, *Race and Class in the Southwest*, 68–69. This settlement resulted in a dramatic increase in the Mexican-born population from 110,393 in 1900 to 700,541 in 1920. Cardoso, *Mexican Emigration to the United States*, 35; García, *Desert Immigrants*, 35.
17. Indeed, Hall and Coerver assert that those entering for permanent residence "formed by far the smallest category of migrants." Hall and Coerver, *Revolution on the Border*, 130. See also García, *Desert Immigrants*, 35. Lorey estimates that from 1910 to 1920, 206,000 Mexican nationals entered as legal immigrants while 628,000 arrived as temporary workers. Lorey, *The U.S.–Mexico Border*, 70.
18. For more information about Chinese and Japanese border crossers and border residents, see the following: Estes, "Before the War"; Benton-Cohen, *Borderline Americans*; Romero, *The Chinese in Mexico, 1882–1940*; Camacho, *Chinese Mexicans*; Delgado, *Making the Chinese*

Mexican; Walz, "The Issei Community in Maricopa County"; Fong, "Sojourners and Settlers"; Du-Hart, "Immigrants to a Developing Society."

19. Along the Arizona–Sonora border, for example, the major industries—mining, ranching, and agriculture—emerged in a binational fashion. American capital funded the construction of mining facilities on both sides of the line, irrigation projects in Mexico that supported farms in the United States, and ranching ventures that participated in transnational grazing arrangements. In Tijuana, American entrepreneurs and Mexican politicians worked together to develop the town's entertainment industry, constructing gambling halls, race tracks, theaters, and spas. Hall and Coerver, *Revolution on the Border,* 29, 41; St. John, *Line in the Sand,* 148–173; Truett, "Transnational Warrior," 249; Vanderwood, *Juan Soldado,* 83, 87; Vanderwood, *Satan's Playground.*

20. Hall and Coerver, *Revolution on the Border,* 93–101; García, *Desert Immigrants,* 5; Sheridan, *Los Tucsonenses,* 6.

21. Ralph J. Totten, Consul General at Large, El Paso, Texas, "Report on Conditions on the Mexican Border," January 20, 1918, file 54152/11, RG 85, National Archives, 15. See also Bureau of Immigration, *Annual Report, Fiscal Year Ended June 30, 1918,* 317–319.

22. Romo notes that over forty Spanish-language newspapers were published in El Paso between 1890 and 1924. Romo, *Ringside Seat to a Revolution,* 18–20.

23. For an account of these mercantile establishments see Romo, *Ringside Seat to a Revolution,* 198–200. See also Delgado, *Making the Chinese Mexican;* Walz, "The Issei Community in Maricopa County"; Fong, "Sojourners and Settlers"; Du-Hart, "Immigrants to a Developing Society"; Delgado, "In the Age of Exclusion"; Estes, "Before the War"; Romero, *The Chinese in Mexico.* For an account of Japanese-owned farms in the outskirts of El Paso and San Diego County, see Estes, "Before the War"; Romo, *Ringside Seat to a Revolution,* 201–202. See also Bureau of Immigration, *Annual Report, Fiscal Year Ended June 30, 1917,* 230; and Bureau of Immigration, *Annual Report, Fiscal Year Ended June 30, 1919,* 408 (explaining that in Southern California, American-born children of Japanese nationals typically held title to the land as a result of California's alien land laws). On Chinese businesses established in Mexico, see Camacho, *Chinese Mexicans,* 23–25; A. E. Burnett, Inspector in Charge to Supervising Inspector, El Paso, April 8, 1920, file 54820/455, RG 85, National Archives.

24. On the history of Chinese immigrants in Mexico, see Romero, *The Chinese in Mexico;* Delgado, *Making the Chinese Mexican;* and Camacho, *Chinese Mexicans.*

25. Romero, *The Chinese in Mexico,* 30–65, 97–145. On Anglo, Chinese, and Mexican economic and social relations in the Arizona–Sonora borderlands see, Delgado, *Making the Chinese Mexican,* 41–72.

26. Merchants were exempted from the exclusionary provisions applied to Japanese (the Gentleman's Agreement of 1907) and Chinese (the Chinese Exclusion Act of 1882) immigrants. The McCreary Amendment of 1893, however, placed strict evidentiary requirements upon Chinese merchants re-entering the United States. On Japanese exclusion, see Daniels, *The Politics of Prejudice.* On Chinese exclusion and the McCreary Amendment, see Salyer, *Laws Harsh as Tigers.* Delgado notes that Chinese Mexican merchants could use their citizenship status as well as their merchant status to gain entry into the United States. See Delgado, *Making the Chinese Mexican,* 26–32; and Camacho, *Chinese Mexicans,* 10–11.

27. Romo, *Ringside Seat to a Revolution,* 145. Prior to the passage of the Volstead Act in 1919, local and state dry laws as well as wartime limits on the manufacture and sale of alcohol also attracted Americans to Mexican border towns. St. John, *Line in the Sand,* 151.

28. The growth of the tourist industry in Tijuana was due, in part, to the dry and mountainous landscape, which rendered it inhospitable to the development of the mining and agriculture industries. Alvarez, *Familia,* 32. See also Vanderwood, *Satan's Playground.*

29. Vanderwood, *Juan Soldado,* 76–81.

30. Vanderwood, *Juan Soldado,* 105.

31. Vanderwood, *Juan Soldado,* 113.

32. Calexico Chamber of Commerce, "Regulations at Crossing of International Boundary at the Port of Calexico, California," n.d., file 54410/331G, RG 85, National Archives.

33. García, *Desert Immigrants*, 7. For a discussion of the raiding activities of Mexican revolution-aries on mines and oil fields in Mexico and the United States, see Hall and Coerver, *Revolution on the Border*.

34. In 1913 Victoriano Huerta, chief of staff to President Francisco Madero, assumed office in a military coup and ordered Madero's assassination. His military dictatorship galvanized revolutionary forces against him and he fled the country a year later. Huerta's resignation, however, did not bring peace to Mexico as revolutionary forces splintered into rival factions, battling each other for control of the state well after revolutionary leader Venustiano Carranza assumed the presidency in 1917. St. John, *Line in the Sand*, 200.

35. Many of these raids were conducted as a part of the Plan de San Diego. Drafted in South Texas in 1915, the plan called for the execution of Anglo-American men; defended the concerns of racial minorities, including African Americans, Mexicans, and Native peoples; and called for the overthrow of the United States in the Southwest. Its implementation led to violent repri-sals by Texas civilians and the Texas Rangers. Johnson, *Revolution in Texas*; St. John, *Line in the Sand*, 200, 206, 216.

36. Retaliating against Wilson's withdrawal of support for a Villa-led government in Mexico, Pancho Villa and his troops killed sixteen Americans traveling on a train in northern Mexico in January 1916. Several months later, they crossed the border into New Mexico and killed another seventeen Americans. Johnson, *Revolution in Texas*, 138–142. On the complex rela-tionship between the *Villistas* and the borderlands, see St. John, *Line in the Sand*, 211–217; Romo, *Ringside Seat to a Revolution*.

37. Briggs, "For the Welfare of Wage Earners," 164; St. John, *Line in the Sand*, 231; Totten, "Report on Conditions on the Mexican Border."

38. Capitalizing on anti-American sentiments in the aftermath of Pershing's expedition, the German foreign minister, Arthur Zimmerman, proposed an alliance that, in the event of a German victory, promised the restoration of Texas and much of the Southwest to Mexico. Along with Germany's declaration of unrestricted submarine warfare, the telegram fueled anti-German sentiment, garnered popular support for the war, and led President Wilson to abandon neutrality for war.

39. García, *Desert Immigrants*, 7.

40. Romo, *Ringside Seat to a Revolution*, 7.

41. For a recent account of the refugee crisis, see Lim, "Immigration, Asylum, and Citizenship."

42. Romo, *Ringside Seat to a Revolution*, 233.

43. During this inspection, city officials found two cases of typhus, and one incidence each of measles, rheumatism, tuberculosis, and chicken pox. Those found ill were forced to take vin-egar and kerosene baths, shave their heads, and burn all of their clothing. Romo, *Ringside Seat to a Revolution*, 231, 234, 235.

44. Romo, *Ringside Seat to a Revolution*, 243.

45. Metz, *Border*, 233.

46. As an omnibus bill, the Immigration Act of 1917 became the foundation of American immi-gration law for the next thirty-five years. While the Immigration Acts of 1921 and 1924 added pivotal features to this nation's immigration laws, the Immigration Act of 1917 continued to serve as the basic outline or organizational structure. Fitzgerald, *The Face of the Nation*, 129, 132.

47. For a history of the literacy test see Higham, *Strangers in the Land, Patterns of American Nativism, 1860–1925*.

48. Higham, *Strangers in the Land*, 190–193; Divine, *American Immigration Policy, 1942–1952*, 5.

49. Briggs, "For the Welfare of Wage Earners," 164.

50. Preston, *Aliens and Dissenters*; Briggs, "For the Welfare of Wage Earners," 164; Divine, *American Immigration Policy*, 8.

51. Under the Immigration Act of 1917, Congress decided not to waive the head tax (increased to $8.00) and the new literacy test for Mexican immigrants as it had in the Immigration Acts of 1903 and 1907. Cardoso, *Mexican Emigration to the United States*, 46.

52. US Congress, House, Committee on Foreign Affairs, *Control of Travel From and Into the United States*, 65th Cong., 2d sess., February 13, 1918, 4–5.

53. Entry and Departures Control Act, 40 Stat. 559 (1918); Executive Order 2932, August 18, 1918 (implementing Act of May 22, 1918). Violators of the Passport Act were subject to criminal penalties, including a maximum fine of $10,000 and a prison sentence of twenty years.

54. For a history of the passport, see Torpey, *The Invention of the Passport*; Robertson, *The Passport in America.*

55. Kang, "The Legal Construction of the Borderlands," 31–41.

56. Cardoso, *Mexican Emigration to the United States,* 46.

57. Cardoso, *Mexican Emigration to the United States,* 46.

58. Reisler, *By the Sweat of Their Brow,* 24.

59. "Report of Supervising Inspector, Mexican Border District," in Bureau of Immigration, *Annual Report, Fiscal Year Ended June 30, 1918,* 317–319.

60. On the supporters and opponents of immigration restriction in the Southwest, see Montejano, *Anglos and Mexicans in the Making of Texas,* 182–186.

61. Totten, "Report on Conditions on the Mexican Border," 17.

62. See, for example, Blocker, American Consul, Eagle Pass to Secretary of State, December 6, 1917, file 54152/1E, RG 85, National Archives; Unsigned Memorandum, January 2, 1918, file 54152/1F, RG 85, National Archives. See also Ruiz, *From Out of the Shadows,* 12.

63. Alvey A. Adee, Second Assistant Secretary of State to Anthony Caminetti, Commissioner General, April 11, 1918, file 54152/1J, RG 85, National Archives (on the American border crossers); Alvey A. Adee, Second Assistant Secretary of State to Anthony Caminetti, Commissioner General, January 24, 1918, file 54152/1G, RG 85, National Archives (regarding Japanese merchants living on Mexican side of border wishing to cross border to purchase goods); F. W. Berkshire, Supervising Inspector, El Paso to Chief, Division of Passport Control, September 9, 1918, file 54410/331B, RG 85, National Archives; A. E. Burnett, Inspector in Charge to Supervising Inspector, El Paso, April 8, 1920, file 54820/455, RG 85, National Archives (Chinese, with American support, seeking crossing privileges between Calexico and Mexicali).

64. Grover C. Wilmoth, Acting in Charge of District, Mexican Border District to Commissioner General, March 31, 1923, file 55301/217, RG 85, National Archives.

65. Telegram to Frank L. Polk, received December 10, 1917, file 54152/1E, RG 85, National Archives. On the history of the Tijuana vice and entertainment industries, see St. John, "Selling the Border," 113–142.

66. Prohibitionists opposed any relaxation of passport regulations for those desirous of crossing the border into Mexico, which they called "a moral plague spot menacing soldiers and civilians alike." Charles C. Selegman, President, Los Angeles Ministerial Alliance to Robert Lansing, Secretary of State, November 23, 1917, file 54152/1E, RG 85, National Archives; W. B. Wheeler, General Counsel, Anti-Saloon League of America to Raymond Fosdick, War Department, April 4, 1918, file 54152/1J, RG 85, National Archives; T. A. Storey, Executive Secretary, Interdepartmental Social Hygiene Board to Bureau of Immigration, March 6, 1920, file 54410/331F, RG 85, National Archives. For an account of how Prohibition impacted border closing times in three different border communities, see Buffington, "Prohibition in the Borderlands," 19–39.

67. C. K. Clarke, General Manager, Imperial Irrigation District to Senator Hiram Johnson, November 19, 1917, file 54152/1E, RG 85, National Archives.

68. Grosvenor Calkins, for Duquesne Mining and Reduction Company to Louis F. Post, Assistant Secretary of Labor, January 17, 1918, file 54152/1G, RG 85, National Archives.

69. F. W. Berkshire, Supervising Inspector, El Paso to Commissioner General, January 1, 1918, file 54152/1F, RG 85, National Archives.

70. George J. Harris, Acting Supervising Inspector, El Paso to Commissioner General, January 10, 1918, file 54152/1G, RG 85, National Archives; Dr. J. A. Wallace to Department of State, Bureau of Citizenship, January 10, 1918, file 54152/1G, RG 85, National Archives.

71. Totten, "Report on Conditions on the Mexican Border," 17.

72. Anthony Caminetti, Commissioner General to Supervising Inspector, Mexican Border District, August 31, 1918, file 54410/331A, RG 85, National Archives.

73. Bureau of Immigration, *Annual Report, Fiscal Year Ended June 30, 1919.*

74. W. W. Husband, Commissioner General, Memorandum for the Second Assistant Secretary, May 17, 1923, file 54275/Gen., Pt. 1, RG 85, National Archives (citing Act of February 5, 1917, ch. 29, § 3, 39 Stat. 874, 876 [1917]).

75. Reisler, *By the Sweat of Their Brow*, 29.

76. Reisler, *By the Sweat of Their Brow*, 30.

77. Under the Selective Service Act of May 18, 1917, foreigners were exempted from the wartime draft. In order to prove their alien status, however, they were required to present proof of foreign citizenship (by means of a birth certificate or the affidavits of two reliable witnesses as to place of birth) to the local draft boards. Uninformed, unable, or unwilling to meet these requirements, thousands of Mexicans repatriated to Mexico. In the Southwest, many of the repatriations were motivated by fear and a deep distrust of the American government given the recent vigilante action undertaken by Anglo-Americans against Mexicans and Mexican Americans in retaliation for the raids of Mexican revolutionaries. Local and state draft board officials only aggravated this distrust by compelling ethnic Mexicans, regardless of their citizenship status, to register for the draft. Johnson, *Revolution in Texas*, 150–153; Cardoso, *Mexican Emigration to the United States*, 50–51.

78. Reisler, *By the Sweat of Their Brow*, 30.

79. Reisler, *By the Sweat of Their Brow*, 33.

80. Reisler, *By the Sweat of Their Brow*, 34.

81. Reisler, *By the Sweat of Their Brow*, 39.

82. Reisler, *By the Sweat of Their Brow*, 40

83. Reisler, *By the Sweat of Their Brow*, 40.

84. George J. Harris to Commissioner General of Immigration, May 24, 1923, file 54275/Gen., Pt. I, RG 85, National Archives.

85. F. W. Berkshire, Supervising Inspector to Commissioner General of Immigration, March 9, 1917, file 54275/Gen., Pt. 1, RG 85, National Archives.

86. W. W. Husband, Commissioner General, "Memorandum for the Second Assistant Secretary," May 17, 1923, file 54275/Gen., Pt. I, RG 85, National Archives (discussing 1917 agency debates regarding use of Ninth Proviso to create an exemption to the literacy test).

87. On May 7, 1917, Washington, DC officials authorized this procedure in the following telegram: "Habitual crossing and recrossing boundary by illiterate aliens residing in United States is permitted by paragraph f, subdivision five, rule four, regarding transit of resident illiterates through contiguous foreign territory but illiterates residing outside the United States cannot be permitted habitual crossing privilege." George J. Harris to Commissioner General of Immigration, May 24, 1923, file 54275/Gen., Pt. I, RG 85, National Archives.

88. A. E. Burnett, Inspector in Charge, Los Angeles to Commissioner General of Immigration, May 28, 1923, file 54275/Gen., Pt. I, RG 85, National Archives.

89. George J. Harris, Supervisor to Commissioner General, May 24, 1923, file 54275/Gen., Pt. II, RG 85, National Archives.

90. United States Department of Labor, Bureau of Immigration, *Immigration Laws, Rules of May 1, 1917*, Rule 4, Subdivision 6 (Washington, DC: US Government Printing Office, 1917), 51. Boards of Special Inquiry provided immigrants with the opportunity to appeal the exclusion decisions of immigration inspectors. While they served as a kind of court of first resort, the Board was not bound by judicial procedures. See Salyer, *Laws Harsh as Tigers*, 141.

91. "Report of Supervising Inspector, District No. 23," in Bureau of Immigration, *Annual Report, Fiscal Year Ended June 30, 1920*, 446. See also Bureau of Immigration file regarding the Board of Special Inquiry hearing for Jesus Reyes, a Mexican citizen who failed the reading test but sought temporary admission for business purposes in 1922, file 55238/12, RG 85, National Archives.

92. "Recommendations and Suggestions for the Betterment of the Service and for Remedial Legislation," in Bureau of Immigration, *Annual Report, Fiscal Year Ended June 30, 1920*, 450. See also J. E. Trout, Inspector in Charge, Laredo, Texas to Supervising Inspector, El Paso, February 12, 1919, file 54410/331D, RG 85, National Archives.

93. W. W. Husband, Commissioner General, Memorandum for the Second Assistant Secretary, May 17, 1923, file 54275/Gen., Pt. I, RG 85, National Archives.

94. W. W. Husband, Commissioner General, Memorandum for the Second Assistant Secretary, May 17, 1923, file 54275/Gen., Pt. I, RG 85, National Archives.

95. As the US Commissioner of Immigration, Montreal, Canada wrote, "When the reading test became effective in 1917, it served to debar large numbers of aliens who patronized the above [railway] lines. Many of those excluded on account of the reading test were shown to be substantial citizens of Canada, who were only desirous of visiting the United States as bona fide temporary visitors. . . . This situation was gone over with former Secretary W. B. Wilson in person, and while declining to modify the Regulations as then drawn, he nevertheless, gave me authority to admit temporarily, in my own discretion, illiterates whose exclusion could be shown to involve the serious hardships referred to above." US Commissioner of Immigration, Montreal, Canada to W. W. Husband, Commissioner General of Immigration, April 2, 1923, file 54275/Gen., Pt. I, RG 85, National Archives; W. W. Husband, Commissioner General, Memorandum for the Second Assistant Secretary, May 17, 1923, file 54275/Gen., Pt. I, RG 85, National Archives.

96. W. W. Husband, Commissioner General to US Commissioners of Immigration, Montreal, Canada and Seattle, Washington; Inspectors in Charge, Immigration Service, Buffalo, N.Y., Detroit, Mich., Winnipeg, Can., Spokane, Wash., Los Angeles, California, and San Antonio, Texas; Supervisor, Immigration Service, El Paso, Texas, June 30, 1923, file 54275/Gen., Pt. I, RG 85, National Archives.

97. "Recommendations and Suggestions for the Betterment of the Service and for Remedial Legislation," in Bureau of Immigration, *Annual Report, Fiscal Year Ended June 30, 1920*, 450.

98. For an account of these interagency disputes see Kang, "The Legal Construction of the Borderlands," 44–45.

99. Confidential Instructions for the Guidance of Officials Connected with the Administration of the Act of May 22, 1918, July 1918, file 54410/331, RG 85, National Archives.

100. Confidential Instructions for the Guidance of Officials Connected with the Administration of the Act of May 22, 1918, July 1918, file 54410/331, RG 85, National Archives.

101. Gerard D. Reilly, Acting Solicitor of Labor, Memorandum for the Acting Commissioner of Immigration and Naturalization, April 15, 1937, file 55883/600, RG 85, National Archives. Holders of Section 13 certificates were exempted from the head tax because the bureau realized that it would be unreasonable for them to pay the tax upon each entry.

102. These cards were also in use on the Canadian border, see Kang, "Crossing the Line," 181.

103. Totten, "Report on Conditions on the Mexican Border," 15.

104. R. W. Flournoy, Acting Chief, Bureau of Citizenship, Department of State to A. W. Parker, Law Clerk, Immigration and Naturalization Service, November 30, 1917, file 54152/1E, RG 85, National Archives.

105. A. Warner Parker, Law Officer, Department of State to Supervising Inspector, El Paso, December 6, 1917, file 54152/1E, RG 85, National Archives.

106. J. E. Trout, Inspector in Charge, Laredo to Supervising Inspector, El Paso District, November 23, 1917, file 54152/1E, RG 85, National Archives.

107. George J. Harris, Acting Supervising Inspector, El Paso to Commissioner General, November 27, 1917, file 54152/1E, RG 85, National Archives.

108. F. W. Berkshire, Supervising Inspector, Mexican Border District to Chief, Division of Passport Control, State Department, September 22, 1920, file 54410/331H, RG 85, National Archives.

109. F. W. Berkshire to Secretary of State, November 6, 1919, file 54410/331F, RG 85, National Archives.

110. A. J. Milliken, Inspector in Charge, Nogales, Arizona to Supervising Inspector, El Paso, January 3, 1918, file 54152/1F, RG 85, National Archives.

111. R. M. Cousar, Inspector in Charge, Nogales, AZ to Supervising Inspector, Mexican Border District, October 5, 1920, file 54410/331I, RG 85, National Archives.

112. For an account of the disparate procedures applied to Chinese national, Chinese American, and Chinese Mexican merchants residing in the United States and in Mexico see, F. W. Berkshire to Inspector in Charge, May 16, 1922, file 51941/10A, RG 85, National Archives, in *Records of the Immigration and Naturalization Service, Series A: Subject Correspondence Files, Part 2: Mexican Immigration, 1906–1930*, ed. Alan Kraut, text-fiche, reel 1, frame 947–949.

113. Because it was easier for bureau officials to conduct extensive background examinations of merchants residing in the United States, Chinese American and Chinese national merchants residing in the United States faced more stringent inspections than Chinese American, Chinese Mexican, and Chinese national merchants residing in Mexico. F. W. Berkshire to Inspector in Charge, May 16, 1922, file 51941/10A, RG 85, National Archives, in *Records of the Immigration and Naturalization Service*, text-fiche, reel 1, frame 947–949.

114. F. W. Berkshire, Supervising Inspector, El Paso to Chief, Division of Passport Control, September 9, 1918, file 54410/331B, RG 85, National Archives.

115. Robert Hamilton, Secretary, Bisbee Chamber of Commerce to Henry Ashurst, June 24, 1925, file 55301/217, RG 85, National Archives, in *Records of the Immigration and Naturalization Service*, text-fiche, reel 1, frame 925.

116. Letter and petition from the Nogales Chamber of Commerce to the Secretary of Labor, March 3, 1922, file 51941/10A, RG 85, National Archives, in *Records of the Immigration and Naturalization Service*, text-fiche, reel 1, frame 976–983; El Paso Chamber of Commerce to the Secretary of Labor, December 5, 1921, file 51941/10A, RG 85, National Archives, in *Records of the Immigration and Naturalization Service*, text-fiche, reel 1, frame 1024; Los Angeles Chamber of Commerce to the Secretary of Labor, May 12, 1922, file 51941/10-13, RG 85, National Archives, in *Records of the Immigration and Naturalization Service*, text-fiche, reel 2, frame 216–218.

117. Robe Carl White, Second Assistant Secretary, Department of Labor to Carl Hayden, April 29, 1924, file 51941/10A, RG 85, National Archives, in *Records of the Immigration and Naturalization Service*, text-fiche, reel 1, frame 1025–1026.

118. See, for example, Robert Hamilton, Secretary, Bisbee Chamber of Commerce to Henry Ashurst, June 24, 1925, file 55301/217, RG 85, National Archives, in *Records of the Immigration and Naturalization Service*, text-fiche, reel 1, frame 925.

119. Commissioner General, Memorandum for the Secretary, June 22, 1920, file 54820/727, RG 85, National Archives.

120. It appears, however, that Chinese Mexican merchants were able to obtain either a Section 6 or a Section 13 certificate. Some bureau officials raised questions about the disparity between the border crossing privileges granted to Chinese Mexican and Chinese American merchants. F. W. Berkshire, Supervising Inspector, Mexican Border District to Inspector in Charge, Los Angeles, California, June 1, 1922, file 51941/10-13, RG 85, National Archives, in *Records of the Immigration and Naturalization Service*, text-fiche, reel 2, frame 211–212.

121. W. G. Becktell, Attorney to Commissioner General of Immigration, San Francisco, May 13, 1920, file 54820/727, RG 85, National Archives (attorney for Sam Poy).

122. Commissioner General, Memorandum for the Secretary, June 22, 1920, file 54820/727, RG 85, National Archives; Memorandum for the Second Assistant Secretary, April 3, 1924, file 51941/10-13, RG 85, National Archives, in *Records of the Immigration and Naturalization Service*, text-fiche, reel 2, frame 27–29.

123. See, for example, Harry L. Blee, Immigrant Inspector to Inspector in Charge, Immigration Service, Los Angeles, April 7, 1920, file 54820/455, RG 85, National Archives (correspondence attaching transcript of examination of Lee Thing).

124. William Kettner, Congressman, Eleventh District, California to Commissioner General, October 22, 1919, file 54410/331F, RG 85, National Archives.

125. H. M. Hubbard, Secretary, Building Trades Council of San Diego to William B. Wilson, Secretary of Labor, October 29, 1919, file 54410/331F, RG 85, National Archives.

126. Juan B. Rojo, Chargé d'Affaires ad interim, Mexican Embassy to Frank L. Polk, Acting Secretary of State, July 1, 1919, file 54261/276A, RG 85, National Archives; Fletcher, Under Secretary of State to Secretary of Labor, October 31, 1921, file 54410/331J, RG 85, National Archives.

127. F. W. Berkshire to Philip Adams, Chief, Division of Passport Control, State Department, September 8, 1920, file 54410/331H, RG 85, National Archives.

128. For an account of the Bureau of Immigration's efforts to enforce the Passport Act, see Kang, "The Legal Construction of the Borderlands," 35–38.

129. Kang, "The Legal Construction of the Borderlands," 45.

130. "Report of Supervising Inspector, Mexican Border District," in Bureau of Immigration, *Annual Report, Fiscal Year Ended June 30, 1918*, 320.

131. Reisler, *By the Sweat of Their Brow*, 38. The bureau, however, doubted the accuracy of these figures. Lacking the force to keep track of agricultural admissions, the bureau relied on the accounting of employers who were believed to be lax in their administration of the farm labor program. Bureau of Immigration, *Annual Report, Fiscal Year Ended June 30, 1920*, 427.

132. Totten, "Report on Conditions on the Mexican Border," 12.

133. George J. Harris, Acting Supervising Inspector, Mexican Border District to Secretary of State, August 6, 1919, file 54410/331F, RG 85, National Archives; George J. Harris, Acting Supervising Inspector to Commissioner General, August 8, 1919, file 54410/331F, RG 85, National Archives.

134. Berkshire to Supervising Inspector, El Paso, October 18, 1920, file 54410/331I, RG 85, National Archives; E. P. Reynolds, Inspector in Charge, Brownsville to Inspector in Charge, Hidalgo, April 25, 1921, file 54410/331J, RG 85, National Archives.

135. F. W. Berkshire, Supervising Inspector, El Paso to Commissioner General, August 9, 1918, file 54152/1L, RG 85, National Archives (describing the confused conditions at Calexico where the Bureau of Immigration, Customs, and the US military all helped to enforce the passport laws).

136. A. A. Musgrave, Inspector in Charge, Calexico to F. W. Berkshire, April 12, 1918, file 54152/1J, RG 85, National Archives.

137. A. A. Musgrave, Inspector in Charge, Calexico to F. W. Berkshire, December 14, 1917, file 54410/331A, RG 85, National Archives; F. W. Berkshire to Supervising Inspector, El Paso, September 10, 1918, file 54152/1F, RG 85, National Archives; George J. Harris to Commissioner General, January 19, 1920, file 54951/5, RG 85, National Archives; Alvey A. Adee, Second Assistant Secretary, Department of State to Anthony Caminetti, Commissioner General, April 6, 1918, file 54152/1I, RG 85, National Archives; R. M. Cousar, Inspector in Charge, Nogales, Arizona to Supervising Inspector, Mexican Border District, October 5, 1920, file 54410/331I, RG 85, National Archives; F. W. Berkshire to Inspector in Charge, El Paso, September 10, 1918, file 54410/331A, RG 85, National Archives.

138. Thomas R. Taylor to D. Bendeen, Foreign Trade Secretary, Chamber of Commerce, El Paso, Texas, February 4, 1927, file 150.126/163, RG 59, National Archives.

139. Letter from R. H. Van Deman, Colonel, General Staff, Chief Military Intelligence Section, War Department to Commissioner General, January 8, 1918, file 54152/1F, RG 85, National Archives (enclosing correspondence from E. McCuley Jr., Commander, US Navy, Assistant Director of Naval Intelligence, December 27, 1917). See also Walter H. Sholes, American Consul, Nuevo Laredo, Mexico to Secretary of State, February 20, 1918, file 54152/1H, RG 85, National Archives; F. W. Berkshire, Supervising Inspector, Mexican Border District to Secretary of State, November 6, 1919, file 54410/331F, RG 85, National Archives.

140. Anthony Caminetti, Commissioner General to the Secretary of Labor, July 9, 1918, file 54261/202B, RG 85, National Archives.

141. Bureau of Immigration, *Annual Report, Fiscal Year Ended June 30, 1920*, 24.

142. George J. Harris, Supervisor to Commissioner General, May 24, 1923, file 54275/Gen., Pt. II, RG 85, National Archives.

143. W. A. Brazie, Inspector in Charge to Inspector in Charge, Los Angeles, January 27, 1920, file 54750/36A, RG 85, National Archives.

144. Bureau of Immigration, *Annual Report, Fiscal Year Ended June 30, 1919*, 24. For an account of the bureau's enforcement efforts against illegal Japanese immigrants, see "Report of Supervising Inspector, District No. 23," in Bureau of Immigration, *Annual Report, Fiscal Year Ended June 30, 1919*, 408–409; "Report of Supervising Inspector, District No. 23," in Bureau of Immigration, *Annual Report, Fiscal Year Ended June 30, 1920*, 440.

145. Department of Labor, Bureau of Immigration, Departmental Order, June 12, 1918, file 54261/202B, RG 85, National Archives (reports need for more manpower to track farmworkers once they have been admitted to the United States); George J. Harris, Assistant Supervising Inspector, Mexican Border District to Commissioner General, August 27, 1918, file 54410/331, RG 85, National Archives (proposes a mobile immigration force

in response to problems created by passport law enforcement); "Report of Supervising Inspector, Mexican Border District," in Bureau of Immigration, *Annual Report, Fiscal Year Ended June 30, 1918*, 319 (general call for border patrol); Bureau of Immigration, *Annual Report, Fiscal Year Ended June 30, 1919*, 26 (call for a "patrol service" in response to illegal Chinese and Japanese immigration); Bureau of Immigration, *Annual Report, Fiscal Year Ended June 30, 1921*, 12 (call for a border patrol to assist in enforcement of the Act of May 19, 1921, popularly known as the Quota Act of 1921).

146. Bureau of Immigration, *Annual Report, Fiscal Year Ended June 30, 1928*, 10.

Chapter 2

1. Harry E. Hull, Commissioner General to I. F. Wixon, Chief Supervisor, Calexico, CA, January 28, 1926, file 55031/81, RG 85, National Archives.
2. J. B. Bristol, Nogales Chamber of Commerce to James J. Davis, Secretary of Labor, Department of Labor, April 19, 1928, file 55637/640, RG 85, National Archives; J. B. Bristol, Nogales Chamber of Commerce to Senator Henry Ashurst, May 7, 1928, file 55637/640, RG 85, National Archives.
3. George W. P. Hunt, Governor, Arizona to James J. Davis, Secretary of Labor, July 23, 1927, file 55301/217, RG 85, National Archives.
4. Harry E. Hull, Commissioner General to I. F. Wixon, Chief Supervisor, Calexico, CA, January 28, 1926, file 55031/81, RG 85, National Archives.
5. Immigration Act of 1924, 43 Stat. 153; Appropriations Act of May 28, 1924, 43 Stat. 240; Act of March 4, 1929, 45 Stat. 1551.
6. National Prohibition Act, 42 Stat. 223 (1919).
7. "The right of the people to be secure in their persons, houses, papers, and effects, against unreasonable searches and seizures, shall not be violated, and no warrants shall issue, but upon probable cause, supported by oath or affirmation, and particularly describing the place to be searched, and the persons or things to be seized." US Constitution, Fourth Amendment.
8. St. John, "Selling the Border," 114–115.
9. St. John, "Selling the Border," 113, 128; Langston, "The Impact of Prohibition on the Mexican–United States Border," 65, 73. For an interesting discussion about how different border towns attracted disparate classes of Americans, see St. John, "Selling the Border," 113.
10. Klein, "The Last Resort," 135.
11. St. John, "Selling the Border," 124–126.
12. St. John, "Selling the Border," 126; Vanderwood, *Juan Soldado*, 105; Martínez, *Border Boom Town*, 59–60.
13. For a detailed account of the economic development of individual border towns, see Martínez, *Border Boom Town*, 63; Kearney and Knopp, *Border Cuates*, 196–197. For an explanation of the broader structural forces, including the economic policies of the Mexican government, that led border towns to rely on the vice trade, see Kearney and Knopp, *Border Cuates*, 197. See also Langston, "The Impact of Prohibition on the Mexican–United States Border," 328.
14. Martínez, *Border Boom Town*, 64.
15. Martínez, *Border Boom Town*, 64.
16. Martínez, *Border Boom Town*, 61, 63; Lorey, *The U.S.-Mexican Border in the Twentieth Century*, 47–48.
17. Lorey, *The U.S.–Mexican Border in the Twentieth Century*, 48; Martínez, *Border Boom Town*, 63.
18. For example, Lorey notes that in the industrial sector, between 1900 and 1940, California experienced a 489 percent increase in industrial employment, Arizona witnessed a 272 percent rise, and Texas reported a 392 percent increase. Lorey, *The U.S.–Mexican Border in the Twentieth Century*, 48; Martínez, *Border Boom Town*, 63.
19. Taxes on liquor production specifically constituted 13 million pesos in 1923; meanwhile federal revenues that year amounted to 250 million pesos. Buffington, "Prohibition in the Borderlands," 25. On state revenues, see St. John, *Line in the Sand*, 159.

20. St. John, "Selling the Border," 133; St. John, *Line in the Sand,* 159; Buffington, "Prohibition in the Borderlands," 26–27.

21. Martínez, *Border Boom Town,* 59; Lorey, *The U.S.–Mexican Border in the Twentieth Century,* 49; St. John, "Selling the Border," 114; Klein, "The Last Resort," 141; Langston, "The Impact of Prohibition on the Mexican–United States Border," 64, 82.

22. Klein, "The Last Resort," 146.

23. St. John, *Line in the Sand,* 169; Klein, "The Last Resort," 146.

24. St. John, *Line in the Sand,* 154–155.

25. St. John, "Selling the Border," 131.

26. St. John, "Selling the Border," 132; Martínez, *Border Boom Town,* 66.

27. For example, by 1926, Americans owned approximately 40 percent of the real estate in Juárez. In Tijuana, fourteen Americans owned most of the town's business establishments. Martínez, *Border Boom Town,* 59–60, 63.

28. St. John, "Selling the Border,"131.

29. St. John, "Selling the Border," 132. Mexico's early closing hours were often created in retaliation against the establishment of analogous policies by American Customs officials. Langston, "The Impact of Prohibition on the Mexican–United States Border," 183.

30. St. John, "Selling the Border," 133.

31. St. John, *Line in the Sand,* 163. For an overview of the difficulties facing the Bureau of Customs in the enforcement of Prohibition, see Prince and Keller, *The U.S. Customs Service,* 195–218.

32. St. John, *Line in the Sand,* 164.

33. For an account of these disparate closing times, see St. John, "Selling the Border," 134; St. John, *Line in the Sand,* 166–167; Buffington, "Prohibition in the Borderlands," 29; Langston, "The Impact of Prohibition on the Mexican–United States Border," 181.

34. St. John, "Selling the Border," 135.

35. St. John, *Line in the Sand,* 165.

36. On the protests against and exemptions to the curfews see St. John, *Line in the Sand,* 159, 171; Martínez, *Border Boom Town,* 65–66; St. John, "Selling the Border," 133; Buffington, "Prohibition in the Borderlands," 26–27; Langston, "The Impact of Prohibition on the Mexican–United States Border," 74, 190, 202, 216; Walter E. Carr, District Director, Los Angeles to Commissioner General, November 19, 1929, file 55630/25, RG 85, National Archives; Harry E. Hull, Commissioner General to Immigration Service, Galveston, Texas, May 14, 1931, file 55630/31A, RG 85, National Archives.

37. St. John, *Line in the Sand,* 165. On Mexico's efforts to attract nonvice tourists, see Middaugh, "Transnational Cultural Market," 139, 193; Klein, "The Last Resort," 60–61, 134–135, 180–181.

38. Lorey, *The U.S.–Mexican Border in the Twentieth Century,* 70–71; Martínez, *Border Boom Town,* 57–77.

39. D. C. Kinne, Inspector in Charge, Douglas, Arizona to District Director, El Paso, April 22, 1925, file 55466/51, RG 85, National Archives.

40. Harry E. Hull, Commissioner General to I. F. Wixon, Chief Supervisor, Calexico, CA, January 28, 1926, file 55031/81, RG 85, National Archives.

41. Grover C. Wilmoth, Memorandum to All Immigration Officers and Employees, Nogales, AZ, May 19, 1928, file 55637/640, RG 85, National Archives.

42. J. B. Bristol, Nogales Chamber of Commerce to James J. Davis, Secretary of Labor, Department of Labor, April 19, 1928, file 55637/640, RG 85, National Archives.

43. George J. Harris, Assistant Commissioner General to District Director, El Paso, June 7, 1928, file 55637/640, RG 85, National Archives.

44. See, for example, "New Immigration Building Sought," *Nogales Herald,* September 23, 1930, file 55598/459, RG 85, National Archives.

45. Walter E. Carr, District Director, Los Angeles to Commissioner General, March 5, 1929, file 55605/911, RG 85, National Archives.

46. William A. Whalen, District Director, San Antonio to Commissioner General, March 22, 1930, file 55630/28, RG 85, National Archives.

47. In Ysleta, the limited port of entry appeared to have opened in 1929. In Fort Hancock, the port opened in 1930. G. C. Wilmoth, District Director, El Paso to Commissioner General,

July 9, 1930, file 55630/25, RG 85, National Archives; G. C. Wilmoth, District Director, El Paso to Commissioner General, July 9, 1932, file 55630/25, RG 85, National Archives.

48. A downtown gate, business leaders vehemently argued, would protect their business interests and real estate values. A gate built to the east of the city, in contrast, would benefit Mexicali, a town south of the border, which was expanding eastward at the time. Randall Henderson, Secretary and Leo S. Watts, Secretary, Calexico Chamber of Commerce to Secretaries of Treasury and Labor, February 12, 1929, file 55639/777, RG 85, National Archives.

49. Grover C. Wilmoth, District Director to Commissioner General, May 31, 1928, file 55610/160, RG 85, National Archives.

50. Grover C. Wilmoth, District Director, El Paso to Inspector in Charge, Tucson, Arizona, January 14, 1927, file 55597/927, RG 85, National Archives.

51. Grover C. Wilmoth, District Director, El Paso to Commissioner General, May 23, 1928, file 55610/160, RG 85, National Archives; Harry E. Hull, Commissioner General to Congressman Claude Hudspeth of Texas, June 20, 1928, file 55610/160, RG 85, National Archives.

52. William A. Whalen, District Director, San Antonio to Commissioner General, March 22, 1930, file 55630/28, RG 85, National Archives.

53. On the anti-Chinese movement in Mexico, see Delgado, *Making the Chinese Mexican*, 104-129; Camacho, *Chinese Mexicans*, 38–83.

54. J. B. Bristol, Nogales Chamber of Commerce to James J. Davis, Secretary of Labor, Department of Labor, April 19, 1928, file 55637/640, RG 85, National Archives.

55. J. B. Bristol, Secretary, Nogales Chamber of Commerce to Congressman Carl Hayden of Arizona, March 14, 1928, file 54933/351E, RG 85, National Archives. For a history of the relationship between INS and state welfare officials, see Fox, *Three Worlds of Welfare Relief*.

56. R. M. Cousar, Inspector in Charge, Nogales, Arizona to District Director, El Paso, May 25, 1928, file 55637/640, RG 85, National Archives.

57. This was particularly the case because immigration inspectors, since World War I, had found that their management of the border crossing population drew their focus and resources away from their enforcement mandate. H. C. von Struve, Consul, Mexicali, Mexico, Department of State to the Secretary of State, April 4, 1925, file 55466/51, RG 85, National Archives.

58. But cognizant of the agency's weak inspection procedures, deported immigrants, this official continued, brazenly recrossed the line at the border ports of entry. R. B. Mathews, Assistant District Director, El Paso, "Semi-Annual Inspection Report," January 26, 1927, file 55396/25A, RG 85, National Archives.

59. Grover C. Wilmoth to Commissioner General, May 24, 1928, file 55637/640, RG 85, National Archives.

60. Lee, *At America's Gates*, 181–186.

61. Lee, *At America's Gates*, 181–186.

62. Act of May 28, 1924, 43 Stat. 240.

63. Coppock, "History: Border Patrol," 5.

64. Those selected from this register were then given an oral examination and physical test. Congress, House, Subcommittee of House Committee on Appropriations, *Appropriations, Department of Labor, 1926*, 68th Cong., 2d sess., January 8, 1925, 97.

65. Lytle-Hernández notes that approximately twenty-five of the new hires were former Mounted Guards who provided the leadership for the new organization. Lytle-Hernández, "Entangling Bodies and Borders," 35.

66. Representative Shreve of Pennsylvania, speaking on Departments of State, Justice, Commerce, and Labor Appropriation Bill, H. R. 11753, on January 20, 1925, 68th Cong., 2d sess., *Cong. Rec.* 66, pt. 3: 2167.

67. Roberts, "The Border Patrol—65 Years of Action," 1, 12–13. See also Bureau of Immigration, *Annual Report, Fiscal Year Ended June 30, 1927*, 17.

68. Ngai, "Illegal Aliens and Alien Citizens," 167. See also Ellis, interview.

69. Bureau of Immigration, *Annual Report, Fiscal Year Ended June 30, 1925*, 15.

70. Lytle-Hernández, "Entangling Bodies and Borders," 4.

71. Stiles, interview.

72. Stiles, interview.

73. Alfred Hampton, District Director, District No. 26 to Commissioner General, August 19, 1924, file 53108/22, RG 85, National Archives. The file contains no response from the Commissioner General.
74. See also Bureau of Immigration, *Annual Report, Fiscal Year Ended June 30, 1925*, 15.
75. Stiles, interview.
76. Congress, House, Subcommittee of House Committee on Appropriations, *Appropriations, Department of Labor, 1926*, 68th Cong., 2d sess., January 8, 1925, 68.
77. R. B. Mathews, Assistant District Director, El Paso, January 26, 1927, file 55396/25A, RG 85, National Archives.
78. Department of Justice, Immigration and Naturalization Service, "The Border Patrol," 53–60.
79. The initial salary was $1,680 per year. Coppock, "History: Border Patrol." In later years, Patrol wages were not competitive with salaries offered by comparable government agencies such as the Customs Border Patrol. Hence, the Immigration Border Patrol found itself losing recruits to other government offices. Department of Justice, Immigration and Naturalization Service, "The Border Patrol," 53–60.
80. Diary of Dogie Wright, Border Patrol, n.d., C. L. Sonnichsen Special Collections Department, University of Texas at El Paso.
81. Bureau of Immigration, *Annual Report, Fiscal Year Ending June 30, 1927*, 19.
82. Perkins, *Border Patrol*, 108–114.
83. As a result of Perkins's inspection at the Laredo office, almost half of the officers were fired or quit. Perkins, *Border Patrol*, 105–114.
84. Ngai, "Illegal Aliens and Alien Citizens," 169.
85. The Rangers conducted these campaigns in retaliation for the incursions of Mexican revolutionaries such as Pancho Villa. For an account of the vigilante violence, see Johnson, *Revolution in Texas*, 108–143; Belenchia, "Cowboys and Aliens," 11 (citing Mary Kidder Rak, *Border Patrol* [Boston: Houghton Mifflin, 1938]); Lytle-Hernández, "Entangling Bodies and Borders," 56.
86. Ngai, *Impossible Subjects*, 70.
87. Memorandum from Commissioner General to Second Assistant Secretary, August 30, 1924, file 53108/22, RG 85, National Archives.
88. Immigrant smugglers faced a minimum one-year sentence in a federal penitentiary. Congress, House, Subcommittee of House Committee on Appropriations, *Appropriations, Department of Labor, 1926*, 68th Cong., 2d sess., January 8, 1925, 5, 72, 74-76.
89. Sentences ranged from one month to several years. After serving their sentences, violators were deported. In some jurisdictions, however, prosecution and incarceration of violators would congest the court system; these individuals were deported directly. Indeed, by January 1925, Border Patrol apprehensions under the Passport Act increased the number of deportees and created a backlog of 1,000 cases for Bureau of Immigration administrators. Congress, House, Subcommittee of House Committee on Appropriations, *Appropriations, Department of Labor, 1926*, 68th Cong., 2d sess., January 8, 1925, 74–76.
90. Explaining the work of the Border Patrol in the administration of the Prohibition laws, Wilmoth defined these common law rights as follows: "1) To take the necessary steps to prevent the commission of a felony; 2) To arrest without a warrant persons who commit or attempt to commit a felony (or for that matter a breach of peace) in their presence, or whom the officers have reasonable grounds to suspect of having committed a felony." Congress, House, Committee on Immigration and Naturalization, *Border Patrol*, 71st Cong., 2d sess., January 6, 1929, 18. See also Bureau of Immigration, *Annual Report, Fiscal Year Ended June 30, 1930*, 36.
91. Sanford, "The Line Rider," 3. Bureau of Immigration General Order No. 63 instructed immigration and Border Patrol officers to enforce the terms of the National Prohibition Act. Bureau of Immigration, General Order No. 63, March 29, 1926, file 55938/943, RG 85, National Archives. In addition to immigration and Prohibition enforcement, Border Patrol officers would assist in the administration of the plant quarantine laws (regarding the illegal importation of agricultural products), the neutrality laws (particularly focusing on the incursion of Mexican revolutionaries into the United States), the Dyer Act (apprehending persons driving stolen cars from one state to another), and the White Slave Traffic Act. Grover C. Wilmoth,

District Director, El Paso to Commissioner General, April 24, 1930, file 55688/876, RG 85, National Archives.

92. Congress, House, Subcommittee of House Committee on Appropriations, *Appropriations, Department of Labor, 1926,* 68th Cong., 2d sess., January 8, 1925, 72.

93. Roberts, "The Border Patrol—65 Years of Action," 1, 12–13. On the violence surrounding Prohibition enforcement, see Sinclair, *Era of Excess,* 188.

94. "New U.S. Police Force Now Combats Smugglers," 25.

95. Roberts, "The Border Patrol—65 Years of Action," 1, 12–13.

96. Perkins, *Border Patrol,* 102–103.

97. Congress, House, Committee on Immigration and Naturalization, *Immigration Border Patrol,* 70th Cong. 1st sess., March 5, 1928, 12.

98. Commissioner General, Memorandum for the Second Assistant Secretary, August 30, 1924, file 53108/22, RG 85, National Archives; Congress, House, Committee on the Judiciary, *To Establish a Border Patrol,* 69th Cong., 1st sess., April 12, 1926, 21; Congress, House, *Immigration Border Patrol,* 70th Cong., 2d sess., March 5, 1928, 6; Congress, House, Committee on Immigration and Naturalization, *Border Patrol,* 71st Cong., 2d sess., January 6, 1929, 18–19. In the 1920s, immigration officials had reasons to be concerned about lawsuits. The Volstead Act made it a misdemeanor for any officer of the United States to conduct a search or seizure of a private home without a warrant and a search and seizure of other buildings without warrant and probable cause. Historian Andrew Sinclair observes that six months after Prohibition went into effect, courts heard over seven hundred search and seizure cases; six hundred of these cases pertained to the Volstead Act. Sinclair, *Era of Excess,* 215. Indeed, as discussed below, the agency later relied on one of these cases, *Carroll v. United States,* 267 US 132, to establish the boundaries of its search and seizure powers vis-à-vis undocumented immigrants.

99. On the congressional intent underlying the new law, see Congress, House, Committee on the Judiciary, *To Establish a Border Patrol,* 69th Cong., 1st sess., April 12, 1926, 21–27.

100. Act of February 27, 1925, 43 Stat. 1049. The new Border Patrol bill was drafted by Senator David Reed of Pennsylvania (cosponsor of the Immigration Act of 1924 and cocreator of the national origins approach to immigration quotas). On Reed and the national origins quota system, see Ngai, *Impossible Subjects,* 22; Higham, *Strangers in the Land,* 322–323. While Reed was an ardent restrictionist who also opposed Western Hemisphere quotas (for the sake of fostering diplomatic relations among Western Hemisphere countries), it is not clear that he presented the new Border Patrol bill in order to promote a restrictionist immigration agenda. At a minimum, the bill appears to have been presented to rectify problems with the language of the original Border Patrol act. On Reed and Western Hemisphere quotas, see Reisler, *By the Sweat of Their Brow,* 202.

101. Congress, House, Committee on Immigration and Naturalization, *Authorization for Increased Power to the Border Patrols,* 70th Cong., 1st sess., May, 21, 1928, 33.

102. Act of February 27, 1925, 43 Stat. 1049.

103. Until the demise of Prohibition in 1933, however, the Border Patrol continued to take into custody Prohibition violators under the common law standards described above.

104. This provision was particularly important due to concerns about the unauthorized entry of noncitizen seamen. Congress, House, Subcommittee of House Committee on Appropriations, *Appropriations, Department of Labor, 1926,* 68th Cong., 2d sess., January 8, 1925, 78, 86.

105. The Supreme Court defined a search as reasonable when undertaken with a warrant supported by probable cause. *Katz v. United States,* 389 US 347, 357 (1967); *Johnson v. United States,* 333 US 10, 14 (1948); *Carroll v. United States,* 267 US 132, 153–154 (1925). See also, Clark, *Deportation of Aliens from the United States to Europe,* 257, 361; National Commission on Law Observance and Enforcement, *Report on the Enforcement of the Deportation Laws of the United States,* 133, 151, 171; Van Vleck, *The Administrative Control of Aliens,* 172–178.

106. While there was much debate pertaining to the appropriations bill itself, there was virtually no debate regarding the Reed amendment. The measure also received very little attention in the national press.

107. Emphasis added. Senator Reed of Pennsylvania, speaking on Departments of State, Justice, Commerce, and Labor Appropriation Bill, H. R. 11753, on February 7, 1925, 68th Cong., 2d sess., *Cong. Rec.* 66, pt. 3: 3202.

108. Through the following statutory language, Congress conferred this power upon Customs officials: "That every collector, naval officer and surveyor, or other person specially appointed by either of them for that purpose, shall have full power and authority, to enter any ship or vessel, in which they shall have reason to suspect any goods, wares or merchandise subject to duty shall be concealed; and therein to search for, seize, and secure any such goods, wares or merchandise." Act of July 31, 1789, ch. 5, § 24, 1 Stat. 29, 43. See also, Rosenzweig, "Functional Equivalents of the Border," 1121; "Legal Analysis of Border Patrol Checkpoints."

109. In *Carroll*, the plaintiffs were convicted for transporting 68 quarts of whiskey and gin in violation of the Volstead Act. Plaintiffs sought a reversal of the conviction, arguing that the evidence was found through an unlawful search of their vehicle. The Supreme Court upheld the conviction, holding that the Prohibition officers had probable cause to search the vehicle. While this case established what legal scholars now refer to as "the automobile exception" to the Fourth Amendment, it also established in *obiter dicta* the "border exception" or "border search exception" to the Fourth Amendment. For more information on the automobile exception, see O'Connor, "Vehicle Searches—The Automobile Exception," 393–434.

110. Beyond the border, however, the Court held that customs officers had to have probable cause prior to conducting a vehicular search without warrant. In *Carroll*, the Court defined probable cause as follows: "On reason and authority the true rule is that if the search and seizure without a warrant are made upon probable cause, that is, upon a belief, reasonably arising out of circumstances known to the seizing officer, that an automobile or other vehicles that which by law is subject to seizure and destruction, the search and seizure are valid." *Carroll v. United States*, 267 US 132, 149. The Bureau of Immigration cited to *Carroll* when it instructed its officers on enforcing the Volstead Act. Bureau of Immigration, General Order No. 63, March 29, 1926, file 55938/943, RG 85, National Archives. Yet while the Court established Fourth Amendment standards for customs searches beyond the border in 1925, no analogous standards existed for immigration searches until 1973. *Carroll v. United States*, 267 US 132, 154 (1925). See also Fragomen, "Searching for Illegal Aliens."

111. Until the Supreme Court decision in *Almeida-Sanchez v. United States*, 413 US 266 (1973), the Border Patrol had the power "to stop any vehicle and search for aliens, within a reasonable distance from the border, without warrant, probable cause or consent. This authority had been upheld by the Circuit Courts of Appeal in the Fifth, Ninth, and Tenth Circuits." In *Almeida-Sanchez* the Court held that "for all vehicle searches conducted by roving patrols of Immigration Officers away from the international border, a warrant, probable cause, or consent would be required." Tiltti, "Non-Border Search and Seizure," 106.

112. Harry E. Hull, Commissioner General, Testimony before the House Committee on Immigration and Naturalization on H. R. 11204, January 15, 1930, file 55688/876, RG 85, National Archives.

113. George J. Harris, Assistant Commissioner General to District Director, El Paso, April 15, 1930, file 55688/876, RG 85, National Archives.

114. Alfred Hampton, District Director, District No. 26 to Inspector in Charge, Gateway, Montana, April 27, 1925, file 53244/1E, RG 85, National Archives.

115. Harry E. Hull, Commissioner General, Testimony before the House Committee on Immigration and Naturalization on H. R. 11204, January 15, 1930, file 55688/876, RG 85, National Archives.

116. *Lew Moy v. United States*, 237 Fed. 50 (1916).

117. Congress, House, Committee on Immigration and Naturalization, *Immigration Border Patrol*, 71st Cong., 2d sess., January 15, 1930, 7.

118. H. C. von Struve, Consul, Mexicali, Mexico, Department of State to the Secretary of State, April 4, 1925, file 55466/51, RG 85, National Archives.

119. I. F. Wixon, Inspector in Charge, Calexico to Commissioner General, January 19, 1926, file 55301/81, RG 85, National Archives; G. C. Wilmoth, District Director, El Paso, "Immigration Patrol Officers Duties and Authority to Act," 12, Manual published for

the Border Patrol Training School, Mexican Border, May 1, 1940, Kelly Lytle-Hernández Collection of Border Patrol Research Papers, Box 13, Folder 16, Chicano Studies Research Center, University of California, Los Angeles.

120. Grover C. Wilmoth, District Director, El Paso to Commissioner General, April 24, 1930, file 55688/876, RG 85, National Archives.

121. Truett, *Fugitive Landscapes*.

122. R. A. Scott, Inspector in Charge to District Director, June 2, 1926, file 55280/25B, RG 85.

123. Congress, Senate, Committee on Immigration, *Illegal Entry of Aliens*, 66th Cong., 1st sess., October 10, 1919, 16. This strategy resembled the interior enforcement strategy that the Mounted Guard put in place in its pursuit of Chinese immigrants during the first decade of the twentieth century. Lee, *At America's Gates*, 186.

124. Harry E. Hull, Commissioner General to District Directors in Charge of Border Patrol, July 20, 1926, file 55409/Gen, RG 85, National Archives.

125. Grover C. Wilmoth, District Director, El Paso, Report re Inspection of District (Border Patrol), June 30, 1926, file 55396/22, RG 85, National Archives.

126. Grover C. Wilmoth to Commissioner General, June 30, 1926, file 55396/25, RG 85, National Archives.

127. Grover C. Wilmoth, District Director, El Paso, Report re Inspection of District (Border Patrol), June 30, 1926, file 55396/22, RG 85, National Archives.

128. See, for example, R. B. Matthews, Semi-Annual Inspection Report (Border Patrol), Nogales, Arizona, January 26, 1927, file 55396/25A, RG 85, National Archives; Walter F. Miller, Semi-Annual Inspection Report (Border Patrol), Marfa, Texas, February 24, 1927, file 55396/25A, RG 85, National Archives; Walter F. Miller, Semi-Annual Inspection Report (Border Patrol), Presidio, Texas, September 22, 1927, file 55396/25A, RG 85, National Archives.

129. See, for example, Grover C. Wilmoth, Semi-Annual Inspection Report (Border Patrol), August 19, 1926, file 55396/25, RG 85, National Archives.

130. See, for example, Walter F. Miller, Semi-Annual Inspection Report (Border Patrol), Casa Grande, Arizona, December 22, 1927, file 55396/25A, RG 85, National Archives.

131. See, for example, Walter F. Miller, Semi-Annual Inspection Report (Border Patrol), San Angelo, Texas, February 24, 1927, file 55396/25A, RG 85, National Archives; Walter F. Miller, Semi-Annual Inspection Report (Border Patrol), Sasabe, Arizona, December 22, 1927, file 55396/25A, RG 85, National Archives.

132. Registry Act of March 2, 1929, 45 Stat. 1512.

133. Perkins, *Border Patrol*, 105.

134. William A. Whalen, District Director, San Antonio, "Mexican Border Problems," in US Department of Labor, Bureau of Immigration, "Problems of the Immigration Service: Papers Presented at a Conference of Commissioners and District Directors of Immigration," Washington, DC, January 1929.

135. Harry E. Hull, Commissioner General to I. F. Wixon, Chief Supervisor, Calexico, CA, January 28, 1926, file 55031/81, RG 85, National Archives; J. B. Bristol, Nogales Chamber of Commerce to James J. Davis, Secretary of Labor, Department of Labor, April 19, 1928, file 55637/640, RG 85, National Archives; J. B. Bristol, Nogales Chamber of Commerce to Senator Henry Ashurst, May 7, 1928, file 55637/640, RG 85, National Archives; George W. P. Hunt, Governor, Arizona to James J. Davis, Secretary of Labor, July 23, 1927, file 55301/217, RG 85, National Archives.

136. Perkins, *Border Patrol*, 102, 104, 106.

137. Perkins, *Border Patrol*, 104, 106.

138. Lytle-Hernández, "Entangling Bodies and Borders," 53–54.

139. Grover C. Wilmoth, District Director, El Paso to Commissioner General, May 24, 1928, file 55637/640, RG 85, National Archives; George J. Harris, Assistant Commissioner General to District Director, El Paso, June 7, 1928, file 55637/640, RG 85, National Archives.

140. I. F. Wixon, Chief Supervisor, Calexico, CA to Commissioner General, February 3, 1926, file 55031/81, RG 85, National Archives.

141. Reisler, *By the Sweat of Their Brow*, 63.

142. Reisler, *By the Sweat of Their Brow*, 63.

143. On the opposition to the program, see Reisler, *By the Sweat of Their Brow*, 61–65.

144. Cardoso notes that immigration restrictionists were unable to garner enough votes to defeat this measure. Cardoso, *Mexican Emigration to the United States*, 141.

145. On Hoover's efforts to promote Pan-American relations through this measure see Cardoso, *Mexican Emigration to the United States*, 141–142.

146. Bureau of Immigration, *Annual Report, Fiscal Year Ended June 30, 1930*, 27–28; Bureau of Immigration, *Annual Report, Fiscal Year Ended June 30, 1931*, 45–47.

147. These forces had also expressed their outrage regarding Wixon's registration program, arguing that it completely undermined the immigration laws. I. F. Wixon, Chief Supervisor, Calexico, CA to Commissioner General, January 20, 1926, file 55031/81, RG 85, National Archives.

148. Representative Box of Texas, speaking on Naturalization, H. R. 349, on March 1, 1929, 70th Cong., 2d sess., 70, pt. 5 (March 1, 1929): 4950.

149. Representative Box of Texas, speaking on Naturalization, H. R. 349, on March 1, 1929, 70th Cong., 2d sess., *Cong. Rec.* 70, pt. 5: 4948.

150. For much of its history, the Border Patrol would suffer from a lack of resources. Historians have observed that even though Congress created the Border Patrol to appease restriction-ists, it failed to provide the organization enough funds to adequately enforce the laws and thereby obstruct southwestern growers' access to a ready supply of Mexican immigrant labor. See Tichenor, *Dividing Lines*, 172.

151. Representative Free of California, speaking on Deportation of Aliens, S. 5094, on February 16, 1929, 70th Cong., 2d sess., *Cong. Rec.* 70, pt. 4: 3620.

152. Representative Hudson of Michigan, speaking on Deportation of Aliens, S. 5094, on February 16, 1929, 70th Cong., 2d sess., *Cong. Rec.* 70, pt. 4: 3621.

153. Representative Blanton of Texas, speaking on Deportation of Aliens, S. 5094, on February 16, 1929, 70th Cong., 2d sess., *Cong. Rec.* 70, pt. 4: 3619.

154. Representative LaGuardia of New York, speaking on Deportation of Aliens, S. 5094, on February 16, 1929, 70th Cong., 2d sess., *Cong. Rec.* 70, pt. 4: 3619.

155. Bureau of Immigration, *Annual Report, Fiscal Year Ended 1932*, 3. See also Clark, *Deportation of Aliens from the United States to Europe*, 269.

156. W. W. Husband, Second Assistant Secretary to Attorney General, September 13, 1932, file 55639/731A, RG 85, National Archives.

157. They also agreed to not prosecute the following: 1) women and children; 2) those whose prosecution would require transportation from one judicial district to another (here, the Immigration Service was attempting to cut back the costs involved with enforcing the Act); 3) those who intended to return to Mexico rather than remain in the United States; 4) those without a criminal record or an "aggravated intent" to violate the law. William A. Whalen, District Director, San Antonio to H. M. Holden, US Attorney, Houston, Texas, May 22, 1933, file 55639/731A, RG 85, National Archives.

158. Immigration officials reported that they handled most violations of the Act of March 4, 1929 as voluntary departures. District Director, San Antonio, June 30, 1930, file 55727/922, RG 85, National Archives.

159. "Border Patrol Work," *El Paso Herald*, July 15, 1929, file 55598/459, RG 85, National Archives; "Border Patrol Work Outlined: Wilmoth Says U.S. Not Making Intensive Drive on Aliens," *El Paso Times*, July 13, 1929, file 55598/459, RG 85, National Archives; Editorial, "Aliens Should Register," *Douglas Arizona Daily Dispatch*, May 12, 1929, file 55598/459, RG 85, National Archives.

160. Grover C. Wilmoth, District Director, El Paso, "Semi-Annual Inspection Report," May 9, 1928, file 55396/25A, RG 85, National Archives; William A. Whalen, District Director, San Antonio, "Mexican Border Problems," in US Department of Labor, Bureau of Immigration, "Problems of the Immigration Service: Papers Presented at a Conference of Commissioners and District Directors of Immigration," Washington, DC, January 1929.

161. Congress, House, Committee on the Judiciary, *To Establish a Border Patrol*, 69th Cong., 1st sess., April 12, 1926, 21. Dry forces in Congress specifically observed that Border Patrol officers refrained from Prohibition enforcement activities because, lacking the statutory au-thority, they were concerned about potential lawsuits. For a brief overview of interagency Prohibition enforcement efforts, see Prince and Keller, *The U.S. Customs Service*, 195–218.

162. It appears that the first consolidation proposal came from the Bureau of Immigration itself. In 1922, Commissioner General Husband put forth such a plan as a means of strengthening both Prohibition and immigration enforcement. (See "Ask United Force to Guard Borders," 10.) During the debates over the Act of February 27, 1925, members of Congress also discussed consolidation as a means of reducing the Border Patrol appropriation. (Representative LaGuardia of New York speaking on Bureau of Immigration, H. R. 11753, on January 20, 1925, 68th Cong., 2d sess., *Cong. Rec.* 66, pt. 3: 2167.) In 1926, Assistant Secretary of the Treasury Lincoln C. Andrews, a vigorous supporter of the Anti-Saloon League, proposed the creation of a 12,000 to 15,000-man border patrol that would catch alien, drug, and alcohol smugglers. With the support of the Women's Christian Temperance Union, Representative Hudson of Michigan presented Andrews's plan in Congress (H. R. 9731). Ultimately, it failed to pass due to the expense involved in the bill's proposal to create a combined force under the aegis of the Coast Guard. This, in effect, would militarize the Patrol and require the construction of barracks along both borders for the housing of the new units. It also failed to pass due to disagreements over whether the Coast Guard ought to supervise the new patrol at all. ("Aid of Congress to Dry Law Wins WCTU Approval," 1; "Fight for Dry Bills Likely to Go Over," 6; "Liquor Buyer Bill Urged by Sheppard," 30.) In 1930, Hudson presented another consolidation proposal, H. R. 11204, which had the backing of President Herbert Hoover (who wanted to improve Prohibition enforcement) and the Wickersham Commission, which publicly opposed the repeal of Prohibition (although its members were divided on this point). ("Alien Crime Bill Voted," 1; "Full Text of the Wickersham Commission Report on Prohibition," 52. On Hoover's enforcement efforts, see Sinclair, *Age of Excess*, 167, 178–219.)

163. Congress, House, Committee on the Judiciary, *To Establish a Border Patrol*, 69th Cong., 1st sess., April 12, 1926, 12–13, 19–20.

164. Representative Mead of New York, speaking on United States Border Patrol, H. R. 11204, on July 1, 1930, 71st Cong., 2d sess., *Cong. Rec.* 72, pt. 11: 12218; Representative Boylan of New York, speaking on United States Border Patrol, H. R. 11204, on July 1, 1930, 71st Cong., 2d sess., *Cong. Rec.* 72, pt. 11: 12218.

165. Congress, Senate, Committee on Commerce, *Hearings on An Act to Regulate the Entry of Persons into the United States to Establish a Border Patrol in the Coast Guard and for Other Purposes*, 71st Cong., 3d sess., December 18, 1930, 37–39; "Border Patrol to be Increased," *San Angelo Morning News, San Angelo, Texas*, May 25, 1930, file 55598/459, RG 85, National Archives.

166. Congress, Senate, Committee on Commerce, *Border Patrol*, 71st Cong., 3d sess., December 18, 1930, January 8, 1931, 14, 37–39, 45.

167. This police force would have the power to enforce all federal laws along the border. Congress, House, Committee on Interstate and Foreign Commerce, *United States Border Patrol*, 71st Cong., 2d sess., June 9, 1930, H. Rep. 1828, 2.

168. Congress, House, Committee on Rules, *Hearings on H. R. 11204*, 71st Cong., 2d sess., June 14, 1930, 607; Congress, House, Committee on Interstate and Foreign Commerce, *United States Border Patrol*, 71st Cong., 2d sess., June 9, 1930, H. Rep. 1828, 4–5.

169. Congress, House, Committee on Interstate and Foreign Commerce, *United States Border Patrol*, 71st Cong., 2d sess., June 9, 1930, H. Rep. 1828, 4–5.

170. Congress, House, Committee on Rules, *Hearings on H. R. 11204*, 71st Cong., 2d sess., June 14, 1930, 607; Congress, House, Committee on Interstate and Foreign Commerce, *United States Border Patrol*, 71st Cong., 2d sess., June 9, 1930, H. Rep. 1828, 6–7.

171. Under Secretary of the Treasury, Ogden L. Mills stated, "An adequate number of points of entry will be maintained at which will be stationed customs, immigration, public health, agriculture, and other officers to administer the various laws applicable to entry into the country. Supervision and inspection of vehicles, pedestrians and merchandise will begin and end at the border, which is the logical place. There will no longer be the liability of interruption of travel on the interior roads by the patrol now maintained there. At the present time persons and vehicles that are several miles from the boundary and may never have been out of the country are subjected to this annoyance in the belief that they may have entered the United States without compliance with the law . . . Examination of persons and property

at the designated border crossings can be careful, thorough, and certain." Congress, House, Committee on Interstate and Foreign Commerce, *Hearings on H. R. 11204*, 71st Cong., 2d sess., April 24, 1930, 5.

172. Congress, House, Committee on Immigration and Naturalization, *Immigration Border Patrol*, 70th Cong. 2d sess., March 5, 1928, 12; Congress, House, Committee on Immigration and Naturalization, *To Amend the Fourth Proviso of the Act of February 27, 1925*, 70th Cong., 1st sess., May 21, 1928, 39.
173. Grover C. Wilmoth, District Director, El Paso to Commission General, March 28, 1931, file 55597/927, RG 85, National Archives.
174. Ngai, *Impossible Subjects*, 70.
175. Congress, Senate, Committee on Commerce, *Border Patrol*, 71st Cong., 3d sess., December 18, 1930, January 8, 1931, 6, 68; Grover C. Wilmoth, District Director, El Paso, "Annual Report for District No. 25, fiscal year ending June 30, 1930," July 18, 1930, file 55727/925, RG 85, National Archives.
176. Congress, Senate, Committee on Commerce, *Border Patrol*, 71st Cong., 3d sess., December 18, 1930, January 8, 1931, 68.
177. Opponents objected to the provisions of the bill that would subject owners of leisure crafts (boats under 15 tons) to untrammeled searches and require the mandatory registration of US citizens crossing the US–Canadian border. "Law Enforcers' Power Limited to Prohibition," *Chicago Daily Tribune*, June 22, 1930, 1. Even more controversial was the provision that rendered it a misdemeanor subject to a $100 fine for American citizens to cross the border without inspection at a port of entry. "House Praises Wickersham Bill for Unified Patrol," 6. See also Representative O'Connor of New York, speaking on United States Border Patrol, H. R. 11204, on July 1, 1930, 71st Cong., 2d sess., *Cong. Rec.* 72, pt. 11: 12229, 12236.
178. Congress, House, Committee on Immigration and Naturalization, *Immigration Border Patrol*, 71st Cong., 2d sess., January 15, 1930, 7.
179. Congress, House, Committee on Immigration and Naturalization, *To Amend the Fourth Proviso of the Act of February 27, 1925*, 70th Cong., 1st sess., May 21, 1928, 31.
180. Congress, House, Committee on Immigration and Naturalization, *To Amend the Fourth Proviso of the Act of February 27, 1925*, 70th Cong., 1st sess., May 21, 1928, 32.
181. Some Border Patrol officers argued that ranch inspections were more effective than interior inspections in the detection and apprehension of undocumented immigrants. I. F. Wixon, Chief Supervisor to Commissioner General, February 15, 1926, file 55409/31, RG 85, National Archives.
182. Grover C. Wilmoth, District Director, El Paso, Draft of Proposed Circular, May 4, 1933, RG 85, file 55597/927, RG 85, National Archives; Congress, House, *Immigration Border Patrol*, 70th Cong., 2d sess., March 5, 1928, 4–5.
183. Congress, House, Committee on Immigration and Naturalization, *Immigration Border Patrol*, 70th Cong. 1st sess., March 5, 1928, 3–6. Indeed, perhaps to emphasize the importance of immigration enforcement vis-à-vis Prohibition enforcement, the 1927 annual report renamed the section concerning alien smuggling to "Bootlegging of Aliens." The Report then compared alien smuggling to liquor smuggling and noted that the two often went hand in hand (liquor smugglers often resorted to alien smuggling when no cash was available to procure illegal contraband). Bureau of Immigration, *Annual Report, Fiscal Year Ended June 30, 1927*, 15.
184. Grover C. Wilmoth, Lecture, "Immigration Border Patrol Officers' Duties and Authority to Act," March 29, 1944, file 56192/582, RG 85, National Archives.
185. The Secretary of Labor's Committee on Administrative Procedure, "The Immigration and Naturalization Service," Washington, DC, May 17, 1940, 9, 74.

Chapter 3

1. D. W. McCormack, Commissioner General to Secretary of Labor, May 26, 1933, file 55884/600, RG 85, National Archives.
2. George J. Harris, Director, General Order 21, March 29, 1933, Kelly Lytle-Hernández Collection of Border Patrol Research Papers, Box 3, Folder 6, Chicano Studies Research Center, University of California, Los Angeles.

3. In the late nineteenth century, litigation filed by the Chinese famously led the Supreme Court to circumscribe the rights of immigrants to judicial review of agency decisions in deportation and exclusion cases. *Chae Chan Ping v. United States* (also known as the Chinese Exclusion Case), 130 US 581 (1889), established the national authority to exclude. *Fong Yue Ting*, 149 US 698 (1893) established the national authority to deport. And *Nishimura Ekiu*, 142 US 651 (1892) affirmed the holding of the Chinese Exclusion Case and virtually precluded judicial review of congressional legislation regarding immigration. Despite these defeats, in the early decades of the twentieth century, the Chinese continued to fight for a modicum of justice and rights within the administrative process itself. Chinese litigation filed in the lower federal courts raised questions pertaining to immigrants' rights to counsel in agency hearings, immigrants' access to the evidence that had been compiled against them, and greater procedural protections (specifically in the form of arrest warrants issued on the basis of probable cause) against deportation raids. See Salyer, *Laws Harsh as Tigers*, 154–156, 214–216.

4. Agency oversight, or self-regulation, can take a variety of forms. More specifically, as Elizabeth Magill explains, agencies self-regulate when they voluntarily "adopt rules, guidelines, and interpretations that substantively limit their options—limiting either the range of outcomes they can reach or the rationales that can be used to defend their choices." In a similar fashion, the INS and the Border Patrol, throughout their respective institutional histories, periodically undertook internal investigations, redrafted operations manuals, and prescribed procedural changes as part of a larger effort to check potential abuses of the agency's discretionary power. Magill, "Annual Review of Administrative Law," 860.

5. These claims draw upon the work of administrative constitutionalists who argue that through self-regulation agencies have played a central role in defining administrative law—a body of law traditionally defined almost exclusively in terms of judicial review of administrative action. More broadly, these scholars assert that, given their ability to define both their daily operations and the very boundaries of their authority, agencies construct an "administrative constitution." In more banal terms, agencies, both past and present, think constitutionally, anticipating the ways in which agency rules might transgress or even expand conceptions of fundamental rights. Mashaw, *Creating the Administrative Constitution;* Magill, "Annual Review of Administrative Law," 860; Bremer, "The Unwritten Administrative Constitution"; Metzger, "Administrative Constitutionalism"; Lee, "Race, Sex, and Rulemaking"; Desai, "Wiretapping Before the Wires." See also the work of Reuel Schiller who, unlike Mashaw, argues that studies of the contemporary administrative state overemphasize the role of legislators and agency officials and underestimate the role of the courts as regulators of agency action and more broadly, policymaking institutions. Schiller, "Enlarging the Administrative Polity" and "The Era of Deference."

6. Balderrama and Rodríguez, *Decade of Betrayal*, 54. (citing to Representative Martin Dies, Jr. [D-Tex], "The Immigration Crisis," *Saturday Evening Post*, April 20, 1935.)

7. Moloney, *National Insecurities*, 97.

8. L. Paul Winings, Acting Deputy Commissioner to Henry F. Ashurst, Senator, Democrat from Arizona, April 17, 1934, file 55739/674A, RG 85, National Archives.

9. Walter E. Carr, District Director, Los Angeles to Commissioner General, June 17, 1931, file 55739/674A, RG 85, National Archives.

10. Cardoso, *Mexican Emigration to the United States*, 146.

11. In addition to this deportation drive, Hoover instructed consular officials abroad to restrict the issuance of visas through an expanded application of the "likely to become a public charge" provision of the immigration laws. Moloney, *National Insecurities*, 96.

12. Hoffman, "Stimulus to Repatriation," 207. Many of these raids were conducted without warrants. Martin, *Madam Secretary*, 25.

13. Hoffman explains that this disparate impact was a product of the high concentration of Mexican immigrants residing in the Southern California region. Hoffman, "Stimulus to Repatriation," 207, fn. 4.

14. Moloney, *National Insecurities*, 92–95.

15. Balderrama and Rodríguez, *Decade of Betrayal*, 64.

16. Balderrama and Rodríguez, *Decade of Betrayal*, 63.

17. While the remainder of this chapter focuses on the ethnic Mexican experience during the Great Depression, it is important to note that the federal government targeted other immigrant

groups in its removal efforts. On the Filipino repatriation drive, see Ngai, *Impossible Subjects*, 96–127.

18. Balderrama and Rodríguez, *Decade of Betrayal*.
19. See James B. Bryant, Inspector in Charge, Galveston, Texas to Commissioner General, October 17, 1919, file 54549/670A, RG 85, National Archives.
20. Grover C. Wilmoth, District Director, El Paso to Harry E. Hull, Commissioner General, March 28, 1931, file 55597/927, RG 85, National Archives.
21. Phil Baldwin, Inspector in Charge to Mr. O. B. Holton, District Director of Immigration, Grand Forks, North Dakota, August 17, 1931, file 55630/18, RG 85, National Archives.
22. F. W. Berkshire to Commissioner General, February 15, 1919, file 54261/202F, RG 85, National Archives; Commissioner General to All Immigration Officers in Charge of Districts, August 19, 1919, file 54261/202F, RG 85, National Archives.
23. Grover C. Wilmoth, District Director, El Paso to All Immigration Stations and Chief Patrol Inspectors, El Paso District, July 11, 1929, file 55853/300, RG 85, National Archives. See also James L. Houghteling, Commissioner General to Grover C. Wilmoth, District Director, El Paso, May 5, 1939, file 55853/300, RG 85, National Archives.
24. Grover C. Wilmoth, District Director, El Paso to All Immigration Stations and Chief Patrol Inspectors, El Paso District, July 11, 1929, file 55853/300, RG 85, National Archives.
25. Grover C. Wilmoth, District Director, El Paso to Harry E. Hull, Commissioner General, March 28, 1931, file 55597/927, RG 85, National Archives.
26. L. Paul Winings, Chairman, Board of Review to Edward Shaughnessy, Deputy Commissioner, May 10, 1933, file 55639/731A, RG 85, National Archives. On the impact of the Great Depression on the agency's budget in general, see G. C. Wilmoth, District Director, El Paso District to US Immigration Service, June 15, 1931, file 55630/25, RG 85.
27. D. W. MacCormack, Commissioner General, Circular Letter to All Commissioners and District Directors of Immigration, August 31, 1933, file 55597/927B, RG 85, National Archives.
28. I. F. Wixon, Deputy Commissioner to Secretary of Labor, March 3, 1937, file 55853/300, RG 85, National Archives; G. C. Wilmoth, District Director, El Paso to Commissioner General, June 3, 1939, file 55853/300, RG 85, National Archives.
29. Unsigned report, n.d., file 55938/943, 6, RG 85, National Archives.
30. Grover C. Wilmoth, District Director, El Paso to Commissioner General, March 28, 1931, file 55597/927, RG 85, National Archives.
31. Grover C. Wilmoth stated that those immigrants subject to deportation were usually detained for 2 to 3 weeks at a cost of $22 per person. Congress, House, Committee on Immigration and Naturalization, *Immigration Border Patrol*, 70th Cong., 2d sess., March 5, 1928, 11.
32. D. W. MacCormack, Commissioner General, Circular to All Commissioners and District Directors of Immigration, August 12, 1933, file 55597/927B, RG 85, National Archives; Grover C. Wilmoth, District Director, El Paso to Commissioner General, March 28, 1931, file 55597/927, RG 85, National Archives.
33. Grover C. Wilmoth, District Director, El Paso, Memorandum, June 7, 1933, file 55597/927, RG 85, National Archives.
34. Statement of Grover C. Wilmoth, District Director, El Paso in Congress, House, Committee on Immigration and Naturalization, *Immigration Border Patrol*, 70th Cong., 2d sess., March 5, 1928, 11. See also Grover C. Wilmoth, District Director, El Paso to Commissioner General, March 28, 1931, file 55597/927, RG 85, National Archives.
35. Bureau of Immigration, *Annual Report, Fiscal Year Ended June 30, 1931*, 10.
36. Bureau of Immigration, *Annual Report, Fiscal Year Ended, June 30, 1931*, 10.
37. Memorandum for the Secretary, May 12, 1933, file 55854/600, RG 85, National Archives.
38. Edward Corsi, Commissioner of Immigration, New York District to Commissioner General, June 7, 1933, file 55854/600, RG 85, National Archives.
39. D. W. MacCormack, Commissioner General to Congressman James Buchanan of Texas, February 17, 1936, file 55739/674A, RG 85, National Archives.
40. Harry E. Hull, Commissioner General to Mr. O. M. Burt, Chairman, Trunk Line Association, Passenger Department, February 19, 1931, file 55739/674, RG 85, National Archives; S. K. Morse, Secretary, Trans-Atlantic Passenger Conference to W. N. Doak, Secretary of Labor, May 19, 1931, file 55730/674, RG 85, National Archives.

41. Ngai, "Illegal Aliens and Alien Citizens," 158–59.
42. D. W. MacCormack, Commissioner General to Secretary of Labor, May 26, 1933, file 55854/ 600, RG 85, National Archives.
43. Reisler, *By the Sweat of Their Brow*, 231.
44. Fox, *Three Worlds of Welfare Relief.*
45. Reisler, *By the Sweat of Their Brow*, 232.
46. Hoffman notes, "it has been shown that the actual movement of thousands of Mexican nationals was not due solely to federal motivations, but was the result of a world of factors spun by acute unemployment, the threat of deportation, the urging of welfare officials, and the acceptance of the repatriation idea, with its lure of colonization projects and free transportation." Hoffman, *Unwanted Mexican Americans*, 125. Dinwoodie writes that "expulsions under federal immigration statutes represented only a small proportion of departures to Mexico, most of which were "repatriations" organized or encouraged by local authorities." Dinwoodie, "Deportation," 195.
47. Kiser and Kiser, *Mexican Workers in the United States*, 60 (citing Memo from John L. Zurbrick, District Director of Immigration, Detroit District to Commissioner General of Immigration, October 20, 1932, file 55784/585, RG 85, National Archives).
48. General Order No. 169, "Removal of Aliens under the Provisions of Section 23 of the Immigration Act of 1917," February 19, 1931, file 55739/674, RG 85, National Archives.
49. Edward J. Shaughnessy, Acting Commissioner General to John L. Zurbrick, District Director, Detroit, October 27, 1932, file 55784/585, RG 85, National Archives. See also Harry E. Hull, Commissioner General to Immigration Service, February 19, 1931, file 55739/674, RG 85, National Archives.
50. Kiser and Kiser, *Mexican Workers in the United States*, 63.
51. Ngai, "Illegal Aliens and Alien Citizens," 219.
52. Edward J. Shaughnessy, Deputy Commissioner General to Congressman Harry B. Coffee of Nebraska, June 4, 1935, file 55854/100, RG 85, National Archives; Commissioner General to John L. Zurbrick, District Director, Detroit, May 13, 1935, file 55854/100, RG 85, National Archives; Commissioner General to M. F. Lence, District Director, Salt Lake City, May 16, 1935, file 55854/100, RG 85, National Archives; District Director, San Antonio to D. W. Brewster, Inspector in Charge, Brownsville, Texas, November 2, 1938, file 55854/100, RG 85, National Archives.
53. Hoffman, "Stimulus to Repatriation," 206–207, 218.
54. Hoffman, "Stimulus to Repatriation," 208.
55. Hoffman, "Stimulus to Repatriation," 212.
56. Hoffman, "Stimulus to Repatriation," 217.
57. Sixty percent of those expelled during the 1930s were US citizens, many of whom were children born in the United States. Balderrama and Rodríguez, *Decade of Betrayal*, 216.
58. Hoffman, "Stimulus to Repatriation," 217; Balderrama and Rodríguez, *Decade of Betrayal*, 53.
59. W. F. Watkins, Supervisor to Robe Carl White, Secretary of Labor, February 21, 1931, file 55739/674A, RG 85, National Archives.
60. In further defense of the agency, Walter Carr asserted, "This office however made an announcement through the press definitely stating that this Service had no intention of considering any activity aimed solely at Mexicans; that any action which this Service might take would not discriminate against any one race; that in any event, persons legally in the United States had nothing to fear; and that we were interested only in the same classes of aliens that have always demanded our attention, that is, any alien of any race actually subject to deportation under the immigration laws." Walter E. Carr, District Director of Immigration, Los Angeles to Commissioner General, June 17, 1931, file 55739/674A, RG 85, National Archives.
61. Hoffman, *Unwanted Mexican Americans*, 106.
62. Balderrama and Rodríguez, 302–313; Moloney, *National Insecurities*, 92.
63. Hoffman, *Unwanted Mexican Americans*, 152–164.
64. Historian D. H. Dinwoodie observes that the Immigration Service specifically assumed a more reactive role during the Great Depression, responding to the demands of local and state officials who took the initiative in the repatriation campaigns. Dinwoodie, "Deportation," 199.

65. On the opposition of private and public organizations in Mexico, see Balderrama and Rodríguez, 147. On the opposition of groups in the United States, see Moloney, *National Insecurities*, 92–93.
66. Balderrama and Rodríguez, *Decade of Betrayal*, 148.
67. Balderrama and Rodríguez, *Decade of Betrayal*, 147.
68. Balderrama and Rodríguez, *Decade of Betrayal*, 147–148.
69. Balderrama and Rodríguez, *Decade of Betrayal*, 148.
70. Sánchez-Walker, "Migration Quicksand," 336.
71. Sánchez-Walker, "Migration Quicksand," 148, 163.
72. These organizations included the American Jewish Committee, the Young Women's Christian Association Immigration Department, the Foreign Language Information Service, the Hebrew Sheltering and Immigrant Aid Society, the International Migration Service, the National Council of Jewish Women, the National Institute of Immigrant Welfare, the National League for American Citizenship, and the New York Travelers Aid Society. In 1934, these groups met in the Joint Conference on Immigration Legislation in New York City to discuss immigration law reform. Sánchez-Walker, "Migration Quicksand," 86, 164.
73. Moloney, *National Insecurities*, 95.
74. Immigration and Naturalization Service, *Annual Report, Fiscal Year Ended June 30, 1934*, 48.
75. In opposition to a federal deportation drive MacCormack wrote, "These figures can not be cited to prove 500,000 illegal entries, or in fact any illegal entries whatever, although it is recognized that there must have been some. On the other hand they show clearly that the great increase in the Mexican population during this decade was due, not to immigration, either legal or illegal, but primarily to the very high birth rate among Mexicans living in the United States. If the facts can be ascertained, I believe that it will be found that a majority of the Mexicans on relief are not aliens, but that they were born in the United States and can claim the privileges of citizenship. This does not render the economic problem less serious, but it precludes mass deportations as a possible remedy." D. W. MacCormack, Commissioner General to James B. Buchanan, January 21, 1936, file 55739/674A, RG 85, National Archives. On MacCormack's appointment by Perkins, see Martin, *Madam Secretary*, 245; and Severn, *Frances Perkins*, 120.
76. D. W. MacCormack, Commissioner General to Secretary of Labor, May 26, 1933, file 55854/600, RG 85, National Archives.
77. Ngai, *Impossible Subjects*, 83. The general tone of the bureau's annual reports changed under MacCormack's tenure, characterized by a more humanitarian rather than restrictionist orientation toward immigrants and immigration.
78. After 1933 the number of deportations and voluntary departures was cut in half from the annual average of 30,000. Dinwoodie, "Deportation," 194.
79. Clark, *Deportation of Aliens from the United States to Europe*; National Commission on Law Observance and Enforcement, *Report on the Enforcement of the Deportation Laws*; Van Vleck, *The Administrative Control of Aliens*.
80. Ngai, *Impossible Subjects*, 77.
81. Ngai, *Impossible Subjects*, 77.
82. Ngai, *Impossible Subjects*, 77.
83. Ngai notes that "one-sixth of aliens in deportation hearings had legal representation." Ngai, *Impossible Subjects*, 77; Van Vleck, *The Administrative Control of Aliens*, 98–99.
84. As Van Vleck observed, "the courts have held that the technical legal rules of evidence do not apply in these administrative hearings." Van Vleck, *The Administrative Control of Aliens*, 107.
85. Ngai, *Impossible Subjects*, 77.
86. Van Vleck, *The Administrative Control of Aliens*, 104.
87. Ngai, *Impossible Subjects*, 78.
88. Clark, *Deportation of Aliens*, 488; National Commission on Law Observance and Enforcement, *Report on the Enforcement of the* Deportation *Laws*, 6–7, 158–165. (There was some dispute, however, among the commission members as to whether deportation ought to be considered a civil or criminal procedure and, hence, subject to higher procedural standards.) See also Van Vleck, *The Administrative Control of Aliens*, 172–174, 219; Dinwoodie, "Deportation," 46; I. F. Wixon, Deputy Commissioner to Secretary of State, March 19, 1937, file 55853/300, RG 85, National Archives.

89. Clark, *Deportation of Aliens*, 488; National Commission on Law Observance and Enforcement, *Report on the Enforcement of the Deportation Laws*, 6, 158–165; Van Vleck, *The Administrative Control of Aliens*, 172–174, 219.
90. Van Vleck, *The Administrative Control of Aliens*, 224.
91. Immigration and Naturalization Service, *Annual Report, Fiscal Year Ended June 30, 1934*, 49.
92. Immigration and Naturalization Service, *Annual Report, Fiscal Year Ended June 30, 1934*, 51.
93. Ngai, *Impossible Subjects*, 77.
94. Edward J. Shaughnessy, Acting Commissioner, Memorandum to All Commissioners and Directors of Immigration Districts, July 25, 1932, file 55597/927, RG 85, National Archives.
95. Immigration and Naturalization Service, *Annual Report, Fiscal Year Ended June 30, 1934*, 52.
96. Immigration and Naturalization Service, *Annual Report, Fiscal Year Ended June 30, 1934*, 52; Ngai, *Impossible Subjects*, 77–89.
97. D. W. MacCormack, Commissioner General, Memorandum, May 23, 1933, file 55639/731A, RG 85, National Archives.
98. Ngai, *Impossible Subjects*, 83.
99. Ngai notes that the studies by Clark, Van Vleck, and the Wickersham Commission "were generally motivated by the Immigration Service's treatment of European and Canadian immigrants." Ngai, *Impossible Subjects*, 77, 85–89.
100. George Coleman to D. W. MacCormack, Commissioner General, September 16, 1933, file 55877/443, RG 85, National Archives.
101. Rafael Fuentes Jr., First Secretary, Mexican Embassy to Edward J. Shaughnessy, Deputy Commissioner General, August 3, 1935, file 55884/66, RG 85, National Archives.
102. George Coleman to D. W. MacCormack, Commissioner General, September 16, 1933, 16, file 55877/443, RG 85, National Archives.
103. George Coleman to D. W. MacCormack, Commissioner General, September 16, 1933, 17, file 55877/443, RG 85, National Archives.
104. George Coleman to D. W. MacCormack, Commissioner General, September 16, 1933, 32, file 55877/443, RG 85, National Archives.
105. George Coleman to D. W. MacCormack, Commissioner General, September 16, 1933, 23, file 55877/443, RG 85, National Archives.
106. Report of Senator Fletcher of Florida, Records of the Wickersham Commission on Law Observance and Enforcement, microfilm reel 6, frame 36, Manuscript Division, Library of Congress, Washington, DC (reporting killing of private citizen by immigration officers). See also National Commission on Law Observance and Enforcement, *Report on the Enforcement of the Deportation Laws*, 133–136.
107. Ngai, "Illegal Aliens and Alien Citizens," 170.
108. Roberts, "The Border Patrol," 12–13.
109. Immigration and Naturalization Service, *Annual Report, Fiscal Year Ended June 30, 1934*, 48.
110. Roberts, "The Border Patrol," 12–13.
111. Grover C. Wilmoth, District Director, El Paso, Draft of Proposed Circular, May 4, 1933, RG 85, file 55597/927, RG 85, National Archives.
112. Ngai, *Impossible Subjects*, 77, 85–89.
113. According to Dinwoodie, deportations and voluntary departures in the Southwest dropped from "about eight thousand in each category to about four to five thousand each throughout the 1930s." Dinwoodie, "Deportation," 194–195.
114. Balderrama, *Decade of Betrayal*, 53.
115. Ngai, *Impossible Subjects*, 83; Dinwoodie, "Deportation," 195–196.
116. Under the statute, Border Patrol officers could arrest without warrant in the following cases: 1) where officers witnessed immigrants in the act of crossing the border illegally; and 2) at any time before the immigrant had reached his or her destination. Conference of the Warrant Committee, Bureau of Immigration, June 2, 1933, file 55597/927, RG 85, National Archives.
117. With respect to the deportation statute, one reformer noted, "Concerning such procedure the [deportation] statutes are virtually silent. There is (1) a provision relating to bail; (2) a limited authorization of arrest without a warrant; (3) a general authorization to inspectors to inquire into the right of any alien to enter or remain in the United States; and (4), of primary importance, the curt statement that an alien of a deportable class 'shall upon the warrant of the Secretary of Labor be taken into custody and deported.'" The Secretary of Labor's

Committee on Administrative Procedure, "The Immigration and Naturalization Service," Washington, DC, May 17, 1940, 61 (hereinafter referred to as the "Dimock Report"). See also Hutchinson, *Legislative History of American Immigration Policy, 1798–1905*, 457.

118. Conference of the Warrant Committee, Bureau of Immigration, June 2, 1933, file 55597/927, RG 85, National Archives.

119. Conference of the Warrant Committee, Bureau of Immigration, June 2, 1933, file 55597/927, RG 85, National Archives. In this scenario, the bureau feared less the consequences for the immigrants than the consequences for its own officers who faced the risk of lawsuits by harassed civilians.

120. L. Paul Winings, Board of Review to Commissioner General, August 7, 1933, file 55597/927B, RG 85, National Archives. After studying the bureau's internal procedures, specifically the *Immigration Laws and Rules*, Winings concluded that even they explicitly prohibited the detention of foreigners without an arrest warrant; he wrote "the rule plainly discloses that an alien is not to be taken into custody until a warrant of arrest has been obtained from the Secretary of Labor." (Winings examined Rule 19 of the January 1, 1930 edition of the *Immigration Laws and Rules*.)

121. In the Southwest, these issues were particularly important because the border districts issued the majority of the arrest warrants within the entire agency; for example, one reformer noted, "Of the total number of warrants of deportation executed in 1938, over one-half originated in the three border districts of El Paso, San Antonio and Los Angeles." Dimock Report, 61.

122. Dimock Report, 62.

123. Dimock Report, 65, 66. See also Van Vleck, *The Administrative Control of Aliens*, 90–96. Again, while reformers recognized that due process standards, such as the Fifth Amendment provision against self-incrimination, applicable to a criminal law proceeding did not adhere to exclusion hearings, they used these as a benchmark to evaluate and critique the deportation process. Van Vleck, *The Administrative Control of Aliens*, 172.

124. Van Vleck, *The Administrative Control of Aliens*, 96, 228–229.

125. On the investigation and arrest, the Dimock report observed, "Of all the aspects of the deportation process, those of investigation and arrest entail by far the greatest problems. The situations which confront enforcement officers are endlessly varied. Apart from this, the procedure of investigation must necessarily be fluid and to a large extent discretionary. To frame formal safeguards of any kind which will leave unhampered the necessary and legitimate methods of enforcement is thus a task of the utmost difficulty. Yet it is in connection with the processes of investigation and arrest that lie the greatest possibilities of abuse of the wide powers entrusted to the Department of Labor under the deportation statutes." Dimock Report, 61.

126. I. F. Wixon, Director of Field Service, Memorandum, June 16, 1933, file 55597/927A, RG 85, National Archives.

127. I. F. Wixon, Director of Field Service to Commissioner General, July 29, 1933, file 55597/927A, RG 85, National Archives.

128. George J. Harris to Commissioner General, September 1, 1920, file 55597/927, RG 85, National Archives. Opponents also reasoned that if law enforcement officers had the power "to take into custody persons either suspected or known to have committed offenses against the law," immigration officers ought to have an analogous power to "[detain] where deemed necessary, aliens known to have violated the immigration law in a manner which rendered them amenable to deportation until warrants could be secured." I. F. Wixon, Director of Field Service to Commissioner General, July 29, 1933, file 55597/927, RG 85, National Archives.

129. W. F. Kelly to Commissioner General, September 20, 1934, file 55877/341, RG 85, National Archives.

130. Van Vleck, *The Administrative Control of Aliens*, 225.

131. Dimock Report, 61; Hutchinson, *Legislative History of American Immigration Policy, 1798–1905*, 457.

132. Van Vleck, *The Administrative Control of Aliens*, 224–225.

133. George J. Harris, Acting Supervising Inspector, Mexican Border District to Commissioner General, September 19, 1921, file 54152/56, RG 85, National Archives.

134. Dimock Report, 61. See also National Commission on Law Observance and Enforcement, *Report on the Enforcement of the Deportation Laws*, 26.

135. While Grover C. Wilmoth told his officers to abide by the new order, he also encouraged them to question suspected undocumented immigrants so as to elicit evidence or a confession as to their illegal entry. Once officers obtained such evidence, they were permitted to make an immediate arrest without warrant. Failing to specify what constituted sufficient evidence, what modes of questioning were acceptable or not, how long the questioning could go on, Wilmoth's instructions were decidedly ambiguous and left a tremendous amount of room for the kind of interrogation tactics that concerned reformers. Van Vleck, for example, cautioned against the procurement of testimony under coercion or intimidation. Wickersham criticized bureau officials for failing to limit their questioning to issues of alienage, instead asking immigrants about their personal matters. Grover C. Wilmoth, District Director, El Paso to Commissioner General, June 19, 1933, file 55597/927, RG 85, National Archives; Van Vleck, *The Administrative Control of Aliens*, 172–173; National Commission on Law Observance and Enforcement, *Report on the Enforcement of the Deportation Laws of the United States*, 172.

136. W. F. Kelly to Commissioner General, September 20, 1934, file 55877/341, RG 85, National Archives.

137. William A. Whalen, District Director, San Antonio to Commissioner General, July 20, 1933, file 55597/927A, RG 85, National Archives. The new procedure presented a novelty not only to Border Patrol officers but also to outside observers. Dinwoodie notes that an immigration attorney for the American Civil Liberties Union expressed his surprise at handling a case where "for almost the first time in my experience they [the Immigration Service] obtained a lawfully issued warrant before taking the alien into custody." Dinwoodie, "Deportation," 195.

138. I. F. Wixon, Director of Field Service to Commissioner General, July 29, 1933, file 55597/927, RG 85, National Archives.

139. F. W. Berkshire, District Director, Los Angeles to Commissioner General, March 6, 1934, file 55597/927B, RG 85, National Archives.

140. Grover C. Wilmoth, District Director, El Paso to Commissioner General, August 16, 1934, file 55597/927C, RG 85, National Archives.

141. Grover C. Wilmoth, District Director, El Paso to Commissioner General, September 18, 1934, file 55877/341, RG 85, National Archives. Kelly wrote, "It is an utter impossibility for the patrol at its present size to function effectively if the only aliens it may arrest without warrants are those who, in its 'presence or view' are entering unlawfully." W. F. Kelly to Commissioner General, September 20, 1934, file 55877/341, RG 85, National Archives.

142. Immigration and Naturalization Service, *Annual Report, Fiscal Year Ended June 30, 1934*, 51.

143. W. W. Brown, Assistant, Immigration and Naturalization Service to District Director, Buffalo, August 14, 1936, file 55883/300, RG 85, National Archives.

144. The telegraphic warrant procedure was highly criticized by reformers. They found it problematic that, under department procedures, the central office did not receive a complete evidentiary record for these warrants until after their issuance. The central office thus generated these warrants on the basis of a series of code words telegraphed by district officials. Reformers further discovered that once Washington administrators received the complete evidentiary record by regular mail, it often failed to support the issuance of the warrant. Van Vleck, *The Administrative Control of Aliens*, 229; National Commission on Law Observance and Enforcement, *Report on the Enforcement of the Deportation Laws of the United States*, 81.

145. This was considered necessary not only to expedite the apprehension of flight risks but also to save the Service detention costs. For specific details of this procedure, see D. W. MacCormack, Commissioner General, Memorandum Covering Bureau Procedure Incident to the Handling of Telegraphic Applications for Warrants of Arrest, July 21, 1933, file 55818/251, RG 85, National Archives.

146. R. J. Powers, Chief, Warrants-Deportation Division, Memorandum for the Commissioner, September 26, 1933, file 55818/251, 6, RG 85, National Archives.

147. R. J. Powers, Chief, Warrants-Deportation Division, Memorandum for the Commissioner, September 26, 1933, file 55818/251, 6, RG 85, National Archives.

148. W. H. Wagner to Edward J. Shaughnessy, Assistant Commissioner General, January 9, 1934, file 55818/251A, RG 85, National Archives.

149. R. J. Powers, Chief, Warrants-Deportation Division, Memorandum for the Commissioner, September 26, 1933, 3, file 55818/251, RG 85, National Archives.

150. R. J. Powers, Chief, Warrants-Deportation Division, Memorandum for the Commissioner, September 26, 1933, 7, file 55818/251, RG 85, National Archives.

151. R. J. Powers, Chief, Warrants-Deportation Division, Memorandum for the Commissioner, September 26, 1933, 5, file 55818/251, RG 85, National Archives.

152. The southwestern offices reported back on the following: 1) the time the request for a warrant was received by an investigating officer; 2) the time the telegraphic warrant was requested from the central office; 3) the time the telegraphic warrant was received by the District Office; 4) the time the warrant was served; and 5) total elapsed time. D. W. MacCormack, Commissioner General, Memorandum Covering Bureau Procedures Incident to the Handling of Telegraphic Applications for Warrants of Arrest, July 21, 1933, file 55818/251, RG 85, National Archives; G. C. Wilmoth, District Director, El Paso to Commissioner General, July 31, 1933, file 55818/251, RG 85, National Archives; William A. Whalen, District Director, San Antonio to Commissioner General, July 31, 1933, RG 85, National Archives; A. E. Burnett, District Director of Immigration, Los Angeles to Commissioner General, August 1, 1933, file 55818/251, RG 85, National Archives; Clyde Campbell, Acting District Director, Galveston to Commissioner General, December 1, 1933, file 55818/251A, RG 85, National Archives.

153. R. J. Powers, Chief, Warrants-Deportation Division, Memorandum for the Commissioner, September 26, 1933, 3–4, file 55818/251, RG 85, National Archives.

154. R. J. Powers, Chief, Warrants-Deportation Division, Memorandum for the Commissioner, September 26, 1933, 7, file 55818/251, RG 85, National Archives.

155. R. J. Powers, Chief, Warrants-Deportation Division, Memorandum for the Commissioner, September 26, 1933, 8, file 55818/251, RG 85, National Archives.

156. R. J. Powers, Chief, Warrants-Deportation Division, Memorandum for the Commissioner, September 26, 1933, 8, file 55818/251, RG 85, National Archives.

157. D. W. MacCormack, Commissioner General, Memorandum to All Commissioners and District Directors of Immigration, October 21, 1933, file 55597/927B, RG 85, National Archives.

158. F. W. Berkshire, District Director, Los Angeles to Commissioner General, August 14, 1934, file 55597/927C, RG 85, National Archives.

159. Telegram, October 24, 1941, file 55883/300B, RG 85, National Archives. See also Lemuel B. Schofield, Memorandum for the Attorney General, October 18, 1941, file 55883/300B, RG 85, National Archives.

160. W. A. Carmichael, District Director, Los Angeles to Commissioner General, July 22, 1949, file 56279/216, 6, RG 85, National Archives.

161. Dimock Report, 18.

162. Dimock Report, 65. On the continued use of informants, historian D. H. Dinwoodie notes, "To provide convincing evidence, heavy reliance continued to be placed on the word of informers. This use of *ex parte* statements was a convenience for the INS since it lessened the need for an investigation which might call the attention of suspects to the presence of Immigration Inspectors. With this dependence on surreptitious information, the Service encouraged the submission of random allegations and rewarded regular informers financially . . . this practice [use of informers] promoted dissemination of unsubstantiated accusations and a consequent atmosphere of fear in Chicano communities over threats of deportation." Dinwoodie, "Deportation," 195–196.

163. Dimock Report, 25, 26, 79.

164. Dimock Report, 50–51.

165. Dimock Report, 50.

166. Dimock Report, 62

167. Dimock Report, 126.

168. Dimock Report, 126.

169. Statement of Mr. Landis, Conference of Immigration and Naturalization Service Officials, September 6, 1941, file 56134/282, RG 85, National Archives.
170. Dimock Report, 128.
171. Ngai, *Impossible Subjects*, 78.
172. It is interesting to note that Immigration Bureau officials made a similar argument with respect to the Act of March 4, 1929 (creating criminal penalties for entry without inspection), calling for the exemption of those arrested and deported prior to the passage of the Act who had applied for readmission to the country. In this case, however, the agency succeeded in attaining an amendment to the legislation (under the Act of June 24, 1929) that mitigated the problematic provisions. Bureau of Immigration, *Annual Report, Fiscal Year Ended June 30, 1930*, 21.
173. In his tour of southwestern immigration stations, Coleman observed, "During my trip I heard many suggestions that discretionary powers should lie in someone, to waive or suspend the immigration laws covering deportations, in individual cases which involved hardship or injustice or were contrary to the recognized laws of humanity . . . A discretionary power of such nature, vested in the Commission of Immigration, seems very desirable. It should permit the Commissioner to temporarily stay the action of any particular section of the law, in individual cases, for such period as is deemed necessary, at the end of which period, if not previously reviewed, the stay should become permanent." George Coleman to D. W. MacCormack, Commissioner General, September 16, 1933, file 55877/443, RG 85, National Archives.
174. Dimock Report, 129.
175. Dimock Report, 125.
176. Salyer, *Laws Harsh as Tigers*, 143.
177. On this point, bureau officials specifically pointed to Section 6 of the Chinese Exclusion Act of 1892, as amended in 1893, which permitted arrest without warrant of Chinese immigrants. Grover C. Wilmoth, District Director, El Paso to Commissioner General, June 20, 1933, file 55597/927, RG 85, National Archives; L. Paul Winings, Memorandum for the Commissioner General, August 7, 1933, file 55597/927B, RG 85, National Archives.

Chapter 4

1. Edward Shaughnessy, Commissioner General, Remarks, April 29, 1944 (Immigration and Naturalization Service Annual Service Conference, 1944, New York, New York, April 19–May 1, 1944), 999, file 56312/675C, RG 85, National Archives.
2. Kennedy, *Freedom from Fear*, 746–797; Cohen, *Making a New Deal*; Brinkley, *New Deal Liberalism in Recession and War*.
3. The debates surrounding the character of the New Deal state are voluminous. For an excellent overview of these debates, see Smith, *Building a New Deal Liberalism*, 1–20.
4. Hawley, *The New Deal and the Problem of Monopoly*, 4.
5. William A. Whalen, District Director, San Antonio to T. B. Shoemaker, Acting Commissioner, January 22, 1946, Kelly Lytle-Hernández Collection of Border Patrol Research Papers, Box 13, Folder 5, Chicano Studies Research Center, University of California, Los Angeles.
6. Craig, *The Bracero Program*; Calavita, *Inside the State*; Tichenor, *Dividing Lines*; Bach, "Mexican Immigration and the American State"; Cohen, *Braceros*; Lytle-Hernández, *Migra!*
7. William J. Blocker, American Consul General to the Secretary of State, April 18, 1944, 3, file 123, box 316, 1944, RG 59, National Archives. Also accompanying Harrison on his visit were representatives of the border chambers of commerce and Mexican border businesses, the deputy commissioner general, the district directors from El Paso, Los Angeles, and San Antonio, and William P. Blocker, consul general at Juárez, Mexico. William P. Blocker, American consul general to the secretary of state, May 8, 1944, file 123, box 316, 1944, RG 59, National Archives (enclosing article written by Commissioner Earl G. Harrison regarding trip along the Mexican–American border).
8. Smith, *Talons of the Eagle*, 39.
9. Wood, *The Making of the Good Neighbor Policy*, 7.

10. Indeed, Hoover privately rejected the Roosevelt Corollary altogether. Schoultz, *Beneath the United States*, 92.

11. Schoultz, *Beneath the United States*, 299, 305–306. It is important to note that Roosevelt's articulation of the policy did not deter the nation from exerting its dominance through other, primarily economic, means. By lowering trade barriers and signing trade agreements, the United States by 1938 had become the primary market for almost every nation in Latin America. Wood, *The Making of the Good Neighbor Policy*, 136, 260–261; Driscoll, *The Tracks North*, 33; González and Fernandez, "Empire and the Origins of Twentieth Century Migration from Mexico to the United States," 47; Smith, *Talons of the Eagle*, 103.

12. Prior to 1939, the US military presence in Latin America was limited to its occupation of several Caribbean nations and a US naval mission in Brazil. Schoultz, *Beneath the United States*, 310.

13. Schoultz, *Beneath the United States*, 310.

14. Schoultz, *Beneath the United States*, 308.

15. By rendering foreign aid an instrument in the diplomat's toolkit, Rockefeller's initiative broke with tradition and, moreover, outlasted the war. As Schoultz notes, "National security considerations required the United States to continue foreign aid for the next half-century, and aid continued after the Cold War, largely because it had become the nation's new tradition." Schoultz, *Beneath the United States*, 309; Smith, *Talons of the Eagle*, 109–111.

16. While the Roosevelt administration was already working to improve US–Mexican trade relations, the onset of World War II accelerated this process. Driscoll, *The Tracks North*, 36; Niblo, *War, Diplomacy, and Development*, 115.

17. The 1938 crisis resulted when the Cárdenas administration nationalized the assets of foreign oil companies in Mexico. An international boycott of Mexican oil ensued while the United States sought compensation from the Mexican government for the lost assets of American companies. On the oil expropriation crisis and its impact on US–Mexican relations, see Wood, *The Making of the Good Neighbor Policy*, 253; Smith, *Talons of the Eagle*, 104–105; Dowling, "The Border at War," 28.

18. On the US–Mexican Commission for Wartime Cooperation, see Lytle-Hernández, *Migra!*, 113; Niblo, *War, Diplomacy, and Development*, 95; Raat and Brescia, *Mexico and the United States*, 164. On the Mexican-American Commission for Economic Cooperation, see Niblo, *War, Diplomacy, and Development*, 106–112. The specific sectors that benefited from the financing of this commission included agriculture, fishing, tourism, public works, and transportation. Driscoll, *The Tracks North*, 37.

19. Wiley and Gottlieb, *Empires in the Sun*, 251.

20. Wiley and Gottlieb, *Empires in the Sun*, 252.

21. Cadava, *Standing on Common Ground*, 21–38.

22. Dowling, "The Border at War," 48–49.

23. Cadava, *Standing on Common Ground*, 30.

24. Juárez Mayor Bermúdez and Brigadier General Quiñones were the two Mexican officials involved in the negotiations. Dowling, "The Border at War," 60.

25. Dowling, "The Border at War," 64–66.

26. Grover C. Wilmoth, District Director, El Paso, Circular to All Inspectors, November 26, 1941, file 55854/217, RG 85, National Archives; Lemuel B. Schofield, Special Assistant to the Attorney General, Circular Letter No. 459, "Non-resident Aliens' Border-Crossing Identification Cards," August 24, 1940, file 55817/902A, RG 85, National Archives.

27. Immigration and Naturalization Service, *Annual Report, Fiscal Year Ended June 30, 1941*, 29–30.

28. Immigration and Naturalization Service, Circular to All District Directors, July 19, 1941, file 56044/951, RG 85, National Archives; Grover C. Wilmoth, District Director, El Paso, Circular to All Inspectors, November 26, 1941, file 55854/217, RG 85, National Archives.

29. Kang, "The Legal Construction of the Borderlands," 163–164.

30. Chris P. Fox, Manager, El Paso Chamber of Commerce, Statement read at Meeting of Sunshine Area Chamber of Commerce, March 25–26, 1944, Before the Assembly and the United States Commissioner of Immigration, and American Consular Officials from Ciudad Juárez, Mexico, file 55817/902E, RG 85, National Archives.

31. Chris P. Fox, Manager, El Paso Chamber of Commerce, Statement read at Meeting of Sunshine Area Chamber of Commerce, March 25–26, 1944, Before the Assembly and the United States Commissioner of Immigration, and American Consular Officials from Ciudad Juárez, Mexico, file 55817/902E, RG 85, National Archives.
32. Grover C. Wilmoth, *Annual Report El Paso District, Fiscal Year Ended, June 30, 1943*, 1, file 56178/564, RG 85, National Archives.
33. Lemuel B. Schofield, Special Assistant to the Attorney General to Honorable Milton H. West, House of Representatives, November 5, 1941, file 55817/902C, RG 85, National Archives; Grover C. Wilmoth, District Director, El Paso, Circular to All Inspectors, November 26, 1941, file 55854/217, RG 85, National Archives.
34. Earl G. Harrison, Commissioner General to District Directors, San Antonio, El Paso, Los Angeles, March 22, 1943, file 55817/902D, RG 85, National Archives (authorizing informal issuance of nonresident alien border crossing cards to illiterate aliens and indicating concurrence of State Department in this procedure). See also Joseph Savoretti, Acting Commissioner of Immigration and Naturalization to Attorney General, August 15, 1944, file 55817/902E, RG 85, National Archives. For the wartime rules on the issuance of nonresident alien and resident alien border crossing cards to illiterate aliens, see Arthur J. Phelan, Assistant to the Deputy Commissioner to Mr. Savoretti, October 12, 1942, file 55817/902C, RG 85, National Archives.
35. Joseph Savoretti, Acting Commissioner of Immigration and Naturalization to Attorney General, August 15, 1944, file 55817/902E, RG 85, National Archives. This action would appease local protests and free the Service from having to hold appeal hearings in such matters. Arthur J. Phelan, Assistant to the Deputy Commissioner to Mr. Savoretti, Deputy Commissioner, October 12, 1942, file 55817/902C, RG 85, National Archives; Joseph Savoretti, Deputy Commissioner to Mr. Crone, October 22, 1942, file 55817/902C, RG 85, National Archives.
36. Earl G. Harrison, Commissioner General to Attorney General, June 27, 1944, file 55817/902E, RG 85, National Archives. See also T. B. Shoemaker, Assistant Commissioner to Earl G. Harrison, Commissioner General, June 12, 1944, file 55817/902E, RG 85, National Archives; US Department of Justice, Immigration and Naturalization Service, Operations Instructions, Sec. 166.13, July 22, 1944, file 55817/902E, RG85, National Archives. Border chambers of commerce were instrumental in changing the validity period of the nonresident alien border crossing cards from six months to a year, and then from a year to an unlimited period of time. Chris P. Fox, Manager, El Paso Chamber of Commerce, Statement read at Meeting of Sunshine Area Chamber of Commerce, March 25–26, 1944, Before the Assembly and the United States Commissioner of Immigration, and American Consular Officials from Ciudad Juárez, Mexico, 4, file 55817/902E, RG 85, National Archives.
37. Mexico declared war on the Axis powers in May of 1942, a few months before the signing of the bracero accords in August 1942. Cohen, *Braceros*, 25–26, 31; Driscoll, *The Tracks North*, 39; FitzGerald, *A Nation of Emigrants*, 48, 50; Wiley and Gottlieb, *Empires in the Sun*, 251.
38. Rodríguez, "Health on the Line," 98, 103. See also Driscoll, *The Tracks North*, 173.
39. For a fascinating look at the braceros' own response to the propaganda surrounding the Bracero Program, see Rodríguez, "Health on the Line," 216, 228–234; Cohen, *Braceros*, 26–27.
40. Kirstein, *Anglo Over Bracero*, 15 (citing to Franklin D. Roosevelt, Press Conference, October 20, 1942).
41. Craig, *The Bracero Program*, 42–43. Under the terms of the Bracero Program, incoming workers were exempted from the literacy test, head tax, contract labor law, visa and passport requirements, the alien registration requirement, and selective service registration. Scruggs, "The Bracero Program," 154; Breckenridge Long, Assistant Secretary of State to Attorney General, Department of Justice, October 9, 1942, file 55854/100F, RG 85, National Archives.
42. Cohen, *Braceros*, 28. On the ways in which Mexico's experience with the repatriation drives of the 1930s informed their demands for worker protections during the Bracero Program negotiations, see Elac, "The Employment of Mexican Workers in U.S. Agriculture, 1900–1960," 73–75.
43. Calavita, *Inside the State*, 19

44. Ngai, *Impossible Subjects*, 140.

45. García y Griego, "The Importation of Mexican Contract Laborers to the United States," 60.

46. On the demerits of grower–bracero contracts, Calavita writes, "A secret US Embassy report in 1950 concluded that "employers had committed mass violations with regard to recruiting, wages, general hiring conditions and utilization of noncontract [undocumented] labor," and that federal agencies were "not enforcing certain wage requirements and assumed a partial attitude in favor of agribusiness." Calavita, *Inside the State*, 29. See also Watson B. Miller, Commissioner General to "Tom," January 31, 1949, file 54246/339D, RG 85, National Archives; Memorandum for the Attorney General, March 23, 1949, 4, file 54246/339E, RG 85, National Archives.

47. On the exploitation and violence surrounding the Bracero Program, see Galarza, *Merchants of Labor*; Flores, "A Town Full of Dead Mexicans," 124–143; McCain, "Texas and the Mexican Labor Question, 1942–1947," 45–64; Hart, "Making Democracy Safe for the World," 49–84.

48. T. B. Shoemaker, Deputy Commissioner, Legal Branch, Immigration and Naturalization Service, Memorandum, September 23, 1941, file 55854/100D, RG 85, National Archives.

49. William A. Whalen, District Director, San Antonio District to Honorable J. J. Mansfield, August 21, 1941, file 55854/100D, RG 85, National Archives.

50. Kirstein, *Anglo Over Bracero*, 13; Fitzgerald, *The Face of the Nation*, 190.

51. I. W. Duggan, Director, Southern Division, Agricultural Adjustment Administration, Department of Agriculture to Lemuel B. Schofield, Special Assistant to the Attorney General, Immigration and Naturalization Service, May 7, 1942, file 55854/100E, RG 85, National Archives; Lemuel B. Schofield to I. W. Duggan, May 12, 1942, file 55854/100E, RG 85, National Archives; A. C. Devaney, Chief Examiner, Adjudications Branch, Memorandum, "Applications submitted to this Service for importation of Mexican labor," May 6, 1942, file 55854/100E, RG 85, National Archives.

52. William F. Blocker, Consul General, American Embassy, Ciudad Juárez, Mexico to George Shaw, Esq., American Consul, American Embassy, Mexico City, May 27, 1942, file 55854/100E, RG 85, National Archives (recounting conversation with Grover C. Wilmoth, District Director, El Paso, concerning labor importation plan).

53. William F. Blocker, Consul General, American Embassy, Ciudad Juárez, Mexico to George Shaw, Esq., American Consul, American Embassy, Mexico City, May 27, 1942, file 55854/100E, RG 85, National Archives. For a comparison of migratory labor programs, both foreign and domestic, during World War I and World War II, see Schwartz, *Seasonal Farm Labor in the United States*.

54. I. F. Wixon, District Director, San Francisco to Joseph Savoretti, Commissioner General, October 20, 1942, file 55854/100G, RG 85, National Archives.

55. Earl G. Harrison, Commissioner General to District Director, El Paso, September 9, 1942, file 55854/100F, RG 85, National Archives.

56. Grover C. Wilmoth to Central Office, September 3, 1942, file 55854/100F, RG 85, National Archives.

57. Grover C. Wilmoth, District Director, El Paso to T. B. Shoemaker, Deputy Commissioner, September 29, 1942, file 555854/100G, RG 85, National Archives.

58. Grover C. Wilmoth, District Director, El Paso to Central Office, September 1, 1942, file 55854/100F, RG 85, National Archives.

59. Kang, "The Legal Construction of the Borderlands," 178–179; Robinson, "Creating Foreign Policy Locally," 154–155.

60. I. M. Brody, Inspector in Charge to Central Office, October 26, 1942, file 55854/100G, RG 85, National Archives.

61. Z. B. Jackson, Acting Supervisor, Special Inspections Division, Immigration and Naturalization Service to District Director, San Francisco, February 2, 1943, file 55854/100I, RG 85, National Archives; W. F. Kelly, Assistant Commissioner, Central Office to District Director, El Paso, August 19, 1948, file 54246/339A, RG 85, National Archives. In 1949, immigration officials reported that former policemen, taxi drivers, bartenders, dance hall owners, and dance band members, none of whom had ever "seen a stalk of cotton," were working the fields. J. F. Delany, Officer in Charge, New Orleans, Louisiana to Watson B. Miller, Commissioner, Central Office, January 12, 1949, file 56246/339D, RG 85, National Archives.

62. Earl G. Harrison, Commissioner General to J. O. Walker, Agricultural Labor Branch, Food Production Division, Department of Agriculture, February 9, 1943, file 55854/100H, RG 85, National Archives.

63. Workers primarily left the job due to their inability to perform the arduous physical labor and abuse suffered at the hands of employers. Other reasons included family emergencies that compelled workers to return home or wage disputes with employers. J. O. Walker to Allen C. Devaney, December 12, 1942, file 55854/100H, RG 85, National Archives.

64. Z. B. Jackson, Acting Supervisor, Special Inspections Division, Immigration and Naturalization Service to District Director, San Francisco, February 2, 1943, file 55854/100I, RG 85, National Archives.

65. Joseph Savoretti, Deputy Commissioner to District Director, San Francisco, October 27, 1942, file 55854/100G, RG 85, National Archives. For a more detailed account of Immigration Service surveillance and apprehension responsibilities see also J. O. Walker to Allen C. Devaney, December 12, 1942, file 55854/100H, RG 85, National Archives.

66. As Cohen writes of the FSA, "The Farm Security Administration (FSA), established in 1935 to alleviate pervasive rural poverty, built labor camps in California to address the migrants' unsanitary living conditions and brought rural poverty to the attention of the nation when the agency's hired photographers, such as Dorothea Lange, Russell Lee, and Jack Delano, captured these hardships in graphic images. FSA personnel taught hygiene, first aide, and food safety to camp residents and trained them to run camps collectively. This drew the wrath of growers, who labeled FSA employees socialists and feared their farm laborers would be susceptible to this supposedly un-American ideology." Cohen, *Braceros*, 41.

67. Z. B. Jackson, Acting Supervisor, Special Inspections Division, Immigration and Naturalization Service to District Director, San Francisco, February 2, 1943, file 55854/100I, RG 85, National Archives.

68. I. F. Wixon, District Director, San Francisco to Commissioner General, February 3, 1943, file 55854/100I, RG 85, National Archives.

69. I. F. Wixon, District Director, San Francisco to Commissioner General, February 26, 1943, file 55854/100I, RG 85, National Archives.

70. I. F. Wixon, District Director, San Francisco to Commissioner General, February 26, 1943, file 55854/100I, RG 85, National Archives. Within the agency, there were clear differences of opinion on the legality of bracero detentions. In the Los Angeles District, District Director Albert Del Guercio refused FSA requests to release to their custody a group of Mexican nationals who had elected voluntary departure. To Del Guercio, voluntary departure did not deter desertion but instead encouraged it by sending the message that the only consequence for leaving the worksite was a free trip back to Mexico. William A. Anglim, Acting Regional Director to Mason Barr, Director, Management Division, Farm Security Administration, March 24, 1943, file 55854/100I, RG 85, National Archives; Albert Del Guercio, District Director, Los Angeles to Commissioner General, March 8, 1943, file 55854/100I, RG 85, National Archives.

71. I. F. Wixon, District Director, San Francisco to Commissioner General, February 26, 1943, file 55854/100I, RG 85, National Archives.

72. I. F. Wixon, District Director, San Francisco to Commissioner General, February 26, 1943, file 55854/100I, RG 85, National Archives.

73. In these cases, a warrant would be served. These immigrants, however, would be given the chance to accept voluntary departure. If they refused, formal deportation proceedings would commence.

74. On this point, the INS did not want to become a labor transportation service for the FSA; "It is emphasized that the responsibility of this Service in the handling of such laborers after entry into the United States does not commence until there is a failure on the part of the laborer to abide by the conditions of his admission, and then only after a refusal on the part of the alien to be repatriated by the Department of Agriculture." T. B. Shoemaker, Assistant Commissioner to Mr. Perry M. Oliver, Director of Administrative Services, April 13, 1943, file 55854/100I, RG 85, National Archives.

75. Memorandum, "Meeting in relation to Mexican Agricultural Workers—Held in the Office of Mr. A. C. Devaney, at 9:30am, March 3, 1943, file 55854/100I, RG 85, National Archives.

76. Scruggs, "The Bracero Program," 150, 153, 164; Craig, *The Bracero Program*, 47; Kirstein, *Anglo Over Bracero*, 16–17; Fitzgerald, *The Face of the Nation*, 190.

77. Craig, *The Bracero Program*, 47; Fitzgerald, *The Face of the Nation*, 191. Created by President Roosevelt, the WFA was charged with coordinating all government food programs in an effort to address criticisms about federal management of wartime food production and distribution.

78. Scruggs, "The Bracero Program," 161.

79. Public Law 45 delineated the authority and duties of the WFA. Scruggs, "The Bracero Program," 166.

80. Calavita, *Inside the State*, 22.

81. Calavita, *Inside the State*, 26, 31.

82. Craig, *The Bracero Program*, 47. See also Calavita, *Inside the State*, 24.

83. Immigration and Naturalization Service, Instruction No. 136, "Temporary admission of certain aliens to the United States with the purpose of performing labor during the present war," May 13, 1943, file 56131/1, RG 85, National Archives.

84. Kang, "The Legal Construction of the Borderlands," 178–180; Cohen, *Braceros*, 273, n. 18. For a detailed account of bracero processing on both sides of the border, see Cohen, *Braceros*, 89–112.

85. As Cohen notes, "When U.S. growers first expressed a desire for imported labor, they envisioned a program like the informal arrangements of World War I. At that time, growers contracted workers directly and set wages and work conditions without state intervention; workers suspected of union activity were quickly repatriated." Cohen, *Braceros*, 27.

86. Public Law 45 replicated the terms of the Ninth Proviso of Section 3 of the Immigration Act of 1917, conferring upon the Commissioner General the administrative discretion, in Kitty Calavita's words, "to admit the inadmissible . . . waiv[ing] the prohibition against contract labor 'for such time and under such conditions' as he shall prescribe." Calavita, *Inside the State*, 23; Kirstein, *Anglo Over Bracero*, 19; Kang, "The Legal Construction of the Borderlands," 178–180.

87. Calavita, *Inside the State*, 23. Under this procedure, Calavita estimates that 2,000 braceros were admitted during May 1943. McCain estimates that 2,000 to 4,000 were admitted in the same period. McCain, "Texas and the Mexican Labor Question," 50.

88. Calavita, *Inside the State*, 23.

89. H. R. Landon, Memorandum for the File, May 13, 1943, file 56163/1, RG 85, National Archives.

90. Calavita, *Inside the State*, 73.

91. Grover C. Wilmoth, District Director El Paso to Commissioner General, June 30, 1946, file 56188/215, RG 85, National Archives.

92. Indeed, the very renewal of the Program between 1947 until 1951 reflected the continuing influence of southwestern growers on American immigration policy. Like the wartime Bracero Program, the statutory authority for the peacetime Bracero Program rested in the Ninth Proviso of Section 3 of the Immigration Act of 1917. Yet, unlike the wartime program, Congress, responding to its agribusiness interests, sustained the Bracero Program through a series of backroom administrative maneuvers. More specifically, on April 28, 1947, Congress passed Public Law 40, which extended the Bracero Program until December 31, 1947 and stipulated its termination no later than January 31, 1948. In December 1947, however, the House Committee on Agriculture met with growers and federal administrators to devise and sanction an extralegal continuation of the Program. During these hearings, the Committee members and the INS agreed that continued postwar labor shortages made it necessary to maintain the Program. Having reached this consensus, the hearing participants quickly moved on to plan the logistical details, ignoring the express stipulation of Public Law 40 that terminated the Bracero Program. Despite the termination clause, the Bracero Program continued by administrative fiat under the plan drafted by the House Committee meeting. Seven months later, Congress officially, yet quietly sanctioned this administrative extension and continued the Program for an additional year (until June 30, 1949) when it passed Public Law 893. Calavita, *Inside the State*, 26–27; Kirstein, *Anglo Over Bracero*, 49–50.

93. J. F. Delany, Officer in Charge, New Orleans to Watson B. Miller, Commissioner General, January 12, 1949, file 56246/339D, RG 85, National Archives. Despite its long-standing reservations regarding grower-bracero contracting, Mexico signed the postwar bracero accords (March 25, 1947, April 2, 1947, February 21, 1948, and August 1, 1949) because it believed that its ongoing participation in the Bracero Program would help deter undocumented immigration, sustain the flow of remittances, which had become an important source of revenue, to Mexico, and act as a safety valve for Mexico's own economic and social problems. Craig, *The Bracero Program*, 53, 57-60.

94. Craig, *The Bracero Program*, 54.

95. Craig, *The Bracero Program*, 54.

96. Public Law 893 appropriated $2.5 million for the Program. Kirstein, *Anglo Over Bracero*, 66.

97. Calavita, *Inside the State*, 73.

98. William G. MacLean, Division of Mexican Affairs, Department of State to W. F. Kelly, Assistant Commissioner for Alien Control, January 8, 1948, file 56246/339, RG 85, National Archives. See "Lovett," Telegram to American Embassy, Mexico City, September 21, 1949, file 56246/339B, RG 85, National Archives.

99. A. R. Mackey, Acting Assistant Commissioner to H. L. Mitchell, President, National Farm Labor Union, January 18, 1949, file 56246/339D, RG 85, National Archives. See also Commissioner General of Immigration & Director of United States Employment Service, Information Relative to Temporary Admission of Nationals of Mexico to the United States to Engage in Agricultural Employment under the Agreement of February 21, 1948 Governing the Migration of Mexican Agricultural Workers, March 1948, file 56246/339A, RG 85, National Archives.

100. Southwestern INS officials appear to have taken on these responsibilities for several reasons, including an effort on the part of USES and INS officials to pool their resources in the face of federal budget cuts for the peacetime Bracero Program; INS efforts to facilitate growers' access to Mexican workers; and, most commonly, a lack of clarity in instructions issued to agency employees in the field. See, for example, Department of Labor, United States Employment Service, Minutes of Organization Meeting of Special Farm Labor Committee, February 20, 1948, file 56246/339, RG 85, National Archives; Commissioner General of Immigration & Director of United States Employment Service, Information Relative to Temporary Admission of Nationals of Mexico to the United States to Engage in Agricultural Employment under the Agreement of February 21, 1948 Governing the Migration of Mexican Agricultural Workers, March 1948, file 56246/339A, RG 85, National Archives; Department of State, Press Release, "Mexican Farm Labor Migration Arrangements," February 26, 1948, file 56246/339, RG 85, National Archives; Robert C. Goodwin, Director, United States Employment Service to Regional Directors, Regions X and XII, March 4, 1948, file 56246/339, RG 85, National Archives.

101. Ugo Carusi, Commissioner General to Congressman Milton H. West, April 18, 1947, file 56216/579, RG 85, National Archives.

102. Whalen said that "farmers would have to agree to pay the prevailing wage and that the prevailing wage would have to be established. I told him that this office had been unable to get anyone in authority to certify or state what the prevailing wage scale was, or that there was a scarcity of labor, but that I had written letters to the TSES [Texas State Employment Service] and the Hidalgo County Agent. He said in the absence of certificates from people in authority, it would be necessary for this Service to send men into the field and question farmers and determine what the prevailing wage is from such investigations." Allan C. Skinner, Officer in Charge, Confidential Memorandum of Telephone Conversation with Mr. Whalen in San Antonio, April 10, 1947, file 56216/579, RG 85, National Archives.

103. Allan C. Skinner, Officer in Charge, Hidalgo, Texas to Bob Lewis, Officer in Charge, McAllen, Texas State Employment Service, April 4, 1947, file 56216/79, RG 85, National Archives; Allan C. Skinner, Officer in Charge, Hidalgo, Texas to William A. Whalen, District Director, San Antonio, April 10, 1947, file 56216/79, RG 85, National Archives; Joseph Savoretti to District Director, San Antonio, April 18, 1947, file 56216/79, RG 85, National Archives; Allan C. Skinner, Officer in Charge, Hidalgo Texas, Confidential Memorandum, April 10, 1947, file 56216/579, RG 85, National Archives.

104. Emphasis in original. Grover C. Wilmoth, Statement prepared by Grover C. Wilmoth, District Director, Immigration and Naturalization Service, El Paso District, for the President's Commission on Migratory Labor, Holding Sessions at El Paso, Texas on August 4 and 5, 1950, file 56302/267, pt. 1, RG 85, National Archives.

105. Commissioner General of Immigration & Director of United States Employment Service, Information Relative to Temporary Admission of Nationals of Mexico to the United States to Engage in Agricultural Employment under the Agreement of February 21, 1948 Governing the Migration of Mexican Agricultural Workers, March 1948, file 56246/339A, RG 85, National Archives.

106. Handwritten note attached to memorandum from Howard L. Field, Acting District Director, Los Angeles to Commissioner General, November 19, 1947, file 56246/339, RG 85, National Archives. The following letters concern authorizations for Mexican laborers to work in agricultural processing and packing plants: A. C. Devaney, Acting Assistant Commissioner to file, April 29, 1947, file 56216/579, RG 85, National Archives; Allan C. Skinner, Officer in Charge, Hidalgo, Texas to William A. Whalen, District Director, San Antonio, Texas, April 10, 1947, file 56216/579, RG 85, National Archives.

107. The standard contract provided that Mexican workers would receive "hygienic lodgings, adequate to the physical condition of the area and of the type used by domestic agricultural workers of the region." In reality, the stipulated standard did not exist since American farmers did not provide domestic workers with housing. This circumstance reflected the broader dispossession of domestic farmers in the United States and their exclusion from the social and economic reforms of the New Deal; as Ngai writes, "agricultural laborers were thus not covered by the National Labor Relations Act of 1935, the Social Security Act of 1935, or the Fair Labor Standards Act of 1938, which recognized the right to organize and bargain collectively, provided for social insurance for the elderly, and established a minimum wage, respectively." Given the absence of wage and working standards for domestic agricultural laborers, the Bracero Program guarantees of conditions equivalent to those of the domestic labor force rang hollow. Ngai, *Impossible Subjects*, 136.

108. J. F. Delany, Officer in Charge, New Orleans to W. F. Miller, District Director, Atlanta, March 4, 1948, file 56246/339, RG85, National Archives.

109. W. F. Miller, District Director, Miami, Florida to J. F. Delany, Officer in Charge, New Orleans, Louisiana, October 22, 1948, file 56246/339C, RG 85, National Archives.

110. W. F. Miller, District Director, Miami, Florida to J. F. Delany, Officer in Charge, New Orleans, Louisiana, October 22, 1948, file 56246/339C, RG 85, National Archives.

111. W. F. Miller, District Director, Miami, Florida to J. F. Delany, Officer in Charge, New Orleans, Louisiana, October 22, 1948, file 56246/339C, RG 85, National Archives.

112. Mr. Robinson to Commissioner General, November 23, 1948, file 56246/339C, RG 85, National Archives.

113. Thus, for example, in a survey of the various ways in which southwestern immigration officials managed the Bracero Program, Commissioner General Watson B. Miller observed that the District Director at El Paso reported human rights violations to the central office while the District Director at San Antonio did not. Memorandum, signed "WBM" (most likely Watson B. Miller), June 7, 1949, file 56246/339E, RG85, National Archives.

114. Memorandum, signed "WBM" (most likely Watson B. Miller), June 7, 1949, file 56246/339E, RG 85, National Archives.

115. Calavita, *Inside the State*, 29. García y Griego states that the 1948 agreement removed INS and USES responsibility for ensuring compliance. García y Griego, "The Importation of Mexican Contract Laborers," 69.

116. This official observed that the USES assigned only one official to manage the state of Arkansas where approximately 14,000 Mexicans were employed and that a single Mexican consular office monitored the working and living conditions of braceros in three states. J. F. Delany, Officer in Charge, New Orleans, Louisiana to Watson B. Miller, Commissioner, January 12, 1949, file 56246/339D, RG 85, National Archives.

117. Grover C. Wilmoth, District Director, El Paso to Commissioner General, June 30, 1947, file 56220/415, RG 85, National Archives; J. F. Delany, Officer in Charge, New Orleans,

Louisiana to Watson B. Miller, Commissioner, January 12, 1949, file 56246/339D, RG 85, National Archives.

118. Report of A. S. Hudson, Chief, Alien Control Section, El Paso in Grover C. Wilmoth, District Director, El Paso to Central Office, July 29, 1949, file 56279/215, RG 85, National Archives.

119. Grover C. Wilmoth to Central Office, June 30, 1947, file 56220/415, RG 85, National Archives.

120. Indeed, due to wartime concerns, Congress granted the Patrol an additional $2 million appropriation for 712 new officers and new equipment in 1940. Immigration and Naturalization Service, *Annual Report, Fiscal Year Ended June 30, 1940*, 111.

121. Immigration and Naturalization Service, *Annual Report, Fiscal Year Ended June 30, 1939*; Immigration and Naturalization Service, *Annual Report, Fiscal Year Ended June 30, 1941*, 19–20; Immigration and Naturalization Service, *Annual Report, Fiscal Year Ended June 30, 1942*, 2–7, 23; Immigration and Naturalization Service, *Annual Report, Fiscal Year Ended June 30, 1943*, 15–16. On the U-boat attack on Atlantic shipping, see Kennedy, *Freedom from Fear*, 568.

122. Hugh Carter, LeRoy B. DePuy, Ernest Rubin, and Marguerite Milan, General Research Unit, Immigration and Naturalization Service, "Administrative History of the Immigration and Naturalization Service during World War II," August 19, 1946 (typed manuscript), 4, Kelly Lytle-Hernández Collection of Border Patrol Research Papers, Box 13, Folder 29, Chicano Studies Research Center, University of California, Los Angeles.

123. Immigration and Naturalization Service, *Annual Report, Fiscal Year Ended June 30, 1944*, 21; Immigration and Naturalization Service, *Annual Report, Fiscal Year Ended, June 30, 1945*.

124. Immigration and Naturalization Service, *Annual Report, Fiscal Year Ended, June 30, 1949*, 36.

125. Albert Del Guercio, District Director, Los Angeles to Joseph Savoretti, Acting Commissioner, October 16, 1944, file 56195/713, RG 85, National Archives.

126. García y Griego, "The Importation of Mexican Contract Laborers," 92, n. 97.

127. FitzGerald, *A Nation of Emigrants*, 51; Cohen, *Braceros*, 214; McCain, "Texas and the Mexican Labor Question," 49, n. 9.

128. FitzGerald, *A Nation of Emigrants*, 51, 54–55.

129. In Mexico, workers, between the ages of twenty and forty, had to supply documentation regarding their character and skills as farmworkers. FitzGerald, *A Nation of Emigrants*, 51. See also Cohen, *Braceros*, 92–93.

130. Cohen, *Braceros*, 96–97.

131. Cohen, *Braceros*, 99.

132. Cohen, *Braceros*, 99–100.

133. Cohen, *Braceros*, 103.

134. Raat and Brescia, *Mexico and the United States*, 166–167.

135. Indeed, bracero remittances were so substantial that, "by the 1950s [they] had become Mexico's third-largest source of hard currency." Cohen, *Braceros*, 214.

136. Cohen, *Braceros*, 90, 202.

137. Cohen, *Braceros*, 29–30.

138. Calavita continues, "from 1942 through 1952, when a total of 818,545 braceros were imported from Mexico, the INS apprehended over two million undocumented workers." Calavita, *Inside the State*, 32.

139. Grover C. Wilmoth, District Director, El Paso, *Annual Report El Paso District, Fiscal Year Ending June 30, 1949*, 1, file 56279/215, RG 85, National Archives.

140. Immigration and Naturalization Service, *Annual Report, Fiscal Year Ended June 30, 1948*, 25.

141. Calavita, *Inside the State*, 34–35.

142. An average of 997 were employed by the Border Patrol during fiscal year 1944. Immigration and Naturalization Service, *Annual Report, Fiscal Year Ended June 30, 1944*, 21. On these congressional budget cuts Calavita observes that they "sent an unequivocal message to the Immigration Service, underscoring the congressional unwillingness to interfere with a plentiful farm labor supply." Calavita, *Inside the State*, 36.

143. Immigration and Naturalization Service, *Annual Report, Fiscal Year Ended June 30, 1945*; Immigration and Naturalization Service, *Annual Report, Fiscal Year Ended June 30, 1946*.

144. Calavita, *Inside the State*, 35.

145. Calavita, *Inside the State*, 35, 37.
146. The INS advised Eastland against the hiring of undocumented immigrants and referred him to the USES for further assistance. A. R. Mackey, Memorandum of telephone call between A. R. Mackey and Mr. Payce, Staff Member for Senator Eastland of Mississippi, September 16, 1948, 1:50 p.m., file 56246/339B, RG 85, National Archives. Even though he was a staunch defender of the national origins quota system, Eastland turned a blind eye to the issue of undocumented immigration along the US–Mexico border. Calavita, *Inside the State*, 36. On the bipolar policy positions of politicians such as Eastland, see Tichenor, *Dividing Lines*, 150.
147. H. R. Landon, District Director, Los Angeles to Commissioner General, August 30, 1950, file 56302/267, pt. 1, RG 85, National Archives.
148. Albert Del Guercio, District Director, Los Angeles to Commissioner General, July 8, 1946, file 56188/216, RG 85, National Archives.
149. Whalen wrote, "the courts have taken into careful consideration the exceptionally strong incentive at this time for Mexican aliens previously deported, to illegally enter the United States; and, the more lenient sentences also reflect the influence upon the courts of the strong public sentiment that our labor supply should be supplemented by temporary admission of Mexican laborers until the war ends in victory." William A. Whalen, District Director, San Antonio, *Annual Report San Antonio District, Fiscal Year Ending June 30, 1943*, 6, file 56178/565, RG 85, National Archives.
150. Grover C. Wilmoth, District Director, El Paso, *Annual Report El Paso District, Fiscal Year Ending June 30, 1946*, 1, file 56188/215, RG 85, National Archives.
151. R. H. Robinson, Operations Advisor to A. R. Mackey, July 25, 1949, file 56246/339F, RG 85, National Archives.
152. W. A. Carmichael, District Director, Los Angeles, *Annual Report Los Angeles District, Fiscal Year Ending June 30, 1949*, 3, file 56279/216, RG 85, National Archives.
153. H. L. Mitchell, President, National Agricultural Workers Union, "Unions of Two Countries Act on Wetback Influx," *The American Federationist*, vol. 61, n. 2 (January 1954), RM-37, Special Collections, Arizona State University Library.
154. H. L. Mitchell, President, National Agricultural Workers Union, "Unions of Two Countries Act on Wetback Influx," *The American Federationist*, vol. 61, n. 2 (January 1954), RM-37, Special Collections, Arizona State University Library.
155. This group also objected to the admission of workers from the British West Indies. California State Federation of Labor, "U.S.–Mexican Unions Ask for Voice in Labor Agreement," *Weekly News Letter*, December 23, 1953, 1, CHI NM-83, Chicano Collection, Arizona State University Library.
156. H. L. Mitchell, President, National Agricultural Workers Union, "Unions of Two Countries Act on Wetback Influx," *The American Federationist*, vol. 61, n. 2 (January 1954), RM-37, Special Collections, Arizona State University Library.
157. H. L. Mitchell, "Why Import Farm Workers?" *The American Federationist*, vol. 56, n. 2 (February 1949), 20, RM-36, Special Collections, Arizona State University Library; See also Craig, *The Bracero Program*, 48, 56, 87, 90.
158. Hawley, "The Politics of the Mexican Labor Issue, 1950–1965."
159. Calavita, *Inside the State*, 37.
160. Lytle-Hernández, "Entangling Bodies and Borders," 84–85, 95.
161. Kirstein, *Anglo Over Bracero*, 52.
162. Kirstein estimates that there were 100,000 out-of-status Mexicans in Texas by 1948. Border Patrol officers counted 115 to 120 unauthorized entries per day. Kirstein, *Anglo Over Bracero*, 55, 69 (citing to an expose published in *Newsweek*, March 11, 1946, 71).
163. Hart, "Making Democracy Safe for the World," 60. See also Guglielmo, "Fighting for Caucasian Rights," 1216; Dowling, "The Border at War."
164. Hart, "Making Democracy Safe for the World," 60; McCain, "Texas and the Mexican Labor Question," 59.
165. McCain, "Texas and the Mexican Labor Question," 59–60.
166. Hart, "Making Democracy Safe for the World." But see Dowling, who argues that in Texas, ethnic Mexicans living on the border experienced less discrimination in this period. Dowling, "The Border at War," 154.

167. Guglielmo, "Fighting for Caucasian Rights," 1223. Guglielmo also explains why and how Mexican Americans in Texas deployed a Caucasian racial identity to defend their political rights.
168. Guglielmo, "Fighting for Caucasian Rights," 1223–1224.
169. Historian Robert Robinson notes that as a reflection of Texans' lack of commitment to Mexican civil rights, "Most of the resolutions were comfortably vague, and the matter of legislation was dealt with by a resolution which simply stated that it should be known that Ambassador de la Colina had requested the GNC to study the possibility of legislation." Robinson, "Creating Foreign Policy Locally," 37, 38–43. For an account of the Texas Good Neighbor Commission, see McCain, "Texas and the Mexican Labor Question," and Dowling, "The Border at War."
170. Robinson notes that this concession lasted for two years—until 1949. Robinson, "Creating Foreign Policy Locally," 36, 61.
171. FitzGerald, *A Nation of Emigrants*, 52–53.
172. Kirstein, *Anglo Over Bracero*, 55, 70.
173. H. P. Brady, Chief, District Alien Control Division, San Antonio, Texas to W. F. Kelly, Assistant Commissioner for Alien Control, August 1, 1944, file 56195/711, RG 85, National Archives; Kirstein, *Anglo Over Bracero*, 52. See also Scruggs, "The U.S., Mexico, and the Wetbacks," 154; Lytle-Hernández, "Entangling Bodies and Borders," 94–95.
174. Scruggs, "The U.S., Mexico, and the Wetbacks," 156.
175. Scruggs, "The U.S., Mexico, and the Wetbacks," 157, 159.
176. Lytle-Hernández, "Entangling Bodies and Borders," 87. On the 1944 campaign, see Otey Scruggs, "The United States, Mexico, and the Wetbacks," 149–165.
177. Calavita, *Inside the State*, 34–35; Earl G. Harrison, Commissioner General to District Directors, San Antonio, El Paso, Los Angeles, April 11, 1944, file 55883/300D, RG 85, National Archives; W. A. Carmichael, District Director, Los Angeles to Commissioner, June 9, 1949, file 56246/339F, RG 85, National Archives; W. A. Carmichael, District Director, Los Angeles to Commissioner, April 25, 1949, file 56246/339E, RG 85, National Archives; "Aliens in U.S. Illegally Caught in Area Search: Mexican Nationals Number More than 130; Buses Take First Offenders to Border," 1, 3. See also Howard L. Field, District Enforcement Officer, Memorandum Concerning Operation for Apprehension of Illegal Aliens at Los Angeles, Commencing Monday, April 11, 1949, April 8, 1949, file 54246/339E, RG 85, National Archives.
178. Calavita, *Inside the State*, 33; García y Griego, "The Importation of Mexican Contract Laborers," 61, 64; Scruggs, "The United States, Mexico, and the Wetbacks," 163; William A. Whalen, District Director, San Antonio to Commissioner General, March 19, 1946, file 56198/14, RG 85, National Archives; W. F. Kelly to Watson B. Miller, May 31, 1949, file 56246/339F, RG 85, National Archives.
179. Albert Del Guercio, District Director, Los Angeles to Joseph Savoretti, Acting Commissioner, October 16, 1944, file 56195/713, RG 85, National Archives. See also Earl G. Harrison, Commissioner General to District Directors, San Antonio, El Paso, Los Angeles, April 11, 1944, file 55883/300D, RG 85, National Archives; J. W. Nelson, Chief, Border Patrol Section to W. F. Kelly, Assistant Commissioner for Alien Control, July 12, 1944, file 56195/711, RG 85, National Archives; Grover C. Wilmoth, District Director, El Paso to Staff Officers, Section Chiefs, Chief Patrol Inspectors, Officers in Charge, El Paso District, April 12, 1948, file 56246/339A, RG 85, National Archives.
180. Kirstein, *Anglo Over Bracero*, 56; Craig, *The Bracero Program*, 59.
181. Allan C. Skinner, Officer in Charge to William A. Whalen, Confidential memorandum, April 11, 1947, file 56216/579, RG 85, National Archives; Allan C. Skinner, Officer in Charge to William A. Whalen, Confidential memorandum, April 13, 1947, file 56216/579, RG 85, National Archives; Albert Del Guercio, District Director to Ugo Carusi, Commissioner General, May 7, 1947, file 56216/579, RG 85, National Archives; "Mexico Plans to Regularize Wetbacks Cited," March 31, 1947, file 56216/579, RG 85, National Archives; Craig, *The Bracero Program*, 59.
182. Douglas Flood, Second Secretary of Embassy to Secretary of State, March 21, 1947, file 56216/579, RG 85, National Archives.

183. Minutes of the Meeting of the Subcommittee on Labor of the Committee on International Social Policy, January 3, 1949, file 56246/339D, RG 85, National Archives; Interim Arrangement for Contracting Wetbacks, January 11, 1949, file 56246/339D, RG 85, National Archives (notes on January 5, 1949 agreement reached with Mexico to contract 4,000 undocumented immigrants at contracting centers in Fresno and Phoenix); Paul J. Reveley, Chief, Division of Mexican Affairs to Watson B. Miller, Commissioner General, January 10, 1949, file 56246/339D, RG 85, National Archives.

184. Craig, *The Bracero Program*, 67.

185. Kirstein, *Anglo Over Bracero*, 56; Craig, *Bracero Program*, 67. For a focused account of these legalization programs in Texas, see Robinson, "Creating Foreign Policy Locally."

186. Kirstein, *Anglo Over Bracero*, 56. US President's Commission on Migratory Labor, *Migratory Labor in American Agriculture*, 53.

187. García y Griego, "The Importation of Mexican Contract Labor," 65.

188. J. F. Delany, Officer in Charge, New Orleans, Louisiana to Watson B. Miller, Commissioner, Central Office, March 4, 1948, file 56246/339, RG 85, National Archives.

189. W. A. Carmichael, District Director, Los Angeles to Commissioner, September 20, 1949, file 56246/339F, RG 85, National Archives.

190. Craig, *The Bracero Program*, 59.

191. Calavita, *Inside the State*, 30.

192. Ngai, *Impossible Subjects*, 153. See also Calavita, *Inside the State*, 29–30; García y Griego, "The Importation of Mexican Contract Laborers," 70.

193. Ngai, *Impossible Subjects*, 153.

194. Of Mexico's withdrawal, Galarza writes, "The Mexican government responded by abrogating the 1948 agreement, formally announcing that it would reserve the possibility of filing claims for damage inflicted upon its agricultural production in the north from the uncontrolled exodus of border resident laborers." Galarza, *Merchants of Labor*, 71. On the impact of the El Paso Incident on the Good Neighbor policy, see Cohen, *Braceros*, 201–203. On the public response to the El Paso Incident in Mexico, see Robinson, "Creating Foreign Policy Locally," 126–128.

195. Calavita, *Inside the State*, 30–31.

196. A. R. Mackey, Memorandum in re Agricultural Laborers, December 30, 1948, file 56246/339D, RG 85, National Archives. See also Minutes of the Meeting of the Subcommittee on Labor of the Committee on International Social Policy held on Wednesday, December 29, 1948 at 2:00 p.m. in room 3215, Department of Labor Building, January 3, 1949, file 56246/339D, RG 85, National Archives; N. D. Collaer, Chief, Border Patrol Section to Watson B. Miller, Commissioner, January 12, 1949, file 56246/339D, RG 85, National Archives. By May 1949 US and Mexican officials agreed to open an additional recruiting center in San Pedro, California. Typed record of telephone conversation with Mr. Bodley of Senator Ecton's office, signed by "MAR," May 25, 1949, file 56246/339F, RG 85, National Archives. See also W. A. Carmichael, District Director, Los Angeles to Officer in Charge, San Diego, July 15, 1949, file 56246/339F, RG 85, National Archives.

197. A. R. Mackey, Acting Assistant Commissioner to District Directors, Los Angeles, San Francisco, El Paso, and San Antonio, January 14, 1949, file 56246/339D, RG 85, National Archives (attaching agreement). On Mexico's agreement to the plan, see Embassy of Mexico, Memorandum, January 5, 1949, file 56246/339D, RG 85, National Archives.

198. R. H. Robinson, Operations Advisor to A. R. Mackey, Deputy Commissioner, July 25, 1949, file 56246/339F, RG 85, National Archives.

199. W. A. Carmichael, District Director, Los Angeles to Commissioner, September 14, 1949, file 56246/339F, RG 85, National Archives. Kirstein notes that Mexico insisted on the inclusion of a legalization provision as a condition of signing a new accord in 1949. Kirstein, *Anglo Over Bracero*, 70.

200. Calavita, *Inside the State*, 28.

201. Calavita, *Inside the State*, 28.

202. W. F. Kelly to Ugo Carusi, Commissioner General Jan. 9, 1947, file 56216/579, RG 85, National Archives.

Chapter 5

1. Argyle R. Mackey, Commissioner General to Mrs. Grover C. Wilmoth, May 7, 1951, file 56302/267, pt. 1, RG 85, National Archives; Maurice J. Tobin, Secretary of Labor, US Department of Labor, "The Recommendations of the President's Commission on Migratory Labor," typed report, Bureau of Labor Standards, April 1952, 4, file 56321/267, pt. 1, RG 85, National Archives.

2. Grover C. Wilmoth, District Director, El Paso, "Mexican Border Procedure, Lecture No. 23," RG 85, file 55875/23; US Department of Justice, Immigration and Naturalization Service, "Grover C. Wilmoth—A Tribute," 113 (authored by Mackey). Wilmoth's report was titled "The Red Menace in the U.S.A.".

3. US Department of Justice, Immigration and Naturalization Service, "Grover C. Wilmoth—A Tribute," 113.

4. Public Law 613, 60 Stat. 864 (1946).

5. For a discussion of the role of mezzo-level agency managers in policy formation, see Carpenter, *The Forging of Bureaucratic Autonomy*, 18–22.

6. In making this claim, I draw upon the work of Daniel Tichenor. Yet whereas Tichenor recounts how Truman, and later Eisenhower, used their executive authority to soften the nation's racially based admission policies, I focus on the ways in which the executive branch sought to create an aggressive border enforcement policy. Tichenor, *Dividing Lines*, 150–207.

7. For the most comprehensive accounts of the commission, see Kirstein, "Agribusiness, Labor, and the Wetbacks." For an account of the relationship between the commission and the Truman administration, see Robinson, "Taking the Fair Deal to the Fields"; Kirstein, *Anglo Over Bracero*, 83–95.

8. Clemens, "Lineages of the Rube Goldberg State."

9. Emphasis in original. C. E. Waller, Chief, Budget and Fiscal Control Section to N. D. Collaer, Chief, Border Patrol Section, July 8, 1949, Kelly Lytle-Hernández Collection of Border Patrol Research Papers, Box 13, Folder 11, Chicano Studies Research Center, University of California, Los Angeles.

10. C. E. Waller, Chief, Budget and Fiscal Control Section to N. D. Collaer, Chief, Border Patrol Section, July 8, 1949, Kelly Lytle-Hernández Collection of Border Patrol Research Papers, Box 13, Folder 11, Chicano Studies Research Center, University of California, Los Angeles.

11. On the use of the radio, see Immigration and Naturalization Service, *Annual Report, Fiscal Year Ended June 30, 1939*. On the use of radar, see unsigned memorandum (most likely from Willard F. Kelly) to Commissioner General, February 3, 1948, file 56245/181A, RG 85, National Archives. On the planelifts, see Lytle-Hernández, "Entangling Bodies and Borders," 96. On patrol plane surveillance, see US Department of Justice, Immigration and Naturalization Service, "Patrolling the Imperial Valley by Plane," 60; W. A. Carmichael, District Director, Los Angeles, *Annual Report Los Angeles District, Fiscal Year Ended June 30, 1949*, 3, file 56279/216, RG 85, National Archives. The service had considered the problem of plane smuggling and the feasibility of using pursuit planes since the late 1920s. See G. C. Wilmoth to Commissioner General, October 16, 1929, file 56364/47.40SW, RG 85, National Archives.

12. Department of Justice, Immigration and Naturalization Service, "Border Patrol Use of Aircraft," 37.

13. G. C. Wilmoth, Lecture, "Immigration Border Patrol Officers' Duties and Authority to Act, March 29, 1944," 1, file 56192/582, RG 85, National Archives.

14. Grover C. Wilmoth, District Director, El Paso, *Annual Report El Paso District, Fiscal Year Ended June 30, 1946*, 2, file 56188/215, RG 85, National Archives.

15. Lytle-Hernández, *Migra!*, 155–156.

16. Lytle-Hernández, "Entangling Bodies and Borders," 93.

17. William A. Whalen, District Director, San Antonio to Commissioner General, August 25, 1933, file 55819/7, RG 85, National Archives.

18. For the agency's position on the roundups, see John Holland, District Enforcement Officer, Immigration and Naturalization Service, testifying before the President's Commission

on Migratory Labor on August 1, 1950, Brownsville, Texas, President's Commission on Migratory Labor, *Stenographic Report of Proceedings*, 351. See also Commissioner General to Mr. Hanavan, September 22, 1952, file 56364/41.11, pt. 1, RG 85, Kelly Lytle-Hernández Collection of Border Patrol Research Papers, Box 3, Folder 3, Chicano Studies Research Center, University of California, Los Angeles.

19. Richard J. Hanavan, Fresno, California to Commissioner General, Immigration and Naturalization Service, May 27, 1952, file 56364/41.11, pt. 1, RG 85, Kelly Lytle- Hernández Collection of Border Patrol Research Papers, Box 3, Folder 3, Chicano Studies Research Center, University of California, Los Angeles.

20. E. T. Yates, Brownsville, Texas to the Secretary of State, May 16, 1952, file 56364/41.11, pt. 1, RG 85, Kelly Lytle-Hernández Collection of Border Patrol Research Papers, Box 3, Folder 3, Chicano Studies Research Center, University of California, Los Angeles.

21. The El Centro facility accommodated 190 prisoners. Albert Del Guercio, District Director, Los Angeles, *Annual Report Los Angeles District, Fiscal Year Ended June 30, 1945*, 2, file 56221/579, RG 85, National Archives.

22. William A. Whalen, District Director, San Antonio to Commissioner General, May 5, 1948, file 56198/14, RG 85, National Archives.

23. William A. Whalen, District Director, San Antonio to Commissioner General, May 5, 1948, file 56198/14, RG 85, National Archives.

24. William A. Whalen, District Director, San Antonio to Commissioner General, March 6, 1946, file 56198/14, RG 85, National Archives. See also William A. Whalen, District Director, San Antonio, *Annual Report San Antonio District, Fiscal Year Ended June 30, 1945*, 2, file 56221/514, RG 85, National Archives.

25. William A. Whalen, District Director, San Antonio to Commissioner General, May 5, 1948, file 56198/14, RG 85, National Archives; William A. Whalen, District Director, San Antonio to Commissioner General, May 4, 1949, file 56198/14, RG 85, National Archives.

26. William A. Whalen, District Director, San Antonio, *Annual Report San Antonio District, Fiscal Year Ended June 30, 1945*, 1, file 56220/414, RG 85, National Archives.

27. William A. Whalen, District Director, San Antonio, *Annual Report San Antonio District, Fiscal Year Ended June 30, 1943*, 30, file 56178/565, RG 85, National Archives.

28. Grover C. Wilmoth, District Director, El Paso, *Annual Report El Paso District, Fiscal Year Ended June 30, 1946*, 5, file 56188/215, RG 85, National Archives; Grover C. Wilmoth, District Director, El Paso, *Annual Report El Paso District, Fiscal Year Ended June 30, 1949*, 1, file 56279/215, RG 85, National Archives.

29. Grover C. Wilmoth, District Director, El Paso, Remarks (Immigration and Naturalization Service Annual Service Conference, 1944, New York, New York, April 19–May 1, 1944), 382–383, file 56312/675A, RG 85, National Archives.

30. Grover C. Wilmoth, District Director, El Paso, Remarks (Immigration and Naturalization Service Annual Service Conference, 1944, New York, New York, April 19–May 1, 1944), 382–383, file 56312/675A, RG 85, National Archives.

31. Grover C. Wilmoth, District Director, El Paso, Remarks (Immigration and Naturalization Service Annual Service Conference, 1944, New York, New York, April 19–May 1, 1944), 290, file 56312/675A, RG 85, National Archives.

32. Grover C. Wilmoth, District Director, El Paso to Commissioner General, September 18, 1934, file 55877/341, RG 85, National Archives; W. F. Kelly to Commissioner General, September 20, 1934, file 55877/341, RG 85, National Archives.

33. Grover C. Wilmoth, District Director, El Paso to Willard F. Kelly, Assistant Commissioner for Alien Control, August 17, 1944, file 56192/582, RG 85, National Archives.

34. As Border Patrol official N. D. Collaer wrote, "Notwithstanding the unprecedented number of Mexican aliens being apprehended in the act of crossing, while working within areas covered by the Patrol or on routes of escape to interior points from such areas, it is reported that thousands have succeeded in reaching the interior." N. D. Collaer, Chief, Border Patrol Section to Watson B. Miller, Commissioner General, January 12, 1949, file 56246/339D, RG 85, National Archives.

35. C. E. Waller, Chief, Budget and Fiscal Control Section to N. D. Collaer, Chief, Border Patrol Section, July 8, 1949, Kelly Lytle-Hernández Collection of Border Patrol Research Papers,

Box 13, Folder 11, Chicano Studies Research Center, University of California, Los Angeles.

36. W. F. Kelly, Assistant Commissioner, Central Office to District Director, El Paso, August 19, 1948, file 56246/339B, RG 85, National Archives.

37. See Kanstroom, *Deportation Nation*, 233–234. Immigrants were also eligible to seek relief through a private bill. Schuck, "The Transformation of Immigration Law," 76.

38. N. D. Collaer, Chief, Border Patrol Section to Watson B. Miller, Commissioner General, January 12, 1949, file 56246/339D, RG 85, National Archives.

39. Savoretti to Winings, November 15, 1944, file 56192/582, RG 85, National Archives.

40. Savoretti to Holtzoff, November 16, 1944, file 56192/582, RG 85, National Archives.

41. Alexander Holtzoff to Mr. Savoretti, Acting Commissioner, November 18, 1944, file 56192/582, RG 85, National Archives.

42. Mr. Reitzel, Acting General Counsel to Mr. Savoretti, Acting Commissioner, November 23, 1944, file 56192/582, RG 85, National Archives. They also considered amending the Act of March 4, 1929 to render a first offense a felony. Savoretti wrote, "we might then raise a question whether Congress would be willing to amend the Act of March 4, 1929 so as to elevate the offense of illegal entry to the status of felony and, perhaps, also to clarify the provisions of Section 8 of the Immigration Act of 1917 with reference to concealing and harboring aliens illegally in the United States." Savoretti to Holtzoff, November 27, 1944, file 56192/582, RG 85, National Archives.

43. Public Law 613, 60 Stat. 864 (1946).

44. Alexander Holtzoff, Memorandum for Honorable Earl G. Harrison, Commissioner, Immigration and Naturalization Service, July 10, 1944, file 56192/582, RG 85, National Archives.

45. Public Law 613, 60 Stat. 864 (1946).

46. G. C. Wilmoth, District Director, El Paso to W. B. Miller, Chief, Border Patrol Section, July 27, 1943, file 56192/582, RG 85, National Archives.

47. G. C. Wilmoth, District Director, El Paso, "Immigration Patrol Officers Duties and Authority to Act," Manual published for the Border Patrol Training School, Mexican Border, May 1, 1940, Kelly Lytle-Hernández Collection of Border Patrol Research Papers, Box 13, Folder 16, Chicano Studies Research Center, University of California, Los Angeles.

48. N. D. Collaer to W. F. Kelly, July 5, 1949, file 55853/300, RG 85, Kelly Lytle-Hernández Collection of Border Patrol Research Papers, Box 13, Folder 6, Chicano Studies Research Center, University of California, Los Angeles. See also N. D. Collaer to C. E. Waller, July 8, 1949, file 56364/47.1, RG 85, Kelly Lytle-Hernández Collection of Border Patrol Research Papers, Box 13, Folder 11, Chicano Studies Research Center, University of California, Los Angeles.

49. N. D. Collaer to W. F. Kelly, July 5, 1949, file 55853/300, RG 85, Kelly Lytle-Hernández Collection of Border Patrol Research Papers, Box 13, Folder 6, Chicano Studies Research Center, University of California, Los Angeles.

50. N. D. Collaer to W. F. Kelly, July 5, 1949, file 55853/300, RG 85, Kelly Lytle-Hernández Collection of Border Patrol Research Papers, Box 13, Folder 6, Chicano Studies Research Center, University of California, Los Angeles.

51. N. D. Collaer to W. F. Kelly, July 5, 1949, file 55853/300, RG 85, Kelly Lytle-Hernández Collection of Border Patrol Research Papers, Box 13, Folder 6, Chicano Studies Research Center, University of California, Los Angeles.

52. N. D. Collaer to W. F. Kelly, July 5, 1949, file 55853/300, RG 85, Kelly Lytle-Hernández Collection of Border Patrol Research Papers, Box 13, Folder 6, Chicano Studies Research Center, University of California, Los Angeles.

53. Ngai, "Illegal Aliens and Alien Citizens," 170.

54. Grover C. Wilmoth, District Director, El Paso to Willard F. Kelly, Assistant Commissioner for Alien Control, August 17, 1944, file 56192/582, RG 85, National Archives.

55. W. F. Kelly, Assistant Commissioner for Alien Control, Memorandum for Mr. Winings, September 16, 1944, file 56192/582, RG 85, National Archives; W. F. Kelly, Chief Supervisor, Border Patrol, Memorandum for Major Lemuel B. Schofield, Special Assistant to the Attorney General, September 9, 1941, file 56085/664, RG 85, National Archives.

56. W. F. Kelly, Assistant Commissioner for Alien Control, Memorandum for Mr. Winings, September 16, 1944, file 56192/582, RG 85, National Archives.

57. W. F. Kelly, Chief Supervisor, Border Patrol, Memorandum for Major Lemuel B. Schofield, Special Assistant to the Attorney General, September 9, 1941, file 56085/664, RG 85, National Archives.

58. W. F. Kelly, Assistant Commissioner for Alien Control to L. Paul Winings, Executive Assistant to the Commissioner, September 23, 1944, file 56192/582, RG 85, National Archives.

59. Emphasis added. Act of February 27, 1925, 43 Stat. 1049.

60. Hudson, "Traffic Inspection."

61. District Directors were required to file a report indicating the following: "1) Topography; 2) Confluence of arteries of transportation leading from external boundaries of the United States; 3) Relative distance from such boundaries; 4) Density of population; 5) Possible inconvenience to the traveling public; 6) Types of conveyances used; 7) Reliable information as to movements of persons effecting illegal entry into the United States; and 8) Unusual circumstances which make the distance reasonable." W. F. Kelly, Assistant Commissioner for Alien Control, Central Office to District Director, San Antonio, Texas, July 9, 1947, file 56192/582A, RG 85, National Archives.

62. Act of February 5, 1917, 39 Stat. 874, § 16.

63. Hudson, "Traffic Inspection."

64. G. C. Wilmoth, Lecture, "Immigration Border Patrol Officers' Duties and Authority to Act, March 29, 1944," 10–11, file 56192/582, RG 85, National Archives. See also W. F. Kelly, Assistant Commissioner for Alien Control to Ugo Carusi, Commissioner General, July 26, 1945, file 56192/582, RG 85, National Archives; G. C. Wilmoth, District Director, El Paso to T. B. Shoemaker, Deputy Commissioner, March 15, 1945, file 56161/109, RG 85, National Archives.

65. Grover C. Wilmoth, District Director, El Paso, *Semi-Annual Inspection Report El Paso District,* December 8, 1944, 2–3, file 56198/15, RG 85, National Archives.

66. G. C. Wilmoth, District Director, El Paso to Commissioner General, July 18, 1928, file 55610/160, RG 85, National Archives; J. D. Bunton, Sheriff, Presidio County, Texas to Commissioner General Harry E. Hull, July 5, 1928, file 55610/160, RG 85, National Archives (charging Border Patrol officers with raiding farms adjacent to the border in pursuit of unauthorized immigrants).

67. Calavita, *Inside the State,* 32–33.

68. Paragraph 15 of the Individual Work Contract stated, "It is agreed that the Consuls of Mexico, or their duly accredited representatives, for the purpose of discussing with the Employer alleged violations of this Contract, shall have free access to the place of employment, and the representatives of the United States Immigration and Naturalization Service and of the United States Employment Service shall likewise have such free access for the purpose of carrying out their respective responsibilities under the laws of the United States, under this Contract and the International Executive Agreement." W. F. Kelly, Assistant Commissioner to District Director, El Paso, Texas, August 1, 1950, file 56192/582A, RG 85, National Archives.

69. Reitzel to Carusi, August 29, 1945, file 56192/582, RG 85, National Archives.

70. Grover C. Wilmoth, District Director, El Paso to Dr. Maurice T. Van Hecke, Chairman, President's Commission on Migratory Labor, August 10, 1950, file 56302/267, pt. 1, RG 85, National Archives.

71. Grover C. Wilmoth, District Director, El Paso to Dr. Maurice T. Van Hecke, Chairman, President's Commission on Migratory Labor, August 10, 1950, file 56302/267, pt. 1, RG 85, National Archives.

72. G. C. Wilmoth, Lecture, "Immigration Border Patrol Officers' Duties and Authority to Act, March 29, 1944," 1, file 56192/582, RG 85, National Archives.

73. If, however, agency officials happened to discover other unauthorized immigrants on the premises in the course of executing the arrest warrant, the INS General Counsel authorized their warrantless arrests when and if agents considered them flight risks. While Patrol officers made such warrantless apprehensions, they sought a clearer statutory basis on which to act. Grover C. Wilmoth, District Director, El Paso to Dr. Maurice T. Van Hecke, Chairman, President's Commission on Migratory Labor, August 10, 1950, file 56302/267, pt. 1, RG 85, National Archives.

74. Lytle-Hernández, "Entangling Bodies and Borders," 116–143.

75. Lytle-Hernández, "Entangling Bodies and Borders," 119, 79, 124.

76. RHR, "Memorandum of Telephone Call from Mr. W. R. Kelly [sic] from McAllen at 2:45 p.m.," July 12, 1951, file 56321/448, RG 85, National Archives.

77. Taylor C. Carpenter, Chief, Adjudications Division, El Paso to G. C. Wilmoth, District Director, El Paso, October 9, 1945, file 56192/582, RG 85, National Archives. See also "U.S. Officials Blast Wetbacks," *El Paso Times*, August 6, 1950, file 56302/267, pt. 2, RG 85, National Archives; Grover C. Wilmoth, District Director, El Paso to Central Office, July 27, 1948, file 56192/582A, RG 85, National Archives; Taylor C. Carpenter, District Adjudications Officer to District Director, El Paso, July 27, 1948, file 56192/582A, RG 85, National Archives.

78. Grover C. Wilmoth, District Director, El Paso, *Annual Report El Paso District, Fiscal Year Ended June 30, 1943*, 15, file 56178/15, RG 85, National Archives.

79. Adams, interview, 13.

80. T. B. Shoemaker, Deputy Commissioner to Grover C. Wilmoth, District Director, El Paso, March 26, 1945, file 56161/109, RG 85, National Archives. See also Joseph Savoretti, Deputy Commissioner to Grover C. Wilmoth, District Director, July 6, 1944, file 56161/109, RG 85, National Archives (instructing Border Patrol officers not to use drainage ditches abutting farm property to detect and apprehend immigrants without warrant).

81. Grover C. Wilmoth, District Director, El Paso, *Semi-Annual Inspection Report El Paso District*, December 8, 1944, 2–3, file 56198/15, RG 85, National Archives.

82. W. F. Kelly, Assistant Commissioner for Alien Control to Ugo Carusi, Commissioner General, July 26, 1945, file 56192/582, RG 85, National Archives.

83. Winings, however, opposed the application of the harboring penalty to private property owners. He noted, "Section 8 of the 1917 Act, which imposes a penalty for harboring an unlawful arrival, is not helpful; for the violation must first be established. It seems evident that we shall continue to be powerless to control the Presidio situation unless it can be established that patrol officers have the right and power to enter upon privately owned lands for the purpose of investigating persons thereon employed without the landowner's consent. It is hardly likely that such consent will be given in many instances." Winings to Carusi, November 7, 1945, file 56192/582, RG 85, National Archives.

84. L. Paul Winings, General Counsel to Ugo Carusi, Commissioner General, November 7, 1945, file 56192/582, RG 85, National Archives.

85. Tichenor, *Dividing Lines*, 178.

86. President, Message, "Returning Without Approval the Bill (H. R. 5678) to Revise the Laws Relating to Immigration and Nationality, and for Other Purposes," H. Doc. 520, 82d Cong., 2d sess. (June 25, 1952), 4 (hereinafter referred to as "Truman, Veto Message").

87. Kang, "The Legal Construction of the Borderlands," 248–251. Congressional opposition to Truman's reform proposals reflected the tense relations between the executive and legislative branches. Truman vetoed 250 bills while in office, including the McCarran-Walter Act of 1952, of which twelve were overridden by Congress. Only FDR and Grover Cleveland vetoed more bills, as historian James T. Patterson notes, "[this] was the most since the days when Andrew Johnson defied the Radical Republicans over Reconstruction." Patterson, *Grand Expectations*, 142.

88. Truman objected to the limits created by the Displaced Persons Act of 1948. Sponsored by restrictionists Senator Patrick McCarran of Nevada and Senator William Chapman Revercomb of West Virginia, the act linked refugee admissions to the quota system. Given the volume of refugee admissions, some quotas were quickly filled and many others were mortgaged for decades. McCarran and Revercomb also drafted provisions that restricted the entry of Jewish refugees from the Soviet Union and other Eastern European countries. Without a more liberal policy, Truman feared that the refugee population would congest a war-torn Europe, creating unmanageable economic and social strains and the kind of mass discontent that led nations on the path to communism. Tichenor, *Dividing Lines*, 187; President, Message to Congress, March 24, 1952 (inserted into the *Congressional Record* by Senator Lehman); Senator Lehman of New York, speaking against S. 2550, on May 13, 1952, 82d Cong., 2d sess., *Cong. Rec.* 98, pt. 4: 5107.

89. Eisenhower followed in Truman's footsteps by invoking the parole power for the benefit of European refugees and authorizing Operation Wetback without the counsel or approval of Congress. Tichenor, *Dividing Lines*, 202.

90. The investigation was also intended to counter the work of McCarran's immigration commission, launched in 1947 as a precursor to his overhaul of the Immigration Act of 1924. McCarran's Subcommittee on Immigration and Naturalization heard testimony from various government officials; and civil, social, and ethnic organizations in Washington, DC, New York, Miami, New Orleans, in towns on the West Coast, the Canadian border, the Mexican border, and Havana, Cuba. In 1950, the Senate Subcommittee reported its findings in a 925-page report, *The Immigration and Naturalization Systems of the United States*. Truman's commission heard testimony in eleven cities over the course of thirty days, publishing a 319-page final report, *Whom Shall We Welcome*. President's Commission on Immigration and Naturalization, *Whom Shall We Welcome: Report of the President's Commission on Immigration and Naturalization* (Washington, DC: US Government Printing Office, 1953).

91. President's Commission on Immigration and Naturalization, *Whom We Shall Welcome*, 285.

92. The national origins quota system was ultimately repealed by the Hart-Celler Act or the Immigration and Nationality Act of 1965, 79 Stat. 911. Tichenor, *Dividing Lines*, 199, 205.

93. Kirstein, *Anglo Over Bracero*, 84.

94. Maurice T. Van Hecke, Professor of Law at the University of North Carolina served as chair of the commission. The other four commissioners included Robert E. Lucey, Catholic archbishop of San Antonio and chairman of the Bishops' Committee for the Spanish Speaking People of the Southwest, Paul Miller, chief of the University of Minnesota extension service, William Leiserson, former chairman of the National Mediation Board, and Peter H. Odegard, professor of political science at the University of California. Varden Fuller, agricultural economist at the University of California served as executive secretary. When Miller resigned, Truman appointed Noble Clark, associate director of the Agricultural Experiment Station of the University of Wisconsin. President's Commission on Migratory Labor, *Migratory Labor in American Agriculture* (Washington, DC: US Government Printing Office, 1951).

95. Kirstein notes that Ernst Schwarz, Executive Secretary of the Congress of Industrial Organizations (CIO) questioned how one could form a labor commission without labor representation. Ultimately, however, most labor unions were satisfied with the final report of the President's Commission. Kirstein, *Anglo Over Bracero*, 86, 92.

96. Truman also considered the appointment of a member of the Mexican American community. Kirstein observes that the NAACP, the Tuskegee Institute, and religious organizations such as the Detroit Council of Churches lobbied in vain for the placement of an African American on the commission. Kirstein, *Anglo Over Bracero*, 85.

97. Kirstein, *Anglo Over Bracero*, 86.

98. Commissioner General Miller wrote, "I entertain some doubt that the Commission could report very much that is not generally known at the present time." Watson B. Miller, Commissioner General to John W. Gibson, Assistant Secretary, Department of Labor, June 14, 1949, file 56302/267, pt. 1, RG 85, National Archives.

99. Agency officials put so much faith in the Bracero Program as a solution to the problem of unauthorized immigration that they worried that the President's Commission on Migratory Labor would disrupt the extension of the peacetime accords. Watson B. Miller, Commissioner General to Attorney General, December 29, 1949, file 56302/267, pt. 1, RG 85, National Archives. See also W. F. Kelly, Assistant Commissioner, Enforcement Division to Watson B. Miller, Commissioner General, June 10, 1949, file 56302/267, pt. 1, RG 85, National Archives.

100. Kirstein, *Anglo Over Bracero*, 87–88.

101. Grover C. Wilmoth, Statement submitted to the President's Commission on Migratory Labor, El Paso, Texas, August 4 and 5, 1950, file 56320/267, pt. 1, RG 85, National Archives.

102. Kirstein, *Anglo Over Bracero*, 89.

103. Kirstein, *Anglo Over Bracero*, 90.

104. Grover C. Wilmoth, District Director, El Paso to Maurice T. Van Hecke, Chairman, President's Commission on Migratory Labor, October 29, 1950, file 56302/267, pt. 1, RG

85, National Archives; Grover C. Wilmoth, District Director, El Paso to Central Office, October 13, 1950, file 56302/267, pt. 1, RG 85, National Archives.

105. Grover C. Wilmoth, "Statement prepared by Grover C. Wilmoth, District Director, Immigration and Naturalization Service, El Paso District, for the President's Commission on Migratory Labor, Holding Sessions at El Paso, Texas on August 4 and 5, 1950," file 56302/267, pt. 1, RG 85, National Archives.

106. Carson Morrow, Chief Patrol Inspector to Grover C. Wilmoth, District Director, El Paso, October 13, 1950, file 56302/267, pt. 1, RG 85, National Archives.

107. The sincerity of Wilmoth's critiques of the Bracero Program is not clear, particularly given Wilmoth's long-standing efforts to supply southwestern growers with easy access to Mexican national workers. The views he expressed during the President's Commission on Migratory Labor may reflect a shift in his viewpoints on immigrant labor or they may have served a more instrumental purpose. Given the attentiveness of the commission to the testimony of labor organizations and the pro-labor stance of its final report, Wilmoth might have curried favor with the commissioners by defending domestic workers in the face of competition from Mexican braceros. Kirstein, *Anglo Over Bracero*, 90.

108. Signed "RHL" (most likely R. H. Landon), Memo for File, July 21, 1950, file 56302/267, pt. 1, RG 85, National Archives.

109. Kirstein, *Anglo Over Bracero*, 88, 90; Tichenor, *Dividing Lines*, 193.

110. "Stiff Migratory Labor Enforcement Urged," *San Antonio Light*, August 2, 1950, file 56302/267, pt. 2, RG 85, National Archives; "Everyday Events," *El Paso Times*, August 8, 1950, file 56302/267, pt. 2, RG 85, National Archives.

111. "Penalties Urged for Employers of Wetbacks," n.d., file 56302/267, pt. 2, RG 85, National Archives.

112. Historian Bernard Lemelin also notes that Celler was concerned about the potential public health problems introduced by the unauthorized immigrant population. Lemelin, "Emmanuel Celler," 96, 107, n. 32.

113. Lemelin, "Emmanuel Celler," 96–97.

114. Lemelin, "Emmanuel Celler," 96–97.

115. Grover C. Wilmoth, District Director, El Paso to Dr. Maurice T. Van Hecke, Chairman, President's Commission on Migratory Labor, August 10, 1950, file 56302/267, pt. 1, RG 85, National Archives.

116. Grover C. Wilmoth to Maurice T. Van Hecke, Chairman, President's Commission on Migratory Labor, August 14, 1950, file 56302/267, pt. 1, RG 85, National Archives (enclosing agency correspondence indicating a sufficient supply of local cotton pickers for El Paso County); W. F. Kelly to Varden Fuller, Executive Secretary, President's Commission on Migratory Labor, October 17, 1950, file 56302/267, pt. 1, RG 85, National Archives (enclosing agency correspondence indicating a sufficient supply of local laborers in Arizona); Grover C. Wilmoth to Maurice T. Van Hecke, Chairman, President's Commission on Migratory Labor, October 19, 1950, file 56302/267, pt. 1, RG 85, National Archives (enclosing agency correspondence indicating a sufficient supply of local laborers in Chavez County, New Mexico); Grover C. Wilmoth to Maurice T. Van Hecke, Chairman, President's Commission on Migratory Labor, October 20, 1950, file 56302/267, pt. 1, RG 85, National Archives (enclosing agency correspondence indicating a sufficient supply of local laborers in Grants, New Mexico and Albuquerque, New Mexico); O. W. Manney, Officer in Charge, Phoenix, Statement before the President's Commission on Migratory Labor, August 7, 8, 1950, file 56302/267, pt. 1, RG 85, National Archives. See also G. J. McBee, Chief Patrol Inspector to District Director, El Paso, November 24, 1950, file 56302/267, pt. 1, RG 85, National Archives; Henry V. Stallings, Patrol Inspector in Charge, Fort Hancock, Texas to G. J. McBee, Chief Patrol Inspector, El Paso, November 22, 1950, file 56302/267, pt. 1, RG 85, National Archives; J. F. Delany, Officer in Charge, New Orleans to W. F. Kelly, Assistant Commissioner, Enforcement Division, September 12, 1950, file 56302/267, pt. 1, RG 85, National Archives; George V. Harrison, Acting Chief Patrol Inspector, Marfa, Texas to District Director, El Paso, November 3, 1950, file 56302/267, pt. 1, RG 85, National Archives; Grover C. Wilmoth, District Director, El Paso to Central Office, November 6, 1950, file 56302/267, pt. 1, RG 85, National Archives; Carson Morrow, Chief Patrol

Inspector, Tucson, Arizona to Grover C. Wilmoth, District Director, El Paso, October 12, 1950, file 56302/267, pt. 1, RG 85, National Archives.

117. In response to a grower's allegation that the Texas Employment Service listed only thirty-five domestic workers available for agricultural work, Wilmoth provided his own figures that showed 2605 workers available in Texas and 3192 workers available in New Mexico. (The Texas Employment Service figures included men and women. Wilmoth's figures included men, women and children. He did not provide the ages of the children.) Grover C. Wilmoth, District Director, El Paso to Maurice T. Van Hecke, Chairman, President's Commission on Migratory Labor, September 20, 1950, file 56302/267, pt. 1, RG 85, National Archives.

118. A. R. Mackey, Acting Commissioner to Peyton Ford, Deputy Attorney General, October 20, 1950, file 56302/267, pt. 1, RG 85, National Archives.

119. "Three U.S. Officials Accuse Farmers of Forcing Illicit Mexican Labor," *New York Times*, August 9, 1950, file 56302/267, pt. 2, RG 85, National Archives (citing to testimony of Carson Morrow, Chief Inspector, Border Patrol, Tucson; O. W. Manney, Chief, Immigration Service, Phoenix; and Fred N. Thomas, Chief Inspector, Border Patrol, Phoenix). See also "Wants Employers of Wetbacks Jailed," *El Paso Herald Post*, August 4, 1950, file 56302/267, pt. 2, RG 85, National Archives; "U.S. Officials Blast Wetbacks," *El Paso Times*, August 6, 1950, file 56302/267, pt. 2, RG 85, National Archives; "Commissioners Question Wetbacks on Labor Inquiry," *El Paso Herald Post*, August 7, 1950, file 56302/267, pt. 2, RG 85, National Archives (reporting testimony of El Paso immigration officials before the Commission).

120. Carson Morrow told the commission, "I get my instructions from the district director in El Paso. No doubt these orders come to him from higher authority. I don't know first hand, but I understand various pressure groups, farm groups, go to Washington and report that their crops will be destroyed unless they get the labor." "Three U.S. Officials Accuse Farmers of Forcing Illicit Mexican Labor," *New York Times*, August 9, 1950, file 56302/267, pt. 2, RG 85, National Archives.

121. "Report Says Braceros Unnecessary," April 8, 1951, file 56302/267, pt. 2, RG 85, National Archives.

122. "Commissioners Question Wetbacks on Labor Inquiry," *El Paso Herald Post*, August 7, 1950, file 56302/267, pt. 2, RG 85, National Archives (reporting testimony of El Paso immigration officials before the commission).

123. Grover C. Wilmoth, District Director, El Paso to Dr. Maurice T. Van Hecke, Chairman, President's Commission on Migratory Labor, August 10, 1950, file 56302/267, pt. 1, RG 85, National Archives.

124. Emphasis in original. Grover C. Wilmoth, District Director, El Paso to Dr. Maurice T. Van Hecke, Chairman, President's Commission on Migratory Labor, August 10, 1950, file 56302/267, pt. 1, RG 85, National Archives.

125. Grover C. Wilmoth, District Director, El Paso to Dr. Maurice T. Van Hecke, Chairman, President's Commission on Migratory Labor, August 10, 1950, file 56302/267, pt. 1, RG 85, National Archives.

126. Grover C. Wilmoth, District Director, El Paso to Dr. Maurice T. Van Hecke, Chairman, President's Commission on Migratory Labor, August 10, 1950, file 56302/267, pt. 1, RG 85, National Archives. If enacted, the proposal had the potential to create a license for Border Patrol officers to not only apprehend those undocumented immigrants they happened to find at the worksite but also to conduct a search of the premises. Since administrative arrest warrants did not permit these types of searches, Wilmoth's intent may have been to transform the administrative arrest warrant into a kind of general search warrant.

127. The public reacted negatively to INS efforts to expand its search and seizure powers. An editorial in the *El Paso Herald Post* charged, "the Immigration Service undertook to repeal the Constitution with a law allowing its inspectors to invade a farm without a search warrant. It is still in effect and should be challenged in the courts." Editorial, "Sense About Wetbacks," *El Paso Herald Post*, August 12, 1950, file 56302/267, pt. 1, RG 85, National Archives.

128. The INS cooperated with the commission in a variety of ways. Los Angeles District Director reported that his office provided commission members with a typist and the use of a car while they were in town. H. R. Landon, District Director, Los Angeles to A. R. Mackey, Acting Commissioner, August 14, 1950, file 56302/267, pt. 2, RG 85, National Archives.

In Brownsville, the commission arranged to collect much of its information about the INS in off-the-record meetings. William A. Whalen reported that as a result only one service official (J. W. Holland) testified at Brownsville. William A. Whalen, District Director, San Antonio to W. F. Kelly, Assistant Commissioner, Enforcement Division, August 7, 1950, file 56302/267, pt. 2, RG 85, National Archives. See also "Alien Labor Study Goes On: Commission Goes Into Field for First Hand Investigation of Conditions," n.d., file 56302/267, pt. 2, RG 85, National Archives. In El Paso, at the request of commission members, local INS officers recommended witnesses. C. W. Manney, Officer in Charge, Phoenix, Arizona to G. C. Wilmoth, District Director, El Paso, August 11, 1950, file 56302/267, pt. 1, RG 85, National Archives.

129. Varden Fuller, Executive Secretary, President's Commission on Migratory Labor to A. R. Mackey, Acting Commissioner, October 6, 1950, file 56302/267, pt. 1, RG 85, National Archives.

130. Varden Fuller, Executive Secretary, President's Commission on Migratory Labor to Willard F. Kelly, September 28, 1950, file 56302/267, pt. 1, RG 85, National Archives; Varden Fuller, Executive Secretary, President's Commission on Migratory Labor to Willard F. Kelly, October 31, 1950, file 56302/267, pt. 1, RG 85, National Archives (enclosing conference agenda).

131. "HBC" (most likely Harlon B. Carter), "Informal to Mr. Kelly," November 2, 1950, file 56302/267, pt. 1, RG 85, National Archives (typed and handwritten list of tentative proposals for legislative reform).

132. "HBC" (most likely Harlon B. Carter), typed notes, November 8, 1950, file 56302/267, pt. 1, RG 85, National Archives.

133. "HBC" (most likely Harlon B. Carter), typed notes, November 8, 1950, file 56302/267, pt. 1, RG 85, National Archives.

134. "HBC" (most likely Harlon B. Carter), typed notes, November 2, 1950, file 56302/267, pt. 1, RG 85, National Archives; "Union Splits with Farmers on Mexicans," *Los Angeles Times*, August 13, 1950, file 56302/267, pt. 2, RG 85, National Archives. See also Tichenor, *Dividing Lines*, 194.

135. Maurice J. Tobin, Secretary of Labor, US Department of Labor, "The Recommendations of the President's Commission on Migratory Labor," typed report, Bureau of Labor Standards, April 1952, 2, file 56321/267, pt. 1, RG 85, National Archives.

136. Of undocumented Mexican workers, the commission wrote, "Last in order of security and first in order of exclusion from the community is the illegal Mexican alien, commonly referred to as a 'wet back.' Under constant threat of apprehension and deportation, his life is one of furtive insecurity. In the hands of employers inclined to make use of the wetback's disabilities, the result is virtually peonage." President's Commission on Migratory Labor, *Migratory Labor*, 5, 65–89, 105, 130, 137.

137. Maurice J. Tobin, Secretary of Labor, US Department of Labor, "The Recommendations of the President's Commission on Migratory Labor," typed report, Bureau of Labor Standards, April 1952, 4, file 56321/267, pt. 1, RG 85, National Archives.

138. President's Commission on Migratory Labor, *Migratory Labor*, 65. Also in defense of bracero workers, the Commission underscored the fact that labor had no representation during the international negotiations over the bracero accords. President's Commission on Migratory Labor, *Migratory Labor*, 51.

139. For example, with respect to federal agency inspections of housing conditions, it found that the US Employment Service "did not want its work complicated by the addition of inspection duties which were thought to be 'administrative.'" President's Commission on Migratory Labor, *Migratory Labor*, 144. See also President's Commission on Migratory Labor, *Migratory Labor*, 64.

140. It characterized worker housing as "grossly inadequate" and it recommended the establishment and enforcement of minimum housing standards for alien workers. With respect to working conditions, the commission found that while agricultural workers suffered the

greatest number of on-the-job injuries and fatalities among all industrial workers, they received no protections under the workers' compensation laws. As result, the commission recommended the enactment of such protections for agricultural workers. Maurice J. Tobin, Secretary of Labor, US Department of Labor, "The Recommendations of the President's Commission on Migratory Labor," April 1952, 11, 13, file 56321/267, pt. 1, RG 85, National Archives.

141. The commission wrote, "Indeed, it is sometimes difficult to distinguish between the recruitment activities of the Farm Placement Service and those of the farm employers themselves." In response, the commission recommended the establishment of minimum wage legislation for farmworkers. President's Commission on Migratory Labor, *Migratory Labor*, 98, 99–100; Maurice J. Tobin, Secretary of Labor, US Department of Labor, "The Recommendations of the President's Commission on Migratory Labor," April 1952, 10, file 56321/267, pt. 1, RG 85, National Archives.

142. President's Commission on Migratory Labor, *Migratory Labor*, 23–24, 56.

143. Calavita, *Inside the State*, 47 (citing President's Commission on Migratory Labor, *Migratory Labor*, 69).

144. President's Commission on Migratory Labor, *Migratory Labor*, 64.

145. President's Commission on Migratory Labor, *Migratory Labor*, 65.

146. President's Commission on Migratory Labor, *Migratory Labor*, 53.

147. Maurice J. Tobin, Secretary of Labor, US Department of Labor, "The Recommendations of the President's Commission on Migratory Labor," April 1952, 7, file 56321/267, pt. 1, RG 85, National Archives.

148. Emphasis added. President's Commission on Migratory Labor, *Migratory Labor*, 52.

149. Emphasis added. President's Commission on Migratory Labor, *Migratory Labor*, 53.

150. President's Commission on Migratory Labor, *Migratory Labor*, 53.

151. The second sentence of the section on legalization stated, "The request to contract wetbacks in the United States was made by the Government of Mexico." Later, the commission wrote that despite Mexican calls for legalization, the INS "saw it as a threat to enforcement of the immigration law and opposed it." President's Commission on Migratory Labor, *Migratory Labor*, 53.

152. President's Commission on Migratory Labor, *Migratory Labor*, 75.

153. "Valley Testimony on Labor is Split," n.t., n.d., file 56302/267, pt. 2, RG 85, National Archives.

154. Benjamin G. Habberton, Acting Commissioner to Dr. Lyle Saunders, Department of Sociology, University of New Mexico, May 31, 1951, file 56249/121, pt. 2, RG 85, National Archives.

155. President's Commission on Migratory Labor, *Migratory Labor*, 86–88.

156. President's Commission on Migratory Labor, *Migratory Labor*, 180.

157. President's Commission on Migratory Labor, *Migratory Labor*, i.

158. President's Commission on Migratory Labor, *Migratory Labor*, 179.

Chapter 6

1. Immigration and Naturalization Service, *Annual Report, Fiscal Year Ended June 30, 1955*, 15.

2. Garciá, *Operation Wetback*, 171 (citing to US Congress, House, *Improper Use of Governmental Equipment and Government Personnel* [Immigration and Naturalization Service], 1956, H. Rpt. 2948, 12).

3. See, for example, Calavita, *Inside the State*; Craig, *The Bracero Program*; Garciá, *Operation Wetback*.

4. Calavita, *Inside the State*, 48, 52.

5. Calavita, *Inside the State*, 45; Craig, *The Bracero Program*, 70.

6. Public Law 78, 65 Stat. 119 (1951). Under Public Law 78, legalization was limited to those who had been in the country for at least five years and could prove good moral character. Typed notes regarding conversation with Argyle Mackey, July 16, 1951, file 56321/448, RG 85, National Archives; W. F. Kelly, Assistant Commissioner, Enforcement Division to Robert T. Creasy, September 20, 1951, file 56321/448A, RG 85, National Archives. See

also Robert Alexander and John L. Ohmans to American Embassy, Mexico City, November 19, 1951, file 56321/448A, RG 85, National Archives; Commissioner Swing to Senator Lloyd Bentsen, August 24, 1954, file 56321/448F, RG 85, National Archives; Commissioner General to Senator Lyndon B. Johnson, August 10, 1951, file 56321/448, RG 85, National Archives. Other major changes under Public Law 78 included a prohibition on blacklisting, the installation of a few border recruitment centers, and the nullification of the prohibition against the importation of contract laborers that was first stipulated by the Contract Labor Law of 1885 (Act of February 26, 1885, 23 Stat. 332). Calavita, *Inside the State*, 43–46; García y Griego, "The Importation of Mexican Contract Laborers," 68.

7. Calavita, *Inside the State*, 44; Craig, *The Bracero Program* 76–77. See also García y Griego, "The Importation of Mexican Contract Laborers," 63.

8. Indeed, the start of the Korean War expedited the passage of the public law. Calavita, *Inside the State*, 45; Craig, *The Bracero Program*, 70; Robinson, "Taking the Fair Deal to the Fields," 389.

9. A. R. Mackey, Acting Commissioner to Senator Pat McCarran (D-NV), Chairman, Senate Subcommittee on Appropriations, April 11, 1953, file 56302/267, pt. 1, RG 85, National Archives; A. R. Mackey, Acting Commissioner to Congressman John J. Rooney, Chairman, House Subcommittee on Appropriations, April 11, 1951, file 56302/267, pt. 1, RG 85, National Archives.

10. Harlon B. Carter to Dale Francis, May 2, 1951, file 56364/44.17, RG 85, National Archives.

11. Peyton Ford, Deputy Attorney General to Frederick J. Lawton, Director, Bureau of the Budget, June 21, 1951, file 56349/121, pt. 2, RG 85, National Archives.

12. Typed notes regarding meeting between Willard F. Kelly and David Stowe at the White House, July 6, 1951, 3:30pm, file 56321/448, RG 85, National Archives.

13. President Harry Truman to Senator Kenneth McKellar (D-TN), Chairman, Senate Committee on Appropriations, September 1, 1951, file 56056/600, RG 85, National Archives.

14. President Harry Truman to Senator Kenneth McKellar, Chairman, Senate Committee on Appropriations, September 1, 1951, file 56056/600, RG 85, National Archives.

15. B. Habberton, Acting Commissioner to Robert C. Goodwin, Executive Director, Defense Manpower Administration, Department of Labor, November 7, 1952, file 56302/267, pt. 1, RG 85, National Archives. In order to support its request for additional appropriations, the service highlighted its efforts to correct those enforcement problems observed by the commission. With respect to the recontracting of undocumented immigrants, the service noted that since the release of the commission report, none had been contracted under the legalization terms of the 1949 bracero agreement. Agency officials further emphasized that the bracero agreement of 1951 prohibited the regularization and hiring of undocumented laborers. It also undertook more vigorous removal operations, conducting airlifts in 1951 that resulted in the deportation of 64,700 to the interior of Mexico. While Congress failed to provide funds for additional airlifts, the INS obtained the cooperation of the Mexican government and conducted trainlift operations in 1953 that resulted in the removal of 23,946 from California and Texas. Despite these efforts, the INS noted, "the Mexican border situation cannot and will not be brought under control until Congress, after approval by the Bureau of the Budget, provides funds for an adequate border patrol force."

16. As a result, the service found itself in a very difficult situation, having begun construction of new detention facilities, hired 300 new Border Patrol officers, and resumed the airlift. Undated, unsigned report with handwritten note indicating that it was printed in the *Congressional Record* at the request of Senator Humphrey on June 26, 1952, file 56364/44.17, RG 85, National Archives. The service planned to employ one hundred of the new Border Patrol officers in a mini-task force operation that would sweep through Texas, Arizona, and California at peak harvest times for two months each year. Harlon B. Carter to Dale Francis, May 3, 1951, file 56364/44.17, RG 85, National Archives.

17. Congress, Senate, Committee on Labor and Public Welfare, Subcommittee on Labor and Labor Management Relations, *Hearings on Migratory Labor*, 82d Cong., 2d sess., March 27, 1952, 739 (testimony of Argyle R. Mackey, Commissioner General). On the agency's need for new detention facilities, see, A. R. Mackey, Acting Commissioner to Congressman John J. Rooney, Chairman, House Subcommittee on Appropriations, April 11, 1951, file 56302/

267, pt. 1, RG 85, National Archives; A. R. Mackey, Acting Commissioner to Senator Pat McCarran, Chairman, Senate Subcommittee on Appropriations, April 11, 1953, file 56302/ 267, pt. 1, RG 85, National Archives.

18. And, as one Senator noted, even if Congress had passed such legislation, the INS would not have been able to enforce it without the increased appropriation. Congress, Senate, Committee on Labor and Public Welfare, Subcommittee on Labor and Labor Management Relations, *Hearings on Migratory Labor*, 82d Cong., 2d sess., March 27, 1952, 739 (testimony of Senator Hubert Humphrey of Minnesota).

19. Calavita, *Inside the State*, 45.

20. Calavita, *Inside the State*, 43–45. See also Typed notes of telephone conversation between Mr. Habberton and Mr. Mackey, July 18, 1951, 4:45pm, file 56321/448, RG 85, National Archives.

21. Robinson, "Taking the Fair Deal to the Fields," 397.

22. The agreement was scheduled to expire on February 11, 1952. It was extended three times: August 8, 1953 (Public Law 237), August 9, 1955 (Public Law 319), and August 27, 1958 (Public Law 779). Under the last extension, the Bracero Program expired on June 30, 1961.

23. Calavita, *Inside the State*, 67.

24. *US v. Evans*, 333 US 483 (1948). During the first session of the 82nd Congress, six bills were presented to rectify the language of Section 8. Hutchinson, *Legislative History of American Immigration Policy, 1798–1905*, 301. For a discussion of the history and efficaciousness of transportation and harboring penalties in American immigration law, see Hutchinson, *Legislative History of American Immigration Policy, 1798–1905*, 594–610.

25. Senator McFarland of Arizona, speaking for Prevention of Illegal Entry of Aliens, S. 1851, on February 5, 1952, 82d Cong, 2d sess., *Cong. Rec.* 98, pt. 1: 798. See also Senator Kilgore of West Virginia, speaking for Prevention of Illegal Entry of Aliens, S. 1851, on February 5, 1952, 82d Cong., 2d sess., *Cong. Rec.* 98, pt. 1: 792, 807; Senator Ellender of Louisiana, speaking for Prevention of Illegal Entry of Aliens, S. 1851, on February 5, 1952, 82d Cong., 2d sess., *Cong. Rec.* 98, pt. 1: 795. According to Calavita, Mexico appeared satisfied with the passage of S. 1851 despite its failure to impose employer sanctions. Citing to contemporary observers, she notes that Mexico itself wanted to renew the Bracero Program and used the passage of S. 1851 to rationalize its ongoing consent to the international accords. Calavita, *Inside the State*, 195, n. 173.

26. Senator Humphrey of Minnesota, speaking for Prevention of Illegal Entry of Aliens, S. 1851, on February 5, 1952, 82d Cong., 2d sess., *Cong. Rec.* 98, pt. 1: 793; Senator Lehman of New York, speaking for Prevention of Illegal Entry of Aliens, S. 1851, on February 5, 1952, 82d Cong., 2d sess., *Cong. Rec.* 98, pt. 1: 794.

27. Senator Douglas of Illinois, speaking for Prevention of Illegal Entry of Aliens, S. 1851, on February 5, 1952, 82d Cong., 2d sess., *Cong. Rec.* 98, pt. 1: 797–798.

28. Calavita, *Inside the State*, 68–69.

29. Senator Douglas of Illinois, speaking for Prevention of Illegal Entry of Aliens, S. 1851, on February 5, 1952, 82d Cong., 2d sess., *Cong. Rec.* 98, pt. 1: 811. For the specific demands made by Texas growers regarding employment penalties, see American Farm Bureau Federation, "Resolution Approved by the House of Delegates, American Farm Bureau Federation, December 13, 1951, on Mexican Farm Labor Program," December 18, 1951, file 56321/ 448A, RG 85, National Archives.

30. Calavita, *Inside the State*, 68.

31. Calavita, *Inside the State*, 68.

32. Immigration and Naturalization Service, Operations Instructions, sec. 115.4, April 1952, file 56321/448B, RG 85, National Archives. See also W. F. Kelly, Assistant Commissioner, Enforcement Division to Wendel Edgren, Chief, Instructions Division, April 4, 1952, file 56321/448B, RG 85, National Archives; Immigration and Naturalization Service, draft of Operations Instructions, March 20, 1952, file 56321/448B, RG 85, National Archives.

33. During congressional debates over S. 1851, Congressman Walter explained that the twenty-five-mile radius was an arbitrary designation. In previous versions of the bill, the provision stipulated a "reasonable distance" from the border. Representative Walter of Pennsylvania, speaking for

S. 1851 for the Prevention of Illegal Entry of Aliens, on February 26, 1952, 82d Cong., 2d sess., *Cong. Rec.* 98, pt. 2: 1419.

34. Representative Fischer of Texas, speaking against S. 1851 for the Prevention of Illegal Entry of Aliens, on February 26, 1952, 82d Cong., 2d sess., *Cong. Rec.* 98, pt. 2: 1418, 1419.

35. Representative Fischer of Texas, speaking against S. 1851 for the Prevention of Illegal Entry of Aliens, on February 25, 1952, 82d Cong., 2d sess., *Cong. Rec.* 98, pt. 1: 1355; See also Representative Bentsen of Texas, speaking against S. 1851 for the Prevention of Illegal Entry of Aliens, on February 25, 1952, 82d Cong., 2d sess., *Cong. Rec.* 98, pt. 1: 1419.

36. Representative Celler of New York, speaking for S. 1851 for the Prevention of Illegal Entry of Aliens, on February 25, 1952, 82d Cong., 2d sess., *Cong. Rec.* 98, pt 1: 1348.

37. Representative Fischer of Texas, speaking against S. 1851 for the Prevention of Illegal Entry of Aliens, on February 25, 1952, 82d Cong., 2d sess., *Cong. Rec.* 98, pt. 1: 1354.

38. Representative Celler of New York, speaking for S. 1851 for the Prevention of Illegal Entry of Aliens, on February 26, 1952, 82d Cong., 2d sess., *Cong. Rec.* 98, pt. 2: 1416.

39. Representative Celler of New York, speaking for S. 1851 for the Prevention of Illegal Entry of Aliens, on February 25, 1952, 82d Cong., 2d sess., *Cong. Rec.* 98, pt. 1: 1348.

40. Representative Shelley of California, speaking against S. 1851 for the Prevention of Illegal Entry of Aliens, on February 26, 1952, 82d Cong., 2d sess., *Cong. Rec.* 98, pt. 2: 1414.

41. Representative Shelley of California, speaking against S. 1851 for the Prevention of Illegal Entry of Aliens, on February 26, 1952, 82d Cong., 2d sess., *Cong. Rec.* 98, pt. 2: 1414.

42. Representative Shelley of California, speaking against S. 1851 for the Prevention of Illegal Entry of Aliens, on February 26, 1952, 82d Cong., 2d sess., *Cong. Rec.* 98, pt. 2: 1414.

43. Representative Walter of Pennsylvania, speaking for S. 1851 for the Prevention of Illegal Entry of Aliens, on February 25, 1952, 82d Cong., 2d sess., *Cong. Rec.* 98, pt. 1: 1354, 1415.

44. House Committee on the Judiciary, *A Bill Assisting in Preventing Aliens from Entering or Remaining in the United States Illegally*, 82d Cong., 2d sess., 1952, H. Rep. 1377, 3.

45. S. 1851 was passed as P.L. 283 or the Act of March 20, 1952, 66 Stat. 26. Its provisions pertaining to the warrantless searches of private lands were incorporated into the Act of August 7, 1946, 60 Stat. 865 (also referred to as P.L. 613). Representative Walter of Pennsylvania, introducing amendment to S. 1851 for the Prevention of Illegal Entry of Aliens, on February 26, 1952, 82d Cong., 2d sess., *Cong. Rec.* 98, pt. 2: 1415, 1418; Representative Fischer of Texas, introducing amendment to S. 1851 for the Prevention of Illegal Entry of Aliens, on February 26, 1952, 82d Cong., 2d sess., *Cong. Rec.* 98, pt. 2: 1420.

46. Benjamin G. Habberton, Deputy Commissioner to All District Directors, March 21, 1952, file 56192/582A, RG 85, National Archives (enclosing copy of INS Operations instructions, sec. 60.28).

47. Senator Barry Goldwater, Republican, Arizona to General J. M. Swing, Commissioner General, December 14, 1955, file 56364/41.12, pt. 1, RG 85, National Archives.

48. Sid L. Hardin to Congressman Lloyd M. Bentsen Jr., March 25, 1953, file 56333/648, RG 85, National Archives.

49. Senator Barry Goldwater, Republican, Arizona to General J. M. Swing, Commissioner General, December 14, 1955, file 56364/41.12, pt. 1, RG 85, National Archives.

50. James W. David to Congressman Lloyd Bentsen, January 13, 1954, file 56333/648, RG 85, National Archives.

51. Kenneth D. Bryant, Patrol Inspector, Albert Conversano, Investigator to George F. Klemcke, Acting Chief Patrol Inspector, Brownsville, Texas, October 31, 1954, file 56333/648, RG 85, National Archives.

52. Joe L. Gavito Jr., Foreman of the Grand Jury, District Court, Cameron County, Texas to Senator [Marion] Price Daniel (D-TX), July 2, 1954, file 56333/648, RG 85, National Archives. The grand jury did not have enough evidence to indict the Border Patrol officer who shot the Mexican immigrant. See also Joseph Swing, Commissioner General to Senator Daniel, July 22, 1954, file 56333/648, RG 85, National Archives. This correspondence indicates that the service was planning to take disciplinary action against a second officer involved in the beating of a local farmer.

53. James W. Davis to Congressman Lloyd M. Bentsen, Jr. (D-TX), April 6, 1954, file 56333/468, RG 85, National Archives.

54. William V. Ausmus to Congressman [*sic*] Lyndon B. Johnson (D-TX), June 16, 1954, file 56333/648, RG 85, National Archives. The service concluded that its officers had no authority to deprive Ausmus of a supply of legal laborers. That decision fell within the jurisdiction of the USES, which took Ausmus's case under review. Frank E. Barton, Operations Advisor to General Edwin B. Howard, July 20, 1954, file 56333/648, RG 85, National Archives.

55. Emphasis in original. John J. Anthony, Port Isabel, Texas to Senator Lyndon B. Johnson, October 12, 1954, file 56333/648, RG 85, National Archives.

56. Argyle Mackey, Commissioner General to Congressman Lloyd Bentsen, March 22, 1954, file 56333/648, RG 85, National Archives; J. W. Holland, District Director to W. F. Kelly, Assistant Commissioner, February 16, 1954, file 56333/648, RG 85, National Archives; Commissioner to Bentsen, n.d., file 56333/648, RG 85, National Archives; R. F. Abbott, Acting District Director, San Antonio, May 15, 1953 to W. F. Kelly, Assistant Commissioner, May 15, 1953, file 56333/648, RG 85, National Archives; H. F. Abbott, Acting District Director, San Antonio, Texas to Frank H. Partridge, Special Assistant to the Commissioner, November 3, 1954, file 56333/648, RG 85, National Archives.

57. Congress, Senate, Committee on Immigration, *Illegal Entry of Aliens*, 66th Cong., 1st sess., October 10, 1919, 16.

58. W. F. Kelly, Assistant Commissioner to Habberton, Acting Commissioner, December 3, 1953, file 56364/44.17, pt. 1, RG 85, National Archives.

59. Public Law 613, 60 Stat. 864 (1946).

60. W. F. Kelly, Assistant Commissioner to Habberton, Acting Commissioner, December 3, 1953, file 56364/44.17, pt. 1, RG 85, National Archives.

61. W. F. Kelly, Assistant Commissioner, Enforcement Division to District Director, El Paso, Texas, October 25, 1951, file 56321/448A, RG 85, National Archives. See also "Regional Conference Held at El Paso, Texas, January 23 through January 26, inclusive, 1952 to Discuss Problems and Procedures in Connection with Public Law 78 and the International Agreement with Mexico Authorizing the Importation of Mexican Contract Workers," file 56321/448B, RG 85, National Archives (record of meeting between INS, USES, and US Public Health Service regarding administration of Bracero Program). On INS responsibilities with respect to contract violators, see LeMont Eaton, Memorandum for File, October 25, 1951, file 56321/448A, RG 85, National Archives; Unsigned memorandum, October 24, 1951, file 56321/448A, RG 85, National Archives; W. F. Kelly, Assistant Commissioner, Enforcement Division to Robert T. Creasey, Assistant Secretary of Labor, October 22, 1951, file 56321/448A, RG 85, National Archives.

62. LeMont Eaton, Memorandum for File, October 25, 1951, file 56321/448A, RG 85, National Archives.

63. J. W. Holland, Acting District Director, San Antonio to A. R. Mackey, Acting Commissioner, March 28, 1951, file 56321/448, RG 85, National Archives. See also "Regional Conference Held at El Paso, Texas, January 23 through January 26, inclusive, 1952 to Discuss Problems and Procedures in Connection with Public Law 78 and the International Agreement with Mexico Authorizing the Importation of Mexican Contract Workers," file 56321/448B, RG 85, National Archives.

64. Ngai, *Impossible Subjects*, 152.

65. H. R. Landon, District Director, Los Angeles to Commissioner General, August 13, 1954, file 56364/44.14, RG 85, National Archives.

66. Clyde Campbell, District Adjudications Officer, San Antonio, Texas to J. W. Holland, District Director, San Antonio, Texas, January 21, 1952, file 56321/448B, RG 85, National Archives.

67. Memorandum for file, March 28, 1952, file 56321/448B, RG 85, National Archives. See also E. J. Murray, Examiner, Enforcement Division, Warrant and Inspections Unit to Mr. Horowitz, Instructions Section, March 25, 1952, file 56321/448B, RG 85, National Archives.

68. A. R. Mackey, Commissioner General to District Directors, San Antonio, El Paso, Los Angeles, July 8, 1952, file 56321/448C, RG 85, National Archives; A. C. Devaney, Assistant Commissioner, Inspections and Examinations Division to District Directors, Los Angeles, San Antonio, El Paso, September 11, 1953, file 56321/448D, RG 85, National Archives.

69. Bruce G. Barber, District Director, San Francisco to Commissioner General, July 22, 1954, file 56321/448E, RG 85, National Archives.

70. Craig, *The Bracero Program*, 103.

71. Craig, *The Bracero Program*, 103–105.

72. Talks broke down over the following issues: the location of border recruitment centers; determination of the prevailing wage; and subsistence payments to unemployed braceros. Calavita, *Inside the State*, 65–66; J. M. Swing, Commissioner General to Assistant Attorney General, Office of Legal Counsel, n.d., file 56321/448G, RG 85, National Archives. The INS made a similar threat during negotiations in Mexico City over what became Public Law 78. Here, Commissioner General Mackey stated that if Mexico did not sign a new agreement, the agency would run the Bracero Program under the Ninth Proviso, issuing border crossing cards to workers. Mackey also threatened to end a 1951 airlift, return workers on foot across the border, and let them recross legally through the ports of entry. Notes of telephone conversation from Mr. Habberton to Mr. Mackey, July 23, 1951, 3:00pm, file 56321/448, RG 85, National Archives.

73. Craig, *The Bracero Program*, 113.

74. Craig, *The Bracero Program*, 114–115. The measure passed by wide margins in both the House and the Senate.

75. Commissioner General to Assistant Attorney General, Office of Legal Counsel, n.d., file 56321/448G, RG 85, National Archives. (This letter most likely originated from General Swing as opposed to Argyle Mackey.)

76. A. C. Devaney, Assistant Commissioner, Inspections and Examinations to Commissioner General, n.d., file 56321/448H, RG 85, National Archives (including draft amendments to Section 101(a)(15)(H) of Immigration and Nationality Act of 1952 and INS Operations Instructions to authorize entry of temporary agricultural laborers as a new class of nonimmigrant admissions). See also L. W. Williams, Acting Assistant Commissioner, Inspections and Examinations Section to R. L. Williams and Paul H. Lindsay, November 15, 1954, file 56321/448H, RG 85, National Archives (ordering preparation of draft amendments to INA of 1952 and Operations Instructions in hypothetical scenario in which Congress failed to pass Public Law 78).

77. It is important to note that, under this plan, the INS admitted agricultural laborers as a special class of temporary workers, not as a class of immigrants (such as those admitted on an H-2 work visa). Calavita explains that nativism informed the opposition of those in Congress, the INS, and southwestern agribusiness to the idea of admitting Mexican workers as anything but *temporary* laborers. Thus, these groups sought to ensure their transient status by admitting them under the auspices of the Bracero Program rather than the immigration laws. Calavita, *Inside the State*, 78–79.

78. L. W. Williams, Acting Assistant Commissioner, Inspections and Examinations Section to R. L. Williams and Paul H. Lindsay, November 15, 1954, file 56321/448H, RG 85, National Archives.

79. A. C. Devaney, Assistant Commissioner, Inspections and Examinations Division to J. M. Swing, Commissioner General, November 8, 1954, file 56321/448H, RG 85, National Archives.

80. The comprehensiveness of the amendments and the accompanying set of operations instructions reflected the agency's fifteen years of accumulated experience with guest worker programs. This document also reflected the agency's awareness of the problems with the Bracero Program and made numerous proposals on how to address them. "Mechanics of Processing and Contracting Braceros Under USES and U.S. INS," n.d., file 56321/448H, RG 85, National Archives.

81. INS officials wrote, "no serious thought can be entertained of transferring from the Department of Justice to the Department of Agriculture the function of guarding the security of the United States by patrolling the land borders to guard against the unlawful entry of persons and the function of inspecting and examining persons applying for entry at the ports." A. C. Devaney, Assistant Commissioner, Inspections and Examinations Division to Raymond A. McConnell Jr., September 28, 1954, file 563321/448G, RG 85, National Archives. Due to budget constraints, the proposal of the President's Commission that the INS take charge of the Bracero Program never made it past the Bureau of the Budget. It is not clear, however, why this later proposal was not pursued further by immigration policymakers. Minutes, Joint Migratory Labor Commission, September 13, 1954, file 56321/448G, RG 85, National Archives.

82. Calavita, *Inside the State*, 74; Langham, "The Eisenhower Administration and Operation Wetback," 120.
83. In so doing, Swing differed from his predecessor Commissioner General Argyle Mackey who focused the agency's attention and resources on its administrative duties. Calavita, *Inside the State*, 75; Langham, "The Eisenhower Administration and Operation Wetback," 187.
84. Garciá also notes that Swing's friendship with Eisenhower gave him easy access to the president during the planning of Operation Wetback. Garciá, *Operation Wetback*, 172.
85. For a discussion of the Administrative Procedures Act of 1946, see Shapiro, *Who Guards the Guardians?*, 39. For a discussion of the immigration agency's exemption from the APA, see Kanstroom, *Deportation Nation*, 170–176; Schuck, "The Transformation of Immigration Law," 30–33.
86. For an extended definition of the notion of bureaucratic autonomy, see Carpenter, *The Forging of Bureaucratic Autonomy*.
87. Garciá, *Operation Wetback*, 157.
88. Garciá, *Operation Wetback*, 159 (citing *Burner's Weekly Magazine*, no. 126 [October 24, 1953], 63).
89. Garciá, *Operation Wetback*, 157.
90. Tichenor, *Dividing Lines*, 201.
91. Langham, "The Eisenhower Administration and Operation Wetback," 87–88.
92. Garciá, *Operation Wetback*, 158.
93. Langham, "The Eisenhower Administration and Operation Wetback," 100.
94. Meanwhile, other Border Patrol officials noted that both divisions routinely competed for funds. Even more concerning to federal officials, the various border districts had long defined policies independently of each other and the authorization of the central office. Langham, "The Eisenhower Administration and Operation Wetback," 101.
95. Langham, "The Eisenhower Administration and Operation Wetback," 101.
96. Langham, "The Eisenhower Administration and Operation Wetback," 93–94.
97. Garciá, *Operation Wetback*, 165. See also Langham, "The Eisenhower Administration and Operation Wetback," 95.
98. Calavita, *Inside the State*, 52.
99. Calavita, *Inside the State*, 51.
100. Garciá, *Operation Wetback*, 171; Craig, *The Bracero Program*, 128.
101. Calavita, *Inside the State*, 82.
102. Commissioner General to Attorney General, September 9, 1954, file 56321/448F, RG 85, National Archives; Marcus T. Neely, District Director, El Paso to A. C. Devaney, Assistant Commissioner, Inspections and Examinations Division, August 6, 1954, file 56321/448E, RG 85, National Archives; Bruce G. Barber, District Director, San Francisco to Commissioner General, August 6, 1954, file 56321/448E, RG 85, National Archives; Bruce G. Barber, District Director, San Francisco to Commissioner General, July 22, 1954, file 56321/448E, RG 85, National Archives; J. W. Holland, District Director, San Antonio to A. C. Devaney, Assistant Commissioner, Inspections and Examinations Division, August 6, 1954, file 56321/448E, RG 85, National Archives; District Director, Los Angeles to Commissioner General, August 5, 1954, file 56321/448E, RG 85, National Archives.
103. Emphasis in original. J. M. Swing, Commissioner General, Remarks, September 20, 1954, file 56321/448F, pt. 2, RG 85, National Archives. See also draft letter from Attorney General to James J. Mitchell, Secretary of Labor, September 23, 1954, file 56321/448G, RG 85, National Archives; Commissioner General to Attorney General, September 9, 1954, file 56321/448F, RG 85, National Archives.
104. Commissioner General to Attorney General, September 9, 1954, file 56321/448F, RG 85, National Archives. In this letter, Swing makes a point-by-point critique of the Bracero Program. He concludes, "The growers are not pleased with the bracero program [*sic*] as it is now being operated and I do not blame them. The program could and should be made attractive to the growers so that there will be no incentive for them to employ wetbacks. We have no antagonism toward the interests of the growers. They have admirably entered into the spirit of converting from wetbacks to legals and we should work with them—not at cross-purposes."

105. J. M. Swing to District Directors (San Antonio, El Paso, Los Angeles, San Francisco), August 25, 1954, file 563321/448E, RG 85, National Archives.
106. Typed notes of telephone conversation between Mr. Williams and Mr. Marshall, August 23, 1954, file 56321/448E, RG 85, National Archives.
107. J. M. Swing to District Directors (San Antonio, El Paso, Los Angeles, San Francisco), August 25, 1954, file 563321/448E, RG 85, National Archives. See also Robert C. Goodwin, Director, Bureau of Employment Security, Department of Labor to All Regional Directors, September 1, 1954, file 56321/448F, RG 85, National Archives (issuing instructions to USES officials on basis of INS directive dated August 25, 1954).
108. J. W. Holland, District Director, San Antonio to All Employers of Mexican Nationals Under the Bracero Program, August 31, 1954, file 56321/448E, RG 85, National Archives. Holland defined specials as tractor drivers and irrigators. Meanwhile, he defined "good" workers as cotton pickers and vegetable workers.
109. Calavita, *Inside the State*, 88.
110. Calavita, *Inside the State*, 88 (citing Commissioner General Swing to Senator Fulbright, July 12, 1955, Accession 58A733, Box 185, RG 85, National Archives).
111. The origins of this plan are not clear. While Calavita claims that Mexico strenuously opposed the I-100 plan, Mexican officials appear to have participated in the creation of the program. Minutes of a Meeting of the American Section, Joint Migratory Labor Commission, August 19, 1954, 11, file 56321/448I, RG 85, National Archives. Other documents suggest that the initiative for the I-100 plan, or what was called the postcard plan, came from Mexican officials themselves. Through the postcard plan, they sought to give employers the power to select their own workers, prevent congestion at the border, and guarantee workers jobs with their former employers. Marcus T. Neelly, District Director, El Paso to J. M. Swing, Commissioner General, September 10, 1954, file 56321/448G, RG 85, National Archives (recounting meeting between Neelly, Mr. Toole, Angel Carvajal, chief officer of the Mexican Cabinet and minister of the Department of Gobernacion, and Jose Rocha. The latter two devised the postcard plan). J. M. Swing, Commissioner General to District Directors San Antonio, El Paso, Los Angeles, San Francisco, September 30, 1954, file 56321/448G, RG 85, National Archives (indicating assent of Departments of State and Labor to the plan). See also L. W. Williams, "Memorandum for file," September 29, 1954, file 56321/448G, RG 85, National Archives. But see, Calavita, *Inside the State*, 91 (describing Mexican objections to I-100 plan circa 1956).
112. J. M. Swing, Commissioner General to Senator Lyndon Johnson, May 20, 1955, file 56321/448I, RG 85, National Archives. To avoid charges that this procedure constituted border recruiting, the INS reasoned that the worker had not lost his contracted status upon his departure from the United States.
113. "Mexican Agricultural Labor Program–Public Law 78," n.d., file 56321/448I, RG 85, National Archives.
114. A. C. Devaney, Assistant Commissioner, Examinations Division to All Regional Commissioners, June 30, 1955, file 56321/448I, RG 85, National Archives.
115. "American Section's Separate Report," October 23, 1954, 14, file 56321/448H, RG 85, National Archives. See also Commissioner General Joseph M. Swing, "Report to the American Section of Joint Commission on Mexican Migrant Labor," September 3, 1954, file 56321/448F, RG 85, National Archives.
116. Walter A. Sahli, District Director, San Antonio, July 28, 1955, file 56364/42.43, RG 85, National Archives; Dulles to American Embassy, Mexico, July 2, 1954, file 56321/448E, RG 85, National Archives; Calavita, *Inside the State*, 74.
117. Marcus T. Neelly, District Director, El Paso to J. M. Swing, Commissioner General, September 10, 1954, file 56321/448G, RG 85, National Archives.
118. Calavita, *Inside the State*, 97.
119. Swing specifically turned to Generals Frank Patridge and Edwin Howard, and Harlon B. Carter of the Border Patrol. Garciá, *Operation Wetback*, 173.
120. W. F. Kelly, Assistant Commissioner to J. Lee Rankin, Assistant Attorney General, August 19, 1953, file 56056/600, RG 85, National Archives.
121. H. R. Landon, District Director, Los Angeles to Commissioner General, August 13, 1954, file 56364/44.14, RG 85, National Archives.

122. Garciá, *Operation Wetback*, 171.
123. Lytle-Hernández, *Migra!*, 185; Langham, "The Eisenhower Administration and Operation Wetback," 123. Although Mexico expressed doubts about its ability to manage the large number of deportees, the American request for assistance was not unprecedented. As Kelly Lytle-Hernández explains, both nations had undertaken coordinated removal drives since 1945. In a series of campaigns that served as strategic precedents for Operation Wetback, the United States transferred custody of detained immigrants to Mexican officials at the international boundary. Although the execution of these collaborative operations was contingent on developments at the bracero negotiating table, when put into effect, they bolstered the shared border enforcement goals of both nations. As Lytle-Hernández notes, binational policing allowed the United States and Mexico to "deny migrants the partial refuge provided by the border." Lytle-Hernández, *Migra!*, 147.
124. Garciá, *Operation Wetback*, 176–177.
125. Garciá, *Operation Wetback*, 185. Southwestern growers also participated in the drive to buttress the wavering support of their political allies. In particular, midwestern growers were beginning to express their resentment toward southwestern farmers, believing that they enjoyed a competitive advantage in their employment of both bracero and undocumented labor. Growers also realized that the public, which began to blame farmers for the problem of undocumented immigration, needed reassurances as well. Garciá, *Operation Wetback*, 187. Finally, border growers in California offered little resistance to Operation Wetback because they were the beneficiaries of a border recruitment station in Mexicali. This station was created in a separate agreement that was signed with Mexico just prior to the passage of P.L. 78. Langham, "The Eisenhower Administration and Operation Wetback," 109, 143.
126. Garciá, however, mentions that Texas news outlets were unwilling to cooperate with the INS by issuing their press releases. Garciá, *Operation Wetback*, 177, 214.
127. Langham, "The Eisenhower Administration and Operation Wetback," 131–132.
128. Garciá, *Operation Wetback*, 210.
129. Calavita, *Inside the State*, 54. See also Parker, interview, 22.
130. H. R. Landon, District Director, Los Angeles to Commissioner General, August 13, 1954, file 56364/44.14, RG 85, National Archives.
131. Garciá, *Operation Wetback*, 174; "Memorandum in re *Laredo Times* Article," June 3, 1953, file 56349/121(1), RG 85, National Archives.
132. Argyle A. Mackey, Commissioner General to R. A. Loughran, Assistant Commissioner, Administrative Division, August 27, 1951, file 56301/574, RG 85, National Archives.
133. Meeting Agenda, "Special Patrol Force," May 19, 1954, file 56364/44.17, pt. 2, RG 85, National Archives.
134. Garciá, *Operation Wetback*, 183.
135. "Patrol Seeks Help in Wetback Hunt: Border Unit Asks Public to Report on Location of Illegal Entrants," *San Diego Evening Tribune*, July 25, 1954, 1, file 56364/43.3SW, RG 85, National Archives.
136. Cavazos, "The Disposable Mexican," 51.
137. Garciá observes that Texans refused to serve meals, sell gasoline, and rent hotel rooms to Border Patrol officers during the campaign. Garciá, *Operation Wetback*, 218.
138. Garciá, *Operation Wetback*, 209.
139. Langham, "The Eisenhower Administration and Operation Wetback," 142, 145.
140. Since Texas farmers refused to grant access to their lands, Border Patrol officials made their sweeps on roads abutting these properties. Garciá, *Operation Wetback*, 207.
141. Langham, "The Eisenhower Administration and Operation Wetback," 159.
142. Many, however, were simply sent across the line where they congregated in border towns and waited for the next opportunity to cross back into the United States. "Border Patrol: Accomplishments," n.d., file 56364/44.17, pt. 2, RG 85, National Archives.
143. Langham, "The Eisenhower Administration and Operation Wetback," 159.
144. Ngai, *Impossible Subjects*, 156.
145. Calavita, *Inside the State*, 54. On the validity of INS apprehension and voluntary departure statistics during the campaign, see Garciá, *Operation Wetback*, 200. Garciá argues that since

congressional appropriations were contingent on agency apprehension rates, the agency had strong incentives to exaggerate these figures.

146. Commissioner General Swing, Statement, n.d. file 56321/448H, RG 85, National Archives.

147. Lytle-Hernández, *Migra!*, 191.

148. In order to contract this huge number of workers, INS officials processed 1,500 brace-ros a day at the same time it conducted Operation Wetback. Typed draft of "Impact of 'Operation Wetback' on the Border States," *Employment Security Review*, January 25, 1955, file 56321/448H, RG 85, National Archives. In just over a month, they processed 50,326 laborers at the Reception Center at Hidalgo. Robert C. Goodwin, Director, Bureau of Employment Security, Department of Labor, "Report on Mexican Labor Situation as Result of Immigration Service Wetback Cleanout," August 13, 1954, file 56321/448E, RG 85, National Archives. The drive also produced a supply of domestic laborers. The Bureau of Employment security reported 35,000 domestic workers in the Rio Grande Valley during the 1954 cotton picking season compared to 19,780 in 1953 for the same period. Robert C. Goodwin, Director, Bureau of Employment Security, Department of Labor, "Report on Mexican Labor Situation as Result of Immigration Service Wetback Cleanout," August 13, 1954, file 56321/448E, RG 85, National Archives.

149. Calavita, *Inside the State*, 55.

150. District Director, Los Angeles to Commissioner General, October 18, 1954, file 56364/45.2, RG 85, National Archives. See also Calavita, *Inside the State*, 59.

151. Swing, "Statement," n.d., file 56321/448H, RG 85, National Archives. These bills were pre-sented in July 1954, during the campaign, as a concomitant to deportation drive.

152. E. A. Wahl, Acting Chief of Border Patrol to H. B. Carter, Acting Assistant Commissioner, July 13, 1955, file 56364/44.17, pt. 2, RG 85, National Archives.

153. The service continued to rely on the mobile task force after Operation Wetback not only because it had been successful but also because it was cost effective. Despite the increased appropriation, the agency remained mindful of cutting costs due to the constant threat of budget cuts. Regional Commissioner, Southwest Region to District Directors, San Francisco, El Paso, San Antonio, March 3, 1955, file 56364/41.23, RG 85, National Archives. See also Chief, Border Patrol Section, Los Angeles District to Acting District Director, Los Angeles, November 23, 1954, file 56364/45.2, RG 85, National Archives.

154. Immigration and Naturalization Service, *Annual Report, Fiscal Year Ended June 30, 1955*, 10; Garciá, *Operation Wetback*, 111.

155. "Border Patrol," n.d., file 56364/43.32, RG 85, National Archives. As in Operation Wetback, the service used the press to inform the public, workers, and farmers of their impending campaigns. District Director, Los Angeles to Commissioner General, October 18, 1954, file 56364/45.2, RG 85, National Archives.

156. Joseph Swing, 1971, Eisenhower Administration Project, Oral History Research Office, Columbia University, New York, 6, 28 (reproduced in Kelly Lytle-Hernández Collection of Border Patrol Research Papers, Box 13, Folder 13, Chicano Studies Research Center, University of California, Los Angeles); Langham, "The Eisenhower Administration and Operation Wetback"; Calavita, *Inside the State*, 75.

157. Immigration and Naturalization Service, *Annual Report, Fiscal Year Ended June 30, 1955*, 10.

158. Walter A. Sahli, District Director, San Antonio, July 28, 1955, file 56364/42.43, RG 85, National Archives; Dulles to American Embassy, Mexico, July 2, 1954, file 56321/448E, RG 85, National Archives; Marcus T. Neelly, District Director, El Paso to J. M. Swing, Commissioner General, September 10, 1954, file 56321/448G, RG 85, National Archives; Calavita, *Inside the State*, 74.

159. John P. Swanson, Chief Enforcement Officer, Southwest Region to Chief Patrol Inspectors, Southwest Region, May 15, 1956, file 56363/42.43, RG 85, National Archives. Calavita explains that Swing's efforts to staunch any sign of labor organizing or labor agitation on southwestern farms were part of his larger goal to stabilize the labor market on the growers' behalf and thereby prevent them from relying on out-of-status workers. Calavita, *Inside the State*, 77–80.

160. Joseph Swing, 1971, Eisenhower Administration Project, Oral History Research Office, Columbia University, New York, 7.

161. Denis E. Wolstenholme, Chief Patrol Inspector, Chula Vista, California to Chief, Border Patrol Section, Los Angeles, October 5, 1954.

162. District Director, Los Angeles to Commissioner General, August 3, 1954, file 56321/448F, RG 85, National Archives.

163. Draft, "Annual Report, Fiscal Year 1956, Enforcement Division," file 56364/43.32, RG 85, National Archives.

164. H. R. Landon, District Director, Los Angeles to Commissioner General, August 13, 1954, file 56364/44.14, RG 85, National Archives.

165. In 1925, 1928, and 1930, the service proposed the construction of a fence at Cordova Island. Grover C. Wilmoth, District Director, El Paso to Commissioner General, May 2, 1930, file 55922/175, RG 85, National Archives.

166. US Congress, House, Committee on Immigration and Naturalization, *Border Patrol*, 71st Cong., 2d sess., January 6, 1930; Secretary of Labor to Harry L. Hopkins, Works Progress Administration, August 26, 1935, file 56364/44.14, RG 85, National Archives.

167. US Congress, House, Committee on Immigration and Naturalization, *Border Patrol*, 71st Cong., 2d sess., January 6, 1930.

168. In 1934, border officials proposed the construction of an 8.6 mile fence between Juárez and El Paso. In 1935, officials recommended the construction of a fence along the most populated regions, specifically San Ysidro and Calexico in California; Naco, Nogales, and Douglas in Arizona; and El Paso, Texas. Nick D. Collaer, Assistant Superintendent, H. C. Horsley, Chief Patrol Inspector to G. C. Wilmoth, District Director, El Paso, February 24, 1934, file 55606/894, RG 85, National Archives; Walter E. Carr, District Director, Los Angeles to Commissioner General, May 10, 1935, file 55660/894, RG 85, National Archives; D. W. MacCormack, Commissioner General to Congresswoman Isabella Greenway of Arizona, July 2, 1935, file 55606/894, RG 85, National Archives.

169. "American Section's Separate Report," October 23, 1954, 63, file 56321/448H, RG 85, National Archives.

170. David Snow, Patrol Inspector in Charge, Brownsville, Texas to Fletcher L. Rawls, Chief Patrol Inspector, McAllen, Texas, March 20, 1953, file 56364/44.14, RG 85, National Archives. Officials also sought new fences at San Ysidro and Calexico because they were riddled with holes bored by migrants. W. A. Carmichael, District Director, Los Angeles to Ugo Carusi, Commissioner General, July 15, 1947, file 56364/42.40SW, RG 85, National Archives; H. R. Landon, District Director, Los Angeles to Commissioner General, August 13, 1954, file 56364/44.14, RG 85, National Archives.

171. Secretary of Labor to Harry L. Hopkins, Works Progress Administration, August 26, 1935, file 56364/44.14, RG 85, National Archives.

172. Conference re Assistance to Department of Justice on Obtaining Cost Estimates for Construction of Boundary Fencing Between Mexico and Texas and Mexico and California to Retard Illegal Entrance into the United States, September 1, 1953, file 56364/44.14, RG 85, National Archives; D. R. Kelley to W. F. Kelley, September 15, 1953, file 56364/44.14, RG 85, National Archives; Donald R. Kelley, Acting Chief, Border Patrol to General Partridge, July 27, 1954, file 56364/44.14, RG 85, National Archives.

173. D. R. Kelley to W. F. Kelley, September 15, 1953, file 56364/44.14, RG 85, National Archives.

174. Press Release, "Exchange of Notes Between the United States and Mexico on Farm Labor," March 10, 1954, file 56321/448E, RG 85, National Archives; "American Section's Separate Report," October 23, 1954, 10, file 56321/448H, RG 85, National Archives.

175. In preparing its report on Operation Wetback, the American Section of the Joint Migratory Labor Commission relied heavily on the following documents prepared by Swing, "Report to the American Section of Joint Commission on Mexican Migrant Labor," September 3, 1954, file 56321/448F, RG 85, National Archives.

176. Garciá, *Operation Wetback*, 167.

177. Mrs. W. J. Williams to President Eisenhower, August 2, 1954, file 56364/45, RG 85, National Archives.

178. Editorial, "For Shame!" n.d., file 56364/45, RG 85, National Archives. Garciá claims that California media coverage was generally favorable before, during, and after the

campaign. He attributes this to Swing's lobbying efforts and to the close connections between the California media and growers. Garciá, *Operation Wetback*, 193–194. For an account of Los Angelenos' response to the campaign, see Molina, *How Race Is Made in America*, 112–138.

179. Editorial, "Good Neighbors?" *Valley Morning Star*, July 28, 1954, file 56364/45, RG 85, National Archives.
180. Gwynevere Marrs, Marrs Early Orange Nursery, Monte Alto-Edcough, Texas to President Dwight D. Eisenhower, August 10, 1954, file 56364/45, RG 85, National Archives.
181. L. Kelley, Chairman, Legislative Committee for the Executive Board, Warehouse Local 6, International Longshoremen's and Warehousemen's Union, Oakland, California, June 23, 1954, file 56364/43.3SW, RG 85, National Archives.
182. Garciá, *Operation Wetback*, 214 (citing Gladwin Hill, "'Wetback' Drive Irks 'The Valley,'" *New York Times*, August 2, 1954, 8).
183. Garciá, *Operation Wetback*, 199.
184. Garciá, *Operation Wetback*, 210.
185. While the INS removed men in roundup campaigns, it offered voluntary departure to women and children. Garciá, *Operation Wetback*, 184, 216.
186. Blanton, "The Citizenship Sacrifice," 299–320; Gutiérrez, *Walls and Mirrors*, 163–165.
187. Draft, "Border Patrol Annual Report, Fiscal Year 1955," file 56364/43.32, RG 85, National Archives.
188. Garciá, *Operation Wetback*, 193–194.
189. Ngai, *Impossible Subjects*, 156 (citing to Testimony of Milton Plumb before House Committee on Agriculture, March 22, 1955, file Wetbacks, 1948–1949, box 45, Sánchez Papers, University of Texas, Austin).
190. Garciá, *Operation Wetback*, 215–216.
191. Ngai, *Impossible Subjects*, 156. See also US Congress, House, Hearings before the Subcommittee on Government Operations, *Reorganization of the Immigration and Naturalization Service*, 84th Cong., 1st sess., 33.
192. Garciá, *Operation Wetback*, 221.
193. Jack Yeaman, "Memorandum in re *Laredo Times* Article, July 3, 1953, file 56349/121, pt. 1, RG 85, National Archives. See also Commissioner General to Martin P. Durkin, Secretary of Labor, n.d., file 56349/121, pt. 1, RG 85, National Archives.
194. Minutes of a Meeting of the American Section, Joint Migratory Labor Commission, August 19, 1954, file 56321/448H, 11, RG 85, National Archives.

Conclusion

1. Graff, "The Green Monster," 1; Meissner et al., *Immigration Enforcement in the United States*, 18, 22.
2. Secure Fence Act of 2006, 120 Stat. 2638.
3. US Customs and Border Protection, "About CBP."
4. Graff, "The Green Monster."
5. Graff, "U.S. Customs and Border Patrol Challenges."
6. Dunn, *The Militarization of the U.S.–Mexico Border, 1978–1992*, 2–3.
7. Nevins, *Operation Gatekeeper*, 68.
8. Dunn, *The Militarization of the U.S.–Mexico Border, 1978–1992*, 2.
9. Nevins, *Operation Gatekeeper*, 68–69.
10. Nevins, *Operation Gatekeeper*, 90.
11. Nevins, *Operation Gatekeeper*, 92.
12. Tichenor, *Dividing Lines*, 284.
13. Tichenor, *Dividing Lines*, 284.
14. By "militarization," Dunn specifically refers not only to an escalation in immigration enforcement efforts but also to a qualitative change in the agency's enforcement authority—or the expansion of its focus to drug traffickers and suspected communists, as well as undocumented immigrants. Dunn, *The Militarization of the U.S.–Mexico Border, 1978–1992*.

15. Tichenor attributes the longevity of this pro-bracero stance to structural features of the American political system. That is, while American public opinion consistently reflected a restrictionist stance on immigration, pro-bracero forces in Congress were able to shield their initiatives from countervailing public attitudes due to their virtual monopoly on the immigration policymaking process. Tichenor, *Dividing Lines*, 284.

16. The legalization program offered temporary resident status to two classes of workers: first, those who had lived in the United States for three years and had worked as agricultural laborers for at least ninety days each of those years; second, those who had worked in agriculture for ninety days between May 1985 and May 1986. Both classes were eligible for permanent residency after two more years of farm work. Those who had worked as agricultural laborers for five years were also eligible for permanent residency. Ultimately, IRCA adjusted the status of three million immigrants. Meanwhile, Congress authorized the admission of 350,000 agricultural workers under IRCA. Tichenor, *Dividing Lines*, 244, 260–261.

17. In their bid for guest worker programs and increased visa quotas, these pro-business forces, Tichenor explains, benefited from the pro-immigration orientation that emerged within Congress during the 1960s. As explained in chapter 5, congressional Democrats, for both economic and ideological reasons, began to adopt a more liberal approach to American immigration policy. Together, pro-business Republicans and pro-immigration Democrats in Congress would form a coalition that defended an expansive immigration policy well into the new millennium. Tichenor, *Dividing Lines*, 284.

18. Tichenor, *Dividing Lines*, 229.

19. For example, while the number of illegal entries increased from 71,000 in 1960 to 345,000 in 1969, Congress refused to authorize an increase in Border Patrol personnel. Nevins, *Operation Gatekeeper*, 36. At the same time that Congress denied the INS the appropriations necessary to fulfill its enforcement mandate, INS administrators themselves fostered a lax enforcement posture in the 1960s and 1970s. Beholden to congressional and grower interests, they adopted a passive stance, declining to request increased appropriations or even acknowledge that there were any problems with the immigration law enforcement infrastructure. Tichenor, *Dividing Lines*, 228.

20. Nevins, *Operation Gatekeeper*, 65 (discussing the US Select Commission on Immigration and Refugee Policy, also known as the Hesburgh Commission).

21. These groups included the Mexican American Legal Defense Fund, LULAC, the ACLU, and religious groups. Tichenor, *Dividing Lines*, 234–235.

22. In response to the 1980 Refugee Relief Act, 125,000 Cuban refugees arrived in Miami. Eligible for public benefits and legal residency under the new law, the public perceived the refugees, as Nevins observes, as "opportunists trying to defraud a system that was 'out of control.' Election campaigns from the local to the presidential level would sound the alarm that Americans had lost control, were losing their country—to crime, to welfare, and to immigration. And the Mariel boatlift had come to symbolize all three." It was in this environment that congressional lawmakers undertook the reform of national immigration laws that produced IRCA. Nevins, *Operation Gatekeeper*, 66.

23. These amendments to the employer penalty proposal "released employers from the responsibility of having to verify the authenticity of their employees' documents." Nevins, *Operation Gatekeeper*, 67.

24. Nevins, *Operation Gatekeeper*, 5. For an assessment of NAFTA after twenty years, see Castañeda, "NAFTA's Mixed Record," 131–141; Hills, "NAFTA's Economic Upsides," 122–127; Wilson, "NAFTA's Unfinished Business," 128–133.

25. Castañeda, "NAFTA's Mixed Record"; Becker, Kraus, and Weiner, "Free Trade Accord at 10," 1.

26. While Mexican industries experienced a boom period in the early years, many, at the turn of the century, closed their operations in the face of competition from overseas. As a result, real wages declined and unemployment, particularly in the border region, soared. One account reported the elimination, since 2000, of 300,000 of the 700,000 new jobs created in the border region during the first seven years of NAFTA. This increased illegal entries into the United

States where wages were six to ten times higher than in Mexico. Becker, Kraus, and Weiner, "Free Trade Accord at 10," 1; Jordan, "Mexican Workers Pay for Success," 1; Sanchez, "Our Sad Neglect of Mexico," 25.

27. Madigan, "Early Heat Wave Kills 12 Illegal Immigrants in the Arizona Desert," 18; Thompson, "U.S. and Mexico to Open Talks on Freer Migration for Workers," 1.

28. Bumiller and Wiener, "At Conference, Fox Backs Bush's Guest Worker Plan," 3.

29. Stevenson, "Bush is Considering Waiver for Mexicans Entering U.S.," 4.

30. The commission, for example, observed delays in processing, the use of nonnetworked computers, and a lack of coordination between the agency's thirty-three districts. National Commission on Terrorist Attacks Upon the United States, *The 9/11 Commission Report*; Schmitt, "The Rube Goldberg Agency," 4.

31. John Mintz, "Tracking 'Terrorist Travel' is a Key Defense," 22.

32. US Customs and Border Protection, "About CBP."

33. Real ID Act of 2005, 119 Stat. 302; Kirpatrick, "House Passes Tightening of Laws on Immigration," 13.

34. Secure Fence Act of 2006, 120 Stat. 2638. The Illegal Immigration Reform and Immigrant Responsibility Act of 1996 (IIRIRA), 110 Stat. 3009 authorized the government to construct border fencing, condemning, if necessary, lands adjacent to the border for that purpose. The Real ID Act of 2005 provided a similar authorization, permitting the secretary of the Department of Homeland Security to waive any laws that might serve as impediments to the creation of border barriers. See Gilman, "Seeking Breaches in the Wall," 259–260.

35. Graff, "The Green Monster." MPI estimates that the combined budgets of CBP and ICE increased at least fifteen-fold between 1986 (when these agencies were a part of the INS) and 2012. Meissner et al., *Immigration Enforcement*, 16.

36. Meissner et al., *Immigration Enforcement*, 18-19.

37. Graff, "The Green Monster," 1. MPI reports that the Border Patrol grew from 10,819 agents in fiscal year 2004 to 21,370 agents in fiscal year 2012, representing a doubling of the force in eight years. Meissner et al., *Immigration Enforcement in the United States*, 22.

38. Between fiscal years 2005 and 2012, the ICE budget grew from $3.1 billion to $5.9 billion. Meissner et al., *Immigration Enforcement in the United States*, 22. For ICE detention statistics, see Meissner et al., *Immigration Enforcement in the United States*, 126.

39. Meissner et al., *Immigration Enforcement in the United States*, 127.

40. Wong, "Hopes and Doubts over Bush Plan," 37. After serving as a congressional representative from California's 50th district from 1993 to 2002 and 51st district from 2003 to 2012, Filner was elected Mayor of San Diego in December 2012. In the midst of multiple allegations of sexual harassment, Filner resigned in August 2013 and served a sentence of three months house arrest and three years probation as part of a plea deal in a sexual harassment suit. Lovett, "Ex-Mayor Sentenced in Harassment Case," 19.

41. Wong," Hopes and Doubts over Bush Plan," 37.

42. Strayer, "Symposium: Making the Development of Homeland Security Regulations More Democratic," 331 (citing Michael Chertoff, Secretary, Department of Homeland Security, Remarks at the Quarterly Meeting of the Advisory Committee on Commercial Operations for US Customs and Border Protection [Aug. 16, 2007], www.dhs.gov/xnews/speeches/sp_1187357854566.shtm). See also Mason, "Business Unusual," 9–16; Department of Homeland Security, "Supporting Travel and Tourism."

43. In an effort to prevent the massive traffic jams that resulted on the US–Canadian border shortly after 9/11, Canada and the United States engaged in talks that resulted in a so-called smart border approach to border management. Later, this approach expanded to the nation's borders in general. In 2005, the Security and Prosperity Partnership of North America supplanted the original agreement between the United States and Canada. Koslowski, "Smart Borders, Virtual Borders or No Borders," 527, 533. The White House reached a similar agreement, the US–Mexican Border Partnership Agreement, with Mexico. The White House Office of the Press Secretary, *Smart Border*.

44. Koslowski, "Smart Borders, Virtual Borders or No Borders," 527–528. Mason, "A New Day," 22–25; Bersin, "Lines and Flows," 401–403.

45. While SENTRI was created in 1995, both SENTRI and NEXUS, which was created in 2002, fulfilled the mandate of the Western Hemisphere Travel Initiative (WHTI) requiring all border crossers traveling between the United States, Canada, and Mexico to carry a passport or other approved travel document. In other words, as a border security measure, it removed the long-standing passport exemption that had been conferred on border residents. SENTRI and NEXUS applicants must undergo extensive background checks for violations of US criminal, customs, immigration, and anti-terrorism laws, and a personal interview with a CBP official. Worrell, "Note and Comment: Free Trade," 117; US Customs and Border Protection, "Fact Sheet: Trusted Traveler Programs"; US Customs and Border Protection, "Fact Sheet: Secure Electronic Network"; US Customs and Border Protection, "Fact Sheet: NEXUS."

46. US Customs and Border Protection, "Fact Sheet: Free and Secure Trade Program (FAST)"; Franklin, "Simplifying Tools for Trade," 28–31. As in the past, however, border residents, particularly Native American tribes whose lands straddle the US–Mexico border, continue to resist the imposition of these new border crossing regulations. See, for example, Daly, "Comment," 157–186.

47. Franklin, "Transformation at Land Border Ports of Entry," 25.

48. Mason, "A New Day," 22–25.

49. Mason, "A New Day," 22–25.

50. Lizza, "Getting to Maybe."

51. Kalhan, "Immigration Surveillance," 54; Giovagnoli, "Overhauling Immigration Law"; Lizza, "Getting to Maybe."

52. Graff, "The Green Monster," 4.

53. Kalhan, "Immigration Surveillance," 75.

54. In many ways, CBP's virtual operations have reconstructed the border once again, expanding the jurisdiction or zone in which it conducts its policing operations. As legal commentators have noted these operations have had the effect of "push[ing] borders out" by conferring upon the CBP the ability to track immigrants and Americans long after their entry and exit from the United States. Koslowski, "Smart Borders, Virtual Borders or No Borders," 528; Kalhan, "Immigration Surveillance," 60–61; Yale-Loehr, Papademetriou, and Cooper, *Secure Borders, Open Doors*, 77.

55. Kalhan, "Immigration Surveillance," 72–78; Shachar, "Territory Without Boundaries," 809–839.

56. With respect to the corruption, Graff notes several instances in which Border Patrol or CBP officers engaged in drug smuggling across the border. Graff, "The Green Monster," 4.

57. The Police Executive Research Forum, *U.S. Customs and Border Protection Use of Force Review*, 8.

58. Criticizing the agency for failing to investigate officers' firearms usage, PERF wrote, "Based on the somewhat limited records that were provided, it appears that CBP is not as diligent with follow up investigation and evaluations of cases where shots were fired and injuries were not confirmed." The Police Executive Research Forum, *U.S. Customs and Border Protection Use of Force Review*, 4.

59. In December 2013, an investigative report conducted by the *Arizona Republic* discovered that no administrative sanctions had been issued for the deaths of forty-two individuals, shot by on-duty CBP and Border Patrol officers since 2005. This investigation explored 12,000 pages of documents issued by the CBP and the Border Patrol regarding 1600 use of force incidents that occurred between 2010 and 2012. Ortega and O'Dell, "Deadly Border Agent Incidents Cloaked in Silence."

In May 2014, an immigrant advocacy group, the American Immigration Council, drew analogous conclusions regarding the use of excessive force and physical violence; in response to 809 complaints filed between January 2009 and January 2012, the agency took administrative action in only 3 percent of these cases. Martínez, Cantor, and Ewing, *No Action Taken*. Reports prepared by the Department of Homeland Security and the Police Executive Research Forum reached similar conclusions. US Department of Homeland Security, "Final Report."

Finally, in an exposé of the CBP published in *Politico Magazine*, Garrett Graff observes that the Border Patrol lacked the legal authority to investigate complaints made against its own officers; more specifically, the post-9/11 reorganization of the INS reserved to ICE officers the power to investigate (1801 authority) and conferred upon CBP officials the authority to enforce the laws only (1811 authority). Turf battles between the DHS and FBI also created obstacles to FBI investigations of Border Patrol excessive use of force complaints. Finally, by the onset of the Obama administration, fiscal concerns rendered investigations of these complaints a low priority. Graff, "The Green Monster," 5.

60. Martínez, Cantor, and Ewing, *No Action Taken*, 3.
61. Ortega and O'Dell, "Deadly Border Agent Incidents Cloaked in Silence." Even before PERF issued its recommendations, CBP officers had the option to carry nonlethal as well as lethal weapons. The latter included pistols, shotguns, and M-4 rifles. The former included pepper spray guns (capable of firing pepper spray balls at long range) and the FN-303 (designed to shoot nonlethal projectiles at long range).
62. The Police Executive Research Forum, *U.S. Customs and Border Protection Use of Force Review*, 9. Meanwhile, the agency itself considers rock throwing to be lethal enough to justify the use of deadly force. Ortega and O'Dell, "Deadly Border Agent Incidents Cloaked in Silence."
63. Given that these recommendations constituted "significant departures from current practice," PERF concluded that a new training procedure would have to be implemented for these new practices to take effect. The Police Executive Research Forum, *U.S. Customs and Border Protection Use of Force Review*, 3, 8.
64. Graff, "The Green Monster," 6.
65. Ortega and O'Dell, "Deadly Border Agent Incidents Cloaked in Silence"; Peralta, "Report Criticizes Border Patrol's Use of Deadly Force."
66. Peralta, "Border Patrol to Limit Use of Deadly Force." Most recently, CBP leaders have rejected recommendations that their officers wear body cameras as a means of preventing agency abuses. See Hennessy-Fiske, "Customs and Border Protection Rules out Body Cameras for Officers"; Lopez, Ma, and Breisblatt, *Body Cameras and CBP.*
67. Graff, "The Green Monster," 4; Ortega and O'Dell, "Deadly Border Agent Incidents Cloaked in Silence."
68. Graff, "The Green Monster," 4.
69. Meissner et al., *Immigration Enforcement in the United States*, 12, 14.
70. *Development, Relief, and Education for Alien Minors Act of 2010*, H. R. 5281, 111th Cong. 2d sess., www.gpo.gov/fdsys/pkg/BILLS-111hr5281eah/pdf/BILLS-111hr5281eah.pdf.
71. In order to bypass an intransigent Congress, Obama, like Truman and Eisenhower, resorted to his executive authority to pass a broad array of immigration measures. For an excellent overview of the broad reforms implemented by the Obama administration, see Grossman, "Hidden in Plain Sight." The most prominent of these measures include the Deferred Action for Childhood Arrivals Program (DACA), created in 2012, to defer deportation for certain individuals who came to the United States as children. In an executive order announced on November 20, 2014, President Obama extended the DACA program and granted temporary reprieve from deportation to the undocumented parents of US citizens and permanent residents. Ehrenfreund, "Your Complete Guide to Obama's Immigration Executive Action."
72. Meissner et al., *Immigration Enforcement in the United States*, 12, 14–15.
73. As further support for this claim, MPI cited to the decline in apprehensions: "Border Patrol apprehensions fell to a forty-year low in FY 2011, bringing the new growth of the resident unauthorized population, which had been increasing at a rate of about 525,000 annually, to a standstill." Meissner et al., *Immigration Enforcement in the United States*, 12.
74. Anthony Caminetti, Commissioner General to Supervising Inspector, Mexican Border District, August 31, 1918, file 54410/331A, RG 85, National Archives.
75. Preston, Rapperport, and Richtel, "What Would It Take for Donald Trump to Deport 11 Million and Build a Wall?"

BIBLIOGRAPHY

Archival and Manuscript Collections

ARIZONA HISTORICAL FOUNDATION, HAYDEN LIBRARY, ARIZONA STATE UNIVERSITY, TEMPE

Ruth Reinhold Aviation Collection.

ARIZONA HISTORICAL SOCIETY, NORTHERN DIVISION, NORTHERN ARIZONA UNIVERSITY, FLAGSTAFF

Ashurst, Henry Fountain. Papers.
Babbitt, George. Papers.
Saunders Collection.

ARIZONA HISTORICAL SOCIETY, TUCSON, ARIZONA

Allianza Hispano-Americana Records.
Arizona Bar Foundation. Oral History Project, Arizona Legal History.
Ashurst, Henry Fountain. Papers.
Baggs, Stanley Chipman. Papers.
Hayden, Carl. Papers.
McKinney, Benjamin Julius. Papers.
Milton, Jeff. Ephemera File.
Morris, Hunter James. Papers.
Morrow, Carson. Ephemera File.
Officer, James E. Papers.
Peck, Arthur. Papers.
Tucson Committee for Interracial Understanding. Papers.
United States Marshal, District of Arizona. Papers.

ARIZONA STATE UNIVERSITY, TEMPE—DEPARTMENT OF ARCHIVES AND MANUSCRIPTS, ARIZONA COLLECTION

Ashurst, Henry Fountain. Papers.
Hayden, Carl. Papers.
Smedley-MacKinnon. Papers.
United States Border Patrol. Papers.

THE BANCROFT LIBRARY, UNIVERSITY OF CALIFORNIA AT BERKELEY

Ashurst, Henry Fountain. Papers.
McWilliams, Carey. Papers.
National Council on Agricultural Life and Labor Records.
Taylor, Paul Schuster. Papers.

CHICANO STUDIES RESEARCH CENTER, UNIVERSITY OF CALIFORNIA
AT LOS ANGELES

Kelly Lytle-Hernández Collection of Border Patrol Research Papers.

EL PASO PUBLIC LIBRARY

Border Patrol. Vertical File.

THE LIBRARY OF CONGRESS, MANUSCRIPT DIVISION

Wickersham Commission on Law Observance and Enforcement Records.

NATIONAL ARCHIVES, COLLEGE PARK, MARYLAND

Records of the US Department of State. Record Group 59. Relating to Internal Affairs of Mexico.
Records of the US Department of State. Record Group 59. Relating to Political Relations between
    the United States and Mexico.
Records of the US Department of State. Record Group 84. Foreign Service Post Files.
    Correspondence between Consulates and the Department of State.

NATIONAL ARCHIVES, WASHINGTON, DC

Records of the Immigration and Naturalization Service. Record Group 85. Subject Correspon-
    dence Files.

NATIONAL ARCHIVES, SAN BRUNO, CALIFORNIA

Records of the Immigration and Naturalization Service. Record Group 85. Subject Index to
    Subject Correspondence and Case Files of the Immigration and Naturalization Service.

SAN DIEGO HISTORY CENTER

Conklin, Ralph L. Biographical File.
Ellis, Frank. Biographical File.
Weddle, Frank. Biographical File.

UNITED STATES BORDER PATROL MUSEUM, EL PASO

Border Patrol. Ephemera File.

UNITED STATES, DEPARTMENT OF HOMELAND SECURITY, CITIZENSHIP
AND INFORMATION SERVICES HISTORICAL REFERENCE LIBRARY

UNIVERSITY OF ARIZONA, TUCSON—SPECIAL COLLECTIONS

Ashurst, Henry Fountain. Papers.

UNIVERSITY OF TEXAS AT EL PASO–SPECIAL COLLECTIONS

Border Patrol. Papers.
Calleros, Cleofas. Papers.
Fox, Chris P. Papers.
Garcia, Mario T. Papers.
Hudspeth, Claude R. Papers.
National Catholic Welfare Conference. Papers.
Sonnichsen, C. L. Papers.

Thomas, R. E. Papers.
Wright, Dogie. Papers.

Government Documents

"Authority of Officers of the Immigration and Naturalization Service to Make Arrests." August 7, 1953. Typed manuscript prepared for use of Immigration and Naturalization Service. United States Border Patrol Museum, El Paso, Texas.

"Border Patrol." n.d. Typed manuscript, INS Historical Reference Library, Washington, DC.

Coppock, Donald R., Deputy Associate Commissioner, Immigration and Naturalization Service. "History: Border Patrol." n.d. Typed manuscript, INS Historical Reference Library, Washington, DC.

Ellis Island Committee. *Report of the Ellis Island Committee*. March 1934.

Franklin, Kathleen. "Simplifying Tools for Trade." *Frontline: U.S. Customs and Border Protection* 5, no. 3 (January 2013): 28–31.

Franklin, Kathleen. "Transformation at Land Border Ports of Entry." *Frontline: U.S. Customs and Border Protection* 6, no. 1 (May 2013): 22–26.

Hudson, A. S., Chief, Border Patrol Section, El Paso District. "Traffic Inspection." February 15, 1950 (rev. by Harlon B. Carter). Typed manuscript prepared for the Border Patrol Training School, State College, New Mexico. United States Border Patrol Museum, El Paso, Texas.

Kraut, Alan, ed. *Records of the Immigration and Naturalization Service, Series A: Subject Correspondence Files, Part 2: Mexican Immigration, 1906–1930*. Research Collections in American Immigration, edited by Rudolph Vecoli. Bethesda, MD: A Microfilm Project of University Publications of America, 1994.

"Legal Analysis of Border Patrol Checkpoints." November 1, 1994. Typed manuscript, INS Historical Reference Library, Washington, DC.

Mason, Marcy. "A New Day: CBP Aims to Help Strengthen U.S. Economy by Modernizing Trade Approach." *Frontline: U.S. Customs and Border Protection* 4, no. 2 (July 2011): 22–25.

Mason, Marcy. "Business Unusual: How CBP's Business Recovery Plans Protect the U.S. Economy." *Frontline: U.S. Customs and Border Protection* 6, no. 1 (May 2013): 9–16.

National Commission on Law Observance and Enforcement. *Report on the Enforcement of the Deportation Laws of the United States*. Washington, DC: US Government Printing Office, 1931.

National Commission on Terrorist Attacks Upon the United States. *The 9/11 Commission Report: Final Report of the National Commission on Terrorist Attacks Upon the United States*. New York: Norton, 2004.

Perkins, Frances, Secretary, United States Department of Labor and D. W. MacCormack, Commissioner, Immigration and Naturalization Service. "Information Concerning Origin, Activities, Accomplishments, Organization and Personnel of the Immigration Border Patrol." January 1936. INS Historical Reference Library, Washington, DC.

Purtell, Dan. "The Immigration and Naturalization Service (INS): An Analysis of Its Reports and Subsequent Effects on Hispanics." July 1986. Draft manuscript prepared for the National Council of La Raza, Washington, DC. INS Historical Reference Library, Washington, DC.

The Secretary of Labor's Committee on Administrative Procedure. "The Immigration and Naturalization Service." May 17, 1940. INS Historical Reference Library, Washington, DC.

US Congress. House. Committee on Appropriations. *An Act Making Appropriations for the Departments of State and Justice and for the Judiciary and the Departments of Commerce and Labor, for the fiscal year ending June 30, 1925*. 68th Cong., 1st sess. H. Rep. 761.

US Congress. House. Committee on Appropriations. *Departments of State, Justice, Commerce, and Labor Appropriation Bill, Fiscal Year 1926*. 68th Cong., 2d sess. H. Rep. 1245.

US Congress. House. Committee on Appropriations. *Hearings on Appropriations Department of Labor, 1926*. 68th Cong., 2d sess., January 8, 9, 1925.

US Congress. House. Committee on Foreign Affairs. *Control of Travel from and into the United States*. 65th Cong., 2d sess., 1918. H. Rep. 485.

US Congress. House. Committee on Foreign Affairs. *Hearing on Control of Travel from and into the United States*. 65th Cong., 2d sess., February 13, 1918.

US Congress. House. Committee on Foreign Affairs. *Hearing on Extension of Passport Control*. 66th Cong., 1st sess., October 7, 8, 9, 10, 1919.

US Congress. House. Committee on Immigration and Naturalization. *Aliens Entering the United States in Violation of Law*. 70th Cong., 2d sess., 1929. H. Rep. 2802.

US Congress. House. Committee on Immigration and Naturalization. *To Amend the Fourth Proviso of the Act of February 27, 1925*. 70th Cong., 1st sess., May 21, 1928.

US Congress. House. Committee on Immigration and Naturalization. *Amending the Immigration and Nationality Act, and for other Purposes*. 89th Cong., 1st sess., 1965. H. Rep. 745.

US Congress. House. Committee on Immigration and Naturalization. *Amending the Law Relating to the Authority of Certain Employees of the Immigration and Naturalization Service to Make Arrests without Warrant in Certain Cases and to Search Vehicles within Certain Areas*. 78th Cong., 2d sess., 1944. H. Rep. 1929.

US Congress. House. Committee on Immigration and Naturalization. *Amending the Law Relating to the Authority of Certain Employees of the Immigration and Naturalization Service to Make Arrests without Warrant in Certain Cases and to Search Vehicles within Certain Areas*. 79th Cong., 1st sess., 1945. H. Rep. 186.

US Congress. House. Committee on Immigration and Naturalization. *Border Patrol*. 71st Cong., 2d sess., January 6, 1930.

US Congress. House. Committee on Immigration and Naturalization. *Deportation of Aliens*. 70th Cong., 2d sess., 1929. H. Rep. 2418.

US Congress. House. Committee on Immigration and Naturalization. *To Establish a Border Patrol, Hearings*. 69th Cong., 1st sess., April 12, 19, 1926.

US Congress. House. Committee on Immigration and Naturalization. *Hearings on Certificates of Arrival, Naturalization Law Amendments, Etc*. 70th Cong., 2d sess., February 12, 1929.

US Congress. House. Committee on Immigration and Naturalization. *Hearings on Immigration Border Patrol*. 70th Cong., 1st sess., March 5, 1928.

US Congress. House. Committee on Immigration and Naturalization. *Immigration Border Patrol*. 71st Cong., 2d sess., January 15, 1930.

US Congress. House. Committee on Immigration and Naturalization. *Immigration Border Patrol*. 71st Cong., 2d sess., January 23, 1930.

US Congress. House. Committee on Immigration and Naturalization. *To Supplement the Naturalization Laws*. 70th Cong., 1st sess., December 15, 1927. H. Rep. 13.

US Congress. House. Committee on Immigration and Naturalization. *To Supplement the Naturalization Laws*. 70th Cong., 2d sess., February 27, 1929. H. Rep. 2763.

US Congress. House. Committee on Interstate and Foreign Commerce. *Hearings on a Bill to Regulate the Entry of Persons into the United States, to Establish a Border Patrol in the Coast Guard, and for Other Purposes*. 71st Cong., 2d sess., April 24, 25, 1930.

US Congress. House. Committee on Interstate and Foreign Commerce. *United States Border Patrol*. 71st Cong., 2d sess., 1930. H. Rep. 1828.

US Congress. House. Committee on the Judiciary. *Assist in Preventing Aliens from Entering or Remaining in the United States Illegally*. 82d Cong., 2d sess., 1952. H. Rep. 1377.

US Congress. House. Committee on the Judiciary. *Assist in Preventing Aliens from Entering or Remaining in the United States Illegally*. 82d Cong., 2d sess., 1952. H. Rep. 1505.

US Congress. House. Committee on the Judiciary. *Hearings Before the President's Commission on Immigration and Naturalization*. 82d Cong., 2d sess., September 1, 2, 6, 7, 8–10, 15, 17, 27, 30 and October 27–29, 1952.

US Congress. House. Committee on the Judiciary. *Immigration and Nationality Act: Conference Report*. 82d Cong., 2d sess., 1952. H. Rep. 2096.

US Congress. House. Committee on Rules. *Border Patrol, Unpublished Hearing*. 71st Cong., 2d sess., 1930.

US Congress. House. *Congressional Record.* 65th Cong., 2d sess., May 3, 4, 1918. Vol. 51, pt. 6: 6029–6032; 6061–6068.

US Congress. House. *Congressional Record.* 68th Cong., 2d sess., January 20, 23, 27, 1925. Vol. 66, pt. 3: 2167–2169; 2385–2386; 2530–2537.

US Congress. House. *Congressional Record.* 70th Cong., 2d sess., February 15, 16, 1929. Vol. 70, pt. 4: 3542–3550; 3614–3621.

US Congress. House. *Congressional Record.* 70th Cong., 2d sess., March 1, 1929. Vol. 70, pt. 5: 4946-4950; 4950-4955.

US Congress. House. *Congressional Record.* 71st Cong., 2d sess., June 30, July 1, 1930. Vol. 72, pt. 11: 12115–12117; 12217–12237.

US Congress. House. *Congressional Record.* 79th Cong., 1st sess., June 4, 1945. Vol. 91, pt. 4: 5504–5505, 5513.

US Congress. House. *Congressional Record.* 82d Cong., 2d sess., February 25, 1952. Vol. 98, pt. 1: 1335–1359.

US Congress. House. *Congressional Record.* 82d Cong., 2d sess., February 26, 1952. Vol. 98, pt. 2: 1413–1421.

US Congress. Senate. Committee on Appropriations. *An Act Making Appropriations for the Departments of State and Justice and for the Judiciary and the Departments of Commerce and Labor, for the fiscal year ending June 30, 1925.* 68th Cong., 1st sess., 1925. S. Rep. 457.

US Congress. Senate. Committee on Commerce. *Hearings on An Act to Regulate the Entry of Persons into the United States to Establish a Border Patrol in the Coast Guard and for Other Purposes.* 71st Cong., 3d sess., December 18, 1930, January 8, 15, 1931.

US Congress. Senate. Committee on Foreign Affairs. *Travel from and into the United States in War Time.* 65th Cong., 2d sess., 1918. S. Rep. 431.

US Congress. Senate. Committee on Immigration. *Hearings on Illegal Entry of Aliens.* 66th Cong., 1st sess., October 10, 1919.

US Congress. Senate. Committee on Immigration. *Making it a Felony with Penalty for Certain Aliens to Enter the Untied States of America under Certain Conditions in Violation of Law.* 70th Cong., 2d sess., 1929. S. Rep. 1456.

US Congress. Senate. Committee on Immigration. *Supplement to Naturalization Laws.* 70th Cong., 2d sess., January 24, 1929. S. Rep. 1504.

US Congress. Senate. Committee on Immigration and Naturalization. *Amending the Law Relating to the Authority of Certain Employees of the Immigration and Naturalization Service to Make Arrests without Warrant in Certain Cases and to Search Vehicles within Certain Areas.* H. R. 386. 79th Cong., 1st sess., 1945. S. Rep. 632.

US Congress. Senate. Committee on the Judiciary. *Admission of Foreign Agricultural Workers.* 81st Cong., 2d sess., 1950. S. Rep. 1474.

US Congress. Senate. Committee on the Judiciary. *Assisting in Preventing Aliens from Entering or Remaining in the United States Illegally.* 82d Cong., 2d sess., 1952. S. Rep. 1145.

US Congress. Senate. Committee on the Judiciary. *To Control Illegal Immigration, Hearing.* 83d Cong., 2d sess., July 12, 13, 14, 1954.

US Congress. Senate. Committee on the Judiciary. *Hearings on S. 272 To Facilitate the Admission of Certain Foreign Workers Desiring to Perform Agricultural Work in the United States.* 81st Cong., 1st sess., July 12, 1949.

US Congress. Senate. Committee on the Judiciary. *The Illegal Employment of Aliens Act of 1954.* 83d Cong., 2d sess., 1954. S. Rep. 2451.

US Congress. Senate. Committee on the Judiciary. *The Illegal Transportation of Aliens Act of 1954.* 83d Cong., 2d sess., 1954. S. Rep. 2452.

US Congress. Senate. Committee on the Judiciary. *The Immigration and Naturalization Systems of the United States.* 81st Cong., 2d sess., 1950. S. Rep. 1515.

US Congress. Senate. Committee on the Judiciary. *Revisions of the Immigration and Nationality Laws.* 82d Cong., 2d sess., 1952., S. Rep. 1137.

US Congress. Senate. Committee on the Judiciary. *Revisions of the Immigration and Nationality Laws, Minority Views.* 82d Cong., 2d sess., 1952, S. Rep. 1137, Pt. 2.

US Congress. Senate. Committee on the Judiciary. Select Commission on Immigration and Naturalization. *History of the Immigration and Naturalization Service.* Report prepared by Sharon D. Masanz, 96th Cong., 2d sess., 1980. Committee Print.

US Congress. Senate. Committee on Labor and Public Welfare. Subcommittee on Labor and Labor-Management Relations. *Hearings on Migratory Labor.* 82d Cong., 2d sess., February 5, 6, 7, 11, 14, 15, 27, 28, 29 and March 27, 28, 1952.

US Congress. Senate. Subcommittee of the Committee on Post Offices and Post Roads. *Hearings Influencing Appointments to Postmasterships and Other Federal Offices.* 71st Cong., 1st sess., June 21, 27, 28, 29 and July 1, 1929.

US Congress. Senate. *Congressional Record.* 65th Cong., 2d sess., May 8, 9, 1918. Vol. 51, pt. 6: 6191–6195; 6246–6248.

US Congress. Senate. *Congressional Record.* 68th Cong., 2d sess., February 7, 1925. Vol. 66, pt. 3: 3201–3202.

US Congress. Senate. *Congressional Record.* 70th Cong., 2d sess., March 1, 2, 1929. Vol. 70, pt. 5: 4872–4873; 5006–5009.

US Congress. Senate. *Congressional Record.* 81st Cong., 2d sess., April 19, 1950. Vol. 96, pt. 4: 5364–5365.

US Congress. Senate. *Congressional Record.* 81st Cong., 2d sess., August 8, 1950. Vol. 96, pt. 9: 11967–11968.

US Congress. Senate. *Congressional Record.* 82d Cong., 2d sess., February 5, 1952. Vol. 98, pt. 1: 791–813.

US Congress. Senate. *Congressional Record.* 82d Cong., 2d sess., May 13, 1952. Vol. 98, pt. 4: 5100-5115.

US Congress. Senate and House. Committees on the Judiciary. Subcommittees on Immigration. *Joint Hearings Before the Subcommittees of the Committees on the Judiciary.* 82d Cong., 1st sess., March 6–9, 12–16, 20–21 and April 9, 1951.

US Department of Commerce and Labor. Bureau of Immigration. *Annual Report of the Commissioner General of Immigration.* Washington, DC: US Government Printing Office, 1903–1911.

US Department of Homeland Security. "Final Report of the CBP Integrity Advisory Panel, March 15, 2016." March 15, 2016. www.dhs.gov/sites/default/files/publications/HSAC%20 CBP%20IAP_Final%20Report_FINAL%20%28accessible%29_0.pdf.

US Department of Homeland Security. Citizenship and Immigration Services. "Early Immigrant Inspection along the U.S.–Mexican Border," by Marian L. Smith. Citizenship and Information Services Historical Reference Library.

US Department of Homeland Security. Citizenship and Immigration Services. "H-2A Temporary Agricultural Workers." December 23, 2015. www.uscis.gov/working-united-states/ temporary-workers/h-2a-temporary-agricultural-workers.

US Department of Homeland Security. Customs and Border Protection. "About CBP." Accessed July 29, 2015. www.cbp.gov/about.

US Department of Homeland Security. Customs and Border Protection. "Fact Sheet: Free and Secure Trade Program (FAST)." Accessed August 5, 2015. www.cbp.gov/sites/default/files/ documents/fast_fact_2.pdf.

US Department of Homeland Security. Customs and Border Protection. "Fact Sheet: NEXUS." Accessed August 5, 2015. www.cbp.gov/sites/default/files/documents/nexus_facts_2.pdf.

US Department of Homeland Security. Customs and Border Protection. "Fact Sheet: Secure Electronic Network for Travelers Rapid Inspection (SENTRI)." Accessed August 5, 2015. www.cbp.gov/sites/default/files/documents/sentri_fact_2.pdf.

US Department of Homeland Security. Customs and Border Protection. "Fact Sheet: Trusted Traveler Programs." Accessed August 5, 2015. www.cbp.gov/sites/default/files/documents/ ttp_factsheet_2.pdf.

US Department of Homeland Security and US Department of Commerce. "Supporting Travel and Tourism to Grow Our Economy and Create More Jobs, Report to the President, A National Goal on the International Arrivals Process and Airport-Specific Action Plans. February 13, 2015. Accessed August 10, 2015. www.whitehouse.gov/sites/default/files/docs/150211_travel_and_tourism_report_final_clean_2.pdf.

US Department of Justice. Immigration and Naturalization Service. *Annual Report of Lemuel B. Schofield, Special Assistant to the Attorney General in Charge of the Immigration and Naturalization Service.* Typed Manuscript. INS Historical Reference Library, Washington, DC, 1940–1942.

US Department of Justice. Immigration and Naturalization Service. *Annual Report of the Immigration and Naturalization Service.* Typed Manuscript. INS Historical Reference Library, Washington, DC, 1943–1948.

US Department of Justice. Immigration and Naturalization Service. *Annual Report of the Immigration and Naturalization Service.* Washington, DC: US Government Printing Office, 1949–1980.

US Department of Justice. Immigration and Naturalization Service. "Border Patrol Use of Aircraft." *Monthly Review* 4, no. 11 (1947): 138.

US Department of Justice, Immigration and Naturalization Service. "Grover C. Wilmoth—A Tribute." *Monthly Review* 7, no. 9 (1951): 113.

US Department of Justice. Immigration and Naturalization Service. "Immigration Patrol Officers Duties and Authority to Act," by Grover C. Wilmoth. Manual published for the Border Patrol Training School, Mexican Border, May 1, 1940.

US Department of Justice. Immigration and Naturalization Service. *An Immigrant Nation: U.S. Regulation of Immigration, 1798–1991.* Washington, DC: US Government Printing Office, 1991.

US Department of Justice. Immigration and Naturalization Service. *Immigration and Nationality Laws and Regulations as of January 1, 1942.* Washington, DC: US Government Printing Office, 1942.

US Department of Justice. Immigration and Naturalization Service. *Immigration and Nationality Laws and Regulations as of March 1, 1944.* Washington, DC: US Government Printing Office, 1944.

US Department of Justice. Immigration and Naturalization Service. *Immigration Border Patrol, El Paso Sector, 1924–1999: Where the Legend Began.* Washington, DC: US Government Printing Office, 2002.

US Department of Justice. Immigration and Naturalization Service. *The Immigration Border Patrol: Its Origins, Activities, Accomplishments, Organization, and Personnel.* Washington, DC: US Government Printing Office, 1948.

US Department of Justice. Immigration and Naturalization Service. *Immigration Manual.* Washington, DC: US Government Printing Office, 1942.

US Department of Justice. Immigration and Naturalization Service. *The Law of Arrest, Search, and Seizure.* Washington, DC: US Government Printing Office, 1983.

US Department of Justice. Immigration and Naturalization Service. *Monthly Review.* Washington, DC: US Government Printing Office, 1943–1952.

US Department of Justice. Immigration and Naturalization Service. "Patrolling the Imperial Valley by Plane." *Monthly Review* 5, no. 5 (1947): 59–61.

US Department of Justice. Immigration and Naturalization Service. "The Border Patrol." *Monthly Review* 2 (November 1944): 53–60.

US Department of Labor. Bureau of Immigration. *Annual Report of the Commissioner General of Immigration.* Washington, DC: US Government Printing Office, 1912–1933.

US Department of Labor. Bureau of Immigration. *Immigration Laws and Rules of May 1, 1917.* Washington, DC: US Government Printing Office, 1917 (rev. 1918, 1920, 1921, 1922).

US Department of Labor. Bureau of Immigration. *Immigration Laws and Rules of July 1, 1925.* Washington, DC: US Government Printing Office, 1925.

US Department of Labor. Bureau of Immigration. *Immigration Laws and Rules of March 1, 1927.* Washington, DC: US Government Printing Office, 1927.

US Department of Labor. Bureau of Immigration. "Mexican Border Problems," by William A. Whalen. In "Problems of the Immigration Service: Papers Presented at a Conference of Commissioners and District Directors of Immigration," US Department of Labor, Bureau of Immigration. Washington, DC, January 1929.

US Department of Labor. Bureau of Immigration. *U.S. Immigration Service Bulletin.* Washington, DC: US Government Printing Office, 1918–1919.

US Department of Labor. Bureau of Labor Standards. "The Recommendations of the U.S. President's Commission on Migratory Labor." Prepared by William L. Connolly, Director. April, 1952. Library of Congress, Washington, DC.

US Department of Labor. Immigration and Naturalization Service. *Annual Report of the Commissioner General of Immigration and Naturalization.* Washington, DC: US Government Printing Office, 1934–1939.

US Department of Treasury. Immigration Service. *Annual Report of the Commissioner General of Immigration.* Washington, DC: US Government Printing Office, 1897–1902.

US Department of Labor. Immigration and Naturalization Service. *Immigration Laws and Rules of January 1, 1930.* Washington, DC: US Government Printing Office, 1929.

US Department of Labor. Immigration and Naturalization Service. *Immigration Laws and Rules of January 1, 1930 with amendments from January 1, 1930 to July 11, 1932.* Washington, DC: US Government Printing Office, 1934.

US Department of Labor. Immigration and Naturalization Service. *Immigration Laws and Rules of January 1, 1930, as amended up to and including December 31, 1936.* Washington, DC: US Government Printing Office, 1937 (rev. 1941).

US Department of Labor. The Secretary of Labor's Committee on Administrative Procedure. "The Immigration and Naturalization Service." May 17, 1940. INS Historical Reference Library, Washington, DC.

US President. "Message from the President of the United States Returning without Approval the Bill (H.R. 5678) to Revise the Laws Relating to Immigration and Nationality, and for Other Purposes." 82d Cong., 2d sess.,1952. H. Doc. No. 520.

US President. Communication. "Proposed Supplemental Appropriation for the Department of Justice, Fiscal Year 1952." 82d Cong., 1st sess., 1951. H. Doc. 208.

US President. Communication. "Proposed Supplemental Appropriation for the Department of Justice, Fiscal Year 1953." 82d Cong., 2d sess., 1952. S. Doc. 152.

US President's Commission on Immigration and Naturalization. *Whom Shall We Welcome: Report of the President's Commission on Immigration and Naturalization.* Washington, DC: US Government Printing Office, 1953.

US President's Commission on Migratory Labor. *Migratory Labor in American Agriculture: Report of the President's Commission on Migratory Labor.* Washington, DC: US Government Printing Office, 1951.

US President's Commission on Migratory Labor. *Stenographic Report of Proceedings.* Washington, DC: Ward and Paul, 1950.

White House Office of the Press Secretary. *Smart Border: 22-Point Agreement—U.S.–Mexican Border Partnership Action Plan.* March 21, 2002. http://2001-2009.state.gov/p/wha/rls/fs/8909.htm.

Oral Histories

Adams, Arthur L. Interview by Jim Marchant and Oscar J. Martínez. August 10, 1977. Interview 646, transcript. Institute of Oral History, University of Texas at El Paso.

Ashurst, Henry Fountain. Interview by George Babbitt. May 19, 1959 and October 9, 1961. George Babbitt Collection. Cline Library, Northern Arizona University, Flagstaff.

Ayala, E. V. Interview by Rodolfo Mares. April 28, 1976. Interview 231, transcript. Institute of Oral History, University of Texas at El Paso.

Calleros, Cleofas. Interview by Oscar J. Martínez. September 14, 1972. Interview 157, transcript. Institute of Oral History, University of Texas at El Paso.

Croxen, Fred W. Interview by Margaret L. Gerow. November 26, 1973. Interview 290, transcript. Arizona Historical Society, Tucson.

Darling, John Hutchinson. Interview by Emil F. Schaaf. February 14, 1972. Interview 201, recording. Arizona Historical Society, Tucson.

Ellis, Frank Garfield. Interview by Edgar F. Hastings. March 28, 1961. Transcript. Oral History Program. San Diego Historical Society.

Frakes, Harold D. Interview by Oscar J. Martínez. October 11, 1978. Interview 698, transcript. Institute of Oral History, University of Texas at El Paso.

Jackson, Armond. Interview by Oscar J. Martínez. February 4, 1975. Interview 172, transcript. Institute of Oral History, University of Texas at El Paso.

Machuca, J. C. Interview by Oscar J. Martínez. May 9, 1975. Interview 152, transcript. Institute of Oral History, University of Texas at El Paso.

Martinez, Bernardo. Interview by Oscar J. Martínez. May 9, 1975. Interview 152, transcript. Institute of Oral History, University of Texas at El Paso.

Newton, David C. Interview by Oscar J. Martínez and Virgilio H. Sanchez. October 9, 1978. Interview 721, transcript. Institute of Oral History, University of Texas at El Paso.

Parker, Ben A. Interview by Douglas V. Meed. July 25, 1984. Interview 661, transcript. Institute of Oral History, University of Texas at El Paso.

Reeves, Edwin M. Interview by Robert H. Novak. June 25, 1974. Interview 135, transcript. Institute of Oral History, University of Texas at El Paso.

Rodríguez, George. Interview by Richard Estrada. August 7, 1975. Interview 412, transcript. Interview of Oral History, University of Texas at El Paso.

Stiles, Wesley E. Interview by Wesley C. Shaw. January 1986. Interview 756, transcript. Institute of Oral History, University of Texas at El Paso.

Weddle, Henry H. Interview by Edgar F. Hastings. February 25, August 20, and December 30, 1959. Transcript. Oral History Program. San Diego Historical Society.

Dissertations and Theses

Anthony, Steven. "The Los Angeles District Office of Immigration: Its Organization, Functions, and Methods of Apprehension." PhD diss., Claremont Graduate School, 1983.

Briggs, Lawrence John. "For the Welfare of Wage Earners: Immigration Policy and the Labor Department, 1913–1921." PhD diss., Syracuse University, 1995.

Cabeza de Baca, Vincent. "Moral Renovation of the Californias: Tijuana's Political and Economic Role in American–Mexican Relations, 1920–1935." PhD diss., University of San Diego, 1991.

Cavazos, Sylvia. "The Disposable Mexican: Operation Wetback 1954, The Deportation of Undocumented Workers in California and Texas." MA thesis, University of Texas, Pan American, 1997.

Dowling, Winifred B. "The Border at War: World War II along the United States–Mexico Border." PhD diss., University of Texas at El Paso, 2010.

Elac, John Chala. "The Employment of Mexican Workers in U.S. Agriculture, 1900–1960: A Binational Economic Analysis." PhD diss., University of California, Los Angeles, 1961.

Gonzales, Adolfo. "Historical Case Study: San Diego and Tijuana Border Region Relationship with the San Diego Police Department, 1957–1994." EdD diss., University of California at San Diego, 1996.

Jarnagin, Richard Tait. "Effect of Increased Illegal Mexican Immigration upon the Organization and Operations of the U.S. Immigration Border Patrol, Southwest Region." MS thesis, University of Southern California, 1957.

Kang, S. Deborah. "The Legal Construction of the Borderlands: The INS, Immigration Law, and Immigrant Rights on the U.S.–Mexico Border, 1917–1954." PhD diss., University of California, Berkeley, 2005.

Klein, Kerwin Lee. "The Last Resort: Tourism, Growth, and Values in Twentieth-Century Arizona." MA thesis, University of Arizona, 1990.

Langham, Thomas Caloway. "The Eisenhower Administration and Operation Wetback, 1953–1956: A Case Study of the Development of a Federal Policy to Control Illegal Migration." PhD diss., University of Texas, Austin, 1984.

Langston, Edward Lonnie. "The Impact of Prohibition on the Mexican–United States Border: The El Paso–Ciudad Juarez Case." PhD diss., Texas Tech University, 1974.

Lytle-Hernández, Kelly. "Entangling Bodies and Borders: Racial Profiling and the U.S. Border Patrol, 1924–1955." PhD diss., University of California, Los Angeles, 2002.

Martínez-Matsuda, Verónica. "Making the Modern Migrant: Work, Community, and Struggle in the Federal Migratory Labor Camp Program," 1935–1947. PhD diss., University of Texas, Austin, 2009.

Mason, Waynelle. "The Immigration and Nationality Amendments Act of 1965: Righting Past Wrongs." MA thesis, University of Tulsa, 1997.

Maxwell, Edward Joe. "The McCarran-Walter Immigration and Nationality Act of 1952." MA thesis, Stanford University, 1962.

Middaugh, Jon S. "Transnational Cultural Market: A Concept for Understanding Cultural Transmission across the Mexico-United States Border, 1920–1946." PhD diss., Washington State University, 2010.

Ngai, Mae M. "Illegal Aliens and Alien Citizens: United States Immigration Policy and Racial Formation, 1924–1945." PhD diss., Columbia University, 1998.

Pittman, Von V., Jr., "Senator Patrick A. McCarran and the Politics of Containment." PhD diss., University of Georgia, 1979.

Robinson, Robert S. "Creating Foreign Policy Locally: Migratory Labor and the Texas Border, 1943–1952." PhD diss., Ohio State University, 2007.

Rodríguez, Chantel Renee. "Health on the Line: The Politics of Citizenship and the Railroad Bracero Program of World War II." PhD diss., University of Minnesota, 2013.

Sánchez-Walker, Marjorie. "Migration Quicksand: Immigration Law and Immigration Advocates at the El Paso-Juárez Border Crossing, 1933–1941." PhD diss., Washington State University, 1999.

Schulze, Jeffrey M. "Trans-nations: Indians, Imagined Communities, and Border Realities in the Twentieth Century." PhD diss., Southern Methodist University, 2008.

Sparks, George F. "The Speaking of Henry Fountain Ashurst." PhD diss., University of Utah, 1953.

St. John, Rachel. "Line in the Sand: The Desert Border between the United States and Mexico, 1848–1934." PhD diss., Stanford University, 2005.

Tiltti, John Thomas. "Non-Border Search and Seizure: Authority of United States Border Patrol Agents Under Section 287-a of the Immigration and Nationality Act." MA thesis, University of Texas at El Paso, 1978.

Whited, Frank Elmer, Jr. "The Rhetoric of Senator Patrick Anthony McCarran." PhD diss., University of Oregon, 1973.

Wojtak, Steven Anthony. "The Los Angeles District Office of Immigration: Its Organization, Functions, and Methods of Apprehension." PhD diss., Claremont Graduate School, 1983.

Woo-Sam, Anne Marie. "Domesticating the Immigrant: California's Commission of Immigration and Housing and the Domestic Immigration Policy Movement, 1910–1945." PhD diss., University of California at Berkeley, 1999.

Published Materials

Abbott, Edith. *Historical Aspects of the Immigration Problem: Select Documents.* Chicago: University of Chicago Press, 1926.

Acuña, Rodolfo. *Occupied America: A History of Chicanos.* New York: Harper and Row, 1988.

Adelman, Jeremy, and Stephen Aron. "From Borderlands to Borders: Empires, Nation-States, and the Peoples in Between in North American History," *American Historical Review* 104, no. 3 (1999): 814–841.

Agrawal, Swati. "Trusts Betrayed: The Absent Federal Partner in Immigration Policy." *San Diego Law Review* 33, no. 2 (1996): 755–829.

Aguila, Jaime R. "Mexican/U.S. Immigration Policy prior to the Great Depression." *Diplomatic History* 31, no. 2 (April 2007): 207–225.

"Aid of Congress to Dry Law Wins WCTU Approval." *Christian Science Monitor,* September 30, 1926.

Alfaro-Velcamp, Theresa. *So Far from Allah, So Close to Mexico: Middle Eastern Immigrants in Modern Mexico.* Austin: University of Texas Press, 2007.

Alfaro-Velcamp, Theresa, and Robert H. McLaughlin. "Immigration and Techniques of Governance in Mexico and the United States: Recalibrating National Narratives through Comparative Immigration Histories." *Law and History Review* 29, no. 2 (2011): 573–606.

"Alien Crime Bill Voted," *Los Angeles Times,* February 17, 1929.

"Aliens in U.S. Illegally Caught in Area Search: Mexican Nationals Number More Than 130; Buses Take First Offenders to Border," *Los Angeles Times,* April 13, 1949.

Almaguer, Tomás. *Racial Fault Lines: The Historical Origins of White Supremacy in California.* Berkeley: University of California Press, 1994.

Alvarez, Robert R. *Familia: Migration and Adaptation in Baja and Alta California, 1800–1975.* Berkeley: University of California Press, 1987.

Andreas, Peter. Border Games: Policing the U.S.–Mexico Divide. Ithaca, NY: Cornell University Press, 2000.

Andreas, Peter. "The Escalation of U.S. Immigration Control in the Post-NAFTA Era." *Political Science Quarterly* 113, no. 4 (1998–1999): 591–615.

Andreas, Peter. *Smuggler Nation: How Illicit Trade Made America.* New York: Oxford University Press, 2014.

Archibold, Randal C. "Arizona Enacts Stringent Law on Immigration." *New York Times,* April 23, 2010.

"Ask United Force to Guard Borders." *New York Times,* September 25, 1922.

Bach, Robert L. "Mexican Immigration and the American State." *International Migration Review* 12, no. 4 (1978): 536–558.

Balderrama, Francisco E., and Raymond Rodríguez. *Decade of Betrayal: Mexican Repatriation in the 1930s.* Albuquerque: University of New Mexico Press, 1995.

Balogh, Brian. *A Government Out of Sight: The Mystery of National Authority in Nineteenth-Century America.* Cambridge: Cambridge University Press, 2009.

Barrera, Mario. *Race and Class in the Southwest: A Theory of Racial Inequality.* Notre Dame: University of Notre Dame Press, 1979.

Becker, Elizabeth, Clifford Kraus, and Tim Weiner. "Free Trade Accord at 10: The Growing Pains Are Clear." *New York Times,* December 27, 2003.

Begley, Sarah. "Donald Trump Hits New High in Poll of Republicans." *Time Magazine,* July 20, 2015. http://time.com/3965192/donald-trump-john-mccain-poll/.

Belenchia, Joanne M. "Cowboys and Aliens: How the INS Operates in Latino Communities." *Peace and Change* 6, no. 3 (1980): 10–19.

Benton-Cohen, Katherine. *Borderline Americans: Racial Division and Labor War in the Arizona Borderlands.* Cambridge, MA: Harvard University Press, 2011.

Bennett, David H. *The Party of Fear: From Nativist Movements to the New Right in American History.* New York: Vintage Books, 1990.

Bernard, William S. *American Immigration Policy, A Reappraisal.* New York: Harper & Brothers, 1950.

Bersin, Alan D. "Lines and Flows: The Beginning and End of Borders," *Brooklyn Journal of International Law* 37, no. 2 (March 2012): 389–406.

Blakemore, Howard. *Special Detail*. Philadelphia, PA: Dorrance and Company, 1944.

Blanton, Carlos Kevin. "The Citizenship Sacrifice: Mexican Americans, the Saunders-Leonard Report, and the Politics of Immigration, 1951–1952." *Western Historical Quarterly* 40, no. 3 (2009): 299–320.

Bosniak, Linda. "Membership, Equality, and the Difference that Alienage Makes." *New York University Law Review* 69, no. 6 (1994): 1047–1149.

Bremer, Emily S. "The Unwritten Administrative Constitution." *Florida Law Review* 66, no. 3 (2014): 1215–1274.

Brinkley, Alan. *New Deal Liberalism in Recession and War*. New York: Vintage, 1996.

Bruce, J. Campbell. *The Golden Door: The Irony of Our Immigration Policy*. New York: Random House, 1954.

Buffington, Robert. "Prohibition in the Borderlands: National Government–Border Community Relations." *Pacific Historical Review* 63, no. 1 (1994): 19–39.

Bumiller, Elizabeth, and Tim Weiner. "At Conference, Fox Backs Bush's Guest Worker Plan." *New York Times*, January 13, 2004.

Cadava, Geraldo L. *Standing on Common Ground: The Making of a Sunbelt Borderland*. Cambridge, MA: Harvard University Press, 2013.

Calavita, Kitty. *Inside the State: The Bracero Program, Immigration and the I.N.S.* New York: Routledge, 1992.

Calavita, Kitty. *U.S. Immigration Law and the Control of Labor: 1820–1924*. London: Academic Press, 1984.

Camacho, Julia María Schiavone. *Chinese Mexicans: Transpacific Migration and the Search for a Homeland, 1910–1960*. Chapel Hill: University of North Carolina Press, 2012.

Camarillo, Albert. *Chicanos in California: A History of Mexican Americans in California*. San Francisco: Boyd and Fraser Publishing Company, 1984.

Cardoso, Lawrence A. *Mexican Emigration to the United States: 1897–1931: Socio-economic Patterns*. Tucson: University of Arizona Press, 1980.

Carpenter, Daniel P. *The Forging of Bureaucratic Autonomy: Reputations, Networks, and Policy Innovation in Executive Agencies, 1862–1928*. Princeton, NJ: Princeton University Press, 2001.

Casteñeda, Jorge G. "NAFTA's Mixed Record." *Foreign Affairs* 93, no. 1 (2014): 131–141.

Celler, Emanuel. *You Never Leave Brooklyn*. New York: John Day Company, 1953.

Chávez, Sergio. *Border Lives: Fronterizos, Transnational Migrants, and Commuters in Tijuana*. New York: Oxford University Press, 2016.

Clark, Jane Perry. *Deportation of Aliens from the United States to Europe*. New York: Columbia University Press, 1931.

Clemens, Elisabeth S. "Lineages of the Rube Goldberg State: Building and Blurring Public Programs, 1900–1940." In *Rethinking Political Institutions: The Art of the State*, edited by Ian Shapiro, Stephen Skowronek, and Daniel Galvin, 187–215. New York: New York University Press, 2006.

Cohen, Deborah. *Braceros: Migrant Citizens and Transnational Subjects in the Postwar United States*. Chapel Hill: University of North Carolina Press, 2011.

Cohen, Lizabeth. *Making a New Deal: Industrial Workers in Chicago, 1919–1939*. New York: Cambridge University Press, 1990.

Colley, Charles C. "Carl T. Hayden–Phoenician." *Journal of Arizona History* 18, no. 3 (1977): 247–257.

Coolidge, Mary Roberts. *Chinese Immigration*. New York: Arno Press, 1969.

Corbin, Helen. "The Sheriff Who Became a Legend: Carl Hayden." *The Arizona Sheriff*, December 1970.

Craig, Richard B. *The Bracero Program: Interest Groups and Foreign Policy*. Austin: University of Texas Press, 1971.

Crawford, William. *The United States Border Patrol*. New York: G. P. Putnam's Sons, 1965.

Daly, Sara. "Comment: Bordering on Discrimination: Effects of Immigration Policies/Legislation on Indigenous Peoples in the United States and Mexico." *American Indian Law Review* 38, no. 1 (2013): 157–186.

Daniels, Roger. *The Politics of Prejudice: The Anti-Japanese Movement in California and the Struggle for Japanese Exclusion*. Berkeley: University of California Press, 1999.

Davis, Kenneth Culp. *Discretionary Justice: A Preliminary Inquiry*. Urbana: University of Illinois Press, 1977.

Davis, Mike. *Magical Urbanism: Latinos Reinvent the U.S. City*. London: Verso, 2000.

Delgado, Grace Peña. "At Exclusion's Southern Gate: Changing Categories of Race and Class among Chinese Fronterizos, 1882–1904." In *Continental Crossroads: Remapping U.S.–Mexico Borderlands History*, edited by Samuel Truett and Elliot Young, 183–208. Durham, NC: Duke University Press, 2004.

Delgado, Grace Peña. *Making the Chinese Mexican: Global Migration, Localism, and Exclusion in the U.S.–Mexico Borderlands*. Redwood City, CA: Stanford University Press, 2012.

Derthick, Martha. *Agency Under Stress: The Social Security Administrative in American Government*. Washington, DC: The Brookings Institution, 1990.

Desai, Anuj C. "Wiretapping Before the Wires: The Post Office and the Birth of Communications Privacy." *Stanford Law Review* 60, no. 2 (2007): 553–594.

Deutsch, Sarah, *No Separate Refuge: Culture, Class, and Gender on an Anglo-Hispanic Frontier in the American Southwest, 1880–1940*. New York: Oxford University Press, 1987.

Díaz, George T. *Border Contraband: A History of Smuggling across the Rio Grande*. Austin: University of Texas Press, 2015.

Dinwoodie, D. H. "Deportation: The Immigration Service and the Chicano Labor Movement in the 1930s." *New Mexico Historical Review* 52 (July 1977): 193–206.

Divine, Robert A. *American Immigration Policy, 1942–1952*. New York: De Capo Press, 1972.

Driscoll, Barbara A. *The Tracks North: The Railroad Bracero Program of World War II*. Austin: CMAS Books, University of Texas at Austin, 1999.

Du-Hart, Evelyn. "Immigrants to a Developing Society: The Chinese in Northern Mexico, 1874–1932." *Journal of Arizona History* 21, no. 3 (1980): 49–86.

Dudziak, Mary L., "Desegregation as a Cold War Imperative." *Stanford Law Review* 41, no. 1 (1988): 61–120.

Dunn, Timothy J. *The Militarization of the U.S.–Mexico Border, 1978–1992: Low-Intensity Conflict Doctrine Comes Home*. Austin: University of Texas at Austin, 1996.

Edwards, Jerome E. *Pat McCarran: Political Boss of Nevada*. Reno: University of Nevada Press, 1982.

Ehrenfreund, Max. "Your Complete Guide to Obama's Immigration Executive Action." *Washington Post*, November 20, 2014.

Elsberger, Angela M. "Florida's Battle With the Federal Government Over Immigration Policy Holds Children Hostage: They Are Not Our Children!" *Law and Inequality* 13, no. 1 (1994): 141–168.

Erb, Richard D., and Stanley R. Ross. *United States Relations with Mexico*. Washington, DC: American Enterprise Institute for Public Policy Research, 1981.

Estes, Donald H. "Before the War: The Japanese in San Diego." *Journal of San Diego History* 24, no. 4 (1978): 425–455.

Ettinger, Patrick. *Imaginary Lines: Border Enforcement and the Origins of Undocumented Immigration, 1882–1930*. Austin: University of Texas Press, 2010.

Farrell, Raymond. "The Role of the Immigration and Naturalization Service in the Administration of Current Immigration Law." *International Migration Review* 4, no. 3 (1970): 16–30.

Fernandez, Raul A. *The Mexican American Border Region: Issues and Trends*. Notre Dame, IN: University of Notre Dame Press, 1989.

"Fight for Dry Bills Likely to Go Over." *New York Times*, June 16, 1926.

Figueroa-Aramoni, Rodulfo. "A Nation Beyond its Borders: The Program for Mexican Communities Abroad." *Journal of American History* 86, no. 2 (1999): 537–544.

FitzGerald, David. *A Nation of Emigrants: How Mexico Manages its Migration*. Berkeley: University of California Press, 2009.

FitzGerald, David, and David Cook-Martín. *Culling the Masses: The Democratic Origins of Racist Immigration Policy in the Americas*. Cambridge, MA: Harvard University Press, 2014.

Fitzgerald, Keith. *The Face of the Nation: Immigration, the State, and the National Identity*. Redwood City, CA: Stanford University Press, 1996.

Flores, Lori A. "A Town Full of Dead Mexicans: The Salinas Valley Bracero Tragedy of 1963, the End of the Bracero Program, and the Evolution of California's Chicano Movement." *Western Historical Quarterly* 44, no. 2 (2013): 124–143.

Foley, Neil. *The White Scourge: Mexicans, Blacks, and Poor Whites in Texas Cotton Culture*. Berkeley: University of California Press, 1999.

Fong, Lawrence Michael. "Sojourners and Settlers: The Chinese Experience in Arizona." *Journal of Arizona History* 21, no. 3 (1980): 1–30.

Foucault, Michel. "Governmentality." In *The Foucault Effect: Studies in Governmentality*, edited by Graham Burchell, Colin Gordon, and Peter Miller, 87–104. Chicago: University of Chicago Press, 1991.

Fox, Cybelle. *Three Worlds of Welfare Relief: Race, Immigration, and the American Welfare State from the Progressive Era to the New Deal*. Princeton, NJ: Princeton University Press, 2012.

Fragomen, Austin T., Jr. "Searching for Illegal Aliens: The Immigration Service Encounters the Fourth Amendment." *San Diego Law Review* 13, no. 1 (1975): 82–124.

Friedman, Lawrence. *A History of American Law*. New York: Simon and Schuster, 1985.

"Full Text of the Wickersham Commission Report on Prohibition." *New York Times*, January 21, 1931.

Galarza, Ernesto. *Merchants of Labor: The Mexican Bracero Story, An Account of the Managed Migration of Mexican Farm Workers in California, 1942–1960*. San Jose, CA: Rosicrucian Press, 1964.

Gamio, Manuel. *Mexican Immigration to the United States: A Study of Human Migration and Adjustment*. New York: Dover Publications, 1971.

García, Juan Ramon. *Operation Wetback: The Mass Deportation of Mexican Undocumented Workers in 1954*. Westport, CT: Greenwood Press, 1980.

García, Mario T. *Desert Immigrants: The Mexicans of El Paso, 1880–1920*. New Haven, CT: Yale University Press, 1981.

García y Griego, Manuel. "The Importation of Mexican Contract Laborers to the United States, 1942–1964: Antecedents, Operation, and Legacy." In *The Border that Joins: Mexican Migrants and U.S. Responsibility*, edited by Peter G. Brown and Henry Shue, 49–98. Lanham, MD: Rowman & Littlefield, 1983.

Geiger, Andrea. "Caught in the Gap: The Transit Privilege and North America's Ambiguous Borders." In *Bridging National Borders in North America: Transnational and Comparative Histories*, edited by Benjamin H. Johnson and Andrew R. Graybill, 199–224. Durham, NC: Duke University Press, 2010.

Gilboy, Janet A. "Penetrability of Administrative Systems: Political 'Casework' and Immigration Inspections." *Law and Society Review* 26, no. 2 (1992): 273–314.

Gilman, Denise. "Seeking Breaches in the Wall: An International Human Rights Law Challenge to the Texas–Mexico Wall." *Texas International Law Journal* 46 (Spring 2011): 259–260.

Gilmore, Grant. "Legal Realism: Its Cause and Cure." *Yale Law Journal* 70, no. 7 (1961): 1039–1048.

Giovagnoli, Mary. "Overhauling Immigration Law: A Brief History and Basic Principles of Reform." Immigration Policy Center. February 14, 2013. www.immigrationpolicy.org/perspectives/overhauling-immigration-law-brief-history-and-basic-principles-reform.

González, Gilbert G. *Mexican Consuls and Labor Organizing*. Austin: University of Texas Press, 1999.

González, Gilbert G., and Raúl Fernandez. "Empire and the Origins of Twentieth Century Migration from Mexico to the United States." *Pacific Historical Review* 71, no. 1 (2002): 19–57.

González-Quiroga, Miguel Ángel. "Conflict and Cooperation in the Making of Texas-Mexico Border Society, 1840-1880." In *Bridging National Borders in North America: Transnational and Comparative Histories*, edited by Benjamin H. Johnson and Andrew R. Graybill, 33-58. Durham, NC: Duke University Press, 2010.

Gordon, Charles. "The Need to Modernize Our Immigration Laws." *San Diego Law Review* 13, no. 1 (1975): 1–33.

Graff, Garrett M. "The Green Monster: How the Border Patrol Became America's Most Out-of-Control Law Enforcement Agency." *Politico Magazine* November/December 2014. www.politico.com/magazine/story/2014/10/border-patrol-the-green-monster-112220.html#.VJnJgMAAcA.

Green, Justin J. "Influence of Administrative Reform on the Immigration and Naturalization Service." *Administrative Science Quarterly* 15, no. 3 (1970): 353–359.

Grossman, Jordan. "Hidden in Plain Sight: Examining the Obama Administration's Discreet Implementation of a Scaled-Down Version of Comprehensive Immigration Reform." *Harvard Law and Policy Review* 8 (Winter 2014): 195–228.

Guérin-Gonzales, Camille. *Mexican Workers and American Dreams: Immigration, Repatriation and California Farm Labor, 1900–1939*. New Brunswick, NJ: Rutgers University Press, 1994.

Guglielmo, Thomas A. "Fighting for Caucasian Rights: Mexicans, Mexican-Americans, and the Transnational Struggle for Civil Rights in World War II Texas." *Journal of American History* 92, no. 4 (March 2006): 1212–1237.

Gusfield, Joseph R. *Symbolic Crusade: Status Politics and the American Temperance Movement*. Urbana: University of Illinois Press, 1963.

Gutiérrez, David G. *Walls and Mirrors: Mexican Americans, Mexican Immigrants, and the Politics of Ethnicity*. Berkeley: University of California Press, 1995.

Gutiérrez, David G. "Migration, Emergent Ethnicity, and the 'Third Space': The Shifting Politics of Nationalism in Greater Mexico." *Journal of American History* 86, no. 2 (1999): 481–518.

Gusfield, Joseph R. *Symbolic Crusade: Status Politics and the American Temperance Movement*. Urbana: University of Illinois Press, 1963.

Hahamovitch, Cindy. *No Man's Land: Jamaican Guestworkers in America and the Global History of Deportable Labor*. Princeton, NJ: Princeton University Press, 2013.

Hall, Linda B., and Don M. Coerver. *Revolution on the Border: The United States and Mexico, 1910–1920*. Albuquerque: University of New Mexico Press, 1988.

Hamm, Richard, *Shaping the Eighteenth Amendment: Temperance Reform, Legal Culture, and the Polity, 1880–1920*. Chapel Hill: University of North Carolina Press, 1995.

Handlin, Oscar. *Race and Nationality in American Life*. Boston: Little, Brown, 1957.

Handlin, Oscar. *The Uprooted*. Boston: Little, Brown, 1973.

Haney López, Ian F. *White by Law: The Legal Construction of Race*. New York: New York University Press, 1996.

Hart, Justin. "Making Democracy Safe for the World: Race, Propaganda, and the Transformation of U.S. Foreign Policy During World War II." *Pacific Historical Review* 73, no. 1 (2004): 49–84.

Harwood, Edwin. *In Liberty's Shadow: Illegal Aliens and Immigration Law Enforcement* Redwood City, CA: Stanford University Press, 1986.

Harwood, Edwin, "The Thin Green Line." n.d. INS Historical Reference Library, Washington, DC.

Hawley, Ellis W. *The New Deal and the Problem of Monopoly: A Study in Economic Ambivalence*. Princeton, NJ: Princeton University Press, 1966.

Hawley, Ellis W. "The Politics of the Mexican Labor Issue, 1950–1965." *Agricultural History* 40, no. 3 (July 1966): 157–176.

Hellyer, Clement David. *The U.S. Border Patrol*. New York: Random House, 1963.

Henkin, Louis. "The Constitution and United States Sovereignty: A Century of Chinese Exclusion and its Progeny." *Harvard Law Review* 100, no. 4 (1987): 853–886.

Henkin, Louis. "The Constitution as Compact and as Conscience: Individual Rights Abroad and at Our Gates." *William and Mary Law Review* 27, no. 1 (1985): 11–34.

Henkin, Louis. "Human Rights and State 'Sovereignty.'" *Georgia Journal of International and Comparative Law* 25, nos. 1 & 2 (1995): 31–45.

Hennessy-Fiske, Molly. "Customs and Border Protection Rules Out Body Cameras for Officers, At Least for Now." *Los Angeles Times*, November 12, 2015.

Higham, John. *Strangers in the Land: Patterns of American Nativism, 1860–1925.* New York: Atheneum, 1963.

Hills, Carla A. "NAFTA's Economic Upsides: The View from the United States." *Foreign Affairs* 93, no. 1 (2014): 122–127.

Hinkle, Stacy C. *Wings Over the Border: The Army Air Service Armed Patrol of the United States–Mexico Border, 1919–1921.* El Paso: University of Texas at El Paso, 1970.

Hirota, Hidetaka. "The Moment of Transition: State Officials, the Federal Government, and the Formation of American Immigration Policy." *Journal of American History* 99, no. 4 (2013): 1092–1108.

Hoffman, Abraham. "The El Monte Berry Pickers Strike, 1933: International Involvement in a Local Labor Dispute." *Journal of the West* 12 (January 1973): 71–84.

Hoffman, Abraham. "The Federal Bureaucracy Meets a Superior Spokesman for Alien Deportation." *Journal of the West* 14 (October 1975): 91–106.

Hoffman, Abraham. "Stimulus to Repatriation: The 1931 Federal Deportation Drive and the Los Angeles Mexican Community." *Pacific Historical Review* 42 (May 1975): 205–219.

Hoffman, Abraham. *Unwanted Mexican Americans: The Great Depression Repatriation Pressures, 1929–1939.* Tucson: University of Arizona Press, 1974.

Horwitz, Morton. *The Transformation of American Law, 1870–1960: The Crisis of Legal Orthodoxy.* New York: Oxford University Press, 1992.

"House Praises Wickersham Bill for Unified Patrol," *Chicago Daily Tribune*, July 2, 1930.

Hugill, Peter T. "Good Roads and the Automobile in the United States, 1880–1929." *Geographical Review* 72, no. 3 (1982): 345–348.

Hutchinson, E. P. *Legislative History of American Immigration Policy, 1798–1905.* Philadelphia: University of Pennsylvania Press, 1981.

Jacoby, Tamar. "A Line Has Been Drawn in the Arizona Sand." *Washington Post*, November 14, 2004.

James, Daniel. *Illegal Immigration—An Unfolding Crisis.* Lanham, MD: University Press of America, Inc., 1991.

Johnson, Benjamin Heber. *Revolution in Texas: How a Forgotten Rebellion and its Bloody Suppression Turned Mexicans into Americans.* New Haven, CT: Yale University Press, 2003.

Johnson, Benjamin Heber, and Andrew R. Graybill, "Introduction: Borders and Their Historians in North America." In *Bridging National Borders in North America: Transnational and Comparative Histories,* edited by Benjamin H. Johnson and Andrew R. Graybill, 1-32. Durham, NC: Duke University Press, 2010.

Johnson, Burke. "Border Patrol—A Rugged Beat." *Arizona Days and Ways*, August 17, 1958.

Johnson, Kevin R. "'Aliens' and the U.S. Immigration Laws: The Social and Legal Construction of Nonpersons." *University of Miami Inter-American Law Review* 28 (Winter 1996): 263–292.

Johnson, Kevin R. "Los Olvidados: Images of the Immigrant, Political Power of Noncitizens, and Immigration Law and Enforcement." *Brigham Young University Law Review* 1993, no. 4 (1993): 1139–1256.

Johnson, Kevin R. "Race, the Immigration Laws and Domestic Race Relations: A 'Magic Mirror' into the Heart of Darkness." *Indiana Law Journal* 73, no. 4 (Fall 1998): 1111–1160.

Johnson, Marilynn S. *The Second Gold Rush: Oakland and the East Bay in World War II.* Berkeley: University of California Press, 1993.

Joyner, W. C. "Immigration and Naturalization." *Our Sheriff and Police Journal* 31 (June 1936): 26.

Joyner, W. C. "Immigration Border Patrol." *Our Sheriff and Police Journal* 31 (June 1936): 23–25.

Jordan, Mary. "Mexican Workers Pay for Success, With Labor Costs Rising Factories Depart for Asia." *Washington Post*, June 20, 2002.

Kalhan, Anil. "Immigration Surveillance." *Maryland Law Review* 74, no. 1 (2014): 1–86.

Kang, S. Deborah. "Crossing the Line: The INS and the Federal Regulation of the Mexican Border." In *Bridging National Borders in North America: Transnational and Comparative Histories*, edited by Benjamin H. Johnson and Andrew R. Graybill, 167–198. Durham, NC: Duke University Press, 2010.

Kang, S. Deborah. "Implementation: How the Borderlands Redefined Federal Immigration Law and Policy in California, Arizona, and Texas, 1917–1924." *California Legal History: Journal of the California Supreme Court Historical Society* 7 (2012): 245–285.

Kanstroom, Daniel. *Deportation Nation: Outsiders in American History*. Cambridge, MA: Harvard University Press, 2007.

Kearney, Milo, and Anthony Knopp. *Border Cuates: A History of the U.S.–Mexican Twin Cities*. Austin, TX: Eakin Press, 1995.

Kennedy, David M. *Freedom from Fear: The American People in Depression and War, 1929–1945*. New York: Oxford University Press, 1999.

Kennedy, John F. *A Nation of Immigrants*. New York: Harper and Row, 1964.

Kettner, James H. *The Development of American Citizenship, 1608–1870*. Chapel Hill: University of North Carolina Press, 1978.

Kirkpatrick, David D. "House Passes Tightening of Laws on Immigration." *New York Times*, February 11, 2005.

Kirstein, Peter N. "Agribusiness, Labor, and the Wetbacks: Truman's Commission on Migratory Labor." *The Historian* 40, no. 4 (1950): 650–667.

Kirstein, Peter N. "American Railroads and the Bracero Program, 1943–1946." *Journal of Mexican American History* 5 (1975): 57–90.

Kirstein, Peter N. *Anglo Over Bracero: A History of the Mexican Worker in the United States from Roosevelt to Nixon*. San Francisco: R & E Research Associates, 1977.

Kiser, George C., and Martha Woody Kiser. *Mexican Workers in the United States: Historical and Political Perspectives*. Albuquerque: University of New Mexico Press, 1979.

Kiser, George, and David Silverman. "Mexican Repatriation During the Great Depression." *Journal of Mexican American History* 3, no. 1 (1973): 139–164.

Klein, Kerwin Lee, "Reclaiming the 'F' Word, or Being and Becoming Postwestern." *Pacific Historical Review* 65 (May 1996): 179–215.

Knauff, Ellen. *The Ellen Knauff Story*. New York: Norton, 1952.

Konvitz, Milton. *The Asian and the Asiatic in American Law*. Ithaca, NY: Cornell University Press, 1946.

Koslowski, Ray. "Smart Borders, Virtual Borders or No Borders: Homeland Security Choices for the United States and Canada." *Law and Business Review of the Americas* 11 (Summer–Fall 2005): 527–550.

Landis, James M. *The Administrative Process*. New Haven, CT: Yale University Press, 2012.

Lawrence, Steve. "Curbs on Illegal Immigration Fail." *Daily Breeze* (Torrance, CA), July 6, 2005.

Lee, Erika. *At America's Gates: Chinese Immigration During the Exclusion Era, 1882–1943*. Chapel Hill: University of North Carolina Press, 2003.

Lee, Erika, and Judy Yung. *Angel Island: Immigrant Gateway to America*. New York: Oxford University Press, 2010.

Lee, Sophia Z. "Race, Sex, and Rulemaking: Administrative Constitutionalism and the Workplace, 1960 to the Present." *Virginia Law Review* 96, no. 4 (2010): 799–886.

Leff, Mark Hugh. *The Limits of Symbolic Reform: The New Deal and Taxation, 1933–1939*. New York: Cambridge University Press, 1984.

Leffler, Melvyn P. *A Preponderance of Power: National Security, the Truman Administration, and the Cold War*. Redwood City, CA: Stanford University Press, 1992.

Legomsky, Stephen H. *Immigration Law and Policy*. Westbury, NY: The Foundation Press, 1992.

Legomsky, Stephen H. "Ten More Years of Plenary Power: Immigration, Congress, and the Courts." *Hastings Constitutional Law Quarterly* 22, no. 4 (1995): 925–937.

LeMay, Michael C. *Anatomy of a Public Policy: The Reform of Contemporary American Immigration Law*. Westport, CT: Praeger, 1994.

LeMay, Michael C. *From Open Door to Dutch Door: An Analysis of U.S. Immigration Policy Since 1820.* New York: Praeger, 1987.

LeMay, Michael C. *The Gatekeepers: A Comparative Immigration Policy.* New York, Praeger, 1989.

Limerick, Patricia. *Legacy of Conquest: The Unbroken Past of the American West.* New York: Norton, 1987.

Lemelin, Bernard. "Emmanuel Celler of Brooklyn: Leading Advocate of Liberal Immigration Policy, 1945–1952." *Canadian Review of American Studies* 24 (Winter 1994): 81–111.

Lim, Julian. "Chinos and Paisanos: Chinese Mexican Relations in the Borderlands." *Pacific Historical Review* 79, no. 1 (2010): 50–85.

Lim, Julian. "Immigration, Asylum, and Citizenship: A More Holistic Approach." *Legal Studies Research Paper Series* (December 8, 2003). St. Louis: Washington University School of Law, 2012.

Limerick, Patricia. *Legacy of Conquest: The Unbroken Past of the American West.* New York: Norton, 1987.

"Liquor Buyer Bill Urged by Sheppard." *New York Times,* June 6, 1930.

Lizza, Ryan. "Getting to Maybe: Inside the Gang of Eight's Immigration Deal." *The New Yorker,* June 24, 2013.

Lockwood, Jim. "Jim Lockwood: Border Patrol." In *New Immigrants: Portraits in Passage,* edited by Thomas Bentz, 81–90. New York: The Pilgrim Press, 1981.

Lopez, James, Jacinta Ma, and Josh Breisblatt. *Body Cameras and CBP: Promoting Security, Transparency and Accountability at Our Nation's Borders.* Washington, DC: National Immigration Forum, 2015.

Lorey, David E. *The U.S.–Mexican Border in the Twentieth Century: A History of Economic and Social Transformation.* Wilmington, DE: SR Books, 1999.

Lovett, Ian. "Ex-Mayor Sentenced in Harassment Case." *New York Times,* December 10, 2013.

Lytle-Hernández, Kelly. *Migra! A History of the U.S. Border Patrol.* Berkeley: University of California Press, 2010.

Madigan, Nick. "Early Heat Wave Kills 12 Illegal Immigrants in the Arizona Desert." *New York Times,* February 16, 2001.

Magill, Elizabeth. "Annual Review of Administrative Law: Foreword: Agency Self-Regulation." *George Washington Law Review* 77, no. 4 (2009): 859–903.

Martin, George. *Madam Secretary: Frances Perkins.* Boston: Houghton Mifflin, 1976.

Martínez, Daniel E., Guillermo Cantor, and Walter A. Ewing. *No Action Taken: Lack of CBP Accountability in Responding to Complaints of Abuse, May 2014.* Washington, DC: American Immigration Council, 2014.

Martínez, Oscar J. *Border Boom Town: Ciudad Juárez Since 1948.* Austin: University of Texas Press, 1978.

Martínez, Oscar J., *Troublesome Border.* Tucson: University of Arizona Press, 1988.

Martínez, Oscar J., ed. *U.S.–Mexico Borderlands: Historical and Contemporary Perspectives.* Wilmington, DE: Scholarly Resources, Inc., 1996.

Mashaw, Jerry L. *Creating the Administrative Constitution: The Lost One Hundred Years of American Administrative Law.* New Haven, CT: Yale University Press, 2012.

McArdle, John. "U.S. Customs and Border Patrol Challenges: Interview with Garrett M. Graff," *Washington Journal,* C-SPAN, December 15, 2014.

McCain, Johnny T. "Texas and the Mexican Labor Question, 1942–1947." *Southwestern Historical Quarterly* 85, no. 1 (July 1981): 45–64.

McCarran, Patrick A. "The Internal Security Act of 1950." *University of Pittsburgh Law Review* 12 (Summer 1951): 481–513.

McClain, Charles J. *In Search of Equality: The Chinese Struggle Against Discrimination in Nineteenth-Century America.* Berkeley: University of California Press, 1994.

McCormick, Thomas J. *America's Half-Century: United States Foreign Policy in the Cold War.* Baltimore: Johns Hopkins University Press, 1989.

McWilliams, Carey. *California: The Great Exception.* Berkeley: University of California Press, 1949.

McWilliams, Carey. *Factories in the Field*. Boston: Little, Brown, 1939.

McWilliams, Carey. *North from Mexico: The Spanish-Speaking People of the United States*. Philadelphia: J. B. Lippincott Company, 1949.

Meissner, Doris, Donald M. Kerwin, Muzaffar Chishti, and Claire Bergenon. *Immigration Enforcement in the United States: The Rise of a Formidable Machinery*. Washington, DC: Migration Policy Institute, 2013.

Metz, Leon C. *Border: The U.S.–Mexico Line*. El Paso, TX: Mangan Books, 1995.

Metzger, Gillian E. "Administrative Constitutionalism." *Texas Law Review* 91, no. 7 (2013): 1897–1935.

Mintz, John. "Tracking 'Terrorist Travel' is a Key Defense." *Washington Post*, April 23, 2010.

"'Minutemen' End Border Patrol But Plan to Return." *New York Times*, May 1, 2005.

Molina, Natalie. *How Race Is Made in America: Immigration, Citizenship, and the Historical Power of Racial Scripts*. Berkeley: University of California Press, 2014.

Moloney, Deirdre M. *National Insecurities: Immigrants and U.S. Deportation Policy Since 1882*. Chapel Hill: University of North Carolina Press, 2012.

Montejano, David. *Anglos and Mexicans in the Making of Texas, 1836–1986*. Austin: University of Texas Press, 1987.

Moore, Commander Alvin Edward, *Border Patrol*. Santa Fe, NM: Sunstone Press, 1988.

Motomura, Hiroshi. "The Curious Evolution of Immigration Law: Procedural Surrogates for Substantive Constitutional Rights." *Columbia Law Review* 92, no. 7 (1992): 1626–1704.

Motomura, Hiroshi. "Immigration Law After a Century of Plenary Power: Phantom Constitutional Norms and Statutory Interpretation." *Yale Law Journal* 100, no. 3 (1990): 545–613.

National Conference of State Legislatures. "Arizona's Immigration Enforcement Laws." July 28, 2011. www.ncsl.org/research/immigration/analysis-of-arizonas-immigration-law.aspx.

Myers, John. *The Border Wardens*. Englewood Cliffs, NJ: Prentice-Hall, 1971.

Myrdal, Gunnar. *An American Dilemma: The Negro Problem and Modern Democracy*. New York: Harper and Row, 1944.

Nadelmann, Ethan A. *Cops Across Borders: The Internationalization of U.S. Criminal Law Enforcement*. University Park: Pennsylvania State University Press, 1993.

Neuman, Gerald L. "The Lost Century of American Immigration Law." *Columbia Law Review* 93, no. 8 (1993): 1833–1901.

Neuman, Gerald L. *Strangers to the Constitution: Immigrants, Borders, and Fundamental Law*. Princeton, NJ: Princeton University Press, 1996.

Nevins, Joseph. *Operation Gatekeeper: The Rise of the "Illegal Alien" and the Making of the United States–Mexico Boundary*. New York: Routledge, 2002.

"New U.S. Police Force Now Combats Smugglers." *New York Times*, May 10, 1925.

Ngai, Mae M. *Impossible Subjects: Illegal Aliens and the Making of Modern America*. Princeton, NJ: Princeton University Press, 2004.

Niblo, Stephen R. *War, Diplomacy, and Development: The United States and Mexico, 1938–1954*. Wilmington, DE: Scholarly Resources, 1995.

Note. "Unenforced Boundaries: Illegal Immigration and the Limits of Judicial Federalism." *Harvard Law Review* 108, no. 7 (1995): 1643–1660.

Novak, William J., *The People's Welfare: Law and Regulation in Nineteenth-Century America*. Chapel Hill: University of North Carolina Press, 1996.

O'Connor, Martin L. "Vehicle Searches—The Automobile Exception: The Constitutional Ride from *Carroll v. United States* to *Wyoming v. Houghton*." *Touro Law Review* 16, no. 2 (1999): 393–434.

Odens, Peter. *The Desert Trackers: Men of the Border Patrol*. Yuma, AZ: Sun Graphics, 1990.

Omi, Michael and Howard Winant. *Racial Formation in the United States: From the 1960s to the 1990s*. New York: Routledge, 1994.

Orren, Karen, and Stephen Skowronek. *The Search for American Political Development*. New York: Cambridge University Press, 2004.

Ortega, Bob, and Rob O'Dell. "Deadly Border Agent Incidents Cloaked in Silence: *Republic* Investigation Finds Little Public Accountability in Southwest Border Killings." *Arizona Republic*, December 16, 2013.

Patterson, James T. *Grand Expectations: The United States, 1945–1971.* New York: Oxford University Press, 1996.

Pegler-Gordon, Anna. *In Sight of America: Photography and the Development of U.S. Immigration Policy.* Berkeley: University of California Press, 2009.

Perales, Monica. *Smeltertown: Making and Remembering a Southwest Border Community.* Durham, NC: University of North Carolina Press, 2010.

Peralta, Eyder. "Report Criticizes Border Patrol's Use of Deadly Force." *NPR*, February 27, 2014. www.npr.org/blogs/thetwo-way/2014/02/27/283455547/report-criticizes-border-patrols-use-of-force.

Perkins, Clifford Alan. *Border Patrol: With the U.S. Immigration Service on the Mexican Boundary, 1910–1954.* El Paso: Texas Western Press, University of Texas, 1978.

Pfaelzer, Jean. *Driven Out: The Forgotten War Against Chinese Americans.* Berkeley: University of California Press, 2007.

Police Executive Research Forum. *U.S. Customs and Border Protection Use of Force Review: Cases and Policies, February 2013.* Washington, DC: The Police Executive Research Forum, 2013.

Pressman, Jeffrey L., and Aaron Wildavsky. *Implementation: How Great Expectations in Washington are Dashed in Oakland; or, Why It's Amazing that Federal Programs Work at All This Being a Saga of the Economic Development Administration as Told By Two Sympathetic Observers Who Seek to Build Morals on a Foundation of Ruined Hopes.* 3rd ed. Berkeley: University of California Press, 1984.

Preston, Julia, Alan Rapperport, and Matt Richtel, "What Would It Take for Donald Trump to Deport 11 Million and Build a Wall?" *New York Times*, May 19, 2016.

Preston, William. *Aliens and Dissenters: Federal Suppression of Radicals, 1903–1933.* Urbana: University of Illinois Press, 1994.

Prince, Carl E., and Mollie Keller. *The U.S. Customs Service: A Bicentennial History.* Washington, DC: Department of the Treasury, US Customs Service, 1989.

Raat, Dirk, and Michael M. Brescia. *Mexico and the United States: Ambivalent Vistas.* Athens: University of Georgia Press, 2010.

Rabin, Robert L. "Federal Regulation in Historical Perspective." *Stanford Law Review* 38, no. 5 (1986): 1189–1326.

Rak, Mary Kidder. *Border Patrol.* Boston: Houghton Mifflin, 1938.

Rak, Mary Kidder. *They Heard the Gates: The Way of Life on the American Borders.* Evanston, IL: Row, Peterson, 1941.

Reimers, David M. "An Unintended Reform: The 1965 Immigration Act and Third World Immigration to the United States." *Journal of American Ethnic History* 3, no. 1 (1983): 13.

Reisler, Mark. *By the Sweat of Their Brow: Mexican Immigrant Labor in the United States, 1900–1940.* Westport, CT: Greenwood Press, 1976.

Reséndez, Andrés, *Changing National Identities at the Frontier: Texas and New Mexico, 1800–1850.* New York: Cambridge University Press, 2005.

Rice, Ross R. *Carl Hayden: Builder of the American West.* Lanham, MD: University Press of America, 1994.

Riley, Dennis D., and Bryan E. Brophy-Baermann. *Bureaucracy and the Policy Process: Keeping the Promises.* Lanham, MD: Rowman & Littlefield, 2006.

Roberts, Dan R. "The Border Patrol—65 Years of Action." *The Tombstone Epitaph*, 1989.

Robertson, Craig. *The Passport in America: The History of a Document.* New York: Oxford University Press, 2010.

Robinson, Robert S. "Taking the Fair Deal to the Fields: Truman's Commission on Migratory Labor, Public Law 78 and the Bracero Program, 1950–1952." *Agricultural History* 84, no. 3 (2010): 381–402.

Romero, Robert Chao. *The Chinese in Mexico, 1882–1940*. Tucson: University of Arizona Press, 2010.

Romo, David Dorado. *Ringside Seat to a Revolution: An Underground Cultural History of El Paso and Juárez*. El Paso, TX: Cinco Puntos Press, 2005.

Roediger, David. *The Wages of Whiteness: Race and the Making of the American Working Class*. London: Verso, 1992.

Rosas, Ana. *Abrazando el Espíritu: Bracero Families Confront the U.S.–Mexico Border*. Berkeley: University of California Press, 2014.

Rosenzweig, Paul S. "Functional Equivalents of the Border, Sovereignty, and the Fourth Amendment." *University of Chicago Law Review* 52 (Fall 1985): 1119–1145.

Ruiz, Vicki. *From Out of the Shadows: Mexican Women in Twentieth-Century America*. New York: Oxford University Press, 2008.

"The Saga of a Southeastern Town." *The Cochise Quarterly* 8, nos. 1 & 2 (1978): 4–47.

Sahlins, Peter. *Boundaries: The Making of France and Spain in the Pyrenees*. Berkeley: University of California Press, 1989.

Salyer, Lucy. *Laws Harsh as Tigers: Chinese Immigrants and the Shaping of Modern Immigration Law*. Chapel Hill: University of North Carolina Press, 1995.

Sánchez, George J. *Becoming Mexican-American: Ethnicity, Culture, and Identity in Chicano Los Angeles, 1900–1945*. New York: Oxford University Press, 1993.

Sanchez, Marcela. "Our Sad Neglect of Mexico." *Washington Post*, May 28, 2005.

Sandmeyer, Elmer Clarence. *The Anti-Chinese Movement in California*. Urbana: University of Illinois Press, 1991.

Sanford, Diana. "The Line Rider." *Cochise Quarterly* 11, no. 2 (1981): 3–7.

Sassen, Saskia. "U.S. Immigration Policy toward Mexico in a Global Economy." In *Between Two Worlds: Mexican Immigrants in the United States*, edited by David G. Gutiérrez, 213–227. Wilmington, DE: Scholarly Resources, 1996.

Saxton, Alexander. *The Indispensible Enemy: Labor and the Anti-Chinese Movement in California*. Berkeley: University of California Press, 1971.

Shachar, Ayelet. "Territory Without Boundaries: Immigration Beyond Territory: The Shifting Border of Immigration Regulation." *Michigan Journal of International Law* 30 (Spring 2009): 809–839.

Schiller, Reuel E. "Enlarging the Administrative Polity: Administrative Law and the Changing Definition of Pluralism, 1945–1970." *Vanderbilt Law Review* 53 (October 2000): 1389–1453.

Schiller, Reuel E. "The Era of Deference: Courts, Expertise, and the Emergence of New Deal Administrative Law." *Michigan Law Review* 106, no 3. (2007): 399–441.

Schmitt, Eric. "The Rube Goldberg Agency." *New York Times*, March 24, 2002.

Schneider, Dorothee. *Crossing Borders: Migration and Citizenship in the Twentieth Century United States*. Cambridge, MA: Harvard University Press, 2011.

Schoenbrod, David. *Power Without Responsibility: How Congress Abuses the People Through Delegation*. New Haven, CT: Yale University Press, 1993.

Schoultz, Lars. *Beneath the United States: A History of U.S. Policy Toward Latin America*. Cambridge, MA: Harvard University Press, 1998.

Schuck, Peter H. "Removing Criminal Aliens: The Pitfalls and Promises of Federalism." *Harvard Journal of Law and Public Policy* 22, no. 2 (1999): 367–463.

Schuck, Peter H. "The Transformation of Immigration Law." *Columbia Law Review* 84, no. 1 (1984): 30–33.

Schuck, Peter H., and Rogers M. Smith. *Citizenship without Consent: Illegal Aliens in the American Polity*. New Haven, CT: Yale University Press, 1985.

Schwartz, Harry. *Seasonal Farm Labor in the United States: With Special Reference to Hired Workers in Fruit and Vegetable and Sugar-Beet Production*. New York: Columbia University Press, 1945.

Scruggs, Otey M. "The Bracero Program Under the Farm Security Administration." *Labor History* 3 (Spring 1962): 149–168.

Scruggs, Otey M. "The First Mexican Farm Labor Program." *Arizona and the West* 2, no. 4 (Winter 1960): 319–326.

Scruggs, Otey M. "The United States, Mexico, and the Wetbacks." *Pacific Historical Review* 30, no. 2 (1961): 149–164.

Severn, Bill. *Frances Perkins: A Member of the Cabinet.* New York: Hawthorn Books, Inc., 1976.

Shapiro, Martin. *Who Guards the Guardians? Judicial Control of Administration.* Athens: University of Georgia Press, 1988.

Sheridan, Thomas E. *Los Tucsonenses: The Mexican Community in Tucson, 1854–1941.* Tucson: University of Arizona Press, 1986.

Sinclair, Andrew. *Era of Excess: A Social History of the Prohibition Movement.* New York: Harper and Row, 1962.

Skocpol, Theda. "Bringing the State Back In: Strategies of Analysis in Current Research." In *Bringing the State Back In*, edited by Peter B. Evans and Dietrich Rueschemeyer, 3-43. Cambridge: Cambridge University Press, 1985.

Skocpol, Theda. *Protecting Soldiers and Mothers: The Political Origins of Social Policy in the United States.* Cambridge, MA: Belknap Press, 1992.

Skocpol, Theda, and Kenneth Finegold. "State Capacity and Economic Intervention in the Early New Deal." *Political Science Quarterly* 97 (Summer 1982): 255–278.

Skowronek, Stephen. *Building a New American State: The Expansion of National Administrative Capacities, 1877–1920.* New York: Cambridge University Press, 1982.

Smith, Jason Scott. *Building a New Deal Liberalism: The Political Economy of Public Works, 1933–1956.* New York: Cambridge University Press, 2009.

Smith, Peter H. *Talons of the Eagle: Dynamics of U.S.–Latin American Relations.* New York: Oxford University Press, 2000.

Smith, Marian L. "The Immigration and Naturalization Service (INS) at the U.S.–Canadian Border, 1893–1993: An Overview of Issues and Topics." *Michigan Historical Review* 26 (Fall 2000): 127–148.

Smith, Marian L. "Race, Nationality, and Reality: INS Administration of Racial Provisions in U.S. Immigration and Nationality Law since 1898." *Prologue* 34 (Summer 2002): 91–107.

Spiro, Peter J. "The States and Immigration in an Era of Demi-Sovereignties." *Virginia Journal of International Law* 35, no. 1 (1994): 121–178.

St. John, Rachel. *Line in the Sand: A History of the Western U.S.–Mexico Border.* Princeton, NJ: Princeton University Press, 2011.

St. John, Rachel. "Selling the Border: Trading Land, Attracting Tourists, and Marketing American Consumption on the Baja California Border, 1900–1934." In *Land of Necessity: Consumer Culture in the United States–Mexico Borderlands*, edited by Alexis McCrossen, 113–142. Durham, NC: Duke University Press, 2009.

Steen, Murphy J. F. *Twenty-Five Years a U.S. Border Patrolman.* Dallas: Royal Publishing Company, 1958.

Stern, Alexandra Minna. "Buildings, Boundaries, and Blood: Medicalization and Nation-Building on the U.S.–Mexico Border, 1910–1930." *Hispanic American Historical Review* 79, no. 1 (February 1999): 41–81.

Stevenson, Richard W. "Bush is Considering Waiver for Mexicans Entering U.S." *New York Times*, March 5, 2004.

Strayer, Robert L. "Symposium: Making the Development of Homeland Security Regulations More Democratic." *Oklahoma City Law Review* 33 (Summer 2008): 331–360.

Suárez-Orozco, Marcelo M. *Crossings: Mexican Immigration in Interdisciplinary Perspectives.* Boston: Harvard University David Rockefeller Center for Latin American Studies, 1998.

Sullivan, Kevin. "An Often-Crossed Line in the Sand: Upgraded Security at U.S. Border Hasn't Deterred Illegal Immigration from Mexico." *Washington Post*, March 7, 2005.

Thelen, David. "Rethinking History and the Nation-State: Mexico and the United States." *Journal of American History* 86, no. 2 (1999): 438–452.

Thompson, Ginger. "U.S. and Mexico to Open Talks on Freer Migration for Workers." *New York Times*, February 16, 2001.

Tichenor, Daniel J. *Dividing Lines: The Politics of Immigration Control in America*. Princeton, NJ: Princeton University Press, 2002.

Torpey, John C. *The Invention of the Passport: Surveillance, Citizenship, and the State*. New York: Cambridge University Press, 2000.

Truett, Samuel. *Fugitive Landscapes: The Forgotten History of the U.S.–Mexico Borderlands*. New Haven, CT: Yale University Press, 2008.

Truett, Samuel. "Transnational Warrior: Emilio Kosterlitzky and the Transformation of the U.S.–Mexico Borderlands." In *Continental Crossroads: Remapping U.S.–Mexico Borderlands History*, edited by Samuel Truett and Elliot Young, 1–34. New York: New York University Press, 2006.

Truett, Samuel, and Elliott Young, eds. *Continental Crossroads: Remapping U.S.–Mexico Borderlands History*. Durham, NC: Duke University Press, 2004.

Turner, Frederick Jackson. *The Significance of the Frontier in American History*. New York: Ungar, 1963.

Twining, William. *Karl Llewellyn and the Realist Movement*. London: Weidenfeld and Nicolson, 1973.

Van Vleck, William. *The Administrative Control of Aliens: A Study in Administrative Law and Procedure*. New York: Commonwealth Fund, 1932.

Vanderwood, Paul J. *Juan Soldado: Rapist, Murderer, Martyr, Saint*. Durham, NC: Duke University Press, 2004.

Vanderwood, Paul J. *Satan's Playground: Mobsters and Movie Stars at America's Greatest Gaming Resort*. Durham, NC: Duke University Press, 2010.

Walz, Eric. "The Issei Community in Maricopa County: Development and Persistence in the Valley of the Sun, 1900–1940." *Journal of Arizona History* 38, no. 1 (1997): 1–22.

Weber, David J. "Conflicts and Accommodations: Hispanic and Anglo-American Borders in Historical Perspective, 1670–1853." *Journal of the Southwest* 39, no.1 (1997): 1–32.

Weber, David. "Turner, the Boltonians, and the Borderlands." *American Historical Review* 91, no. 1 (1986): 66–81.

Weissinger, George. *Law Enforcement and the INS: A Participant Observation Study of Control Agents*. Lanham, MD: University Press of America, 1996.

White, Richard. *"It's Your Misfortune and None of My Own": A New History of the American West*. Norman: University of Oklahoma Press, 1991.

White, Richard. *Railroaded: The Transcontinentals and the Making of Modern America*. New York: Norton, 2012.

Wiebe, Robert. *The Search for Order, 1877–1920*. New York: Hill and Wang, 1967.

Wiley, Peter, and Robert Gottlieb. *Empires in the Sun: The Rise of the New American West*. New York: Putnam, 1982.

Wilmoth, G. C. "Halt Alien Horde at U.S. Border: Immigration Service Guided by High Ideals." *Arizona Peace Officers' Magazine* 1 (April 1937): 10, 26.

Wilson, James Q. *Bureaucracy: What Government Agencies Do and Why they Do It*. New York: Basic Books, 1989.

Wilson, Michael. "NAFTA's Unfinished Business: The View from Canada." *Foreign Affairs* 93, no. 1 (2014): 128–133.

Wilson, Roscoe G. "The Old 'Mounted Guards' Gave Way to the 'Border Patrol.'" *Arizona Days and Ways*, September 18, 1960.

Wong, Edward. "Hopes and Doubts over Bush Plan." *New York Times*, June 9, 2002.

Wood, Bryce. *The Making of the Good Neighbor Policy*. New York: Columbia University Press, 1961.

Worster, David. *Rivers of Empire: Water, Aridity, and the Growth of the American West*. New York: Pantheon Books, 1985.

Worrell, Erin M. "Note and Comment: Free Trade, Free Migration: A Path to Open Borders and Economic Justice in the North American Free Trade Agreement and the Security and

Prosperity Partnership of North America." *Temple International and Comparative Law Journal* 23 (Spring 2009): 113–142.

Wrenn, Lisa. "On Patrol." *Lifetime*, September 16, 1979.

Wunder, John R. "The Chinese and the Courts in the Pacific Northwest: Justice Denied?" *Pacific Historical Review* 52, no. 2 (1983): 191–211.

Yale-Loehr, Stephen, Demetrious G. Papademetriou, and Betsy Cooper. *Secure Borders, Open Doors: Visa Procedures in the Post-September 11 Era*. Washington, DC: Migration Policy Institute, 2005.

Yans-McLaughlin, Virginia. *Immigration Reconsidered: History, Sociology, and Politics*. New York: Oxford University Press, 1990.

Zanger, Maggy. "Planes, Training and Automatic Weapons: Marines Give Border Patrol Agents Some Rambo-Style Tips on Battling Drug Smugglers." *Tucson Weekly*, April 4, 1990.

Zolberg, Aristide. *A Nation by Design: Immigration Policy in the Fashioning of America*. Cambridge, MA: Harvard University Press, 2009.

INDEX